The Fasces

The Fasces

A History of Ancient Rome's Most Dangerous Political Symbol

T. COREY BRENNAN

OXFORD
UNIVERSITY PRESS

OXFORD
UNIVERSITY PRESS

Oxford University Press is a department of the University of Oxford. It furthers
the University's objective of excellence in research, scholarship, and education
by publishing worldwide. Oxford is a registered trade mark of Oxford University
Press in the UK and certain other countries.

Published in the United States of America by Oxford University Press
198 Madison Avenue, New York, NY 10016, United States of America.

Library of Congress Cataloging-in-Publication Data
Names: Brennan, T. Corey, author.
Title: The fasces : a history of Ancient Rome's most
dangerous political symbol / T. Corey Brennan.
Other titles: History of Ancient Rome's most dangerous political symbol
Description: New York, NY : Oxford University Press, [2023]
Identifiers: LCCN 2022008598 (print) | LCCN 2022008599 (ebook) |
ISBN 9780197644881 (hardback) | ISBN 9780197644904 (epub)
Subjects: LCSH: Signs and symbols—Italy—History, | Fasces—History.
Classification: LCC CR572 .B74 2023 (print) | LCC CR572 (ebook) |
DDC 929.60945—dc23/eng/20220222
LC record available at https://lccn.loc.gov/2022008598
LC ebook record available at https://lccn.loc.gov/2022008599

DOI: 10.1093/oso/9780197644881.001.0001

1 3 5 7 9 8 6 4 2

Printed by Sheridan Books, Inc., United States of America

Contents

Acknowledgments

ABOUT THIRTY-FIVE YEARS ago, sometime in the 1985–1986 academic year, my dissertation director Ernst Badian (1925–2011) suggested two possible topics for a Ph.D. thesis. One was the role of the magistrate called the praetor in the Roman Republic. The other was the staff of the praetor in that same era, including the lictors, the attendants who carried his most important insignia of office, the fasces. At the time, the difference in significance between the two projects seemed to me practically laughable, and on the spot (for better or worse) I chose the first. I did not give much thought to the second until August 2017, while trying to process the shocking "Unite the Right" rally of extremists held in Charlottesville, Virginia. I was stunned to see from news reports that some of the participating hate groups had chosen a Roman-style fasces as their symbol. The thought then occurred to me that Professor Badian, as so often, had identified a genuinely compelling subject for study, one with real contemporary relevance. Hence the present book.

For six weeks in the fall of 2019 I had the excellent fortune to hold the Lucy Shoe Meritt Residency in Classical Studies and Archaeology at the American Academy in Rome (AAR). It certainly seems providential that I spent a good portion of my time at the AAR in its superb Library gathering materials for this book, since starting in March 2020 (and indeed, right through the completion of this manuscript) the global public health crisis has made this type of in-person research almost impossible. I thank the organizers of the Glasgow University conference "Women, Wealth and Power in the Roman Republic," the Center for the Humanities at Temple University, the Classical Association of Scotland (Edinburgh and South-East Centre), an AAR-sponsored panel at the Society for Classical Studies / Archaeological Institute of America joint annual meeting, and the University of Gothenburg for the opportunity to share some of the findings of this book in 2021 via remote presentations. I am also grateful for invitations to lecture on this subject in 2020 at Roehampton University, the Institute of Classical Studies

(London), and the Charterhouse School (Godalming, Surrey); each of these events was canceled due to COVID-19. I also express my thanks to Rutgers University, its School of Arts and Sciences, and the Department of Classics for its warm support in general, and in particular for waiving my teaching in fall 2019 so that I could take up the AAR Residency. In other visits to Rome over the past years, HSH Prince Nicolò (1941–2018) and HSH Princess Rita Boncompagni Ludovisi most generously allowed me to make their historic Villa Aurora my scholarly base, for which I feel greatly honored and indebted.

I thank especially the following individuals for specific help and guidance in connection with this project over the years, without wishing to implicate them in any of the errors in fact and interpretation this book may contain: T. Aidonis (Westminster School); E. Badian† (Harvard); M. Beard (Cambridge); H. Becker and J. A. Becker (Binghamton); M. T. Boatwright (Duke); W. W. Briggs (South Carolina); D. Chiekova (The College of New Jersey); M. G. D'Amelio (Rome Tor Vergata); E. Dench (Harvard); J. Dugan (Buffalo); H. I. Flower (Princeton); V. Follo (AAR); C. Fried (Harvard); G. Fried (Boston College); A. Giardina (Scuola Normale Superiore, Pisa); J. P. Hallett (Maryland); K. K. Hersch (Temple); S. Hierl (AAR); S. L. James (UNC Chapel Hill); M. Koortbojian (Princeton); L. Lancaster (Ohio); J. Linderski (UNC Chapel Hill); M. Lotts (Rutgers); B. Lundquist (Tidskriften Medusa); J. Ma (Columbia); C. Maciver (Edinburgh); A. Majanlahti (Rome); P. Montserrat (Temple); D. Nousek (Western); B. Nygren (Loyola Maryland); J. Ochsendorf (MIT); I. Östenberg (Gothenburg); D. Padilla Peralta (Princeton); P. Pedinelli (Rome); G. Ponti (IES Rome); C. Raddato (Frankfurt); M. V. Ronnick (Wayne State); P. Rudy (Missouri-Kansas City); E. J. Shepherd (Aerofototeca Nazionale, ICCD); C. Steel (Glasgow); A. Summerscale (Cambridge, MA); K. Tempest (Roehampton); and L. Webb (Oxford). I am more generally indebted to each of my colleagues in the Rutgers Department of Classics: J. McGlew (chair), and S. Al Kuntar, E. Allen-Hornblower, K. Chew, S. Connolly, T. J. Figueira, J. Fisher, B. Perruzzi, T. Power, J. Ulrich, and A. Yadin-Israel.

Dorothy Bauhoff expertly copy-edited this book, and Brent Matheny (Oxford University Press) and Dharuman Bheeman (Newgen Knowledge Works) patiently guided it through production. I must also register my warmest thanks to Stefan Vranka, Executive Editor at Oxford University Press, for his many years of interest, support, and wise counsel, spanning now three books.

But I offer my deepest appreciation to my beloved wife, Dr. Antonia Fried, and our children Samuel, Nicholas, and Allegra, to whom I dedicate this work.

List of Illustrations

I

Introduction to the Roman Fasces

WITH A CONTINUOUS history stretching at least some twelve hundred years over a vast geographic area, the fasces—derived from the Latin word for "bundle"—must be counted as the most significant and recognizable symbol of authority that the Romans came to use. The fasces was an assemblage of wooden rods, typically about a meter and half long, bound by leather straps together with a singled-headed axe—the equipment needed to inflict either corporal or capital punishment. In our era, that historical emblem is inseparably associated with its ubiquity in the years 1919 through 1945 as the principal sign of Italian Fascism.

Significance of the Fasces

It is hard to overstate the importance of the fasces in the ancient world. For all periods of Roman antiquity, the fasces remained the most distinctive tangible sign of the public authority of holders of *imperium*, a term which in its basic sense denoted full civil and military power. In 70 BCE, Cicero accused the ex-magistrate Gaius Verres of not understanding, during his tenure of Sicily, what the fasces symbolized and what responsibilities they entailed. The governor did not receive "those rods and axes, that crushing weight of authority, that position of majestic splendor," chides Cicero, "that you might use their force and their authority" for personal gratification and gain.[1]

Indeed, "the fasces" is a common periphrasis for Roman high public office in general, especially the top regular office of consul.[2] Greeks as early as the second century BCE were in the habit of calling the praetor—a junior colleague of the consuls—"six axes" (*hexapelekus*). In like fashion, in Latin literature of all periods "the twelve fasces" very frequently stands for "the consulship."[3]

The Fasces. T. Corey Brennan, Oxford University Press. © Oxford University Press 2023.
DOI: 10.1093/oso/9780197644881.003.0001

At the same time, the fasces represented also the power of Rome itself. Cicero is explicit on this. When Verres as governor of Sicily established himself at Syracuse, so did "the name and fasces of the *imperium* of the Roman People." As such, the fasces had to be handled with care. In the early first century CE, the writer Valerius Maximus offers a grandiose definition of the symbol. In these insignia there resided, he asserts, "the highest glory of the Senate and the order of Knights and the entire People and by whose nod Latium and the powers of all Italy were governed."[4] Hence recipients of the fasces who are deemed unworthy of them, or who are alleged to have gained them improperly, or who mishandle them once in office, routinely draw the ire of our ancient sources.[5]

Rome's Fasces-Bearing Lictors

On the folks who physically had to carry the fasces—the lictors—our (largely elite) literary sources get us only so far. Epigraphy provides welcome evidence on their professional organization and social status, at least in the Empire. Yet the broad consensus among our literary authors—Republican and Imperial, Greek and Latin, prose and poetry—is that lictors were low-born and prone to thuggish behavior, over and above the unnerving actions that their formal duties might involve. "It was every man's own imagination that made them great and awe-inspiring," Livy has a rabble-rousing speaker say in 473 BCE of the consuls' lictors, whom he points out were (merely) plebeians. Examples of open social disdain for lictors persist into the literature of late antiquity.[6]

Then there was the violence and cruelty of lictors, which can be regarded as proverbial, throughout the antique period. As early as Plautus's comedy the *Asinaria*, first produced sometime between 212 and 205 BCE, two slaves compliment each other in a comically inflated dialogue on their ability each to withstand beatings at the hands of "eight fierce rod-men (*virgatores*)" or "lictors," the latter armed "with flexible elm rods." Each seems to be exaggerating the details of mundane domestic punishment—hence the humor of the exchange. Yet patently the figure of the fierce lictor was already a well-established trope. Not much in this regard changes over the next five and a half centuries. Writing after the death of the emperor Julian (363 CE), the sophist Libanius evokes the image specifically of an official "escorted by lictors who lash out with their rods and create alarm," in contradistinction to his own claims of moderation as a private citizen.[7]

To convey all the more vividly the qualities perceived in lictors and the nature of the commands they received, ancient authors regularly personify the fasces themselves. So Cicero says the insignia "produced fear"; Horace (followed by Statius) calls them "arrogant"; Valerius Maximus tags them as "domineering."[8] A crucial reference to the "fasces and their cruel axes" appears already in Lucretius, in a passage in which he critiques the Sisyphean desire of politicians for high office. Vergil then takes Lucretius's phrase and expands it, for a central passage of *Aeneid* Book 6—and indeed for the epic as a whole— in the context of describing Rome's transition from monarchy to Republic. "Would you also see the Tarquin kings, the proud spirit of Brutus the avenger, and the fasces regained?," asks Anchises in the underworld, as he offers his son Aeneas a visual tutorial in the destiny of Rome. Anchises then points out Lucius Iunius Brutus (consul in 509 BCE, the first year of Rome's Republic). "He first shall receive a consul's power and the cruel axes, and when his sons would stir up revolt, the father will hale them to execution in fair freedom's name." In this way the permanence of the figure was guaranteed.[9]

There is no obvious endpoint for the study of the ancient fasces. Lictors followed Rome's top authorities wherever they went, and use of the fasces was extended to municipal magistrates and, in time, certain priesthoods and even Rome's empresses. We find the fasces also as an attribute of office in the Byzantine period, and in an attenuated form, utilized by the emperor's body-guard probably down to 1453.

Post-Classical Interpretation of the Fasces

So ubiquitous are the fasces in ancient sources that we find Renaissance humanists and artists readily comprehending the emblem's basic appearance, use, and official symbolism. However, what demonstrably made less of an im-pression on thinkers of this and indeed later ages was the psychological terror generated by the original Roman fasces. For that development, we can blame a learned conflation in the Renaissance era of an antiquarian understanding of the fasces with a famous ancient moralizing tale of Greek origin. The story is first found in the Greek author Babrius (second century CE), was attached to Aesop's collection of *Fables*, and is known variously as "The Old Man and his Sons" or "The Bundle of Sticks." The larger context is that an aged father's sons habitually quarreled. Since he could not persuade them to stop through an appeal to reason, he devised this participatory exercise with the sticks. "'O my sons,' concludes the father in the fable. "If you are all of the same mind, then no one can do you any harm, no matter how great his power. But if your intentions differ from one another, then what happened to the single rods is what will happen to each of you!"[10]

Within the genre of fable, the story of the bundle of sticks has an unde-niable immediacy, since it is placed directly in the sphere of human relations, and not mediated (as so often in Aesop) through animal actors. Indeed, a particularized version of this tale crops up in the later Roman-era *Sayings of Kings and Commanders*, that has come to us in Plutarch's collection of *Moral Essays*. There we get a name for the father—Scilurus, a king of Scythia who reigned in the late second century BCE—and a specific application of the lesson to the political sphere. When the king was on the point of death, we are told, he handed a bundle of javelins to each of his eighty sons in turn, with an order to break the assemblage. "After they had all given up, he took out the javelins one by one and"—despite his infirmity—"easily broke them all, thereby teaching the young men that, if they stood together, they would continue strong, but that they would be weak if they fell out and quarreled." The parable even passed beyond Greek and Roman literature, to find a rec-ognizable place, e.g., in the *Secret History of the Mongols*, composed in the thirteenth century.[11]

In Europe, the basic fable as recorded in Babrius enjoyed deep popularity in the Renaissance and beyond, inevitably with small changes along the way—for instance, the identification of the father's occupation, the origin of the sons' quarreling, and inevitably the ethical point of the tale. In a popular early sixteenth-century collection of fables widely circulated in the Low Countries (compiled by Louvain humanist Martinus Dorpius, and published starting in 1509), we find the lesson summed up in a Latin phrase adapted from Sallust's *Jugurthine War*: *concordia parvas res crescere, discordia magnas dilabi* ("with harmony small matters grow, with discord great ones are ruined"). In the original text, it is spoken by the Numidian king Jugurtha's uncle Micipsa; it reached the status of a key aphorism on the evils of discord even before the Renaissance. This memorable sentiment later also would become an almost canonical formulation of the Aesopic story's moral.[12]

It must be stressed that, in historical terms, there is no close connec-tion between the Roman fasces and the Aesop fable of the old man and his sons—other than the attractive coincidence that each involves a bundle of sticks. However, beginning in the course of the sixteenth century, the fasces and the fable became inextricably linked. And this in turn opened up whole new vistas in the centuries to follow for the interpretation of the fasces, es-pecially as connoting unity. Even Mussolini took the equation for granted. Just weeks after his "National Fascist Party" seized power in Italy in October 1922, he decided to devote significant public resources to investigating what was the most "authentic" form of the Roman fasces, and then to propagating the image that emerged from that research. When that effort was complete, he still insisted—despite a complete absence of ancient testimony—that what the fasces represented was the imposition of political unity by means of authority.

Structure and Contribution of this Study

The story of the ancient Roman and (in less detail) Byzantine fasces occupies the core of this book, Chapters 2 through 6. The rest of this work concerns the thorny tale of the post-classical afterlife of the fasces, especially in Italy, France, and the United States, and to a lesser extent, Great Britain. Chapter 7 assesses medieval and Renaissance knowledge of the insignia. In Chapter 8, I investigate how a series of iconological treatises in the early modern period sought to disengage the resonances of the rods with axe, but in the process imposed a few concepts on the symbol quite unfamiliar to the Romans. Chapters 9 and 10 seek to trace how the fasces entered the popular mainstream in Europe and the Americas in the seventeenth through twentieth centuries, and after 1789 won a central place as a political symbol in both the United States and France, independently of each other. Chapter 11 studies the attempts in Fascist Italy to recover the "authentic" form of the Roman insignia, with special emphasis on Mussolini's exploitation of the symbol, which escalated especially after December 1926, when the fasces was formally made the national emblem. In conclusion, Chapter 12 concerns itself with efforts to obliterate the emblem before and following the fall of Fascism in 1943, especially in Italy but also the United States. It also offers a brief case study of the only public monument constructed in the twenty-first century I have found that un-ironically presents a fasces, followed by some concluding comments on some current aggressive manifestations of the symbol.

The fasces as a marker of legitimate power had an astonishingly long run in the Roman world, and today remains—when it can be spotted and recognized—a potent symbol. However, there is no true global synthesis of this Roman institution and its afterlife, in any language. This work aims to make a start toward filling that gap, with a focus throughout on recovering details and assigning them to phases of development. Here I place special emphasis on tracing the connection between the original significance of the symbol and its post-antique uses—though admittedly in a much more restricted geographical area than I had originally researched. I conclude that there are surprisingly few direct lines to be drawn, and that paradoxically Mussolini ran roughshod over the ancient Roman tradition he supposedly cherished by making the fasces his actual symbol of state. My overarching argument is an unsurprising one: today's understanding of the fasces necessarily is mediated by layers of significance accrued over the centuries, and in assessing individual appearances of the symbol, context is key.

Many aspects of the story of the fasces have received expert treatment, as my bibliography should suggest. My sense is that this book would at least double in size if, at each point in the discussion, I were to list systematically in the notes every relevant item of modern scholarship. Instead, my practice has been to write directly, so far as is possible, from the primary sources and to cite in the notes only the secondary items that have substantially shaped my argument. The bibliography contains all the items I have used. As it happens, I have discussed the fasces, mostly from a different perspective, at some length in some of my earlier works, especially *The Praetorship in the Roman Republic* (2000). In some respects, the first half of this volume forms a pendant to that longer study.

In spirit, however, I feel this book is closest to a compact analysis offered by A. J. Marshall in a 1984 journal article, "Symbols and Showmanship in Roman Public Life: The Fasces." Page for page, Marshall offers the most stimulating treatment yet of why the fasces mattered, and how the dynamism and drama associated with this symbol made its impact felt in Rome's Forum, the streets, and the field, with some invaluable remarks also on its modern reception. He closes with the admonition that "a more empirical investigation into the impact of symbols and showmanship as an element in public life should be undertaken." One wishes that the author had lived long enough to write a full-length study of his topic. In this book I enthusiastically emulate Marshall's approach, seeking to apply it well beyond the ancient period, from the medieval through the Renaissance and down through the mid-twentieth century, when Mussolini's totalitarian regime ended up universally—and I think permanently—discrediting the fasces as a living symbol.

So it is hard to suppress shock that, starting in the early 2000s, a number of American white supremacist groups began to incorporate the fasces in their logos.[13] In a sense, the complex global history of the fasces offers to extremists what one may call plausible deniability in reviving images of the regalia. As I show in this book, it would be hard to eradicate the symbol of the fasces in America without dismantling a good bit of the US Capitol, the principal components of the Jefferson Memorial, and countless other public structures and monuments nationwide. But context clearly matters. There is nothing "fascist" about the fasces in Daniel Chester French's statue of a seated Lincoln in his Memorial, dedicated in Washington, DC, on May 20, 1922, seven months before Mussolini's "March on Rome" by which he seized political power in Italy. Wearing a T-shirt emblazoned with the fasces to a hate rally in 2022 is a different matter.

This book has turned out to be not so much a comprehensive treatment of the fasces—my original and frankly naïve intention—as an impressionistic sketch of what the symbol meant to the Romans and some of those who looked back at the history and insignia of their ancient society, sometimes through multiple interpretive layers. I am convinced that the topic of the fasces is an important and timely one, not least since October 2022 marks the centenary of Mussolini's March on Rome. There is of course universal awareness of the word "fascism," but in my experience not much understanding how the original fasces worked in ancient Rome, and still less the pervasiveness of the fasces in modern-era political culture outside of Mussolini's Italy, and the struggle in the twenty-first century to control the symbol's meaning. These are the areas where I hope this study has made at least an initial contribution.

2

Origins of the Fasces

The Etruscan "Tomb of the Lictor"

In the early 1930s the tiny Tuscan hamlet of Vetulonia, some 200 kilometers northwest of Rome, was aiming to build its own "Casa del Fascio"—a local headquarters for the National Fascist Party (PNF). To help fund the construction, postcards were sold that highlighted a striking find from the town's Etruscan past, discovered in 1897 by the archaeologist Isidoro Falchi. Though clearly archaic in date, the object had a strong contemporary relevance, in that it was the oldest known representation of a fasces (Figure 2.1).

What is pictured on the card is in fact an early model of a fasces, made completely of iron, that served as a marker of status in a male burial from Etruscan-era Vetulonia. Though heavily oxidized and fragmentary—the vertical portion had crumbled into three segments, and lost some elements—one readily discerns a double-headed axe with its long handle surrounded by rods, originally perhaps seven or eight in number.

Falchi had found this fasces in the necropolis of Vetulonia, in a tomb with a simple decorative program. But the burial included bronze fragments evidently of a chariot harness, as well as rich Orientalizing grave goods, datable to the latter half of the seventh century BCE. So the deceased must have been a high-status individual. All the same, Falchi dubbed his burial place the "Tomb of the Lictor" from that distinctive find of the fasces, for the sake of convenience.[1]

In examining the three broken segments of the fasces, Falchi surmised that at "the two points of the break there was a choke-point designed to receive the lace that kept the sticks tied to the central axis, to which the axe was attached and clenched at the top." The object must have been merely symbolic, for its dimensions were obviously reduced from those of a real instrument. It would

The Fasces. T. Corey Brennan, Oxford University Press. © Oxford University Press 2023.
DOI: 10.1093/oso/9780197644881.003.0002

FASCIO LITTORIO ETRUSCO - VI sec. a. C. - rinvenuto nella
Necropoli di Vetulonia l'anno 1898 nella " Tomba del Littore ,,
(oggi al Museo Archeologico di Firenze)

. . . . I Vetuloni
Vetusto onor delle meonie terre
Pria d'ogni altro costor sei fasci e sei
Mandâr innanzi al console, e di scuri
Altrettante aggiungeano il terror muto :
D' avorio le curuli alte fregiaro,
Della porpora tiria essi la toga
Primi listâr, e accesero le pugne
Co' suoni della tromba. . . . . . .
Silio Italico " Le Puniche ,,
(Trad. di O. Occioni)

FIGURE 2.1. Postcard (1937) showing fasces-like decorative element (60 cm in length, with double-headed axe joined to rods, all in iron) found in 1898 in "Tomb of the Lictor" at the Etruscan site of Vetulonia.

Credit: Collection of T. C. Brennan.

have reached only about 60 centimeters in length, with the span of the twin blades at the top almost half that measure.

On the face of things, this assemblage of axe and rods and binding would seem to confirm a unanimous ancient tradition, that the Etruscans used the fasces as an insignia of legitimate power, and that the Romans derived the institution from them. Indeed, the postcard joined the image of this proto-fasces with a passage from the poet Silius Italicus (later first century CE), in which he posits that the Romans adopted their chief emblems of magisterial status—namely the fasces, the portable stool with curved legs known as the "curule chair," the purple-bordered toga, and the trumpet—specifically from Vetulonia. "From that city," wrote Silius, "came the twelve bundles of rods that are borne before the consul"—i.e., Rome's chief regular magistrate—"and also the twelve axes with their silent menace." Here the poet of course necessarily implies that lictors, the attendants who wielded the fasces, also owed their origin to Vetulonia.[2]

To be sure, this was quite a heady legacy in the general context of 1930s Italy. As we shall see, even before Mussolini's Fascist party seized power in late October 1922, it relentlessly had promoted the rods with axe as their key symbol, and indeed had intensified its efforts after securing the fasces' status as Italian national emblem in December 1926. So the postcard was a modest but clever way for tiny Vetulonia, which at the time had a population of just over 1,000, to leverage its perceived contribution to Rome's system of political symbols for a practical end. The town indeed got its Casa del Fascio, with construction starting in 1934. It is hard to see how the proceeds of the postcards alone could have made much of a difference. But the image certainly broadcast the Tuscan town's role as the ultimate origin of the *fascio littorio*, the lictors' fasces.

Today the consensus view is that the date of the "Tomb of the Lictor" at Vetulonia can be narrowed to 630–625 BCE. So its fasces must be anterior, if only slightly, to the traditional date of Rome's fifth king, and first Etruscan ruler, Tarquinius Priscus, conventionally said to have reigned 616–579 BCE. What is safe to say is that the fasces was recognized as an emblem of power and prestige in central Italy already during the regal period in Rome. That in turn would seem to confirm the unanimous testimony of our literary sources that Rome's kings had lictors and fasces, at least starting with the elder Tarquinius.

The Fasces of the Kings at Rome

The ancient tradition on the fasces of regal Rome is quite specific. Our literary sources agree it was the chief physical symbol of the kings' essentially undefined and unlimited civil and military power, technically known as *imperium*. This absolute power, vested in the person of the king alone, entitled him to do whatever he thought fit in the public interest. Wherever the king went, the lictors processed before him with axes mounted in their bundles of rods, even in the city itself. The social status of those lictors hardly mattered, with the important proviso that they had to be citizens.[3]

A word of further explanation. For the Romans, the story of *imperium* started on April 21, 753 BCE, give or take a year or so. It was activated by the auspication (literally, "bird watching") undertaken by Romulus on the day of the city's foundation—and confirmed by Jupiter through his sending of twelve vultures. Possessing *imperium*, and with it, the "public auspices" of the Roman people, entailed the competence to request, observe, and announce Jupiter's signs regarding an important act, and then to complete what was intended. Since auspication preceded every major action taken on the state's behalf, it formed the basis of regal, and then, in the Republic, magisterial power.

So did the ancients think that Romulus, as Rome's founder and first king, instituted also the fasces? The most fulsome and detailed testimony on Roman kings and the fasces comes from a Greek antiquarian of the late first century BCE, Dionysius of Halicarnassus. He firmly believed that the Etruscans were the source of that institution, as well as other signs of monarchical power found in old Rome, such as the gold crown, ivory throne, scepter tipped with an eagle, and purple dress. If Romulus chose to represent his power by axes and rods, as some authorities had posited, Dionysius insists he must have derived the idea from Etruria.

Furthermore, Dionysius of Halicarnassus takes special pains to explain why the Romans had precisely twelve lictors precede their kings, and later, after their expulsion, the two annual magistrates who headed Rome, known as consuls. Again, for him the practice has an Etruscan origin. There were twelve principal Etruscan cities, Dionysius relates, and the king of each community had one lictor at home. "Whenever the twelve cities undertook any joint military expedition," he continues, it was usual "for the twelve axes to be handed over to the one man who was invested with absolute power." This, asserts Dionysius, is the background to a tradition that Etruscan legates brought Tarquinius Priscus a set of axe and rods from each of the twelve cities when he became Rome's sovereign.

"Tarquinius, however, did not avail himself of these honors as soon as he received them," Dionysius says is the majority view of his Roman sources, "but left it to the Senate and people to decide whether he should accept them or not." Once validated, "twelve lictors, bearing the axes and rods, attended him when he sat in judgment"—one understands at home in Rome—"and preceded him when he went abroad" in the military sphere, setting a precedent for subsequent kings. Cicero also offers the first part of the (surely anachronistic) picture that Dionysius sketches, of a Tarquinius Priscus preoccupied with establishing a constitutional process for the assumption of his own rule.[4]

For Dionysius's contemporary Livy, there is no doubt that Romulus and all subsequent kings had the fasces. Yet he too endorses the origin story of the twelve Etruscan communities, against a variant view that made the symbol purely Roman. Apparently some of Livy's predecessors argued that the dozen auspicious vultures which appeared to Romulus at the foundation of Rome inspired him to represent his kingship with a like number of lictors.

In subsequent eras, not all authors agree on an Etruscan source of the fasces. In the later first century CE, Statius characterizes the fasces as coming from Latium. More than three hundred years later, so does Claudian, who also calls the insignia "Romulean." Meanwhile his contemporary Prudentius ascribes them to "Ausonia" (i.e., Italy in general). Writing in the early fifth century CE, Macrobius acknowledges the Etruscans, but with a martial twist. The Romans did not so much copy the insignia from their neighbors, but rather took them as spoils of victory, well before Tarquinius stepped foot in Rome. "After the Etruscans had been defeated in war," says the antiquarian, "Tullus Hostilius, the Romans' third king, instituted the practice of using at Rome the curule seat, lictors," as well as special types of decorated togas to show status.[5]

So where are we? The descriptions of Tarquinius Priscus's minute attention to constitutional procedures of course strain credulity. However, given the archaeological evidence from Vetulonia, there is no good reason to reject the possibility that this king processed with lictors and fasces. Indeed, that spectacle must be regarded as the most distinctive and revealing aspect of the public presentation of the kings of Rome—at least the later, Etruscan ones of the sixth century BCE—that we can reliably recover.

The institution clearly was meant to leverage memories of regal prestige in Etruria—where many communities already had replaced kings with elected magistrates. It also signaled the king's preparedness to enforce obedience to commands (a power that the Romans later called *coercitio*, or "coercion"), even through exercising capital jurisdiction. But the most visceral effect of the ceremonial parade of what the Romans at least later called lictors was the injection of pure psychological terror into what was in some important respects a politically regressive community.[6]

The Fasces: Etymology and Parallels

A word about the origins of the words "fasces" and "lictor." The etymology of Latin *fascis* (*fasces* is its plural) is not in doubt. Its Indo-European root is **bhasko-*, to be glossed as a "bundle," or a "band." Though the overwhelming number of instances of the word in Latin texts occur in the plural and refer to the insignia of authority, the singular is occasionally found, especially in farming contexts (a "bundle of reeds," or the like). An important secondary meaning of the singular *fascis*, mostly in later Latin, is a heavy or onerous thing, found already in Vergil's *Eclogues*, where one shepherd says to another, "I will relieve you of this burden (*fasce*)," in this case of young goats.[7]

But where does the title "lictor" come from? The ancients didn't know for certain. Writing in the latter half of the second century CE, the scholarly miscellanist Aulus Gellius reports two quite different views. Tiro (died 4 BCE), the learned freedperson of Cicero, is said to have derived the word from a type of belt (Latin *licium*) or apron (*limus*) that these attendants wore. In contrast, a younger contemporary named Valgius Rufus said it was the "binding" (*ligare*) the lictors did to those they intended to discipline that gave rise to the name.

"When the magistrates of the Roman people had given orders that anyone should be beaten with rods," says Gellius in championing Valgius's explanation, "his legs and arms were always fastened and bound by an attendant." For this, Valgius had adduced Cicero himself as support, citing a line in his *Defence of C. Rabirius* (63 BCE), "Lictor, bind his hands" (*i, lictor, conliga manus*).

Writing probably under the emperor Trajan (reigned 98–117 CE), the inquisitive Greek author Plutarch had included both these explanations in his *Roman Questions*, as well as a third (absurd) possibility, that the attendants once were called "litores," which he glosses as "public servants," based on a supposed Greek cognate. Modern scholarship has added its own guesses, for instance, that somehow *licere* ("to be allowed") lies at the root of the word. However, on balance, it does seem that Valgius Rufus got it right, and that the lictors' name came from one their unsettling duties, namely binding persons to be punished with the leather straps on the fasces.[8]

In the ancient world, the concept of official attendants using rods to enforce order was hardly unique to the Etruscans and Romans. The Athenian comic poet Plato, who wrote in the later fifth century BCE, had a (now wholly lost) play with the title *Rhabdouchoi* ("staff bearers"), which is how later Greeks through the Byzantine period translated Latin "lictores." In this case, the reference was surely not to the Roman institution, but rather to security personnel in the Athenian theater. The Hellenistic-era historian Hippias of Erythrae says that in the archaic era, when a trio of oligarchs seized control of his Ionian home town, they dressed in purple, sported gold, and "forced some of the citizens to carry them in litters, others to serve as staff-bearers"—again, *rhabdouchoi*—"and still others to clear the streets" of crowds.

There is more. The Greek historian Polybius wrote that in 205 BCE the Egyptian Greek noblewoman Oenanthe relied on the protection of female attendants armed with staves. This bodyguard, however, ultimately was of little help when angry Alexandrians tore her and her family to pieces. Several Greek sources imagine that the early fifth century BCE Roman exile Coriolanus retained fasces and lictors when he led a Volscian army from southern Latium against Rome. Livy seems to suggest that in Italy also the Samnites had lictors. Sallust ascribes a lictor to the Numidian king Jugurtha (reigned 118–105 BCE). Pliny the Elder reported that a sacred Egyptian ox at Memphis had lictor-like attendants to clear a path.[9]

However, the Etruscan-style fasces, with rods, straps, and an axe, is clearly a quite different instrument than a simple staff. This "portable kit for flogging and decapitation"[10] allowed the kings' lictors to inflict multiple simultaneous beatings, or even executions, wherever the king went. As such, the fasces were much more than an abstract badge of status. Rather, they must reflect the Etruscan outsiders' efforts to rule a potentially resistant Latin people and control their aristocracy by a combination of intimidation and spectacle. In a sense, the fundamental task of lictors was to project their superior's official power assertively into the public sphere while keeping him safe, and to ensure subjection to his authority while sparing his personal engagement in that process. In this, the display of fasces was obviously central.

Rome's Etruscan Kings and the Fasces

It must be said that when our literary sources narrate the history of Rome's monarchy—writing in the late Republic, centuries after the events they purport to describe—there is no special emphasis on the latent violence of the fasces. Rather, they seem to imagine that the kings' lictors functioned essentially as in their own day, as a defensive bodyguard. Consider Livy's account of the assassination of Tarquinius Priscus and his succession, which his wife Tanaquil engineered, by Servius Tullius.[11] As Livy tells the story, the lictors are more effective at enforcing silence in Tarquinius's court than protecting him against a stealthy axe attack during a hearing. And when Tanaquil hides the death of her husband from the public, and introduces Servius as acting in his place, the lictors comply in this dodgy transition without a fuss. However, as I hope to show, our sources have plenty to say in retrospective notices about the terror produced by the regal display of fasces.

After the expulsion from the city (traditionally dated to 509 BCE) of Rome's seventh king, Tarquinius Superbus, the monarchy was gone once and for all. Henceforth two magistrates—at least later to be known as consuls—were chosen from among the senatorial caste of patricians to head the new Republic. Each of the consuls received full public auspices and undefined *imperium*. But they differed from the kings in that their office involved collegiality (in case of conflict, the negative voice prevailed) and annual succession. And now both the Senate and especially the people—i.e., Roman citizens in their organized assemblies—grew in importance.

Fasces in the First Year of the Republic

There is a unanimous tradition that when the Romans replaced their monarchy with a Republic, they retained the lictors and fasces as the principal marker of legitimate power. The full complement of fasces remained notionally at the regal dozen, but the institution was rationalized, for each of the two consuls who now formally headed the state had a right to the insignia. We can judge the fasces' effectiveness from the fact that this arrangement then lasted in its essentials for more than a millennium to come.

Though each of the two consuls was entitled to the twelve fasces of the king, Livy is emphatic that from the start of the Republic there was instituted an awkward system of taking turns with the insignia when the chief magistrates found themselves together. Indeed, as we shall see, a long series of literary sources consistently point up the transgressive aspects of displaying more than twelve fasces in the city.

As tradition has it, 509 BCE, the first consular year of the Republic, actually saw five consuls. The first two were the pair Lucius Tarquinius Collatinus, whose wife Lucretia by her suicide had inspired a revolution against the monarchy, and Lucius Iunius Brutus. Livy narrates that the two consuls agreed that Brutus would be the first to have a turn with the lictors bearing fasces. Yet he and his consular colleague had to face down an instant crisis. They quickly needed to quash a conspiracy to restore the deposed Tarquinius Superbus. Ironically, two of Brutus's sons are said to have joined in the attempt to bring back the Etruscan king. For this, they were tried in Rome's Forum and, when their guilt was clear, were decapitated by lictors on the spot.

As Livy tells the tale, both consuls ascended a tribunal and ordered their lictors to carry out the execution. But the bulk of our sources (including Vergil in his *Aeneid*) make Brutus the protagonist. Plutarch, writing in the late first or early second century CE, imagines a grisly scene where little more than a nod from this consul is enough to prompt the lictors into action.

"[They] straightway seized the young men, tore off their togas, bound their hands behind their backs, and scourged their bodies with their rods. The rest could not endure to look upon the sight, but it is said that the father . . . watched the dreadful punishment of his sons until the lictors threw them on the ground and cut off their heads with the axe. Then he rose and went away, after committing the other culprits to the judgment of his colleague."

But Collatinus—a relative of the Tarquins, and whose nephews are said to have had a part in the attempted coup—ended up abdicating or having his *imperium* abrogated; Publius Valerius Publicola, who had served as a judge in the conspiracy case, was chosen consul in his place. Then Brutus himself was killed in battle, against Etruscans. To fill his post, Publicola saw to the election of one replacement, who soon died, and then another, before the year ran out.[12]

This anecdote of the punishment of Brutus's sons is a powerful one. What it most immediately communicates, of course, is the patent brutality of a father against his sons, combining a spectacle of corporal and capital punishment, inflicted in the name of raising public over private concerns. Yet it is also of critical importance to note that here a member of the Latin aristocracy is using the fasces to signal official dominance over supporters of a would-be Etruscan usurper. So this legendary episode captures the precise moment when the Romans made an Etruscan institution henceforth their own.

The story of Brutus and his sons also represents a flashing moment when the fasces of the Republican consuls were at their most regal. For Publicola, the new suffect (i.e., replacement) consul was to earn the reputation of reshaping how henceforth the fasces would be deployed. The family of the Iunii Bruti of the late Republic understandably made much of the belief that its putative ancestor was the first man in the post-regal period to receive the king's most important insignia, and the last to display them without modification in the city. A denarius that the young Marcus Iunius Brutus, as moneyer, minted in 54 BCE shows on its obverse a female head of "Liberty" (duly tagged as such), and on the reverse the ancient Brutus (again, with identifying legend) in a simplified representation of a procession, walking toward the left. Heading the group is the magistrate's personal attendant (Latin *accensus*). Then comes the consul, placed between two lictors, who on their left shoulders carry fasces—complete with axes (Figure 2.2).

The tradition, reported by Livy, that Brutus had the first turn with the fasces "by his colleague's consent," seems to be highly relevant for the

FIGURE 2.2. Denarius (silver) of M. Iunius Brutus, 54 BCE. The reverse shows his claimed ancestor, the consul (509 BCE) L. Iunius Brutus, between two lictors, preceded by an *accensus* (magistrate's attendant), all walking left; BRVTVS in exergue = *RRC* 433/1. Credit: Classical Numismatic Group, Inc. Triton XXV, Lot 739 (January 11, 2022).

interpretation of this coin. What is clear is that this denarius was the first to depict lictors in ceremonial procession, and demonstrably made quite a splash. As we shall see, not many years later (before ca. 25 BCE), a Danubian dynast decided to copy the type on a gold coin issue. His minters omitted from the scene the *accensus*, but kept the axes fixed in the fasces, which would have been their expected aspect outside of Rome.[13]

So Lucius Iunius Brutus as consul for 509 BCE earned lasting fame as the first in the new Roman Republic to put the fasces to work, indeed to their fullest and most terrifying potential. In this connection his name is regularly invoked even in later antiquity.[14] Yet this first consular year still offered more lore on the rods and axes. Put briefly, the tradition is that Publius Valerius Publicola, who was elected as a substitute consul under Brutus's presidency to replace Collatinus, took pains to emphasize that the Roman people be recognized as the source of the fasces. In all, we see our sources attach to his suffect consulship of 509 BCE up to four "popular" measures specifically in regard to the insignia.

The question of what prompted this blizzard of legislation invited some ancient speculation. The third-century CE consul and historian Cassius Dio, in a late summary, suggests that Publicola positively had to come up with his package of popular reforms, and quickly too. When he found himself as sole consul, it is alleged, the Romans suspected that he was aiming at kingship, and would have murdered him with their own hands had he not cleverly made a show of deference. This is of course obvious rationalization; Publicola's name ("cherisher of the people") seems enough in itself to explain how he received the reputation of reformer in our annalistic accounts.

Cicero in his dialogue *On the Republic*—written between 54 and 51 BCE—is our earliest detailed source on what Publicola was supposed to have done. The two relevant passages make it hard to assess Cicero's understanding of the relative order of these reforms. But his clear implication is that they came in quick succession, precisely once Brutus's death in battle left Publicola as sole consul. In Cicero's work, the famed general and statesperson Scipio Aemilianus (consul in 147 and then 134 BCE) professes surprise at how the Romans in the first year after the expulsion of the Tarquins expressed their new liberty. Among other developments, says Scipio, Publicola instituted a custom that the fasces be lowered in the presence of the Roman people "when he began to speak." Livy describes how Publicola "summoned the people to a council, and with lowered fasces mounted the speaker's platform." Other sources confirm that it was Publicola who first did this when he entered a popular assembly. Among these is Plutarch, who adds that it is a practice that "the consuls observe to this day."

Furthermore, Scipio in Cicero's dialogue notes that the first consular year brought "rights of appeal in all things." The reference here is to a provision that Roman citizens sentenced to capital or corporal punishment by a magistrate henceforth had the right of appeal (in Latin, *provocatio*) to the Roman people. Subsequent measures, especially the series of Porcian laws of the second century BCE, reinforced this basic right. In other words, the ability to appeal to the people served as a curb on the magistrate's use of his lictors.

Later Scipio again brings up the *provocatio*, and adds two more items on the reforms, this time with some welcome signposts. "Publicola, as soon as that law of his in regard to the right of appeal was passed," we read, "ordered the axes to be removed from the bundle of rods; and the next day he caused Spurius Lucretius [Tricipitinus] to be elected as his colleague and ordered his own lictors to be transferred to Spurius as his senior in age." Why would he do that? Cicero's Scipio explains: "Publicola also introduced the rule that the lictors should precede each consul alternately for one month, so that the insignia of executive power might not be more numerous in the free state than they had been under the monarchy."

Cicero is squeezing quite a lot of consequential measures into Publicola's portion of the year 509 BCE. His Scipio Aemilianus clearly links the requirement that the consuls' lictors remove the axes from the fasces within the city boundary with the citizens' new right of appeal. Dionysius of Halicarnassus relates it more generally to Publicola's desire to emphasize popular sovereignty: "this was in order that the terrifying sight, as one employed against their enemies or slaves, might give as little offense as possible to the citizens."

The treatment of the rotation of the fasces, however, allows for some head scratching. In contrast to Livy, who regards the consular "turn" as original to the first beginnings of the Republic, Cicero presents it as an adjustment. Evidently, he is imagining a scenario where the first consular pair each always had twelve lictors and fasces fitted with axes. The early imperial anecdotist Valerius Maximus, who closely follows Cicero's dialogue in a sketch of Publicola's studied moderation, in fact speaks of that early consul "withdrawing axes from the fasces, lowering them in assemblies of the people, and halving their number."[15]

Then there is the bit on how the twelve lictors were distributed. Cicero's Scipio posits that the first consular rotation came when Publicola transferred his fasces-bearing lictors to a newly elected, older colleague. Priority of a consul in age, order of election, or even number of children was indeed an attribute of later eras when determining which of a consular pair should first hold the fasces. Whether any of these factors obtained in the earliest Republic is anyone's guess—and indeed, whether the consular "turn" even dates to this era. The custom, however, does seem to have survived not just the Republic, but the imperial era into late antiquity.[16]

Still, all our literary sources are agreed that the reforms of 509 BCE stuck, and more or less permanently set the tone for Roman political life. Execution of citizens by a lictor's axe-blow within the narrow circuit of the formal city boundary disappears. One notes that when describing the suppression in 500 BCE of a conspiracy in the city, Dionysius of Halicarnassus imagines that the lictors used swords for that purpose. There is a more consequential development. That popular favor grants the emblem of the fasces and the power it represents can be regarded as a commonplace in Republican and even imperial authors, of all genres. Ironically, one of its most famous expressions is in the negative, namely the satirist Juvenal's complaint in the early second century CE that the Roman people "that once used to bestow *imperium*, fasces, legions, everything, now limits itself. It has an obsessive desire for two things only—bread and circuses."[17]

The Roman Dictator's Fasces

It took all of eight years, according to the Roman historical tradition, for Publicola's reforms on the display of fasces to allow for a major exception.

Fear of a war with the Latins, we are told, led one of the consuls of 501 BCE to appoint a certain Titus Larcius Flavus as Rome's first "dictator"—a supreme emergency magistrate meant to privilege the capacity for initiative in one person, but for a period of just six months, notionally the length of a campaigning season. It does seem that a consul lost his power in the presence (loosely defined) of the dictator, and had to lay down his fasces. But a consul probably was unaffected, perhaps even in his symbolism, when not serving directly in proximity to the dictator.

The institution of a dictator aided by a "master of the horse" took hold, and is found used almost 90 times over the course of the next 300 years, with more than half of the instances falling in the fourth century BCE. Overuse (if not abuse) of the dictatorship during the Second Punic War (218–201 BCE) seems to have led to its retirement as an expedient in the second century. However, in 82/81 BCE, Lucius Cornelius Sulla, after imposing himself as master of Rome, revived the office for himself. That in turn set a precedent for Julius Caesar, named dictator four times in the period 49–44 BCE, in the second and third instances for a full year, and in the final instance, at most seven weeks before his assassination, as "perpetual dictator." That was in addition to four consulships held in the same span (48 and 46 through 44 BCE).[18]

So how were the fasces used to convey the special nature of the dictator's power? Writing in the mid-second century BCE, the Greek historian Polybius tells us that twenty-four lictors accompanied the dictator. On the other hand, a late summary of a lost portion of Livy relates that Sulla "as dictator appeared in public accompanied by twenty-four fasces, which no one had ever done." This emphatic statement may be reconcilable with Polybius's report if Sulla was the first to be preceded by twenty-four within the city's sacral boundary, known in Latin as the *pomerium*. Earlier dictators will have had twelve in Rome, like the old kings and the individual consuls; the twenty-four fasces can have been outside the city.

In truth, Polybius may be a bit confused. He demonstrably had never seen a living dictator. But he will have been present in Rome at the aristocratic funeral processions where masked and costumed actors brought back to life the deceased's distinguished ancestors who had reached high office. As Polybius tells us, such actors accompanied the bier to the speaker's platform in the Forum, all of whom "ride in chariots preceded by the fasces, axes, and other insignia by which the different magistrates are wont to be accompanied according to the respective dignity of the honors held by each during his life; and when they arrive at the rostra they all seat themselves in a row on ivory [i.e., "curule"] chairs." The mention of chariots and axes within the city underlines that such parades aimed at an especially assertive display of power. Naturally, the families who had a dictator will have claimed the full complement of fasces for the occasion—hence perhaps Polybius's notion.[19]

As so often for the earlier Republic, in reconstructing the fasces of the original dictator, we have to combine our available sources with a bit of historical imagination. To be sure, the dictator's insignia had to convey the special nature of his superior status to all other magistrates. However, the kings of Rome had represented their absolute power with twelve fasces. Logically it is hard to see how the dictator received more. The key must be that the dictator was not subject to the consular rotation, and so always had the capacity for independent action. It also appears that the dictator's lictors kept axes in their fasces even within the city.[20]

So how are we to suppose the system worked? Presumably, when a dictator was in the city, both consuls were escorted by lictors without full fasces, indicating that their *imperium* lay dormant. If one of the consuls were to continue to be preceded by the fasces, there would be no significant way by which to distinguish his insignia (and powers) from those of the dictator. In the field, where rotation usually did not have to be observed, the dictator had twenty-four lictors to mark him clearly as the full equal of a consular pair, with the ability to give either consul orders. Since the dictator was not a colleague of the consuls, no consul alone could effectively veto his actions. Livy, for one, thinks that a dictator could order an individual consul simply to send his lictors away. And suppose both consuls stood in the way of the dictator? The Romans probably viewed the fact that one of the two consuls was meant to choose and "name" the dictator as a sufficient safeguard against such dangerous conflict.[21]

This reconstruction, however, only hopes to explain the original form of the dictatorship, down to its last incumbent in 202 BCE. After the long intermission in the office, and its revival by Sulla and then Caesar in a significantly new form, there probably was not much genuine tradition about it. Sulla probably claimed that a dictator's powers were superior to consular (i.e., regal) *imperium*, to judge from his twenty-four lictors. Caesar, after his victory in the civil warfare of the early 40s, almost certainly tried to represent his status as such. For his "quadruple triumph" of April 46 BCE, marking the end of four wars (Gaul, Egypt, Pontus, Numidia), the Senate voted that Caesar could cumulate lictors from his three dictatorships to date, for a total of seventy-two. The spectacle backfired, according to the historian Cassius Dio, writing more than two and a half centuries after the event. "The lictors, on account of their numbers, appeared to [the people of Rome] a most offensive multitude, since never before had they beheld so many at one time."[22]

Early Administrative Experiments with Fasces

This admittedly dry discussion of the number of fasces is essential for our inquiry. For there is every indication that demarcating the attributes of official insignia was a serious concern during the Republic. Livy offers an instructive narrative on the harm unregulated fasces might do—almost certainly drawing on memories of Caesar in 46 BCE. It concerns the "decemvirs" ("members of a college of ten") of 451 and 450 BCE, ostensibly created for codifying the laws of Rome's nascent Republic. This extraordinary magistracy supplanted the consuls for those two years, and as such received their insignia. But how were the ten men meant to share them? In 451, relates Livy, only one decemvir had the fasces at a time. One can see the rationale behind this type of rotation, since it was supposed that early Rome had a ten-month calendar. But Livy says the sequence was determined not by months but by days. "Sitting each one day in ten they administered justice to the people. On that day he who presided in court had twelve fasces; his nine colleagues were each attended by a single orderly" (Latin *accensus*).

However, in the second year the system broke down, we are told, and each decemvir appeared in public to enter office with his own set of twelve fasces. And so "a hundred and twenty lictors crowded the Forum," narrates Livy, "and before them, bound up in the rods, they carried axes." (The implication is that such axes had not been seen within the city's sacral boundary since the days of the kings.) "And indeed the decemvirs explained that there had been no reason for removing the axe, since the office to which they had been chosen was without appeal." One notes that during the decemvirate even the plebeians—i.e., Rome's non-patricians, who after 494 BCE formed a sort of state within the state—ceased to elect tribunes to represent them, removing an important protection against official abuse.

Livy continues, explicitly stressing the psychological effect that this show of immunity from appeal created. "They seemed like ten kings; and the terror they inspired, not only in the humblest citizens but in the leaders of the Senate, was intensified by the belief that the decemvirs were merely seeking a pretext and an opening for bloodshed, so that if anybody should pronounce a word in praise of liberty, either in the Senate or before the people, the rods and axes might instantly be made ready, were it only to frighten the rest." Perhaps worst of all, the decemvirs "had further agreed not to interfere with each other's decisions," and so Rome's populace had no hope even for the veto inherent in collegial offices.

The antiquarian Dionysius of Halicarnassus offers essentially the same account as his contemporary Livy of the decemvirs of 450, but adds a dynamic detail of his own. The Romans were filled with terror at the sight within the city of 120 lictors with axes attached to the fasces in the regal fashion, who "with blows forced the throng back from the streets." The axes made the populace think "that they had lost their liberty and [had] chosen ten kings instead of one," whereas the decemvirs "made up their mind that they must rule them by fear thereafter." But as Livy and Dionysius describe, they found themselves overthrown when they attempted illegally to retain power—and with it, their insignia—into 449 BCE.[23]

The story has a sequel of sorts. Just five years after the Romans deposed the decemvirs, we learn they experimented with another multiplication of the chief magistracy. They dubbed these officials "military tribunes with consular power," evidently avoiding use of the word *imperium*. They appear sporadically in place of consular pairs in the years 444 to 367 BCE. Livy considered the consular tribunes, who materialize variously in colleges of three, four, or six, to have had lictors. Did they parade with the full complement of twelve fasces? Livy reports a variant view that "some" authorities thought these men "enjoyed both the consuls' *imperium* and insignia." Leaving aside the question of the *imperium*, the numbers of these consular tribunes—always factors of the number twelve—suggest that they divided the regal fasces among themselves. If so, a college of six consular tribunes would have just two lictors each, at least in the city.

For 443 BCE, our record suggests another instance of sensitivity to capping the annual number of fasces. In that year, the Romans created the office of the censor, a patrician magistracy with wide-ranging powers in the city, held for a period of eighteen months notionally every five years. Censors wore (significantly) the purple toga of the old kings, and enjoyed the same use of the honorific "curule" chair and minor attendants (*apparitores*) that Rome's higher magistrates had. But since censors did not have *imperium*, they received no lictors.[24]

Clearly the incident of the decemvirs of 450—who are said to have dispensed with rotation of insignia, multiplied the regal complement of fasces by ten, ignored Publicola's prohibition of axes in the civil space of the city, suspended the right to appeal, agreed not to veto each other, brutalized private citizens, and eventually refused to relinquish office—evoked for Livy and Dionysius the worst attributes of an absolute monarchy. In short, the tale amply explains why there should be public control of the fasces.

This is particularly so of the final episode, where (as we shall explore in more detail) the decemvirs of 449 BCE saw challenges to their legitimacy and thus resistance to their use of insignia. Indeed, this imaginative story of transgression may shed some light on a real, core problem of the regal era. Recent research on the actual historical situation of sixth century BCE Latium stresses "the strong tradition for the continued presence of independent, war-like clans, often led by so-called *condottieri*."[25]

Given that the received story of regal Rome is essentially a series of attempted or realized usurpations (e.g., Macstarna, Tarquinius Priscus, Lars Porsenna), one must consider that in the regal era competing individuals might simultaneously lay claim to sets of fasces. The same holds true for the first generations of the Republic, with the tradition of a trio of would-be tyrants, namely Spurius Cassius, Spurius Maelius, and Marcus Manlius (said to be killed in 486, 439, and 385 BCE, respectively). And as we shall see, actual usurpation of insignia is lavishly attested for the later Republic, the Triumviral period, and for the Empire as late as the mid-fifth century CE.

This political volatility, I argue, is the root of the tradition of early Republican regulations concerning how consuls should display their fasces. And when use of the fasces was extended in the Republic to officials other than consuls, it seems worth suggesting that cultural memory, as well as the theology of power and practical concerns, shaped the development of the elaborate system of guardrails and protocols we actually find.

The Double-Axed Fasces

To return to the earliest origins of the institution. Whether the poet Silius Italicus is correct that it was precisely Vetulonia which gave the fasces to the Romans must remain an open question. It happens that the archaeologist Isidoro Falchi's find in the Vetulonian necropolis still stands in total isola-tion in our record for the Etruscans of the archaic and classical periods, and so no material comparanda are available to reconstruct how the symbol got to Rome.[26]

To be sure, starting in the early Hellenistic age (late fourth century BCE) in Etruria we find representations of lictors (usually in pairs) bearing fasces in a variety of settings and media, especially in tomb paintings of processions and banquets. But the gap in the archaeological record of close to 300 years of fasces of any type argues against its continuity in Etruria as an institution. Rather, it suggests that the Etruscans of the late fourth century BCE staged a revival, in all likelihood stimulated by practice in Rome itself, or in the territories elsewhere under its control. Local officials in Italian municipalities, Roman colonies, and (later) in provincial cities often had lictors as attendants. At first they commonly equipped these attendants with staves. But in the imperial period these local lictors regularly carried fasces.[27]

There is another apparent sticking point for accepting Silius Italicus at his word on Vetulonia as the source for Rome's chief emblems of power. Falchi's discovery shows a double axe, which our extant literary and iconographic sources never offer as a Roman form of the fasces. However, we hardly have enough information to insist on original and then continuous use at Rome of fasces with a single axe. No actual Roman fasces have come to us from any era, and it is not until at least two and a half centuries after the end of the monarchy that we find our first artistic representations of the emblem.

So there really is no telling what the situation was in regal Rome. It seems conceivable, for instance, that Rome's kings had their lictors display a double axe, and that with the foundation of the Republic, the insignia was "split" into two for the annual pairs of consuls. As we have seen, other modifications of the regal fasces are ascribed to the first year of Rome's Republic, such as a requirement that the consuls somehow rotate the fasces among themselves when they are together, and that lictors remove the axes from the fasces within the city boundary.

3

Images of the Roman Fasces

Funerary Fasces in the Republic

This investigation of the form of the fasces in archaic Rome is necessarily quite speculative. As it happens, the earliest securely datable image of a Roman fasces is a relief sculpture found more than three hundred years later than the early developments we have so far discussed, and some 20 kilometers southeast of Rome. It belongs to a spectacular funerary monument whose rock facade overlooks Lake Albano from the slope of its eastern shore, below the modern Villa Palazzola.

The antiquarian Giovanni Antonio Riccy (1760–1808) was the first to deduce that this site almost certainly commemorates the *pontifex maximus* (i.e., chief priest of the state religion) Gnaeus Cornelius Scipio Hispallus, consul in 176 BCE. Livy tells us he died soon after discharging one of the first formal tasks of his consulship, the performance of the Latin Festival at the temple of Jupiter on Monte Albano. This massive pyramid-shaped monument, integrated into the promontory's side (Figure 3.1), may mark the spot where Hispallus first fell ill.

Here the large hillside relief sculpture, though unfortunately now quite eroded, still plainly shows twelve long fasces—the number marks consular office—each with a single laterally inserted blade. The fasces are displayed upside down, which later literary sources tell us was a sign of mourning. They are arranged in two groups of six, each fasces seemingly hanging from a loop that extends from its handle, flanking a near-illegible tableau of further emblems of the deceased's status. Riccy discerned in this central space between the fasces the curule chair of a high magistrate, the headgear of a *pontifex*, and a scepter (in Latin, *scipio*) topped with an eagle astride a globe. This mix of elements led him to the clever and compelling conclusion that Scipio Hispallus was the

The Fasces. T. Corey Brennan, Oxford University Press. © Oxford University Press 2023.
DOI: 10.1093/oso/9780197644881.003.0003

FIGURE 3.1. Giovanni Battista Piranesi (1720–1778), *Opere* Vol. 11: *Antichita d'Albano e di Castel Gandolfo; Descrizione e disegno dell'Emissario del lago Albano* (1762) Tav. III, showing the tomb of Gnaeus Cornelius Scipio Hispallus, who died as consul in 176 BCE.

Credit: University of South Carolina, Irvin Department of Rare Books and Special Collections.

honorand. What matters most for our present investigation is not the precise composition on the Hispallus monument of those centrally placed symbols. Rather it is that, already by the mid-second century BCE, a relief sculpture showing simply twelve inverted fasces, without lictors, could communicate a man's status as consul and the fact of his demise.[1]

We can presume that the patrician Scipio Hispallus, who died during his consulship of 176 BCE, had his fasces figure at his actual funeral. And that would be in addition to the other customary honors—including the display of ancestors' fasces—that Polybius tells us Rome's nobles (originally, those descended from holders of highest *imperium* in the male line) received at their death. This was a principal means of differentiating nobles from non-nobles, and recalling the men in the deceased's family who had reached high office. Indeed, when calculating the impact of this insignia in Roman society, we have to factor in their display in the constant series of these aristocratic funerals, already long traditional by Polybius's day in the mid-second century BCE. For Rome's highest nobility, one can readily imagine the ceremonial fasces numbering in the many dozens. The overall effect might have resembled the impact that Livy says the decemvirs made in 451–450 BCE.

By the early first century BCE, the fasces also figured prominently at the funerals of Roman noble women. It probably began with Quintus Lutatius Catulus, a protégé of the famed military man Gaius Marius and consul in 102 BCE, who about that time was the first to pronounce a funerary enco-mium over his mother Popillia, of an especially distinguished consular family. Then there is the case of Iunia, probably from the family of Iunii Bruti, who died in 91 BCE, whose funeral included (like those of noble men) actors role-playing her (male) ancestors with appropriate personal masks (*imagines*). Next attested for us is Julius Caesar, just starting out in his political career in 69 BCE, who staged a similar display for his aunt Julia, who was married to Marius. We are specifically told that his fasces were displayed at that event. Caesar seems to have offered a similar display in the next year at the funeral of his wife Cornelia, the daughter of a three-time consul. In the decades to follow, the spectacle must have grown more and more common, and indeed more elaborate. By the time we get to the reign of the emperor Tiberius, the death of another Iunia—this one the sister of Brutus, and wife of Cassius—saw in 22 CE the "celebration of her funeral with a panegyric at the Rostra and the rest of the customary ceremonies. The *imagines* of twenty great houses preceded her to the tomb"—pointedly excluding Brutus and Cassius themselves.[2]

One example can suffice to show the varied ways in which the fasces might be integrated into a public funeral. In 79 BCE, the presentation of magisterial insignia formed an integral element of the dictator Lucius Cornelius Sulla's cremation ceremony, even though he died as a private citizen. The second-century CE Greek historian Appian tells us that Sulla's body was placed in a golden litter and carried "in a procession throughout Italy" that terminated in Rome's Forum, headed by "all the standards and the fasces that he had used while living and ruling." And for Sulla's pyre, Plutarch reports that Rome's women contributed a quantity of spices that filled 210 litters (i.e., portable couches), in addition to enough frankincense and cinnamon to shape a large, combustible image of Sulla himself, "and another image of a lictor"—the latter surely holding a fasces. At some point before the mid-first century BCE it be-came customary, as Cicero indicates, that even managers of more elaborate funerals—ones that involved the celebration of games—be provided with actual lictors, plus the type of orderly known as an *accensus*.[3]

The Evidence of the Arieti Tomb

Fortunately, from the era of the consul of 176 BCE Cornelius Scipio Hispallus, we have roughly contemporaneous visual evidence for the fasces, and specifically how the lictors might bear them, at least in ceremony. It comes from a necropolis on the Esquiline hill in Rome, where in 1875 excavations not 300 meters east of S. Maria Maggiore yielded a rectangular tomb with a simply executed but spectacular mural painting cycle. This "Tomba Arieti" (named after its discoverer) originally showed, at a minimum, three distinct episodes. These were the torture and execution of a bearded and naked standing prisoner; a battle that features both cavalry and infantry, where the adversary is armed with oblong shields; and a distinctly Roman victory celebration, that of the triumph. That last scene has six lictors bearing fasces, preceding a commander in a four-horse chariot (Latin *quadriga*).[4]

An excavator's watercolor captured the procession scene with lictors when still in place and intact. Today the fresco fragments, housed in Rome's Centrale Montemartini Museum, present just four of the six lictors; the horses, chariot, and *triumphator* have not survived. Still there is quite enough to visualize the details of this section of the wall painting.

The artist has rendered the lictors schematically, largely without distinctive individual features, and with their bodies and faces oriented toward the viewer. They are in loose formation, and (despite the frontality of their

FIGURE 3.2. Watercolor of fresco scene (now partially lost) in the "Tomba Arieti" (Rome, Esquiline), showing a Roman triumph, with six lictors bearing fasces, preceding a commander in a four-horse chariot (Latin *quadriga*).

From Giatti (2007), 80 fig. 2.

depiction) plainly moving to the left. Each lictor holds upright in his right hand a single long rod at its base, and in his left hand, and resting on his upper left arm, a thin fasces with a single blade protruding from the bundle's upper left side. The fourth lictor in the series appears closer than the others, and is the only one of the figures to point his rod toward the left, evidently directing the others.

Laureled Fasces

What comes as a bit of a surprise is that the fasces of the Arieti Tomb lictors do not show any trace of decoration. Our literary sources on the triumph make much of how lictors of militarily successful generals—at least starting in the late second and earlier first century BCE—festooned their fasces with laurel. They did so the moment their commander won a qualifying victory in the field and heard his troops hail him with the charismatic appellation "imperator." The lictors then maintained the decoration as they returned to Rome, for the hoped-for celebration of a triumph.

As one might imagine, there was some elasticity to the notion of what qualified one for a triumph. For example, Cicero's consular colleague of 63 BCE, Gaius Antonius Hibrida, is said to have adorned his fasces with laurels even for a victory in Etruria against Romans, namely over the renegade senator Catiline and his insurrectionists in 62 BCE. Yet it was not this decoration per se that earned Antonius criticism. Rather, it was the fact that he then took his laureled fasces to his territorial province of Macedonia, where he was soundly routed by the tribe of the Dardani. As a late writer in the Livian tradition is keen to stress, the laurel turned out to be "an omen of victory to his enemies . . . that he ought to have deposited on the Capitol."[5]

The mention of a commander dedicating his laurels on the Capitol requires some technical explication. The Romans gave a spatial distinction to the spheres where public auspices were exercised. The sacral boundary—known as the *pomerium*—that formed a tight ring around Rome's innermost historic core served as a dividing line between the urban and extra-urban zones. Magistrates with *imperium* could not exercise their extra-urban ("military") auspices in the space of the "city." Another feature of the *pomerium* was that it caused higher magistrates who had been extended past their year of office ("prorogued") or those who had been voted extraordinary commands to lose irrevocably their complement of powers upon crossing into the "city."[6]

For this principle, take the example of Titus Otacilius Crassus in 215 BCE, whom Livy relates held a special praetorian command in Sicily, and then returned to Rome late that year to stand in the consular elections. Those were held in Rome's Campus Martius, in an area which lay (barely) outside the *pomerium*. There the presiding officer, his own father-in-law, Quintus Fabius Maximus—who held the consulship that year, his third—allegedly skewed the election by harshly criticizing his unexceptional performance. "While Titus Otacilius was fiercely and noisily shouting that Fabius wanted to have his consulship prolonged," narrates Livy, "the consul ordered the lictors to go up to him, and, as he had not entered the city, having gone without a halt directly to the Campus"—the implication is that in contrast, his son-in-law had already crossed the *pomerium*, thereby forfeiting his military insignia—"he warned Otacilius that the fasces carried before the consul had their axes."[7]

Otacilius Crassus was correct, at least about his father-in-law's political motives. Fabius in fact wanted (and got) the consulship for himself, and the former Sicilian commander had to console himself with the lesser office of a praetorship for 214. Yet the detail that Fabius threatened to execute his son-in-law for his remonstrations is jarring. Among other things, the incident reminds us that it was the rather tight circuit of the *pomerium*, not the larger occupied urban space of Rome, that placed a limit on the display of the full fasces.

A vote in the Senate, followed by popular ratification, entitled a Roman commander to cross the *pomerium* and enter the historical city center through a special gate—the *porta triumphalis* ("triumphal gate")—which was in essence a hole in the auspical space. A general who properly entered through it was entitled to retain his military auspices and axed fasces in the city (originally for a single day, later for multiple days), so as to make a formal procession to the Temple of Jupiter on the Capitoline, where he sacrificed in thanksgiving, and customarily dedicated that laurel from his fasces. In the late Republic we see commanders waiting outside Rome for periods up to almost five years in the hope of obtaining the requisite vote for that privilege, which brought lofty lifelong status. Oddly, in the meantime, their magisterial powers automatically remained valid.[8]

It is Cicero who offers us our most detailed examples of how seriously Roman commanders took the customs surrounding the bid for a triumph, including the decoration of fasces. One of Cicero's harshest criticisms of his political enemy Lucius Calpurnius Piso (consul in 58 BCE, later commander in Macedonia) is that the man despaired of a triumph, despite his acclamation in his province as *imperator*. Indeed, the man let the laurel wither on his lictors' fasces, and before entering Rome personally tore off the few leaves that remained and dumped them at the Esquiline gate. So says Cicero, with evident distortion, in the published version of an invective he delivered in the Senate in the latter part of 55 BCE.

When given the chance, Cicero showed himself ready to make more of far less. Expecting the vote of a triumph for his (meager) military activities in the southern Anatolian province of Cilicia (51/50 BCE), he made a serpentine path with his lictors and their laureled fasces for almost three full years, even crossing from Italy to Greece and back again. It was only in October 47 BCE, on Italy's east coast at Brundisium in the presence of Caesar, that he dismissed his lictors and waived his claim to a triumph. For soldiers, too, the laureled fasces mattered as a symbol, for they served as a reminder of their military success under their commander—and rewards they expected from him once returned to Rome. And for those who successfully entered the city? Several authors detail how the *triumphator* placed that laurel in the lap of the cult statue of Jupiter Optimus Maximus in his temple on the Capitoline. We have seen Cicero's consular colleague Gaius Antonius criticized for his inability to do so. The emperor Augustus himself, in the long inscription that serves as his political autobiography, boasts that multiple times he had "deposited upon the Capitol the laurels which adorned my fasces."[9]

At some point after the accession of the emperor Nero (54–68 CE), the lictors of Rome's emperors and even consuls carried laureled fasces in a wider range of ceremonies, and eventually for what seems to be routine use. For emperors, this really was an inexorable development. Pompey in 63 BCE and Julius Caesar after his victory in southern Spain at Munda in 45 BCE had been voted the right to appear in the guise of a "triumphator" at games in Rome's Circus Maximus, surely with laureled fasces, providing a precedent. And starting with Augustus, all of Rome's emperors after accession carried "impe-rator"—i.e., the laurel-qualifying title—as the first element of their names.[10]

What stands quite apart in our tradition, however, is the third-century CE historian Cassius Dio's report that the emperor Caligula, soon after his acces-sion in 37 CE, conveyed the remains of his mother Agrippina the Elder and older brothers Nero and Drusus to Rome, "and wearing the purple-bordered toga and attended by lictors, as at a triumph, he deposited their remains in the tomb of Augustus." The second-century CE imperial biographer Suetonius adds the macabre detail that Caligula had the human remains carried in pro-cession to Augustus's Mausoleum as if they were spoils in war. At the time of this event, the emperor had no military successes for which he would have earned triumphal insignia—which one assumes would have included laureled fasces.[11]

The Dress of Roman Lictors

But we have strayed quite far from the evidence of the second-century BCE Arieti tomb frescoes. There the remnants have preserved their details and colors reasonably well, which makes us sure about the absence of laurel on the fasces. Moreover, the paint reveals a crucial detail. Each lictor is dressed in a short red cloak that shows a broad white stripe down the center, and seems also to have a belt or clasp at his midsection. This distinctive outfit must be the military garb known as the *sagum*, open at the front, and showing a white tunic underneath. The poet Silius Italicus portrays lictors in the field in this dress. Before his treatment of the battle of Cannae (216 BCE), he has the Carthaginian Hannibal recognizing the Roman commander at a distance, from "a lictor in his scarlet robe (*sagulo . . . rubenti*) moving round him."[12]

It is worth noting what the Arieti lictors are not wearing, namely the *paludamentum*, a type of long, open-fronted cloak that marked Rome's commanders in the field, and which their lictors' uniforms mirrored and amplified. This garment was essentially a cape, colored so as to be readily recognizable—we hear of purple as well as red and even white—and secured off-center at the right shoulder by a clasp. Its use was prohibited within the sacral boundaries of Rome, even in the late first century CE.

Indeed, the act of a commander taking vows on the Capitoline and then, with his lictors, donning this distinctive cloak formed an important part of the ceremonial of transition from the civil to the military sphere. (Strictly speaking, in the view of Roman public religion, the "military" area was everything outside Rome, including all the territorial provinces, no matter how tranquil.)

The combination of *paludamentum* and lictors with the fasces was the chief signal that one held military *imperium*. This is apparent from an episode of 321 BCE, when the Samnites of south-central Italy trapped a large Roman army under both consuls of the year at the Caudine Forks (near modern Benevento). On the Romans' surrender, the first disgrace inflicted on the commanders was the order that their lictors should depart and they be stripped of their military cloaks. In another instance, when a consul of 177 BCE neglected the departure ritual of assuming the *paludamentum*, he was compelled to repeat it, returning with his lictors from Histria (a peninsula in the north Adriatic, now mostly Croatian territory) to Rome—a round trip of over 1,300 kilometers. On re-entering the city from the field, there was a corresponding necessity to doff the *paludamentum*. So the lack of *paludamenta* in this tomb painting confirms what we would otherwise expect, that the scene is set within the city of Rome.[13]

Fractional Grants of Fasces

The date of the images of the Arieti Tomb is difficult to pin down. The most thorough study of the tomb in its totality, taking into account stratigraphic, structural, and decorative aspects, can offer only "second century BCE" for the narrative wall paintings. Subject matter is another thorny issue. Granted, the three scenes might simply be generic, even given the distinctive representation of the enemy. Yet one must at least consider that the paintings commemorate a historical event, either from the same era as the building of the tomb or dating to a previous generation. Here the combination of the triumphal four-horse chariot and six lictors may offer a way forward. That was the number of lictors which accompanied the praetor, a junior colleague of the consuls who also held *imperium*, though of a lesser sort. As such, this magistrate was assigned half the consular complement of lictors, to signal that his *imperium* was subordinate to that of the consuls in case of proximity or actual personal conflict.

Now, the concepts of "lesser *imperium*" and a single praetor were introduced well before the probable date of this tomb—in the year 366 BCE, as part of a complex political and social compromise between Rome's patricians and the emerging plebeian nobility. This office was a clever invention, and proved a success. The number of praetors was doubled ca. 247 BCE, doubled again ca. 228, and by 197 had reached six. The praetor's reduced number of lictors was so distinctive and familiar that by the mid-second century BCE Greeks could call this magistrate simply the *hexapelekus*—"the six axes."

The first years of the second century BCE introduced a twist that helps us narrow the subject of the Arieti wall paintings, assuming it is indeed historical, and that the original number of lictors depicted was six. From 197 BCE on, the praetors who were sent to distant and dangerous commands in two newly created provinces in the Iberian peninsula regularly received grants of enhanced *imperium* at the consular level, and so twelve fasces. This in fact institutionalized a practice sometimes used in the Hannibalic War; in this way, it seems, the Romans imparted to such commanders the consuls' (previously exclusive) power to delegate *imperium* to others. This bears on our iconographic question in that it excludes from consideration triumphs that praetorian commanders celebrated from the provinces of Nearer or Further Spain.

The first individual with praetorian *imperium* to triumph was in 257 BCE, for a naval victory in the First Punic War. In the next century and a half, only three individuals with this degree of *imperium* are known to have celebrated a full triumph for fighting on land, which evidently is what is depicted in the Arieti Tomb: in the years 200 (against Gauls), 172 (against Corsicans, with the triumph held in protest on the Alban Mount, 21 kilometers southeast of Rome), and 167 BCE (against Illyrians).

The upshot of all this? If these mural paintings from the Esquiline necropolis reflect a historical event, it is likely to be one of these three Roman victories. The first in the series (i.e., that of 200 BCE) has the strongest claim, to judge from the tomb's battle scene where the enemy carries long oblong shields, which the Romans firmly associated with Gauls. At any rate, we can with some confidence refer the six lictors here to a praetorian triumph of the first third of the second century BCE, a bit earlier than or loosely contemporary with the funerary monument of the consul Scipio Hispallus that displays a dozen carved fasces. One notes that these two unrelated representations, in two different media, each in a funerary context, present the same form of the fasces: a single axe showing its blade from the side of the upper portion of a tall, slender bundle of rods. It is safe to regard that as the standard form of the assemblage in the second century BCE.[14]

Fasces and the Roman Citizen's Right of Appeal

One item in the Arieti Tomb fresco demands further comment. Why are the lictors walking in the triumphal procession with a single rod in their right hands? By chance, we find a lictor similarly illustrated on the reverse of a Roman denarius of the late second century BCE, minted by one Publius Porcius Laeca. The moneyer meant for the coin to advertise his family's connection to a series of three "Porcian laws" passed in the second century BCE, that concerned the right of appeal (*provocatio*) against physical punishment, including by those condemned in a criminal trial. The issue is to be assigned to the year 110 or 109 BCE, and must count as our third oldest datable image of a Roman fasces.

On the coin, a military commander with cuirass and sword stands at center facing left, raising his right hand and forearm above the head of a male, presented in smaller scale, clad in a toga. That man, presumably a Roman citizen, is raising his right arm in response. To the right of this pair, behind the commander, is the lictor. He is presented similarly as a reduced figure, in a short cloak, and approaches ready with his rods. However, the lictor holds one rod in his right hand, and apparently has unbundled his fasces, for he balances another two against his left arm; there is no axe. Below this design is the Latin legend PROVOCO—"I appeal."

This reverse offers a clever and dramatic composition, in that it captures the power dynamic between a Roman private citizen and public official, and the precise moment when the citizen appeals the corporal punishment that the authority has ordered the lictor to deliver. Indeed, the scene illustrates well Cicero's summation of the Porcian legislation: "the *lex Porcia* removed the rod from the body of any Roman citizen . . . [it] wrested the liberty of the citizens from the lictor." The image portrays the lictor as a mere instrument of power, and one liable to abuse, from which the citizen might need formal protection.[15]

To return to the gesture of the lictors in the Arieti Tomb painting. The single rods they brandish in their right hands, as in the depiction of the eager lictor on the denarius, are known as *virgae*, or switches. Strictly speaking, they are not part of the magistrates' formal insignia. Rather, these were sticks that lictors kept handy for their own practical use, attached to brackets on the fasces for quick access when needed. (The lictor on the coin seems to have one of these *virgae* plus rods from his bundle.)

In any case, the Arieti Tomb rods must also show the lictors' readiness to inflict punishment. On whom? Here our written sources offer limited help. Only the second-century CE Greek author Appian explicitly notes the presence of lictors in the triumphal procession at Rome. His aim is to describe a triumph of 201 BCE, which he however stresses is relevant to the ceremony in his own day. First, says Appian, came trumpeters; then carts laden with spoils, representations of the victories, and prize crowns; followed by sacrificial oxen, captured animals of war (in this case elephants), and prominent prisoners. Next the lictors "in purple tunics" preceded the commander, though not directly, Appian explains. In between the lictors and the chariot came "a chorus of harpists and pipers, in imitation of an Etruscan procession," followed by "a number of incense-bearers."[16]

The Arieti Tomb does not depict such a festive scene. Rather, one wonders whether the lictors here are signaling their eagerness to batter the foreign captives customarily displayed in the triumph, and which Appian in his procession places just ahead of the lictors. After all, the fragmentary frescoes portray the torture and execution of a bearded, and presumably non-Roman, male.

One additional point: during the celebration of a triumph, the commander (uniquely) kept his full military powers even though he was within the city, and so his lictors retained their functions from the field. Polybius offers a glimpse of this, in describing a praetorian triumph from the year 167 BCE. He relates a wild tale in which one of the commander's lictors lowered the tone of the celebratory games by a bizarre command to famed Greek musicians imported to Rome for the occasion: he ordered them not to play their instruments, but rather to fight each other with them on stage. Surely the lictor was not acting on his own authority, but on that of the *triumphator*. And we can imagine that he directed the musicians to change their tune, so to speak, with at least the implicit threat of force. In a word, the anecdote shows the behavior that Roman lictors might exhibit in the provinces playing out quite literally on the public stage in Rome.[17]

The Fasces on Republican Coinage

So where are we so far? Though material evidence for the Roman fasces before 100 BCE is scant, the few items we have—a relief sculpture, a tomb painting, and a numismatic depiction—suggest that a visual system for their display was firmly in place by the early second century BCE. One notes that each of these representations is found in a context meant to aggrandize the personal status of individual Romans, or (in the case of Porcius Laeca's coin) of a Roman family. In none of these early instances do we see the fasces used as an abstract emblem of the state per se. What is more, the Porcius coin of ca. 110 BCE—the first appearance of the fasces in a mass-market medium—depicts the lictor in a negative light, in that it celebrates how his ability to carry out a magistrate's order was curtailed by a citizen's right to appeal.

After the moneyer Porcius Laeca in the late second century BCE, it took another quarter century for the fasces to reappear on Roman coinage—again, on a personal "family" issue. This one is a denarius assigned to the year 83 BCE, minted amid bitter civil conflict between the political factions loyal either to Sulla or the son of Gaius Marius. The moneyer is a young Gaius Norbanus (a future consul of 38 BCE), who minted a denarius on a massive scale in two closely related types. The obverse of each presents a diademed head of Venus; the reverse shows variously a prow-stem, fasces with axe, caduceus (i.e., Mercury's wand, a symbol of peace), and grain ear; or a fasces with axe between a grain ear and caduceus. It is widely presumed that the moneyer here is aiming to honor his father, a consul in 83 BCE. The senior Norbanus had reached the praetorship by 90 BCE, and then found himself stuck as commander in Sicily for at least six full years, before reaching the consulship as an adherent of the Marian party. Though the reverses lack a legend, they seem nicely to idealize Norbanus's tenure of *imperium* in Sicily during the Social War and beyond. Cicero supplies the particulars: in making his case against a later governor of Sicily, Gaius Verres (praetor in 74), he takes pains to emphasize that Norbanus, in contrast, kept his province and its ports free of disturbances and effectively supplied Rome's armies.[18]

Norbanus's denarius issues of 83 BCE in fact mark a new start in artistic representations of the fasces. It would seem that previous Roman moneyers deliberately avoided the symbol—even after the year 137 BCE, when many abandoned conventional numismatic iconography and instead competed against each other with highly "personal" types. It is noteworthy that when Porcius Laeca in 110/109 BCE needed a lictor for the *provocatio* scene on his denarius, he pictured the attendant with unbound rods. So Norbanus was a pioneer in placing a full fasces with axe on his coins, though he chose to surround it with other symbols of provincial governance.

Imitation was almost immediate. A couple of years later, in 81 BCE, we find a noble Aulus Postumius Albinus minting a denarius with an obverse that shows the veiled head of a personified "Hispania" (i.e., Roman Spain), and a reverse with a strident display of *imperium*. There a man in a toga stands left, turning toward a legionary eagle, to which he raises his left hand as if in salute. What dominates the scene, however, is an outsized fasces with axe that stands to the right, taller than the human figure. This coin offers for us the first depiction of what would become an exceptionally common emblem of Roman power, the fasces paired with an eagle. What is especially worth noting is the scale of the rods and axes on the reverse, deliberately represented as much larger than life. It would seem that the process of actual fetishization of the fasces had begun, soon (in 79 BCE) reinforced by Sulla's pyre with its spice-statue of a lictor.[19]

Yet in the next and last generation of the Republican era, we find just five more significant instances of fasces on coins, four minted at Rome and an isolated example from the province of Asia.[20] In a joint issue of 70 BCE, the moneyers Quintus Fufius Calenus and Mucius Cordus chose for their obverse jugate heads of a personified "Honor" (laureate) and "Virtue" (helmeted). Their reverse shows two standing female figures, explicitly labeled Italia and Roma, clasping their right hands—apparently a celebration (or at least an expression of hope) of their reconciliation after the bloody fighting of 91–88 BCE, when the Italian allies rose against Rome in a conflict known as the "Social War." Italia represents peace and plenty. Behind her is a caduceus, and she holds a cornucopia in her left arm. But Roma plainly is the dominant partner in the alliance. She is rendered taller than Italia, and balances a long, thin, medial-axed fasces in her left arm while she poises her right foot on a globe, a double symbol of domination. The type is unusually significant for our larger study, in that it is the first to show an allegorical figure with the fasces. However, the iconography is a unicum for the Republican period.[21]

On a prolific issue minted at Rome in the politically turbulent year 63 BCE, a Lucius Furius Brocchus chose for his obverse an allusion to the grain supply (a head of Ceres between a wheat-ear and barley-corn), and for the reverse design, two thin fasces with axes flanking a curule chair. We have seen this basic composition before, though executed in a much more elaborate fashion: in the funeral monument of the consul 176 BCE Scipio Hispallus at Lago Albano. For his part, Brocchus placed his name prominently above the chair, a not-so-subtle expression of ambition for high political office. It evidently didn't work, since we never hear of him again in this (well-attested) period.[22]

A few years later, the fasces makes its first appearance on a Roman provincial coin of the Republican period. In that year, Gaius Septimius (praetor 57), as governor of Asia in 56 BCE minted high-denomination tetradrachms at Pergamum, Tralles, and Ephesus. The reverses of each feature as their central image a Dionysiac emblem familiar from the old Hellenistic kingdom of Pergamum, two serpents entwined around a bow and bowcase. However, for coins produced at Ephesus, Septimius inserted above the snakes a platform supporting two facing fasces with axes. Doubtless his aim here was to indicate the city's status as his provincial capital. Yet the effect strikes one as crass, since (as we shall see) Ephesus as a free city should have been exempt from the display of fasces. Notably, Septimius's successor in Asia, Gaius Claudius Pulcher (praetor 56), in the years 55–53 BCE coined in the same three cities, but dropped the fasces symbolism altogether from his tetradrachms. Nor do later Republican magistrates who mint in Asia restore it to their coins.[23]

We have already discussed the denarius that Marcus Iunius Brutus minted in 54 BCE that shows his ancestor, consul in the first year of the Republic, processing between two lictors with rods and axes. Finally, early in the year 44 BCE the moneyer Lucius Aemilius Buca produced for Julius Caesar, now titled "perpetual dictator," a portrait coin with a reverse displaying a complicated ensemble of symbols. At the center is a fasces—significantly, without an axe—crossed with a winged caduceus, each of equal size. Smaller emblems are placed in the interstices: clasped hands to the left (signifying concord), a globe above (a symbol of world domination), and a priest's axe below (a reference to Caesar's role as *pontifex maximus*, the head of the Roman state religion). The moneyer Buca's composition strikes one as a mix of Caesar's personal

insignia and political sloganeering, showing closer contact to Caesarian propaganda coinage of the earlier 40s BCE than the fasces-issues of the previous
forty years. The overall message? A balanced reminder of Caesar's power (the
rods, globe, priest's implement), with a promise of good fortune (the winged
caduceus), stemming from moderation (the axe-less fasces) and reconciliation
(the two hands). As such, it stands in contrast to the other relevant issues in
our brief survey, especially that of Brutus, who unusually chose to show lictors
and axed fasces in action—indeed, at the historical moment when the consuls
stood closest to the kings in their insignia.[24]

The overall impression one gets from the Republican coins minted before the death of Caesar is that of reticence on the part of Rome's moneyers
to deploy the fasces in their designs. Though symbols of political power
and military success are ubiquitous on the coinage of the Republic in all
eras, moneyers demonstrably favored other elements of iconography (e.g.,
personifications of Victory, or representations of trophies) to convey these
themes. These moneyers were young men who counted on their coins minted
at Rome to advance their political careers. When it came to representing the
terrifying fasces, which magistrates could use on Rome's citizens and allies as
well as its enemies, it evidently was hard to get the tone right. One observes
that each of these items has a different iconography; no two of the reverses are
alike. Brocchus's coin of 63 BCE, however, with its twin fasces framing a curule chair, clearly inspired some imitations. In 54 BCE, one moneyer placed a
priestly implement and a wreath on either side of the seat; in 45 BCE, another
used grain-ears in the same way. Finally, we may note that when moneyers do
include the fasces on their money, they generally treat them as freestanding
insignia. In one striking instance, the "reconciliation" coin from 70 BCE, a
personified Roma holds the fasces. Lictors very rarely are represented—just
twice on the Republican coinage (Porcius Laeca in 110/109 BCE; Brutus in 54
BCE), and the first of these approaches a negative caricature.[25]

The Fasces on Coins of the Triumviral Era

The first emergence of what we regard as a conventional fasces reverse type
emerges only after Caesar's assassination, which set off a new era of excited
political messaging on coins. In the year 42 BCE, a group of four moneyers
minted a large and complex issue in gold and silver on behalf of the three men
("triumvirs") who now headed the state—Antony, Octavian, and Lepidus—
mixing in personal types of their own. One of them, Lucius Livineius
Regulus, for an aureus and denarius series, revived Brocchus's assertive reverse

design of 63 BCE, with a curule chair flanked by fasces, with centering of the moneyer's name.

However, Livineius's composition differs from that of Brocchus in that the fasces are now axe-less, and variously appear as a pair (with the reverse legend PRAEF(ectus) VRB(i) = "prefect of the city") or expanded to three on each side. Why the differing number of fasces? The obverses of these types may provide the key: they all feature a portrait of a Regulus identified as "praetor" who must have been the moneyer's father. As mentioned, praetors normally had six lictors (i.e., half the consular complement). City prefects—Caesar named six or eight in the year 45 BCE—seem to have had two. The most natural supposition is that the senior Regulus held both the praetorship (presumably before 49 BCE) and Caesar's city prefecture (45 BCE). His son thought that reminding the Romans of those distinctions would help in his own political career.[26] This triumviral revival of the obscure Brocchus's reverse type seems to have made a bit of an impression, to judge from its reception far outside Rome.[27]

Other representations of fasces on coins in the triumviral period and the early Empire can all be regarded as outliers. Most puzzling is the derivative gold coinage of a "Koson," generally identified with the Dacian king Cotiso, who reigned approximately between 50 and 25 BCE, and with whom Octavian is said to have once contemplated a marriage alliance. This money, which seems to have been minted in the area of modern Transylvania (northern Romania), is exceedingly common considering the metal. For his obverse, Koson modifies Marcus Iunius Brutus's denarius of 54 BCE that shows his consular ancestor in procession with an official attendant (*accensus*) and protected by two lictors with axed fasces. Meanwhile, the reverse is adopted from an unrelated Roman coin of 70 BCE that shows a standing eagle with scepter and wreath. The message the king meant to convey here seems to be a generalized image of his political power, to which each of the individual borrowed features, including the fasces, seems incidental.

The other items admit closer interpretation. A certain Crassus (no title) found in Cyrenaica and Crete minted a higher-denomination bronze at Cnossus with the starkest image of this emblem yet found on a Roman coin. One of his two known issues, by far the rarer, features a laureate head of Apollo on obverse and a single axed fasces on reverse, with the legend CRA(ssus). He is likely to be Marcus Licinius Crassus, eldest son of the famous consular Crassus (consul in 70 and 55 BCE). This young man was an adherent of Marc Antony who switched sides to Octavian before the decisive battle of Actium in 31 BCE and was made consul for the following year.

The iconography of both of this Crassus's coins seems connected to the run-up to the final confrontration between Antony and Octavian at Actium—though it is hard to say from these items which side he was then supporting. The Thracian king Rhoemetalces I (12 BCE–12 CE), a passionate admirer of Augustus, also minted a coin with a single axed fasces in a field, but plainly indicating its meaning with the Greek legend SEBASTOU ("of Augustus"). This king honored the emperor on other issues by placing a large single fasces amidst a capricorn with globe, readily recognizable symbols of his reign in Rome.[28]

The Fasces on Coinage of Rome's Emperors

It is noteworthy that Augustus and, for that matter, Tiberius did not picture the fasces or lictors on their coins. Other than those few scattered and frankly quite minor provincial or foreign items mentioned above, numismatic depictions of the insignia are wholly lacking from their reigns. The same is true of even the openly autocratic Caligula, as well as Claudius, Nero, and indeed—with one slight exception—all the emperors through the Flavians (Vespasian and his sons Titus and Domitian, who reigned 69–96 CE) and then Nerva (96–98 CE). That reckoning includes all the coins minted at Rome, at the imperial mint at Lugdunum (modern Lyon), and in the provinces, which cumulatively total a massive number of coin types. This comes very much as a shock, since lictors and fasces prominently appear on some of the most important official relief sculptures of these same emperors.[29]

The apparent numismatic exception? The reverse of a bronze coin of Nero's successor Galba, minted in December 68, and so late in his short seven-month reign, which came to an end with his assassination on January 15, 69 CE. It is a lively scene of the emperor delivering a military address (*adlocutio*) from a short podium. There, before the podium, one can make out two lictors (rendered only partially) and their fasces, plus a third set of rods and various legionary ensigns sticking out from the crowd, not readily connected to specific figures.[30]

Given the fact that Republican moneyers at least sporadically integrated the fasces into their reverse designs, the avoidance of the symbol on coinage by a long series of Rome's earlier emperors must have been deliberate. It is only with the reign of Trajan (98–117 CE) that one finds substantial representations of lictors and fasces on imperial-era coins. Indeed, the reign of Trajan produced two separate types that featured the fasces. And most of the emperors who followed, through Alexander Severus (reigned 222–235 CE),

had at least one issue that portrayed the insignia. The total number of imperial types in this series is not large—several dozen in all, with many of them
closely related in terms of iconography. Yet it provides enough material for us
to suspect that something new was afoot.

The design of one of Trajan's fasces-coins is already perfectly familiar to
us. The emperor during his reign "restored" or revived about fifty Republican
denarius issues; in this he was continuing a policy of Titus, Domitian, and
Nerva. Among the coins Trajan chose for his program was Marcus Iunius
Brutus's denarius of 54 BCE that showed the consul of 509 BCE in procession
with an attendant and two lictors. Minted probably ca. 107 CE in a limited
run, this really was the first artistically prominent representation of the fasces
on a coin minted in Rome in a century and a half.

The second coin featuring a fasces follows later in Trajan's reign, and is associated with the first phase of the emperor's eastern campaign of 114–117 CE,
during which he died. It is a reverse type that was used in the years 114 and 115
to commemorate three separate instances where he was hailed with the charismatic military title "imperator." It is also in a sense derivative, since the composition of the scene clearly owes much to Galba's bronze of late 68 CE that
depicts a military address. Here Trajan is seated next to two standing officers
on a high podium, before which one spots the partial figure of a lictor holding
the fasces on his left shoulder. From the platform, the emperor extends a hand
toward a group of soldiers with standards and shields, accepting their acclamation. The image was demonstrably effective, for the coin found imitators a
full century later under the Severans.[31]

Trajan's successor Hadrian (ruled 117–138 CE) struck out in a different direction, and introduced a wholly novel reverse type, in two main versions,
that were the first Roman coins ever to center attention on a lictor (see Figure
3.3). These coins, all in bronze, date to the period soon after Hadrian assumed
his third consulship in January 119 CE. The reverses share a common legend
that advertises his decision to cancel old debts owed to the treasury, which
it is said amounted to nine hundred million sesterces, i.e., roughly enough
money to pay all of Rome's legionaries for six years. The later fourth-century
CE biographical collection known as the *Historia Augusta* in fact mentions
Hadrian's bid to seek popularity by this measure, and adds that he had the
promissory notes burned in the Forum of Trajan "to increase the general sense
of security."

To be sure, the iconography of these reverses shows a strong thematic link
with a pair of carved balustrades discovered in the Roman Forum excavations
in 1872, variously attributed to the reign of Trajan or (somewhat more

FIGURE 3.3. Bronze sestertius of Hadrian (*RIC* II 590b), struck 119–121 CE, showing (on obverse) a laureate portrait bust of the emperor facing right, and (on reverse) a lictor standing left, holding fasces, setting fire to heap of bonds with torch. The lictor is deliberately shown with lack of distinctive facial features.

Credit: Classical Numismatic Group, Inc. Auction 97, Lot 655 (September 17, 2014).

compellingly) Hadrian. One of these pictures two lictors engaged in burning bundles of arrears that a long line of soldiers, extending through the old Forum, hauls to them. The other depicts the emperor on a platform flanked by six lictors addressing a crowd of Roman citizens, again in this Forum.

But the coins present an image that is like nothing we have seen before, in any medium. In all the versions of the bronze, a lictor, clad in a short tunic with cloak, stands left, balancing an axed fasces on his left shoulder; with his right hand he extends a torch to ignite a pile of debt papers before him. Some types have a small audience facing the lictor, composed of variously two or three citizens, signaling their approbation. Elsewhere the lictor stands alone, occupying the better part of the field of the coin. What comes as a surprise is not just the centrality of this figure, but also the fact that in this numismatic debut he is doing something unconnected to the lictor's basic duties, with no superior in sight. The rendering of the lictor is impressive enough that in the nineteenth century authorities commonly misidentified him as the emperor himself.[32]

Hadrian did not develop a lictor or fasces motif further on his coins. But this representation, as well as Trajan's acclamation type, and the balustrade reliefs (whoever their patron), clearly struck a chord. Later emperors drew on these basic models—lictor as guardian of the emperor on his podium, and lictor as agent of the emperor's benefactions—sometimes also combining the two, with markedly increased focus on the role of the lictor. Whatever the activity, these multitasking lictors never put down their fasces.

Particularly notable in this regard is Hadrian's successor Antoninus Pius (reigned 138–161). On an issue of 140–144 CE, he represented himself with his heir Marcus Aurelius as joint consuls in 140, seated on curule chairs on a podium, each extending their right hands; on the ground flanking the pair on the daïs are two lictors who face each other with axe-less fasces, each holding a stick or wand pointed downward in his right hand. Though the lictors' facial features are (purposefully) indistinct, it seems that their heads are turned toward their superiors, ready to execute their orders.[33] Engravers use the motif later in the second century CE, and put one or both of the two attentive lictors on the podium, or pair a lictor with another officer to attend the emperor.[34]

Antoninus also dramatically introduced the lictor in a new guise on the coinage—as an agent of "Liberalitas," the personified goddess of cash handouts, whom Trajan and Hadrian had promoted heavily. The latter emperor especially highlighted her on his coinage, and was followed in this by Antoninus Pius. Put briefly, to advertise their cash disbursements, Hadrian and Antoninus each regularly invoke a representation of the personified Liberalitas with her main symbolic attributes. In the developed iconography, that is often an abacus or military banner in her right hand, a cornucopia in her left. On the reverses she either stands by herself, or on the emperor's podium, where she variously appears statue-like or interacts with citizens eager to receive largesse.

So how does the fasces figure into the iconography of Liberalitas? At first, a bit remotely. On a coin minted in 145–147 CE celebrating the fourth largesse of Antoninus's reign, Liberalitas is joined on the podium by a figure who is recognizably a lictor, positioned with his fasces behind the seated emperor. That form of the distribution scene proved immensely influential, with revivals under Lucius Verus (co-ruled 161–169 CE) and Marcus Aurelius (161–180 CE), Marcus's son Commodus (180–192 CE), Septimius Severus (193–211 CE), and then indeed most later rulers into the late third century, including the Romano-British emperor Carausius (286–293). In truth, the engravers of these later issues did not always render the attendant distinctly as a lictor. Yet well into the mid-third century, one can still discern on this reverse type a man with a fasces, e.g., on an aureus minted at Lugdunum in early 262 CE by Postumus (260–269 CE).[35]

Yet Antoninus Pius went even further. The reverse of an aureus struck in 152–153 CE commemorates the emperor's seventh distribution of cash to the people. The design has a tall lictor, wearing a short tunic and cloak, standing left, as the sole figure in the field; he incongruously holds up a coin-counter (abacus) in his right hand. Yet lest we forget his core function, the long fasces

the lictor balances on his left shoulder sports a prominent axe. This experimental design did not catch on. For his next (eighth) largesse, Antoninus
returned to a conventional image of a standing Liberalitas emptying coins out
of a cornucopia. Nor do we again find the lictor standing in for the goddess.

Indeed, in 161 CE, not long before his death on March 7 of that year,
Antoninus minted for his adopted son Marcus Aurelius (not yet emperor) a
bronze which conspicuously restores the attendant to his most familiar role.
The reverse of the coin shows a lictor in tunic and cloak standing left, with his
expected equipment. He extends with his left hand an axed fasces, as if putting it on or taking it off his shoulder; he holds a wand in his right, pointing
it downward. Strange to say, this image of a lictor, which fills the entire field
of the coin, is the first and indeed will remain only portrait in the Roman
coinage of a solitary lictor acting more or less as he is expected to be acting. It
seems not too much to suggest that the depiction of the figure, with the fasces
visibly not touching his shoulder, refers to the anticipated transition.[36]

For the (admittedly narrow) sub-genre of portrayal of lictors on Roman
coins, Antoninus Pius's reign can be regarded as the high-water mark. After
his reign, no one attempts a full-scale representation of a lictor; henceforth
they show up only in ensemble scenes, especially those related to military
addresses and imperial benefactions. What seems completely lacking from
the imperial coinage as a whole is the depiction of fasces for their own sake,
which was the predominant model in the Republic. No allegorical figures are
introduced to bear the fasces to convey Roman power, nor are the fasces displayed in isolation from the lictors. In addition, none of the issues we have
surveyed was minted in Rome's provinces. The general focus seems to be on
the lictor in Rome and in the camp, now seemingly rebranded as an important element in the emperor's philanthropy.

The Fasces in Later Antiquity

With the Severan era comes a surprising development—what appears to be
a redesign of the fasces, after more than seven centuries of continuous use in
Rome. A sestertius struck between 202–204 CE offers early evidence. On the
reverse, the emperor Septimius Septimius and his son Caracalla are seated
right on a platform; an officer stands behind, and an attendant stands before
the pair, holding what looks like a long curved stick. The evidence of late antique sculpture and engraving suggests the object he is holding is a fasces.[37]

The proof is abundant. In the fifth and sixth centuries CE, in both Rome and
Constantinople, which now each provided one of the two annual consuls, the

fasces consistently appear as long curved rods bound in a pair. A prime piece of evidence comes from the east side of the pedestal of the column of Arcadius (reigned 395–408), dedicated in Constantinople in the year 421. This monument was badly damaged by an earthquake and largely pulled down in 1719, and its program of reliefs is now known principally from earlier drawings. On the pedestal, a surprising total of fourteen lictors were shown flanking the emperor, seven on each side. Each of their tall, curving fasces has two blades, one above the other. On a ceremonial silver dish that commemorates the western consulship of Flavius Ardabur Aspar in 434, personifications of Rome and Constantinople stand with the same type of long fasces, that shows a single axe-blade. The idea is not that the cities are serving the new consul as lictors—as some have suggested—but rather are the source of the fasces that they confer on him. That scene of the cities and consul, with the same style of the insignia, later adorns several consular diptychs in ivory from the East (consuls of 513, 518, and 525). On two additional diptychs, for western consulships (that of Astyrias in 449, and an anonymous diptych at Bourges), a pair of diminutive lictors hold the long fasces.[38]

The new-look fasces have only a few points of resemblance to the traditional kit. The lower portion is now housed in a sleeve, and on the upper tip hang ribbons or straps. Modern authorities often speak of a "flag" affixed to the rods, sometime decorated. However, what is being depicted is certainly an axe (albeit a stylized one). Our literary sources for this period are insistent that the fasces were colored purple; it may be that in addition to dyed ribbons, the rods themselves were painted. One advantage of fasces of this sort is that they would rise well above heads in a crowd, and also could be spotted at a good distance. The disadvantage is that the insignia now had lost all functional use.[39]

Writing in the mid-sixth century CE, and obviously speaking of the situation of his own day, the Byzantine antiquarian John Lydus singles out the visibility of the fasces as their prime attribute. In his *On Magistracies*, he speaks of insignia consisting of "long rods evenly bound together" as a continuing custom, and is insistent on the fasces having axes. Rome's consuls, he tells us, had among their insignia "axes raised to a height preceding them; a multitude of men carrying rods from which scarlet-dyed straps had been suspended." After offering a wacky origin story for the rods and axe (he says the fifth-century BCE Roman dictator Cincinnatus's farm equipment inspired them), Lydus concludes that in any case "an axe is indicative of authority."[40]

In the mid-sixth century CE, the statesperson and scholar Cassiodorus shows abundantly that the Ostrogothic Amali dynasty in Italy, under King

Theoderic (reigned 493–526), and then his daughter Amalasuntha and her son Athalaric (526–534), prioritized the maintenance of ancient Roman traditions, including that of the fasces. References in Cassiodorus's erudite collection of letters known as the *Variae* show at least five different offices enjoying the privilege of the insignia under Ostrogothic reign, including in provincial commands. A letter of Athalaric to the Senate even praises the aristocratic family of the Decii for having a collection of laureled fasces in the forecourts of their homes. Whether actual ones, or artistic representations, we are left to imagine. But they might have been the real thing. In the late fifth century, the aristocratic bishop and poet Sidonius Apollinaris mentions the domestic decor of his friend Magnus Felix, who proudly displayed the patrician hat known as the *apex* of his ancestor Philagrius, and also that of Sygarius, whose estate evidently contained an archive of his family's magisterial emblems—including even curule chairs of ivory.[41]

Fasces in the Byzantine Era

For the Eastern Empire and the long stretch of Byzantine rule, the picture is a bit fuzzier. After the testimony of Lydus for the age of Justinian I (reigned 527–565 CE), we are not so well informed on the particulars of the actual use of fasces. In part this is because the lack of a distinctive Greek word for the insignia makes precise identification of the institution in our texts difficult. Even Latin sources on the Byzantine court present a challenge. For example, for the year 565, the Latin poet Corippus describes a display of imperial regalia by Justin II soon after his accession that year, and its impact on a delegation of Avars from the north Caucasus region. The emperor's insignia, we are told, included lances and "cruel axes." The latter may be fasces, or more conventional military weapons.

On the available evidence, the traditional fasces do not seem to have played an appreciable role in Byzantine ceremonial practices. A contributing factor here may be the astounding range of ever-evolving insignia that Byzantine emperors employed, which over time shows an increasing emphasis on the presentation of the ruler's body (clothing, headgear, footwear).[42] But lictor-like attendants most certainly lived on, in the form of various imperial guard groups. We hear plenty about the emperor's orderlies, who were armed with rods (*rhabdouchoi*), staves (*magglabitai*), or axes (*pelekephoroi*), into the early fifteenth century. It seems something of the spirit of the old-style Roman lictors also persevered. For the year 1103, the Byzantine princess and historian Anna Komnena reports witnessing the macabre and gruesome aftermath of a conspiracy against her father, the emperor Alexios I Komnenos. The perpetrators had their eyes gouged out and then were forced into a mock triumph-like procession; rod-bearers walked before them, singing an obscene song that aimed for comic effect, and urged the public to come out to witness the spectacle.

A proper account of lictor-like attendants in the age of Byzantium is impossible here, since it would involve surveying a good chunk of the history of palace security in that long and lavishly attested era. Of special importance were the *magglabitai*, a group of bodyguards who first appear in the later eighth century, and are found as late as the eleventh century, armed with staves (*magglabia*) or swords. They preceded the emperor on both land and sea, and had the power to inflict summary punishment. In the late Byzantine period the axe-wielding Varangians, recruited especially from Scandinavians and (from the late eleventh century) English-speaking Anglo-Saxons, occupied a prominent role in the court and its ceremonial. They had privileged status above other contemporary groups of guards (of which there were at least five), and the most proximity to the emperor. When the ruler left his palace (inevitably) on horseback, the Varangians walked beside him, toting axes on their shoulder; when the emperor presided at ceremonies in the palace, they took a position with their axes nearest him. They seem to have slept within the palace, and their responsibilities extended to guarding its prison.

Most suggestive for the studied survival of Roman practice may be the testimony of Ignatius of Smolensk, a Russian pilgrim to Constantinople who on February 11, 1391, witnessed the coronation of the emperor Manuel II Palaeologus (who reigned to 1425) at Hagia Sophia. He describes a procession of three hours within the basilica in which "twelve men-at-arms"—generally identified as Varangians—"walked on either side of the emperor, all in mail from head to foot." The conclusion? The mention of these dozen attendants implies that at least a memory of the use of the fasces persisted for some time in the Eastern Empire, albeit in an attenuated form.[43]

4

Roman Fasces in Action

Rotation of the Fasces

The evidence is plain and abundant that the Romans used the lictors and their fasces to mark the hierarchy of magistrates and quasi-magistrates. In the Republic, the dictator (at least in his original form, down to 202 BCE) and a consul each had a dozen fasces, but it seems the latter lost his in the presence of the former. When two consuls were together in the city, only one at a time was preceded by lictors with true fasces, to show who had initiative of action. The other would be preceded by the attendant known as the *accensus* and was followed by lictors bearing sets of fasces reduced in some form, an arrangement which would alternate each month. The man who held the full fasces at a given moment seems to have been known as the ' "greater (Latin *maior*) consul." It was only he who had the right to independent action, though his colleague retained the negative power of obstruction. This arrangement had significant political consequences. A good example comes from Livy's account of the year 339 BCE. When the Senate deemed it expedient that a dictator be named, it was the consul who then held the fasces who had the choice—though in this case he diplomatically named his consular colleague to the office.[1]

So which member of a consular pair ought to have received the fasces first? For our earliest Republic, we have seen the tradition that Publicola in 509 BCE offered precedence in the fasces to his colleague who was more senior in age. In the later Republic, however, our record strongly suggests that it was priority of election that determined who held the fasces in January—and, according to the rules of rotation, in the subsequent odd-numbered months of the year. At least that was the model. The fact that Julius Caesar as consul in 59 BCE is said to have "revived" the practice implies it was not always followed.

The Fasces. T. Corey Brennan, Oxford University Press. © Oxford University Press 2023.
DOI: 10.1093/oso/9780197644881.003.0004

This principle had real political consequences. In the administrative calendar of the later Republic, January was relatively free of set Senate business, such as the hearing of embassies (which fell in February), and rich in "comitial" days when popular assemblies might meet (which were sparser in February). So the consul who first held the fasces had more latitude than his colleague in securing decrees of the Senate for favored legislation. He also had a better opportunity, should he wish, of personally putting favored proposals to a popular vote. (In practice this was infrequently exercised; the tribunes of the Plebs passed the bulk of legislation in Republican Rome.) Another advantage for the "greater" consul came from the fact that he will have held precedence during the odd-numbered month of July, which regularly saw the election of major magistrates. It is amply attested that the consul who conducted the elections had at least some influence over the results. All the same, there are some indications that the first-elected consul could waive his prerogatives and allow his colleague to take precedence with the insignia.

Under Augustus in 18 BCE came a significant revision of the mechanisms of the consular turn. The emperor's principal motivation here was not to ensure the smooth functioning of the state. Rather, Augustus sought to leverage the prestige of the fasces for a novel use—to promote social legislation. Specifically, Augustus introduced a new provision on the consuls' alternation of insignia as part of a complex law that encouraged marriage and childbirth among Rome's upper echelons. This reform of the rotation pointedly ignored the established criterion of first electoral place—which was now much less relevant, since the emperor tightly controlled both candidacies and outcomes. Rather, as the second-century CE miscellanist Aulus Gellius explains, "priority in assuming the emblems of power is given . . . to him who either has more children under his control than his colleague, or has lost them in war." Henceforth, the consul who was married with children had the best chance of receiving the fasces first.

Snags in this scheme seem inevitable, but Gellius implies that Augustus's law tried to anticipate some of them. What if both consuls have the same number of kids? "The one who has a wife, or is eligible for marriage, is preferred." Suppose both are already married, and equal in respect to size of family? For that eventuality, Augustus invoked an alleged precedent of the era of Publicola: "the elder is first to assume the rods."

Gellius then notes some gaps in the law. Oddly, there was no insistence on priority of age in instances "when both consuls are without wives and have the same number of sons, or are husbands but have no children." More consequentially, the consular pair themselves seem to have retained discretion to arrange matters among themselves, regardless of what the law prescribed. "I hear that it was usual," says Gellius, "for those who had legal priority to yield the rods for the first month to colleagues who were either considerably older than they, or of much higher rank, or who were entering upon a second consulship." One assumes that when an emperor held the office, his consular colleague always deferred to him, regardless of marital or parental status.

That is not the end of the complications. In the imperial period, the two "ordinary consuls," i.e., the ones who entered office on January 1 and gave their names to the year, rarely held office for more than half a year. They usually saw succession by a pair of "suffect" or substitute consuls, who themselves might be replaced any number of times. For instance, under the emperor Nero in the year 55 CE, we find a total of twelve consuls in all for the year, with each pair (one "ordinary," including the emperor himself, then five "suffect") holding office for two months. It seems inevitable that each transition required working out the rotation of fasces according to the Augustan rules. We are entitled to suspect that these new stipulations about what qualified one to take precedence as "greater" consul with the fasces and the expectation that there be at least four consuls per year (and sometimes, many more) cumulatively cheapened the office, very much to the advantage of the emperor.[2]

What about outside of Rome? On the (rare) occasions that two consuls were in command of the same army, a stark visual system was positively needed to delineate the hierarchy of power. As it happens, there are indications from the era of the Second Punic War (218–201 BCE) that the consular "turn" obtained also in the field. But the solution was an awkward one: the fasces would rotate among a consular pair each day.[3]

Reductions and Enhancements in the Number of Fasces

The fasces signaled other types of power relationships in the Roman political system, although precisely how they did so is even more vexing. Take the case of the praetor, a lesser colleague of the consul created first for 366 BCE. This magistrate was known to Greek authors such as Polybius in the mid-second century BCE, and Posidonius and Diodorus writing in the first century BCE, as "the holder of six axes," i.e., half the consular complement. Indeed, the original praetor (at least later called "urban") must have had six lictors at the inception of his office, at least when outside of the city. That goes as well for a praetor introduced ca. 247 BCE primarily to serve outside

Rome, the "peregrine praetor." Hence the generalization of the "six axes" tag for all praetors in the field, where these Greek authors most readily will have observed them—eliding the fact that after 197 BCE those bound for the Spanish provinces received the enhanced *imperium* of a consul and thus twelve lictors.[4]

Imperial references to "six fasces" as standard for governors of provinces administered by the Senate are numerous. They range from the Jewish historian Josephus, who has a speaker contrast mid-first-century CE practice in Greece and Macedonia with Asia, which (as in the Republic) received a consular complement of fasces, to the aristocratic poet Rutilius Namatianus, who notes the six fasces his father Lachanius received as governor of Tuscia and Umbria in the 380s CE.

Lachanius's distinction was worth a boast. In senatorial provincial administration in the later imperial era, most governors held the rank of *praeses* (literally "superintendent"), an equestrian military post that did not entail fasces; or *consularis*, which, as the name implies, would normally be held by ex-consuls. *Consulares* typically received five lictors—as we shall see, a number long used to denote delegated power—but on occasion six. Writing in the 540s CE in Ostrogothic Italy, Cassiodorus relates a formula (surely traditional for much of late antiquity) for the appointment of a *consularis*. The opening sentences dwell at some length on this governor's brilliant insignia. "For the axes and the rods, which antiquity ordained for that high office, are known to be set aside for your ornaments, so that a silent or rather understood authority is exercised over the provinces." After a full millennium of use, the fasces even at half the regal total were still felt to produce a powerful psychological effect.

Yet the practice of enhancing the number of fasces to twelve for certain senatorial governors also continued until late antiquity. For example, in a letter of ca. 375 CE, the senator and orator Symmachus boasts to his father of his precocious attainment of "twice six fasces" through his recent administration of Africa. Though Symmachus here does not use the term, his title will have been "proconsul"—ranking above *consularis*, and reserved for the governors of Africa and Asia. He held that office in 373–374 CE, well before his actual consulship of 391 CE. The rank of *proconsul* is found also in the administrative system of the Eastern Empire. In 536 CE, when Justinian established three new proconsulates in the East, the prerogatives of the governor for at least Cappadocia included a carriage decorated with silver and the fasces. Whether these fasces numbered the expected dozen is unknown; the notable thing is that they still served as one of the markers of high office.[5]

Here is the puzzling bit. Oddly, at some point in the mid-Republic—certainly by the first years of the second century BCE—it was decided for some reason that a routine retinue of six lictors was too large for urban praetors, or conceivably all praetors, when in the city—or at least when engaged in certain tasks within the city. The received text of a tribunician law passed by one Marcus Plaetorius (date unknown, but perhaps as early as the mid-third century BCE) stipulates that the urban praetor when hearing cases at law should do so with two lictors. In Plautus's comedy *Epidicus* (ca. 190 BCE), a fellow slave of the title character latches onto his name (which roughly means "adjudicator") and jokes that Epidicus is acting like the urban praetor, except in one regard: he lacks "two lictors and the two bundles of elm rods." This passage in fact is our earliest datable literary reference to the fasces, and is doubly welcome, in that it specifies what their material might be.[6]

Much later, in a public speech of 63 BCE, Cicero also speaks of two lictors as the normal number for the urban praetor at Rome. In an aside on the conduct of certain magistrates in Capua at the time of the Social War (91–88 BCE) between Rome and its Italian allies, he relates: "these men wished to be called 'praetors,' though in other colonies they were called duovirs . . . also, lictors walked before them, not with staffs (*bacilli*), but paired, with fasces—as they precede urban praetors here."

When and why in the Republic urban praetors had their lictors reduced to two remains a mystery. On the face of things, such a change should reflect a real innovation in the nature of regular magistrates with *imperium*. The creation of a second "peregrine" praetor in the early 240s BCE—and with it, the introduction of the designation "urban" for the originai praetor—is just one of several possible occasions for a recalculation in the number of lictors. If two praetors found themselves in the city, each with six lictors, and alongside the consuls, one can see the complications—especially with the consul who was out of turn in the alternation of fasces. But other possible occasions for this puzzling reform present themselves, such as the year 227 BCE, when two additional praetors were created for Sicily and Sardinia, or (perhaps) 197 BCE, when the number of praetors was raised to six to provide also for two new Spanish provinces.

However, there is the possibility that the two lictors applied to the urban praetor only in connection with his activities in the sphere of jurisdiction, which was just one of the many tasks he performed. A pair of lictors may have been enough to maintain order in legal proceedings involving Roman citizens, if there were concerns that a presiding magistrate with six fasces might seem imperious in this setting. But this is just a guess from our sparse sources on the reform, and Cicero implies the urban praetor had two lictors also when he was on the move. Furthermore, it is unknown whether during the Republic other praetors when in the city had their insignia trimmed in this way. In the Empire, praetors do seem to have been accompanied by six lictors in Rome. They practically needed them to be recognized, given Augustus's open-handedness with grants of fasces to all sorts of minor officials.[7]

Yielding the Fasces

Throughout the Republic and Empire, through at least the sixth century CE, it seems fair to say that the presence of lictors and fasces was the essential sign that one held high office. Writing ca. 55 CE, the philosopher Seneca describes how Roman children role-play as magistrates: "in make-believe [they] have their purple-bordered toga, fasces and tribunal." Of these three core attributes, only the fasces seem crucial.

The point is readily demonstrated. Consider Livy's account of the short and extraordinary dictatorship of the aged Marcus Fabius Buteo (a consul of 245 BCE). He was appointed in the crisis year 216 BCE, without the customary subordinate master of the horse, for a narrow task—specifically to revise the roll of the Senate following catastrophic losses occasioned by the ongoing Hannibalic War. In Rome's Forum, we are told, "Fabius mounted the Rostra [i.e., speaker's platform] with his lictors," which for a dictator would have been (as we have seen) not less than twelve in number. As Livy tells it, after complaining vociferously about the nature of his appointment, Fabius announced the names of 177 new senators he had chosen. And then "at once [he] abdicated his office and came down from the Rostra a private citizen, after ordering his lictors to leave him." The passage offers a rare glimpse of a procedure that the Romans would have taken for granted, namely how a holder of *imperium* might depart from office. The dictator does not take off his bordered toga. Rather, it is the act of sending away lictors that signals his abdication. He does this while standing on the platform and thus still in an official capacity.

There is another instance of an official terminating his *imperium* from a raised platform in Appian's account of the violence that followed Sulla's settlement of 88 BCE. In short, Sulla's opponent Lucius Cornelius Cinna found himself expelled, though consul, from Rome in 87 BCE. Appian says he headed south to Capua, where he attempted to win over a Roman army, their officers, and whatever senators were present. His form of persuasion? He called an assembly as consul, mounted a speaker's platform, and then staged a ceremony of abdication "where he laid down the fasces as though he were a private citizen." Next, a tearful speech. "From you, citizens, I received this authority. The people voted it to me; the Senate has taken it away from me without your consent." Appian is quite clear that Cinna's main aim here was to rile up his audience, exciting feelings of pity and indignation. But ordering his lictors to put aside the fasces was just the start. "He tore his garments, leaped down from the platform, and threw himself on the ground before them, where he lay a long time." The tactic worked with the military and the senators. "Entirely overcome they raised him up; they restored him to the curule chair; they lifted up the fasces and bade him be of good cheer, as he was consul still, and lead them wherever he would."

A third (probable) example of an official announcing from a platform that he was laying down his *imperium* comes just eight years later, and is arguably the most famous abdication of the Republican period. In early 79 CE, Appian says Lucius Cornelius Sulla as dictator in Rome "when he was laying down his office in the Forum, he also added that he would account for what had happened if anyone required him to." In this case he surely was speaking from the Rostra. Next, "he had the rods and axes removed, dismissed his bodyguard," and henceforth ostentatiously walked to the Forum "with only his friends."[8]

Obviously, the key element of abdicating an office that involved *imperium* was the formal dismissal of lictors with the fasces. The act also seems to have been reversible, if the Senate decreed it. This emerges from the praetorship of Julius Caesar in 62 BCE. Caesar worked closely in Rome with the plebeian tribune Quintus Metellus Nepos to push through two bills that favored Pompey, then holding an extraordinary consular command in the East: one allowing him to stand for the actual office of consul in absence, another to give him the chief military role in the fight against the revolutionaries who followed the recreant senator Catiline. That second bill included the provocative detail that Pompey, against every precedent, would be allowed to retain his military *imperium* within the city. The measures led to vetoes from Metellus's colleagues in the tribunate (which Caesar and his ally ignored), and eventually a decree of the Senate suspending both tribune and praetor from office.

Caesar initially tried to defy the Senate by holding onto his insignia. "Caesar had the audacity to continue in office and to hold court," reports the biographer Suetonius, "but when he learned that some were ready to stop him by force of arms, he dismissed his lictors, laid aside his robe of office, and slipped off secretly to his house." The Senate later rescinded its measure, and restored Caesar to his praetorship; Metellus for his part had already fled to Pompey. There are ample later parallels for magistrates broadcasting or renouncing their claims to legitimate power through their lictors.

More than a century and a half later, the civil warfare of 69 CE saw a magistrate separated from his fasces in even more dramatic fashion before he got them back. When soldiers loyal to the new emperor Vitellius decided to release the suffect consul Aulus Caecina Alienus from imprisonment at Cremona, a summarizer of the historian Cassius Dio reports they restored to him his robes and fasces before sending him to mediate between their faction and that of Vespasian. Evidently Alienus's mere physical presence in the negotiations was felt to be not enough.[9]

Finally, let us spend a moment on the intriguing case of the ordinary consuls of 212 CE, Gaius Iulius Asper and his son Gaius Iulius Camillus Asper, who assumed office just a few days after the emperor Caracalla had murdered his brother Geta on December 26, 211. For a father and son, from a new senatorial family at that, to hold simultaneous ordinary consulships was a signal honor. Plus this was the second consulship for the elder Asper; his first was some years previous, under the emperor Commodus (reigned 180–193 CE). Caracalla, says a summarizer of Cassius Dio, at first conspicuously honored Asper "and his sons." Puffed up with pride, the elder Asper "paraded about surrounded by ever so many fasces at once"—but found himself abruptly exiled by the emperor.

What was the nature of the transgression? After the previous year's fratricide, one can imagine that the spectacle of a non-imperial father having his son as a consular colleague was a welcome one to all social orders, and that the pair made the most of it. There is good reason to believe that the father while consul also may have held the office of prefect of the city. Perhaps he cumulated the insignia of his two offices in some unprecedented or inappropriate way. What does seem certain is that Caracalla sensed it all had gone too far. For we are told the emperor "suddenly insulted [Asper Senior] outrageously and sent him back to his native town" of Tusculum in the nearby Alban Hills, "with abuse and in terrible fear." A natural supposition is that Caracalla stripped the man of his fasces, of which he had been so proud. This is admittedly guesswork, since that is all we are told of Asper's disgrace and exile, which Caracalla rescinded five years later when he needed the experienced consular's help in Asia. At the very least, the anecdote underlines the continuing importance of the fasces as the political symbol par excellence, with its own protocols, even in the Severan period.[10]

Succession of Fasces

The presumed deep antiquity of the fasces contributed much to their mystique. The Romans imagined that, from the very foundation of Rome, there was an unbroken continuity in the handling of public auspices that in turn were the basis of *imperium*. This chain stretched from Romulus, as the city's founder and first king, to the high officials of their own day. In an isolated anachronism, Vergil makes it extend back even centuries earlier, before Aeneas even came to Italy. In *Aeneid* Book 7, he represents the palace of Picus in Latium as the site where "it was auspicious for kings to receive the scepter, and first uplift the fasces," serving as the functional equivalent of the Capitolium in Rome.[11]

An important visual aspect of this theology of *imperium* was the ceremony at the beginning of the administrative year, when consuls on their accession first "took up" or "raised" their fasces—or, more accurately, had lictors do it for them. Indeed, all holders of *imperium*, even extraordinary ones, are said to enter into their command in this fashion. Two epigraphic calendars of the early imperial period note the date that Octavian "first assumed the fasces" in 43 BCE. Conversely, a late calendar lists April 21 as the date when ordinary consuls "lay the fasces down," i.e., to be replaced by suffects. In later antiquity, the ceremony maintained its importance; poets of the later fourth and fifth centuries make much of the act. For the year 379 CE, to cite just one of many relevant items, a shorter personal poem of Ausonius bears the title "Prayer as consul-designate on the eve of 1 January when the fasces are assumed."[12]

We are not so well informed on the practical aspects of the actual entrance ceremony. Writing in the mid-first century CE, the philosopher Seneca implies that in a succession, the lictors "pass from one magistrate to another" amid the exchange of compliments; in the fourth century CE, the historian Ammianus Marcellinus is specific that they do, "as custom requires." Other sources (in verse) seem to imagine two sets of fasces. What is apparent, however, is that lictors played a key role in these transitions of power. One notes the third-century CE senator Rogatianus, who abruptly declined the ceremony for entering his praetorship "though the lictors were already there," and subsequently withdrew from public life to study philosophy. Rogatianus's behavior here seems highly performative, and obviously made an impact, since even we know about it. Probably no magistrate-designate in the previous seven centuries had ever nixed his lictors' chance to shoulder the fasces.[13]

Commands to Lictors

The fact that the lictors' display of fasces was such an old, ubiquitous, and expected public symbol of power paradoxically makes it difficult to study, since it only occasionally attracted comment for its own sake. Yet one matter in which ancient authors do seem to take an interest is the ritual and performative aspects of a magistrate's orders to these attendants. Those orders usually took the form of blunt imperatives to the lictors to take physical action of one sort of another. The impression one gets is that these brusque formal commands were regarded, whether correctly or not, as an archaic survival that went back to the very start of the Republic, and before that, the era of Rome's monarchy.

Writing in the late first or early second century CE, the Greek author Plutarch implies as much in describing how Lucius Iunius Brutus in 509 BCE punished his sons for seeking to overthrow the new Republic. After deciding on their guilt, we are told, Brutus "turned to the lictors and said, 'It is yours now to do the rest.'" Plutarch does not feel the need to add explicit directions to the lictors for what to do next. Rather, he supposes that a long-familiar tradition would dictate their movements and use of the constituent parts of the fasces. "They straightway seized the young men," says Plutarch of Brutus's lictors, "tore off their togas, bound their hands behind their backs, and scourged their bodies with their rods." Finally, "the lictors threw them on the ground and cut off their heads with the axe."[14]

We have seen that in Livy's account of early Roman history, even Romulus had twelve lictors in the Etruscan style. So did each of the senators who served as provisional rulers in the year-long interregnum said to follow Romulus's death, before Numa succeeded him as king. When we get to Rome's third monarch, Tullus Hostilius, the reader finds lictors already receiving formulaic commands. "Publius Horatius, I adjudge you a traitor; go, lictor, bind his hands" pronounces a legal official whom the king delegated to try a thorny capital case.[15]

Indeed, Livy in his narrative prominently underscores the dramatic effect of holders of *imperium* shouting out extreme orders to their lictors. "Go, lictor, remove the mob and open a way for the master to seize his slave!" says the imperious decemvir Appius Claudius in 449 BCE, ordering a minion to abduct the young plebeian Verginia from the Forum. The first part of the command (*submove turbam*, "clear the crowd") was customary, and has ample parallels. Yet what follows plainly was meant to make Appius seem criminal.

One of the most notorious commands to a lictor crops up in Livy's account of the battle in southern Latium in 340 BCE that marked the beginning of a war against Rome's neighbors in Latium. There Livy details how the consul Titus Manlius Imperiosus Torquatus had his own son decapitated for breaking ranks to engage the enemy. "Go, lictor, bind him to the stake" is said to have been the shocking command preliminary to the execution of the young man, despite his winning glory in single combat. Livy further explains that the "Manlian orders" to the lictor became proverbial in later generations, shorthand for Roman military discipline at its most severe.

For 325 BCE, Livy offers another story of a subordinate fighting against orders but with success, in this case an ultra-patrician master of the horse defying his dictator, Lucius Papirius Cursor. The emotional high point in the narrative comes when Papirius utters the words, "Stand ready, lictor" and gives the order "to strip the master of the horse and make ready rods and axes." Soldiers manage to protect the noble victim of the dictator's wrath, and so he "escaped from the clutches of the lictors with his clothes in tatters," eventually making his way to Rome to plead his case. It seems he had good reason to be fearful. Papirius Cursor had the reputation of being quick to use the fasces, a few years later (319 BCE) famously also threatening the chief magistrate of allied Praeneste with decapitation.[16]

In one instance, during a peak crisis year of the Hannibalic War in Italy, we hear of a consul commanding a herald to relay an order of execution to a lictor. The circumstances are extraordinary. They concern the punitive measures of 211 BCE that the consul Gnaeus Fulvius Centumalus Maximus, accompanied by the consular commander Appius Claudius Pulcher, inflicted on Capuan senators arrested in the Campanian towns of Teanum and Cales. Livy describes the Romans as adhering to the form of a public execution, with the erection of a tribunal on which Fulvius sat (explicit for Cales), and lictors binding the Capuan aristocrats to stakes (Cales) before flogging (Teanum) and decapitation (Teanum, Cales). Yet despite the formal elements, this was more of a massacre than a judicial sentence, with a reported fifty-three Capuan senators meeting their death.

Indeed, even though at Cales a messenger from Rome interrupted the proceedings with the delivery of a decree of the Senate on the matter, "Fulvius . . . took the letter, but without breaking the seal . . . commanded a herald to order the lictor to carry out the legal punishment." The impression one gets from Livy's extensive narrative of the episode, complete with variants, is that the consul Fulvius wanted this bloody spectacle to serve as a deterrent to wavering allies. The fact that he employed a herald to direct his own lictors—the aim here evidently was to make the commands ring out as loudly as possible—will have accentuated still further the scale of Rome's reprisals.[17] Examples of dire directives straight from commander to lictor can readily be multiplied.[18]

What was essential to a commander's dignity was that he leave the grim work of punishment to his lictors, and not personally engage himself. For the early Republic, it is worth examining the case of one Publius Postumius Albinus Regillensis, a consular tribune of 414 BCE, to whom Livy attributes the memorable phrase "woe unto my soldiers should they not keep quiet." As the story goes, Postumius took the hostile town of Bolae (probably 35 kilometers southeast of Rome), but broke a promise to his soldiers about the distribution of booty. When called temporarily to Rome—where he uttered his threat to his troops in a public assembly—he left a quaestor behind at Bolae with at least one lictor. (The reference to this type of delegation is almost certainly anachronistic.) That was not enough to keep order in the camp, or from the quaestor being hit with a stone.

In Livy's account, Postumius returned to punish the mutineers. The mode of execution was through suffocation: rocks were heaped onto a wooden hurdle that trapped the condemned. When soldiers tried to interrupt the executions, Postumius himself scurried down from his tribunal to intervene, and "the lictors and centurions assailed the mob and tried to drive them back." In the scuffle, a volley of stones killed Postumius. The epilogue raises an eyebrow. So as not to inflame the Plebs at Rome, we are told, the Senate took a minimalistic approach to punishing the guilty—much as they did in the dangerous era of the Social War against the Italian allies, in 89 BCE, when soldiers stoned to death a consular Aulus Postumius Albinus, the clear inspiration for Livy's whole tale.[19]

The reign of the emperor Tiberius offers another negative example. To illustrate the cruelty and intemperance of Gnaeus Calpurnius Piso senior (blamed for the death of Germanicus in 19 CE), the philosopher Seneca tells the story of how as a provincial commander ("proconsul") he condemned three innocent soldiers to death. When Piso grew impatient with the slow pace of the executions, he jumped down from his tribunal—even tearing his clothes in the process—and snatched the fasces from the lictor. This dramatic episode throws into high relief more mundane instances of magistrates losing patience with their lictors.[20]

Armed with the fasces and usually organized in groups, lictors themselves probably did not have to say much to work their will on individuals or even crowds. Ancient authors are fulsome on the psychological effect that the mere presence of lictors caused. Their aspect would be especially terrifying outside Rome, where they displayed axes fixed in the bundle of rods, and wore military garb. Non-Roman citizens had particular reason to fear these attendants, against whom in both law and practice they had few protections.[21]

That said, the evidence is abundant that lictors had their own traditional cries and calls. They also issued sharp orders on behalf of their superior when the occasion demanded—or when they felt it did. Plautus's *Poenulus*, a comedy that premiered in Rome probably in the latter half of the 190s BCE, offers one of our earliest literary references to a lictor. And here the point is to tell him to be quiet. The actor delivering the prologue to the play represents himself as "an *imperator* of the stage" who has a series of edicts to announce, meant to ensure peace in the theater. Among them: "let not the lictor nor his rods utter a single word." One presumes that Plautus had in mind lictors of the official who produced the festival, who had the greatest stake in ensuring that spectators remained attentive for the performance. But lictors would accompany any higher magistrate who entered the space of the theater and joined the audience. Whatever the case, the pseudo-edict warns them not to push their weight around. It also implies that the sound of their rods whacking flesh was a familiar one.[22]

The Lictors and Crowd Control

A basic function of lictors was to clear the way for magistrates on the move, and plainly they often barked orders while doing it. The younger Pliny gushes over the emperor Trajan for not making too much of a show of it. In his *Panegyric* (100 CE) on the emperor, Pliny recounts how he entered Rome for the first time after his accession, returning from the Danube in 99 CE: "you moved in the midst of the élite of the senators or knights . . . and your lictors quietly and courteously cleared your path."[23] The same duties obtained outside Rome. There the lictors had to maintain the commander's authority amid a crowd of official and unofficial personnel in his retinue. They guided his way on often unfamiliar roads, cleared his path, and in general determined who got access to their superior. In a pinch, it seems a commander might employ them as heralds or messengers.[24]

But what lictors were best at was showing force. In Rome, magistrates sometimes ordered them to flex their muscles even in the Senate. Obnoxious foreign envoys were one target. For 216 BCE, Livy found a report that a Campanian embassy demanded as a price of aiding Rome against Hannibal an annual share in the consulship. The upshot, says Livy, was that the envoys found themselves expelled from the Senate house. It must have been lictors who showed them the door. For the Greek historian Appian relates that it was these attendants who sent packing (at least for a brief time) a high-ranking Carthaginian embassy to the Senate in 149 BCE, on the eve of the Third Punic War. But that was not the end of the humiliation for the Campanian envoys. A lictor was charged to escort them out of the city, to make sure they complied with a traditional interdiction that the Senate ordered, departure from Roman territory before nightfall.[25]

Perhaps inevitably, we find senior magistrates setting their lictors on political enemies in the Senate itself. Cicero relates at some length a heated debate in September 91 BCE over the limits of political language. Matters came to a head when the presiding consul, Lucius Marcius Philippus, tried to discipline an unusually distinguished ex-consul, Lucius Licinius Crassus, by seizing his property as surety. Crassus weaponized his considerable wit and eloquence to get the consul to back down, and even succeeded in securing a Senate decree hostile to Philippus. The early imperial writer Valerius Maximus adds a plausible detail not found in Cicero, namely that the consul ordered a lictor to initiate the legal action against Crassus. Julius Caesar as consul revived the tactic as consul in 59 BCE, when he had a lictor put an end to a speech by the younger Cato by haling him off to prison. At this, "the entire Senate" promptly followed Cato, says Valerius Maximus, which broke the consul's resolve.[26]

It was believed that as far back as the regal period, lictors had the task of verbally enforcing order in a judicial court.[27] For the historical era, our sources emphasize that lictors had a special responsibility to maintain the dignity of the magistrate's tribunal, down to arranging the position of the curule chair. An important task was physically to protect the tribunal during official proceedings, and if need be, quash challenges to its authority. An unlikely challenge came in the year 42 BCE, when the triumvirs Antony, Octavian, and Lepidus jointly occupied a tribunal from which they heard an energetic appeal against a new war tax they had levied on Rome's 1,400 wealthiest women. At the head of the women's delegation was Hortensia, daughter of a famous consular and orator, and in all likelihood then the adoptive mother of Caesar's assassin Brutus. Her speech on the occasion found an audience even in later years. The triumvirs' first response to Hortensia and the women's collective? "They ordered the lictors to drive them away from the tribunal," says Appian. But a popular outcry caused the triumvirs to call off their lictors and reconsider the matter; the next day they trimmed the tax list to 400. For lictors to silence these leading women by forcibly driving them away from the triumvirs' tribunal seems needlessly brutal.[28]

Indeed, for lictors to handle Roman matrons in this way also may have been unlawful, or at least in gross violation of accepted practice. A second-century CE grammarian, drawing on an Augustan-era source, suggests that Roman women of good standing had immunity against lictors roughing them up. "Matrons used not to be removed by magistrates," we are told, "so that they would not seem to be hit or fondled, nor shaken while pregnant." Indeed, if a husband was sitting in a carriage with his wife, that afforded even him a measure of protection against the magistrates' coercion. In the early empire, the writer Valerius Maximus also attests that one could not touch a matron's body while enforcing her presence in court. Prostitutes evidently did not enjoy such privileges. Indeed, it seems clear that the lictors' role in this particular public spectacle of official power served to create and reinforce power relations between men and (certain) women, and also heightened class consciousness and distinctions among women.[29]

Psychological Effects of the Fasces

On the whole, the public spectacle of lictors seems so regular and expected that our literary sources for all eras understandably take little special interest in the routine duties of these attendants. Occasionally, however, a chance notice can offer perspective on the psychological effect that lictors with their fasces must have produced in the populace. Livy offers a famous instance, where he uses a lictor's everyday gesture as a springboard for his dramatic narrative of the last stage of patrician-plebeian conflict in Rome. According to this author, the great social and political compromise that resulted in the Licinian-Sextian legislation of 367 BCE, which for the first time opened the consulship to plebeians, had a personal and petty origin. A decade earlier, we are told, the wife of the plebeian Gaius Licinius Stolo had become jealous of her sister, who was married to a patrician Sulpicius, then serving in Rome's top magistracy.[30]

"It fell out that the sisters Fabia were together in the house of Servius Sulpicius, then consular tribune"—the office was an early experimental substitute for the consulship—"and were whiling away the time in talk . . . when a lictor of Sulpicius, who was returning from the Forum, rapped on the door, in the usual manner, with his rod. At this the younger Fabia, being unused to the custom, went pale, which made the elder laugh with surprise at her sister's ignorance. But that laugh rankled in the other's mind, for a woman's feelings are influenced by trifles."

On the face of things, the anecdote makes little sense. The father of the two Fabia sisters, the patrician Marcus Fabius Ambustus, himself held the consular tribunate in 381 BCE, and so will have had lictors. Plus plebeians were eligible for the office since its inception, and had held it as recently as 379. Furthermore, Livy elsewhere describes lictors escorting their superior to his home. There is no reason to doubt the item here, that one of them would rap on a door with their equipment to signal the magistrate's arrival.[31]

By Livy's account, this mundane detail of a private affair had far-reaching repercussions. As his story goes, the younger Fabia complained to her father Ambustus, and he with his son-in-law Licinius and a friend Lucius Sextius Lateranus made plans to introduce legislation to make plebeians eligible for the consulship. Licinius and Sextius entered the plebeian tribunate first in 376, and then—being re-elected year after year—dragged out the struggle for plebeian participation in the top regular magistracy for ten years, including five in which they annually vetoed the elections for the chief offices, resulting in quasi-anarchy.

More inherently plausible is a detail that Livy offers in his account of how in 186 BCE Hispala Fecenia, a freedwoman who worked as a prostitute, helped disclose the activities of Bacchic cells to the consul Spurius Postumius Albinus. Suspecting that Hispala was well-informed on the Bacchanalia, Postumius asked his (patrician) mother-in-law Sulpicia to invite the woman to her home.[32]

"On receiving the message," relates Livy, "Hispala was frightened—without knowing why, she was being summoned by a woman of such distinction and dignity—and when she caught sight of the lictors in the forecourt, the crowd around the consul and then the consul himself, she almost fainted. She was taken to the interior of the house where the consul, in his mother-in-law's presence"—but apparently without lictors—"informed her that she need not be alarmed if she could bring herself to tell the truth. . . ." Eventually Hispala confesses that while still enslaved she indeed had been initiated into the Bacchic cult, but did not remain active in it.

So the younger Fabia was alarmed by a lictor's loud knock on her sister's door. And Hispala panicked at spotting the consul's (dozen) lictors packed into the vestibule of his mother-in-law's home. In these anecdotes, Livy recreates the individual's perspective on the terror of the fasces. He also implies that lictors increased that terror when they encroached on private space.

It seems to have been expected that when a magistrate entered a private residence, his lictors waited outside or just inside the door. To bring a lictor further into the interior evidently doubled the dread, as a notorious anecdote of a dining room execution attached to the year 192 BCE demonstrates. The story involves Lucius Quinctius Flamininus—younger brother of the famed Titus Flamininus who four years previous presented himself in Greece as its "liberator"—banqueting as consul in Cisalpine Gaul. It is a gruesome tale, which sought to explain why, in 184 BCE, seven years after his command, the censors (i.e., occasional senior magistrates whose tasks included supervision of public morals) expelled him from the Senate. The continued discussion of this case in the rhetorical schools of the early Empire also offers for us a wealth of material on the expected formulas that a commander used to drive his lictor into action, and the terror that the attendant's fasces generated.

Livy reports two versions of the substance of the incident, each of which places the younger Flamininus in a symposiastic setting, and neither of which mentions a lictor. Livy sources his favored account to a speech by one of the censors of 184, Cato the Elder. Here the consul Flamininus, to gratify a young male Carthaginian lover at a wine-soaked feast, orders a high-ranking Gallic deserter to be introduced among the diners, and then himself grabs a sword and brutally slays him. Livy then rejects a variant he found in the Roman historian Valerius Antias (first century BCE), in which Flamininus has a prisoner decapitated among the diners—we are not told by whom—to oblige a female courtesan who had asked to see an execution. Yet Cicero had already endorsed Antias's basic version, as later would Valerius Maximus. So does Plutarch (in two separate biographies he authored), arguing that Cato was exaggerating to strengthen his case, though accepting his detail that Flamininus's lover was a young male. Plutarch also is explicit that the consul summoned one of his lictors into the dining hall to perform the act—a detail he presumably found in Antias.

So Livy's preferred version of the case of Lucius Flamininus stands alone. Indeed, already in the earliest Empire, the rhetorical schools had adopted as a stock theme Valerius Antias's telling of the Flamininus scandal—i.e., the consul ordering the execution of a prisoner by lictor's axe, at the request of a courtesan at a drunken banquet. The one major twist is that they assessed the situation (anachronistically) through the lens of *maiestas* (roughly, "treason") law from their own day. The elder Seneca in a rhetorical treatise lists fully twenty-four Roman declaimers active under Augustus and Tiberius who had tackled the topic, with quotations from their treatments, adding a half-dozen Greek attempts too. His compilation shows that these orators focused largely on amplifying the lurid charges against the commander (whom they consistently and carelessly call "praetor"), and how those reflected precisely on the majesty of the Roman people.

One of the declaimers succinctly summarizes the accusations against Flamininus as "keeping a whore, and killing someone indoors, at night, at a party, at the request of the whore." The consensus among the speakers making the case against Flamininus is that even if he had reason to execute the condemned man, he did so in the wrong place, at the wrong time, and for the wrong reason. As one of Seneca's orators explains by way of comparison, "one is allowed to go into a brothel; but if a praetor, preceded by his axes, is escorted into a brothel, he will be harming majesty (i.e., of the Roman people) even though he is doing something he is allowed to do." Flamininus at his dinner introduced among "private goblets . . . the edge of a public axe." And so he disgraced himself as governor of a province, and indeed—as the declaimer Capito is said to have emphasized— the rods and axes of Roman *imperium*, by taking prerogatives of "the Forum into a feast."

"Capito went on to describe how different is the manner of beheading in the Forum" of a provincial town, recalls Seneca. What follows is a glimpse into how lictors of a provincial commander were expected to execute the condemned, in the Augustan age and surely well before. "The praetor ascends the tribunal, beneath the gaze of the province. The guilty man's hands are tied behind his back; he stands there, as all look intently and grimly on. Silence is enforced by the herald. Then the ritual words are pronounced. The trumpet sounds from the other side."

So much for proper procedure. Seneca cites a half-dozen other declaimers who seized precisely upon the perversion of the role of the lictor for a dining room execution. Perhaps there was an improvised tribunal, and the lictor as well as Flamininus were drunk, suggests one. Two others imply that the lictor could not believe the order which came from his commander, evidently under the courtesan's control. Nor do the guests at the banquet escape blame in the orators' imagining of the grotesque spectacle: "because he had struck a good blow, they drank a toast to the lictor."

Several peppered their speeches on the Flamininus theme with ironic subversions of the formulaic commands to the lictor traditional at an execution, glossing the commander's imperatives with their own caustic annotations. Seneca quotes one as saying: " 'Remove.' Do you hear, lictor? Remove the whore from the praetor. . . . 'Strike.' But make sure your rods don't smash our glasses. 'Strip.' Whore, do you recognize the word? Certainly the province does." Still another is cited for chiding Flamininus for debasing the order: "Act according to the law." "You know the meaning of that? Act by day, act in the Forum. The lictor is aghast—he says the same as your whore: he has never seen such a thing."

In Seneca's sample, the most penetrating accusation of Flamininus comes from the declaimer Albucius Silus, who offers a stark and revealing assessment of the purpose of lictors with their fasces. The commander at his provincial dinner party "made a game out of the terror inspired by the empire of Rome . . . remember that the aim of your power is terror, not diversions for frivolous women." Paradoxically, the intrusion of a public mode of supreme punishment into a private space served as a cheap shock, that ultimately lessened the impact of the magistrate's insignia.[33]

So these Augustan-era declaimers who animated the grisly case of Flamininus are in broad agreement on proper procedure. The sense we get is that Roman executions were supposed to be public, the competent official was expected to be the one giving the orders, and the lictor when wielding his axe acted only on his superior's explicit commands. These basic rules seem to have remained in place well into late antiquity.

Lictors and Military Justice

Camp justice had its own protocols. Our literary sources relish describing how lictors dispensed justice in the military sphere, where there was no formal right of appeal. For example, Livy and Appian describe how in 206 BCE Publius Cornelius Scipio—the future Africanus, then trying to wrest southeastern Spain from the Carthaginians—punished the leaders of a mutiny, about thirty-five in number. It was a serious affair, launched at the Roman fort at Sucro when it was rumored that Scipio had died at New Carthage (modern Cartagena), probably some 180 kilometers south. The mutineers appointed two obscure men from their number as their leaders, and even equipped them with fasces. "Nor did it occur to them," says Livy, "that those rods and axes, which they caused to be carried before them to frighten others"—a stark gloss on the purpose of the insignia—"were hanging over their own backs and their own necks."[34]

Appian is especially lavish with the details on how Scipio lured the ringleaders to New Carthage and had them summarily executed. Stealthily surrounding an assembly with armed guards, Scipio "ordered his attendants to divide the crowd in two parts." He then had the senators in his camp drag the chief mutineers into the gap, and ensured that his military tribunes instantly killed anyone who uttered a word in support of the ringleaders. Then came the work of what must have been Scipio's lictors. "Scipio caused the wretches who had been dragged into the middle to be beaten with rods, those who had cried for help being beaten hardest, after which he ordered that their necks should be pegged to the ground and their heads cut off."

This gruesome literary sub-genre continues well into the Empire. Writing in the late fourth or early fifth century CE of the pretender Avidius Cassius (rebelled and killed 175 CE), the author of the *Historia Augusta* claims he took his lictors to savage extremes. Amid details of some horrific (and frankly unbelievable) novel punishments that Avidius inflicted on errant soldiers, we learn that "after openly beating them with the lictors' rods in the forum and in the midst of the camp, he beheaded those who deserved it with the axe." That in itself sounds credible, but it is not all. "And in numerous instances [he] cut off his soldiers' hands"—presumably also with a lictor's axe.[35]

Intrusions by Lictors into the Domestic Sphere

In handling lictors outside Rome, there was a still worse accusation than severity toward Roman soldiers. Cicero in his lengthy speech for the prosecution of Gaius Verres (a praetor of 74 BCE) makes much of the charge that the man as praetorian governor in Sicily (73–71) shockingly misused his lictors, granted to him for public business, for private motives.[36] Indeed, Cicero argues that Verres seriously abused the fearsome public insignia of Roman office even early in his career, before he was properly entitled to the fasces. The accusation concerns Verres's conduct as a commander's legate to the Roman province of Cilicia in 80–79, especially his transit to and from southeast Anatolia. The case from Verres's earlier career deserves setting out in full.

After pestering the governor Gnaeus Cornelius Dolabella for the position, Verres traveled in such a fashion, Cicero tells us, that he seemed not a legate of the Roman people, but a walking calamity. In transit through Greece, he extorted money from local magistrates, stole from temple treasuries, and stripped communities of their public art. Crossing through Roman Asia, he continued his predations. But the commander for that province, Gaius Claudius Nero, could not punish Verres, who technically was a legate for Cilicia (which he hadn't even reached yet). Later, returning from his province via Athens, Verres allegedly bought a praetorship, now having one million denarii in his pocket to pay bribe money up front.

Much of this seems hyperbolic at best, especially the last bit about walking right into a praetorship. (Verres must have departed from Cilicia by early 78 BCE, and was elected praetor only four years later, for the year 74 BCE.) However, there is one episode from Verres's legateship that Cicero tells at great length, emphasizing several items that clearly were a matter of public record. It concerns his visit to the city of Lampsacus in Asia in 80 or 79 BCE, and reveals a crucial fact—that even as a legate, Verres had been granted at least one lictor, who lost his life in a melée.

We can briefly sum up the essentials of the story. Once in Cilicia, Verres prevailed on his superior Gnaeus Dolabella for leave to see to business with the kings of both Bithynia and Thrace. Verres's journey took him and his entourage to the city of Lampsacus on the Hellespont. There Cicero says he formed the design of abducting the daughter of one Philodamus, its most distinguished citizen. The occasion chosen for the crime was a dinner in Philodamus's home, attended by the legate's entire staff; Verres did not attend with his subordinates, "but gave them instructions what to do." Philodamus ordered his slaves to resist; and within the home, "Cornelius, a lictor of Verres, who with some of Verres's slaves had been posted . . . at the strategic point for abducting the woman, lost his life."

The next day, in response, the outraged citizens of Lampsacus tried to burn down the home where Verres was lodged. The result? Verres escaped, and the governor of Asia tried and convicted Philodamus and his son for the murder of the lictor. The Cilician commander Dolabella is said to have participated in the process, held evidently for his convenience at Laodicea in Phrygia, leaving his province to serve on Claudius Nero's judicial council. "The man selected as prosecutor," relates Cicero, "was a Roman citizen, one of the Lampsacus money-lenders, who might expect the help of Dolabella's lictors in extorting his money from his debtors, provided he said what Dolabella ordered him to say." The Lampsacene father and son were judged guilty, and Nero had them beheaded in the forum of Laodicea, well over 500 kilometers to the southeast of their home city.

In this sordid tale, the only reason we hear of the role of the lictor Cornelius is that he was killed. Yet the basic elements of this incident and its aftermath illustrate the latitude that Rome's representatives had for exercising their official power in the provinces. It must be stressed that Verres was not entitled to this attendant by virtue of his legateship. Dolabella must have granted him one—or possibly more—as a favor, whether for his whole term as legate (as the alleged crimes en route to Cilicia may suggest), or specifically for his business with the kings of Bithynia and Thrace. For the incident at Lampsacus, Cicero sketches a scenario where Cornelius works apart from his superior Verres, in concert with his slaves, and violates provincial hosts within their own home, causing them to retaliate in self-defense. And when the Cilician commander Dolabella shows up for the murder trial, Cicero claims that he was prepared to have his lictors assist a local money-lender in his shakedowns, in a province that was not even his own.

Whatever the precise circumstances of the lictor Cornelius's appointment and deployment, his violent death clearly was deemed a grave affair. The trial that ensued involved a capital charge; Dolabella felt obliged to absent himself from fighting in Cilicia to participate in the proceedings. One can imagine how the condemnation of Philodamus and his son also served to emphasize to Rome's provincial subjects the horror of the fasces. Though Cicero does not expressly point it up, it must have been the lictors of Nero, the governor of Asia, who with their axes carried out the execution order. Cicero does term the beheading in Laodicea "a cruel spectacle . . . which caused all the province of Asia profound unhappiness and distress." In essence, in one of the judicial centers of the province of Asia, lictors very publicly avenged the death of a fellow lictor.[37]

Cicero throughout his *Verrines* means to shock his audience with graphic descriptions of Verres's career-long abuse of public authority for private aims. Now, a competent magistrate was perfectly within his rights ordering a lictor to make an arrest. But the perception of excessive force was inevitable, and Cicero in his prosecution speech repeatedly capitalizes on it. So do later writers. In imperial fiction, Apuleius in the mid-second century CE makes much of scenarios in which local Thessalian magistrates with their lictors show brutish behavior in the administration of law. We see them feeling free to intrude in the private sphere, bursting into a house to conduct a search or to make an arrest, as well as to intervene in the public market, by destroying overpriced fish. Even in court, on a magistrate's order, lictors roughly handle a defendant.[38]

In the later Republic, at least, it seems that lictors could enter private homes even when an official was not present. The saga of Verres's lictor at Lampsacus offers our first certain example. The imperial biographer Suetonius describes how Julius Caesar as dictator strictly enforced his sumptuary legislation (46 BCE), positioning guards in the market to seize prohibited luxury foods, "and sometimes he sent his lictors and soldiers to take from a dining-room any articles which had escaped the vigilance of his watchmen, even after they had been served."

Imperial-era declamation offers a somewhat more fantastical example of a lictor entering the domestic sphere. In one such exercise, a rape victim has the choice of either marrying her rapist or having him put to death. She chooses the former; the wedding ceremony is characterized as a type where a lictor has to escort the bride to the husband's home. Though fictional cases such as these have only occasional contact with Roman legal realities, the natural supposition is that a magistrate ordered the lictor to ensure that this punitive marriage took place. Whether the image has any grounding in actual Roman practice is another matter.[39]

Still, some Christian writers take special pains to emphasize the savagery of lictors, representing them as practically synonymous with prison torturers and executioners. Prudentius (writing in 403 CE) and later Sidonius (in 468 CE) depict lictors as appointed to strangle their victims in dungeons. In 370 CE, the priest and scholar Jerome narrates the story of how a cruel lictor "whose responsibility was the criminally condemned," ended up fearing capital punishment from his own commander, a consular governor for Cisalpine Gaul. His crime? Failure to decapitate a Christian woman falsely accused of adultery. Jerome terms this lictor—who unsuccessfully attempted his grim duties clad in the characteristic military cloak (*paludamentum*)—also a "spy" (*speculator*), as well as a "murderer" (*percussor*) and "butcher" (*carnifex*), and eventually even compares him to the Devil.

The setting of Jerome's tale is Vercellae, some 60 kilometers west of Milan. It was not in the town's forum, relates Jerome, but just outside its walls where the governor delivered a hasty verdict, expecting executions of two alleged lovers promptly to follow. Yet so outraged were the Vercellans at the cruelty of the (irregular) process that they took up arms against the governor and his staff, and for a time prevented the lictor from accomplishing the second of the two decapitations, that of the woman. In the end, says Jerome, divine protection miraculously preserved the life of this Christian, though her neck received a total of seven blows—from a sword, one notes, rather than an axe.[40] As we have seen, a change in the form of the fasces in (probably) the third century CE had reduced the characteristic axe to mere ornament.

5

The Roman Fasces

LIMITS AND DISCONTINUITIES

Institutional Curbs on the Fasces: The Plebeian Tribunes

The lictors with their fasces functioned as the extension of the person of their superior. In the field, we common see a magistrate's lictors giving commands to foreign envoys, and orders to kings, even casting them into chains.[1] Lictors readily issue directives to another Roman holder of *imperium*, if his status was deemed inferior.[2] Yet lictors plainly had their limits, for the Republican system placed basic structural curbs on how their superiors might exercise their official authority. Chief among them was the institution of the plebeian tribunes, said to be created in 493 BCE to defend and support the Roman Plebs. Livy presents a situation in which the Plebs had offered unorganized physical resistance to Rome's consuls and their lictors even before they had tribunes to represent them. What is clear is that the institution of the tribunate served to massively leverage this latent political power.

The tribunes possessed a bundle of rights that ultimately rested on their peculiar status, ritually established at the creation of the office, as sacrosanct, that is, inviolable as to their persons. It was the plebeians themselves who guaranteed that inviolability of their leaders during their year in office. In essence, the Plebs and their elected representatives, who eventually numbered ten, formed (as we have noted) a state within a state in the Roman polity. This created a problem category for higher magistrates and their lictors, since they could not physically enforce orders to the tribunes of the Plebs within the latter's sphere of competence, which extended to the first milestone from the city.

The Fasces. T. Corey Brennan, Oxford University Press. © Oxford University Press 2023.
DOI: 10.1093/oso/9780197644881.003.0005

On the other hand, to assault a magistrate's lictor was viewed as a serious affront. "Let anybody strike a lictor," says an ultra-patrician ex-consul in Livy's account of the year 494 BCE, "knowing that the right to scourge and behead him rests with that one man whose majesty he has violated!" Dionysius of Halicarnassus has patricians in 473 BCE suggest that the offense deserved the death penalty, indeed by hurling the perpetrator from the Tarpeian Rock.[3]

Rome's annalistic historians consistently show a lively interest in domestic conflict. So naturally they enthusiastically illustrated how the display of *imperium* only went so far in handling plebeian tribunes, a theme that offered significant literary possibilities. For this purpose, the record of the years 477–468 BCE, at a high point for the struggle of the patrician and plebeian orders, but largely devoid of major external events, proved ideal for Rome's annalists.[4] The narratives of Livy and Dionysius of Halicarnassus (and later, that of Cassius Dio) draw directly on earlier annalists' efforts, which can be regarded as a blend of historical fiction with actual constitutional principles observable at least from later Republican practice.

Livy and Dionysius offer their readers the picture of a near-intractable power struggle between patricians and plebeians that starts in earnest in the year 476 BCE.[5] A central figure in all this is the plebeian hero Volero Publilius, an ex-centurion who in 473 protests against being pressed into military service as a common soldier. And his adversaries on that occasion are the consuls' lictors, who are ordered to arrest, strip, and beat him for his refusal. The accounts of Livy and Dionysius are roughly congruent. The consuls ignored Publilius's appeal to stand trial—though he of course was a free Roman citizen—and the tribunes failed to stop his summary punishment. So the man took matters into his own hands. Livy says that Publilius obtained help from the crowd in repelling one lictor who was stripping off his clothes; Dionysius describes him single-handedly felling two in a row. When the consuls ordered still more lictors to nab Publilius, by the account of both authors it turned into a melée. The plebeians present attacked these attendants, pointedly broke their rods, and then chased the consuls themselves out of the Forum.

As Livy tells it, the Plebs in a growing dispute over the levy had already noted the consuls' vulnerability, in that they were attended solely by twenty-four lictors, who themselves were plebeian. "It was every man's own imagination that made them great and awe-inspiring," an unnamed speaker is made to say. Throughout this section of his narrative, Livy amplifies that point for literary effect. At the beginning of 473 BCE, two ex-consuls who faced prosecution hyperbolically term "the consular fasces, the purple-bordered toga, and the curule chair" as dooming their recipients to death; a consul was nothing more than an attendant (*apparitor*) of the tribunes. Later that year, after the plebeians actually attacked the lictors to save the ex-centurion Publilius, the consuls more realistically are described as "quickly convinced of the insecurity of majesty when unaccompanied with force."[6]

This incident of Volero Publilius in 473 shows the plebeians acting very much in their unorganized form, without the involvement of tribunes, to push back spontaneously against what they viewed as an unjust application of official violence. In contrast, the tradition on a pitched fight in 471 BCE over the mode of tribunician elections introduces a constitutional clash between lictors and a tribune of the Plebs. In brief, the tribune Gaius Laetorius from the speaker's platform in Rome's Forum sought to remove those not eligible to vote from the relevant assembly, which (we are told) included the patrician consuls. One of them, Appius Claudius, most defiantly refused to depart, claiming that Laetorius was not a proper magistrate and so not competent to make him move. So Laetorius sent his summoner (*viator*) to hale away the consul; the consul in turn sent a lictor to lay hands on the tribune.

In Livy's account, conciliatory gestures by Appius's consular colleague defused this highly volatile situation, evidently before anyone was touched. Dionysius offers a different and even more dramatic version. There Appius surrounds himself with lictors and members of his entourage and stands his ground in the assembly. Laetorius sends an attendant to arrest the consul, but the first of his lictors strikes a blow that drives that man back. The tribune himself then gathers a group to advance on Appius. Yet the other consul manages to insert himself between the two hostile parties, and successfully puts an end to the fracas.[7]

In the city of Rome during the Republic, contention between magistrates with *imperium* and plebeian tribunes was a constant, in all eras. Here the magistrates of the People were at a technical disadvantage, since their lictors properly could not physically interact with the inviolable tribunes, or even their attendants. The tale that they did so in the squabbles of 471 BCE is meant to shock. That is clear from a reported incident of the mid-450s, again from the annalists, which Livy briefly alludes to, but Dionysius describes at some length.[8]

In the year 456 BCE, so we hear, the plebeian tribunes, led by Lucius Icilius, were pressuring the consuls to convene the Senate to discuss a measure to assign Rome's Aventine hill to the Plebs. Eventually Icilius sent his attendant to force them into action. "And when one of the lictors at the orders of the consuls drove away the attendant," reports Dionysius, "Icilius and his colleagues in their resentment seized the lictor and led him away with

the intention of hurling him down from the (Tarpeian) rock"—a cliff on the
south slope of the Capitoline hill. This would be a first; as Dionysius points
out, no lictor had ever faced death for following his superior's command.

In this situation, the consuls had no recourse except—and this is
important—to seek the help of a member of the tribunician college, which
was not forthcoming. In the end, the tribunes released the captive lictor,
we learn, reluctant both to set a horrifying precedent and further provoke
the patricians. The tribunes indeed got their Senate meeting, where Icilius
spoke and sought to justify the tribunes' actions toward the lictor, "citing
the sacred laws which did not permit either a magistrate or a private citizen to offer any opposition to a tribune"—or, we may add, his personal
representative.

The maintenance and protection of the tribunes' personal inviolability
was crucial, for that is what allowed them to attend to their most important core function, namely assisting members of the Plebs against patricians
and magistrates of the Roman people as a whole. The Plebs, as the source
of the tribunes' power, plainly felt competent to intervene forcibly not just
on behalf of their leaders, but even in anticipation of their aid, when necessity demanded it. And a chief way in which plebeians in the city asserted
their strength vis-à-vis holders of *imperium* was to take their fasces and
smash them.

Our sources describe precisely such an instance of popular resistance
when the decemvirate—a special college of ten men with consular power—
that prepared the Twelve Tables illegally extended its commission of 451–450
BCE into a third year. In the annalistic tradition, this constitutional experiment revived some of the worst attributes of the monarchy, multiplied by ten.
The decemvirs displayed fasces with axes within the city, against which citizens had no appeal, and plebeians had no tribunes to protect them—hence
the narratives of spontaneous mass action that we find in greatest detail in
Livy and Dionysius of Halicarnassus.

For these authors, the criminal conduct of the decemvir Appius Claudius
on his tribunal in Rome dominates the first part of the year 449 BCE. Through
a complicated legal ruse, Appius sought to ensnare the schoolgirl Verginia,
engaged to the ex-tribune Lucius Icilius. Her father, however, forestalled
the plot by killing the young woman on the spot, openly in the Forum.
Public outrage—at the decemvir Appius—leads to a plebeian secession to
the Aventine, and nearly sparks civil war. In the end, all the decemvirs are
compelled to abdicate, and a re-established Republican government punishes
them through legal means for their various crimes.

Livy and Dionysius both portray Appius as a full-blown autocrat, whose use of his lictors characterizes the excesses of the decemviral period as a whole. For example, Livy has Verginia's father offer a fiery indictment of this "perpetual decemvir," who fortified his tribunal with "executioners (*carnifices*) not lictors," and "wreaked his vengeance on the goods, the backs, and the lives of the citizens, threatening all indiscriminately with the rods and axes."

Our two main narratives take every opportunity to highlight the imbalance in power between decemvirs and citizens, represented especially in the gratuitous use of axe-bearing fasces. When Icilius initially intervenes for his fiancée at Appius's tribunal, the decemvir's lictors attempt to push him back. Livy pens for Icilius a defiant reply: "summon all the lictors of all your colleagues"—the decemvirs had of course 120 in all, counting those of Appius—"give orders for the axes and rods to be in readiness." Unnerved, Appius adjourns proceedings to the next day. But then he shockingly judges Verginia to be the long-separated slave of one of his clients. Livy says that the decemvir sent a lictor to clear a path so that the man could take her into his possession; Dionysius goes further, and has Appius promise an escort in the Forum of "12 axes." Verginia never left the Forum, for that is where her father slays her.

What follows in our accounts is a violent confrontation around the corpse of Verginia, a tumultuous public meeting, the embarrassment of the decemvir, and ultimately the fall of the decemvirate. Throughout, the fasces are made to express the vicissitudes of the volatile political situation. In summary, Appius tries to disrupt protesters in the Forum with his lictors, ordering them to drag away Verginia's body and arrest the principals of the opposition. Instead, the lictors are routed. Livy specifies that the tipping point in the clash came when Appius's lictors attacked two patricians who had sided with the popular resistance, Lucius Valerius Potitus and Marcus Horatius. In defense of these men, the crowd broke up the lictors' fasces. Calling an impromptu assembly, Appius tried to whip up sentiment against his adversaries, but was shouted down. Livy has the private citizen Valerius then make a decisive intervention. "Assuming the tone of authority, [he] ordered the lictors"—we must remember that they had just lost their fasces—"to cease attendance on one who held no official position." Appius, stripped of his insignia and in fear for his life, decides to skulk away. When over the next days the plebeians apply further pressure, including a secession that a speaker in Livy wittily says left "a greater number of lictors in the Forum than of all other citizens put together," the decemvirs decide to abdicate. The established forms of the Republic return under Valerius and Horatius, now elected as consuls.[9]

Unorganized Resistance to the Fasces

Of course, Livy and Dionysius, in narrating all this rough-and-tumble, are indulging in an imaginative historical reconstruction of the state under the decemvirs, aided by what they found in earlier annalists, themselves not anywhere near contemporary to the events described. Yet by the time we get to the mid-Republic, our sources underline the difficulties that Roman magistrates—even those with *imperium*—sometimes had in enforcing their will. And the overall record amply confirms that in extreme situations Romans might resist the coercive power of magistrates by seizing and smashing their fasces.[10]

In the contentious tribunician elections of the summer of 133 BCE, the breaking of rods is described as a decisive turning point that tipped a riotous public assembly into open violence. The proceedings, now in their second day, took place on the Capitol near the temple of Jupiter Optimus Maximus. One or more holders of *imperium* must have been on the spot, since Appian says "partisans of Tiberius Gracchus"—the elder of the famous Gracchi brothers, then a plebeian tribune, and seeking election to an atypical second term—"seized the fasces in the hands of the lictors and broke them in pieces. They drove the rich out of the assembly with such disorder and wounds that the tribunes fled from their places in terror, and the priests closed the doors of the temple." Whose lictors? Probably those of a praetor, for at the time of the disturbances, the consul Publius Mucius Scaevola (who was favorable to Gracchus) was presiding over a Senate meeting at the nearby temple of Fides. The chaos only intensified. Later that same day, a mob led by Rome's *pontifex maximus* (i.e., head of the Roman state religion) killed Gracchus himself before the doors of Jupiter's temple.

Authorities both ancient and modern count the assassination of the (technically inviolable) tribune Tiberius Gracchus as destroying a fragile political consensus in the Roman state and causing a dramatic shift in the tone of Republican politics. The event certainly changed attitudes toward murder as a political tool, previously quite rare. For instance, the Greek author Plutarch reports that in 88 BCE the Senate dispatched two praetors—a Brutus and a Servilius—to forbid the consul Sulla's advance on Rome. Sulla's troops took offense at their directives, and came close to killing them. In this instance there was a change of mind, and they chose rather to debase the pair symbolically. The soldiers "contented themselves with breaking their fasces, stripping them of their senatorial togas, insulting them in many ways"—we are left to imagine how—"and then sending them back to the city." Plutarch adds that the sight of two praetors stripped of their insignia shook the resolve of Rome to withstand Sulla and his forces.

Later incidents within the city of Rome flipped this scenario, with fasces-smashing as a preliminary to further violence. In a raucous legislative assembly of 67 BCE where a far-reaching tribunician bill was up for a vote, a mob broke the consul Gaius Cornelius Piso's fasces and threatened to tear him apart, reports the third-century CE historian Cassius Dio. The presiding tribune forestalled a debacle only by dissolving the meeting. Asconius, writing in a historical work of the first century CE, offers a more detailed and nuanced version of what caused the assembly to be suspended. In his telling, the consul Piso sent a lictor to arrest individuals in the crowd who had threatened to lay hands on him. In response, "his fasces were broken and stones were hurled at the consul from the rear of the gathering," before the crowd was dispersed.

Several Greek sources from the imperial period detail how a mob in 59 BCE set on the consul Marcus Calpunius Bibulus when he entered the Forum to keep his colleague Julius Caesar from passing his second agrarian law of the year. The bill, which provided for distribution of Campanian land to veterans and certain members of the urban Plebs, seems to have been promulgated and voted on within the month of May—an odd-numbered month, when Caesar as the first-elected consul will have had the full fasces and thus priority of action. In addition to his lictors, Bibulus had a number of senators and several plebeian tribunes in his entourage, evidently expecting that their presence would protect him against Caesar's adherents.

Cassius Dio specifies that Caesar was speaking on the podium of the temple of Castor and Pollux when his colleague sought to obstruct him. Bibulus utterly failed in his object. "He was thrust down the steps, his fasces were broken to pieces, and the tribunes as well as others received blows and wounds." Plutarch mentions the incident in two different biographical works, adding some details: when the crowd set on Bibulus's lictors, someone dumped on his head a basket of feces; in the aftermath, it was two tribunes who were wounded, among others. Appian takes pains to emphasize Bibulus's bravery when he lost his insignia, defiant against the Caesarians who had wounded the tribunes and threatened the consul himself with their daggers.[11] Yet the result of this bloody and humiliating skirmish was that Bibulus almost immediately withdrew from the public performance of his consular duties for the rest of the year. It seems to have been the first occasion in the historical period when a consul experienced the loss of not just a single lictor's fasces, but apparently his entire complement in the city of Rome itself.

The latter months of the year 58 BCE offered another first, on which Cicero has much to say, though at the time he was removed from Rome in exile, thanks to the efforts of the demagogic tribune Publius Clodius Pulcher. In that year both consuls found themselves physically attacked, with one seeing his fasces smashed. The spark came from an unlikely source: the tribune Clodius's corrupt release of a high-level foreign prisoner, whom Pompey had taken to Rome. When Clodius came into conflict over this with the consul Aulus Gabinius, their rival gangs clashed in the streets. Cicero tendentiously characterizes this as leading to a state of near anarchy in the city, though (or rather because) he was not there to see it. One of the specifics that Cicero offers us, in a series of short impressionistic sketches of daily "weapons, stonings, and flights," is that a riotous mob broke Gabinius's fasces and wounded his fellow consul Lucius Calpurnius Piso (presumably after attacking also his lictors).[12]

It is easy to see why lictors, who after all were proxies for their superiors, offered such attractive targets in such violent brawls. One wonders, however, what impression the news of their humiliation in domestic conflicts made on Rome's subjects and adversaries. Indeed, it is fair to say that throughout the entire antique period, non-Romans instantly recognized, always feared, and widely hated their insignia. It is a commonplace in our Roman literary sources to say that such-and-such a foreign locale regarded the fasces with fear.[13]

Foreigners' Fear of the Fasces

Yet outsiders voice this sentiment, too. Significantly, second century BCE historian Polybius reckons that the culmination of all calamities to befall Greece came in the years 150–146, when through their transgressions—and subsequent panic—"the Peloponnesians, the Boeotians, the Phocians, the Euboeans, the Locrians, some of the cities on the Ionian Gulf, and finally the Macedonians . . . lost every shred of honor, and for various reasons consented to receive the Roman rods and axes into their cities." Two and a half centuries after Polybius, the satirist Juvenal offers some details about what Rome's subjects might expect from governors who indulge their ambition and caprice. It is especially aristocrats, he argues, who should put limits on their sadism in the provinces. "If you break your rods in the blood of allies, if you get a kick out of blunted axes and exhausted lictors"—i.e., from serial floggings and executions—"then the nobility of your ancestors themselves starts to work against you and to hold a bright torch over things you should be ashamed of." Even much later, in the latter half of the fourth century CE, Prudentius characterizes ambitious political figures of his day in much the same way. Such men count as a success their ability "to break the fasces on poor wretches' bodies and wield the terror-striking axes of the law."[14]

In principle, cities that Rome deemed "free" maintained their sovereignty—even if they were located within organized provinces under Roman *imperium*—and as such were exempt from lictors. Some of these communities had their status guaranteed by formal treaties, others did not. Commanders also could make ad hoc grants of certain rights to cities, subject to later ratification on their return to Rome. Yet such technical distinctions carried only so much weight when it came to the display of insignia. Where we can check, it seems that individual Roman commanders largely did what they wanted when outside Rome to make their presence felt.

For the gradual erosion of legal categories in the face of growing Roman power, the province of Africa offers a striking example. Upon the destruction of Carthage in 146 BCE, the city of Utica found itself with the best port, and soon became by far the richest and most important city in the province. Though Utica was technically a free city, by the early 80s BCE it nonetheless became the center of Roman administration, where governors must have kept at least some of their lictors, with their fasces and axes.

Now, one way that Rome's commanders broadcast sensitivity to local rights was to reduce the number of lictors to what they considered to be a bare minimum. Livy reports that in early 197 BCE Titus Flamininus (a consul of 198) approached Thebes in Boeotia with a single lictor—but in this case, to deceive the city as to his intentions while he brought up a sizable component of his military force. It was proposed in 57 BCE that Pompey be sent on a sensitive commission to (independent) Egypt with just two lictors and no army; the senators who successfully opposed the plan alleged that such an escort was insufficient for his safety. The triumvir Antony, while wintering in Athens in 39/38 BCE, altogether eschewed lictors, though in early spring reassembled them at his door, which served (we are told) only to increase their impact.

The same holds true for the Principate. When the future emperor Tiberius retired to Rhodes (6 BCE–2 CE), reports Suetonius, he affected an unassuming manner by "from time to time" walking within the confines of a gymnasium without a lictor or messenger. Tacitus says Germanicus (died 19 CE) used a single lictor in (free) Athens, which he still counts as an admirable gesture of self-restraint. Suetonius too praises Germanicus for his conspicuous modesty, yet says he "always entered free and federate towns without lictors." Even if Suetonius is correct in this, his obvious implication is that by the early Empire such exemplary behavior was quite unexpected.[15]

Occasionally we hear of pushback. In 47 BCE, when Julius Caesar entered Egyptian Alexandria preceded by apparently all his lictors, it sparked a bloody riot. Caesar himself recounts that "the whole crowd was shouting that this amounted to a slight on the [Egyptian] king's majesty," and that the disturbances extended several days, with several Roman soldiers killed "in every district of the city."[16]

Mockery of the Fasces

Rome's open enemies of course had wide latitude in expressing their feelings about the fasces. One avenue for that seems to have been the ironic appropriation of captured insignia. In the preliminaries to the battle of Zama in 202 BCE, Livy has Publius Cornelius Scipio (the future Africanus) state that Hannibal made a display of marching behind the fasces that he had captured from fallen Roman generals, whose number topped those that Rome's legitimate commanders then possessed. It is perfectly possible that this was the case. The first-century CE Latin poet Silius Italicus, for one, takes it as a given and expands upon it, introducing a nightmare scenario in which Carthage would celebrate a Roman-style triumph in North Africa, complete with axes and "blood-stained" rods. More than a half century after Zama, the Lusitanian rebel Viriathus, before his death in 139 BCE, is said to have incorporated captured Roman fasces into his victory trophies.

In early 88 BCE, Quintus Oppius—a commander in Cilicia with enhanced (i.e., consular) *imperium* and thus twelve fasces—found himself hemmed in at Laodiceia in Phrygia. The town eventually surrendered Oppius to the Pontic king Mithridates VI, who ostentatiously paraded him as his prisoner until Sulla secured his release in 85. Appian relates that the Laodiceans had "led Oppius to Mithridates with his lictors marching in front of him by way of ridicule." The townspeople obviously knew how a Roman holder of *imperium* paraded in public, and so in mockery they made him exit from their gate into captivity in precisely the same way he earlier had entered it. There is every reason to imagine that Mithridates maintained the ironic spectacle for the next three years, as he dragged Oppius (and surely his lictors) all through western Anatolia.[17]

In the next generation, this type of cruel cleverness is taken to a new level by the Parthian general Surena, who at Carrhae (modern Harran in Turkey) in 53 BCE crushed a large invading force under Marcus Licinius Crassus. Though the Roman commander lost his life in a parley that followed the battle, Surena sent word to the great city of Seleucia on the Tigris—some 700 kilometers to the southeast, near today's Baghdad—"that he was bringing Crassus there alive." For his entrance into the city, Surena decided on a grotesque parody of the essentials of the Roman triumph, in which some captive lictors would play a key role. He chose a Roman prisoner who was a Crassus lookalike, put him on a horse, and told him to answer to the title "imperator." Before him rode "trumpeters and a few lictors borne on camels; from the fasces of the lictors, purses were suspended, and to their axes were fastened Roman heads newly cut off." In the place of soldiers who customarily followed the *triumphator* and engaged in ritual mockery, Surena recruited prostitutes of Seleucia to sing decidedly non-ironic verses of abuse about Crassus. In short, the Parthian leader showed detailed familiarity with Roman military spectacle—balancing elements of pageantry, comedy, and horror—which he turned upside down against the vanquished. Indeed, Surena seems to have been too effective in his display at Seleucia, for we are told the Parthian king Orodes II soon suspected his ambition and had him executed—whether by beheading, we are not told.[18]

Seizure and Usurpation of Fasces

In the Republic, the more or less orderly annual succession of consuls' fasces was occasionally altogether interrupted. This happened when the state fell into an *interregnum* from the failure to elect magistrates in time for the start of the administrative year. For much of the mid-Republic, that was a date in March; after 153 BCE, it fell on January 1, which then served as the civil "new year's day" all through the Empire. In the troubled latter half of the 50s BCE, there were three such *interregna* in just a four-year span—in 55, 53, and 52. In the last of those years, tribunician obstruction prevented even the Senate's selection of an *interrex*—a patrician caretaker of the state in the absence of magistrates—until well into the third week of January. During that time, the city would not have seen any individual displaying fasces within its sacred perimeter.

For the troubled year 52 BCE, a turning point came early. On the 18th of January the demagogue Publius Clodius was murdered outside Rome in a scuffle with his rival Titus Milo's retinue. The next day Clodius's followers brought his corpse into the Senate house to cremate, which set the structure itself on fire. They also attacked the home in Rome of the newly appointed *interrex*, as well as that of Milo (then a candidate for the consulship, but absent from the city). Finally, the mob headed to the sanctuary of Libitina, the goddess of funerals. Located probably just outside the Esquiline Gate, it served as the center of Rome's undertaker industry.

Why there? The historian Asconius discloses that is where the fasces were then located, and the crowd wanted to confer them on enemies of Milo. "They then took the fasces from the grove of Libitina," and carried them to the home of two other candidates for the consulship of 52. Presumably these men rebuffed the Clodian group, since it next made its way "to the gardens of Gnaeus Pompeius," probably on Rome's Pincian hill, "hailing him now as consul, and now as dictator." As it happens, Pompey already was in possession of twelve fasces, thanks to extension of *imperium* from his consulship of 55 BCE. Through an extraordinary arrangement, at the time he resided just outside the civic center, and was governing the two Spanish provinces through legates. Presumably the mob in calling Pompey "dictator" wanted him to assume a dozen fasces in addition to the consular complement he already had.

It is telling that the crowd knew where to go to seize the fasces, and succeeded in finding them and carting them off. To be sure, during the *interregnum*, temporary storage was needed for most of these insignia; a dozen fasces will have gone to the *interrex*, but the rest awaited the proper election of two consuls and eight praetors. What seems most likely from Asconius's offhand reference is that the grove of Libitina was the base not just of the city's undertakers, but also of the lictors, and that is where they created, maintained, and stored the tools of their trade. One notes that when the emperor Claudius ordered high-profile executions by the axe, he is said to have used the area of the Esquiline. This further suggests that Libitina's sanctuary is likely to have hosted the lictors' headquarters. If true, this adds yet another level of terror to the fasces as symbol.

In the event, the mob had no takers for its impromptu offer of the fasces. Despite extreme disorder bordering on anarchy, eventually an *interrex* was able to hold the elections of higher magistrates. There Pompey was returned (most unusually) as sole consul, a full 58 days after Clodius's death.[19]

It is hard to imagine what inspired Clodius's supporters in their illegal attempt to confer the magisterial insignia. Granted, in late 66 BCE, there was a persistent rumor that two men would seize the fasces in Rome, after disappointment in the consular elections for the following year. More precisely, the two successful candidates—Publius Cornelius Sulla and Publius Autronius Paetus—found themselves tried and then convicted of electoral bribery. Under the terms of a recent law, the pair forfeited their right to enter office and were disbarred from future candidacy; selected in their place were their competitors Lucius Aurelius Cotta and Lucius Manlius Torquatus. Cicero in 62 BCE dismisses as absurd the notion that in response the condemned men hatched an elaborate plot: to kill Cotta and Torquatus as they prepared to assume office on the Capitoline hill on January 1, take over their fasces, and in their stead descend into the Forum as consuls with lictors. Still, several other sources portray the alleged plot as a serious crisis averted.

The item certainly confirms the formal importance of the ceremony on the Capitol through which consuls entered office. Strange to say, it also suggests this mode of usurpation was at least conceivable. How it all was supposed to work is another question. Are we to suppose that the conspirators had the intention of suborning the legitimate outgoing or incoming consuls' lictors? Or would bring their own men to overpower the lictors and take their fasces? Of course, the biggest question is how either the Senate or people would acquiesce in such a violent power grab, and how the rogue "consuls" could possibly perform even the expected rites on the Capitol necessary for entering office—never mind secure their position beyond the first day of the year.[20]

Indeed, the details of this alleged plot to seize the consular fasces may be colored by a notorious sequence of events that belongs to the last months of Cicero's consulship of 63 BCE, after Lucius Sergius Catilina was defeated in the consular elections for the second year in a row. In late October of that year one Gaius Manlius rose up in armed revolt in Etruria, at the head of what can be described as a debtors' army that eventually swelled (we are told) to some 20,000 men. Cicero claims that Catiline, to show his support and signal his intentions, sent Manlius a military emblem—a silver eagle—that he had cherished at his home, as well as "arms, axes, fasces, trumpets, military standards."

Other sources mention illicit fasces and other insignia playing a role in the insurrection, but with a different chronology. When Catiline himself finally fled Rome, Plutarch reports that he took with him "three hundred armed followers, assumed the fasces and axes as though he were a magistrate, raised standards," and in this way proceeded to join Manlius. A contemporary to the events, the historian Sallust, asserts that Catiline proceeded to Manlius's camp via Arretium (modern Arezzo), with "the fasces and other emblems of authority." This caused the Senate, adds Sallust, to proclaim both these men enemies of the state. We have already seen how this turned out for the rebels. In early 62 BCE Cicero's consular colleague Gaius Antonius, on his way to Macedonia, met and defeated Catiline in the field, near Faesulae. For that action, Antonius—surprisingly and it would seem improperly—received an imperatorial acclamation and also the Senate's declaration of a thanksgiving feast, each prerequisites to the later vote of a triumph.

In describing that battle, Sallust offers a provenance for Catiline's silver eagle: the army of Gaius Marius had fought under it when they faced down the invading Germanic Cimbri at Vercellae in 101 BCE. Where Catiline got his fasces and the rest of the insignia is anyone's guess. Perhaps they were an inheritance from his patrician ancestors, or relics of his own praetorian command (67 BCE) in the Roman province of Africa. What does emerge plainly from Sallust's account is that Catiline fully assumed the role of a Roman commander with *imperium* in the fighting, and so we can presume he displayed himself with all the relevant accoutrements.[21]

Indeed, it seems Catiline established himself as a byword for usurping the fasces. That emerges from Cicero's fourteenth *Philippic*, delivered before the Senate on April 21, 43 BCE, on the "shepherds' feast" of the Parilia and the birthday of Rome itself. At the time, both consuls and Octavian were at Mutina (modern Modena), engaged in lifting Antony's siege of the city, then held by one of Caesar's assassins, Decimus Brutus. In this context, Cicero takes considerable pains to dispel a prevalent and rather ironic rumor—that he had been planning "to descend with the fasces," i.e., from Rome's Capitol to the Forum, indeed on that specific day. Such a rumor, says Cicero, might make sense if cooked up against "a gladiator or a bandit or a Catiline." But was it really likely that the consul who destroyed Catiline "should suddenly reveal myself a Catiline?"

Cicero then spells out the practical obstacles to believing this report. "With what auspices was I, an augur [i.e., a member of the priesthood concerned with interpreting the auspices], to have accepted those fasces, how long was I going to keep them, to whom should I have handed them over?" The point here, for once, is plain and direct, though it needs some expansion. Usurped fasces would stand outside of what was, at least in principle, an unbroken line of auspical succession established by Romulus. An individual who simply claimed the fasces would have no legitimacy from the viewpoint of the augural law. Cicero, as a member of the college of augurs, was hardly going to violate the discipline of the auspices that he had been charged to maintain.

Cicero's crescendo as "a gladiator or a bandit or a Catiline" is more slippery. As we shall see, Rome would have some experience with low-status outlaws or foreign enemies who got their hands on fasces and paraded with them, usually far outside the city. They did this with varying degrees of irony, whether to enhance their status, advertise their pretensions, or provocatively mock Roman power. Very occasionally we find Roman citizens making dubious claims to magisterial insignia, especially in the context of revolts, but also as a last-chance lifeline in political chaos. It would seem that the example of Catiline belongs to this latter category. What made Catiline's display of fasces especially dangerous is that he was a charismatic patrician senator of praetorian status with recent experience of provincial command, and that he had a significant following within the city, as well as substantial armed support in nearby Etruria. His fasces also came from a larger set of authentic insignia, including at least one item from his personal collection—Marius's silver eagle standard, with its deep historical and indeed emotional resonances. And it was in central Italy that he was flaunting these emblems of official power.

As it happens, Cicero when addressing the Senate in April 43 BCE had more recent instances of fasces irregularities that he could cite. Two notable cases belonged to just the previous year, in the swirl of events that followed the consul and dictator Julius Caesar's assassination on March 15, 44. The early imperial historian Velleius Paterculus reports that the suffect (i.e., substitute) consul elected to replace Caesar, Publius Cornelius Dolabella, assumed his office prematurely, "snatching up" his fasces and other insignia. And Appian describes how late in that year "the soldiers of Octavian furnished him lictors provided with fasces"—and urged him to claim an extraordinary praetorian command. Octavian, then aged nineteen, deferred the matter to the Senate, which—as we have noted, on the urging of Cicero himself—regularized his command with a vote of praetorian *imperium*.

On January 7, 43 BCE, the young Octavian "for the first time took up the fasces," as an epigraphic calendar duly notes. The elder Pliny adds the item that he assumed the insignia in Umbria, at Spoletium (modern Spoleto). "When sacrificing" on that day, says Pliny, "the livers of six victims were found with the bottom of their tissue folded back inward, and this was interpreted to mean that within a year he would double his *imperium*"—i.e., from praetorian to consular, which indeed came with Octavian's election as suffect consul on August 19, 43 BCE.[22]

Amid such unprecedented volatility, Cicero amply confirms how widespread was the suspicion that he himself plotted to seize power in Rome in 43 BCE. In his speech to the Senate, he describes how a friendly tribune of the Plebs convened a public assembly specifically to allay fears about Cicero's political intentions, and (it seems) to elicit an informal vote of confidence for the ex-consul. Cicero also floats an elaborate theory that seeks to explain how the talk of his usurpation started in the first place. Anti-Senate forces, he says, had plotted to take over the city, but also counted on the populace to rally to Cicero as their natural leader. "And so . . . they spread this rumor about the fasces." An explication follows. The Senate's enemies "were even going to offer me the fasces, and when this had been done as though at my own wish, an attack upon me by a hired gang was planned, as if upon a despot." Finally,

Cicero underlines the relevance of all this to his audience. "From this there would have followed a massacre of all you senators."[23]

That last detail is obvious nonsense. Nevertheless, in this political climate, anxiety about improper use of the fasces and the power they represented seems quite comprehensible. Of course, opportunities for abusing insignia of public office increased dramatically in civil strife, and the further one traveled from Rome.

Indeed, the landscape shifted as soon as one left the city. The peoples of Italy evidently had much to fear from the fasces while they were still largely excluded from Roman political life, a situation resolved only by the Social War between Rome and its Italian allies that ended in 88 BCE. Before that, the corporal punishment of the allies was a perennial issue, one that the re-former Gaius Gracchus—the younger of the famous Gracchi brothers— seized upon in his tribunates of 123 and 122 BCE. In the latter of those years, a consul executed the Senate's decision to drive non-citizens out of Rome be-fore Gracchus's proposals came to a vote; Plutarch suggests that on this occa-sion Rome's friends and allies saw rough treatment at the hands of his lictors. Matters did not improve for some decades. The Greek historian Diodorus Siculus relates that just before the Social War broke out in 91 BCE, an actor of Latin origin defused the Picentines (i.e., inhabitants of the modern Marche) in a theater who wanted to murder him by reminding them "that I am no Roman, but, subject to the fasces as you yourselves are, I traipse around Italy" as a mere entertainer.[24]

Once equipped with this symbol of power, even patent imposters could overawe local populations. In 104 BCE, the city praetor Lucius Licinius Lucullus had to leave Rome to put down a well-organized slave revolt at Capua. A local Roman knight, one Titus Minucius Vettius, had attempted to escape his creditors by putting himself at the head of a renegade army composed initially of his own slaves, arming some 400 in all. Amazingly, as Diodorus reports it, Vettius chose to model his insignia and indeed methods not on contemporary Roman magistrates, but on the city's old kings. "Having assumed the diadem and a purple cloak, together with lictors and the other appurtenances of office . . . proclaimed himself king, he flogged and beheaded the persons who were demanding payment. . . ." Furthermore, he put to death anyone on neighboring estates who opposed his efforts to recruit more slaves to his cause. Vettius even constructed a fortified camp to which he welcomed fugitives, whom he started to organize in the manner of the Roman military. The Roman praetor Lucullus, however, smashed these efforts before Vettius's support considerably broadened. More dangerous were instances where minor Roman officials set themselves up as faux magistrates in the provinces, found in both the mid-80s and mid-70s BCE.[25]

This type of bluster sometimes worked even closer to Rome. Writing in the early empire, Valerius Maximus tells how in 43 BCE or soon after, a Sentius Satuminus Vetulo disguised himself as a praetor, and so managed to escape from the triumvirs' proscriptions. He suborned confederates to walk before him, playing the part of lictors, *apparitores*, and public slaves. But that was just the start of it, according to Valerius. Making his way to Puteoli and its port, "he seized vehicles, took possession of lodgings, removed people coming his way," and finally requisitioned ships, which brought him and his entourage to safety in Sicily. Appian reports that a Pomponius used a similar ruse, in his case claiming to be an envoy sent by the triumvirs to Sextus Pompeius. "He passed through the city as a praetor attended by lictors"—who were in reality his slaves—"his attendants pressing close to him lest he should be recognized. At the city gates he took possession of public carriages and traversed Italy," and eventually used a public ship to cross to Sicily.[26]

To judge from our literary sources, the misappropriation of fasces comes off largely as a Republican phenomenon. But it would seem that the often-tumultuous history of the Empire afforded many opportunities for fasces fraud. As late as the year 619, the eunuch Eleutherius, who had charge of the Byzantine province (exarchate) of Ravenna, is said to have "scorned the patriciate with the fasces" and in this way signaled his claim to the imperial throne. His attempted rule was short, for he was killed in the next year.[27] An imperial succession crisis could also cause technical problems across the administrative system, upsetting the fasces protocols of lesser offices involving *imperium*. We hear of one such case for early 457 CE, when a governor for the Gallic provinces felt compelled "to take up the fasces" and assume his position before receiving his official patent of office.[28]

Loss of Fasces

There is one further discontinuity in the fasces that needs discussion—that occasioned by death. In the field, it is an open question how effective the lictors were in any era at protecting their superiors. In truth, our sources usually note the presence or absence of these attendants only when something bad happens to their commander or to them. The annalistic record of the Second Punic War offered two such mishaps, each in the context of ambushes. In the latter instance, one of the consuls of 208 BCE was killed and the other mortally wounded near Tarentum. Of the consuls' twenty-four combined lictors, we are told the Carthaginians killed an indeterminate number and captured five alive.[29]

Such disasters were not confined to major wars. Take, for instance, transit to Rome's two Spanish provinces: four or five months to get there with an army by land, which included crossing the Alps. And several times we hear of commanders losing their lives to bellicose tribes on the dangerous coastal road that cut through the area now known as the French Riviera. For example, in 189 BCE, the praetor Lucius Baebius Dives was wounded by Ligurians while he was making his way to Further Spain. He soon died at Massilia (modern Marseilles). Livy reports that Baebius had escaped to the town "with a few comrades and without his lictors." At this time, praetorian commanders for Spain had twelve lictors; presumably all were killed.[30]

Worse was yet to come, and not at the hand of Rome's external enemies. During the civil warfare of 87 BCE, a junior cavalry commander managed to pursue the consul Gnaeus Octavius and his lictors to Rome's Janiculum hill, and then behead him. Octavius's head "was suspended in the Forum in front of the rostra, the first . . . of a consul that was so exposed"—a shocking demonstration of even a consul's vulnerability, to a form of punishment closely associated with his own lictors. A few years later in this civil conflict, in 84 BCE, the four-time consul Lucius Cornelius Cinna is said to have been killed in a clash with mutineers whom his lictors failed to control.[31]

In the 70s and early 60s BCE, significant insults to lictors and the fasces only accelerated, now at the hands of some unnerving adversaries. A praetor Publius Varinius of 73 BCE, who apparently had enhanced *imperium* and thus twelve lictors, suffered a series of defeats against Spartacus and his rebel gladiators and slaves, evidently in the area of Campania and Lucania. Several of Varinius's subordinates also were worsted. In the end the praetor lost his camp, his horse, and his lictors to Spartacus's ragtag forces. Plutarch reasonably suggests that the symbolism of these humiliating losses added greatly to Spartacus's prestige. Spartacus, for his part, seems to have prized the acquisition of these official insignia. On his ultimate defeat in 71 BCE, the Livian tradition reports that there were recovered from his camp "five Roman eagles and twenty-six standards . . . along with much other booty, including five sets of rods and axes."[32]

The loss of a commander's fasces to an adversary signaled deep debasement. The absolute nadir in this line of development came a few years after Spartacus's revolt, in the early 60s BCE, when we find pirates raiding the coast of Italy and even venturing into the interior. The chief national disgrace came with the pirates' capture of two praetors, Sextilius and Bellienus, with their full insignia of office—including their lictors and attendants, which Cicero explicitly says yielded twelve fasces in all. (Even Spartacus, in three years of brilliant fighting, got his hands on only five.) We need not assume that the two praetors, who apparently had the charge of protecting the coast, were captured together. But the sources do suggest they belong to the same year, one not long before the Gabinian law of 67 BCE that gave Pompey a sweeping command against the pirates, which he executed with startling success. It is evident that the symbolism of the fasces made lictors an especially attractive target for adversaries. Numbers of captured insignia plainly were registered and remembered, even in civil conflict: for example, in March 45 BCE Caesar put a premium on the number of military standards and fasces he captured from the Pompeians he thoroughly defeated at Munda in southern Spain.[33]

Lictors and Bodyguards

Perhaps inevitably, some powerful Romans thought that the protection of mere lictors saddled with their fasces was not enough. Cicero claims in his *Philippics* that Antony in 44 BCE was the first ever in the city's history to surround himself with a guard that openly displayed their weapons. "Our kings did not do this, neither did those who after the expulsion of the kings have tried to usurp the kingship." Cicero then adds his own eyewitness testimony. "I remember Cinna, I saw Sulla, recently Caesar, the three who since Lucius Brutus liberated the community have possessed more power than the entire Republic. I cannot say that no weapons surrounded them, but this I do say: there were not many, and they were hidden."[34]

Other sources confirm that these three holders of *imperium* formed a personal guard in addition to their lictors. Here Lucius Cornelius Sulla as dictator in the years 82–80 BCE seems to have been the real innovator. Appian notes that he was preceded in public by twenty-four lictors "and he had a large bodyguard around him also." Subsequently we sometimes find the consuls formally receiving an armed guard in the city, over and above their lictors. Caesar notoriously had no such protection on the Ides of March in 44 BCE, when his escort to the fateful Senate meeting "had consisted simply of his lictors, most of the magistrates and a further large throng made up of inhabitants of the city, foreigners and numerous slaves and ex-slaves."[35]

One imagines that a commander would significantly diminish his own aura of authority if he were to give his lictors their own guard in the camp or the field. In principle, lictors were a commander's most trusted attendants. As such, he depended on them for enforcing the most difficult cases of camp discipline and provincial justice. They attended him in sensitive or dangerous conferences.[36] And in a crisis, they represented his last hope for protecting his person. Naturally, we are more likely to hear about failures in this regard rather than routine successes. Consider the general Fabius Valens, a supporter of the emperor Vitellius in the tumultuous year 69 CE, who at Ticinum (modern Pavia) found his soldiers second-guessing his command decisions. "Valens sent his lictors among them and tried to check the mutiny," says Tacitus. Apparently this order exposed the general's vulnerability. "Thereupon the troops attacked Valens himself, stoned him, and pursued him when he fled." The denouement? The commander disguised himself as a slave and waited out the riot in the tent of one his cavalry officers. But then, says a summarizer of Cassius Dio, Valens charged this man with stealing money from his baggage, and had him executed—presumably by his lictors.[37]

By the time we get to the third century CE, it seems to have been unusual for a provincial governor's retinue to consist solely of his lictors. And in the year 400 CE, the poet Claudian thinks the military commander Stilicho worthy of praise for dispensing with an armed guard in Rome, and appearing in public "accompanied only by his lictors . . . guarded only by a people's love".[38]

6

Carrying the Fasces

Expansion of Access to the Fasces

There is every indication that use of the fasces continued without interruption for the entire antique period. But the system hardly remained static. Our sources suggest, especially for the Republic, an ever-evolving system of protocols, including multiplied or fractional grants of fasces, designed to mark individual rank in Rome's political universe, and at the same time meant to reduce conflict and curb the possibilities of abuse. The later Republic and early Principate also saw a massive broadening in the range of positions entitled to the fasces. Naturally, one consequence of these developments was an expansion of the numbers of citizens needed to carry all those bundles. And with that, we would assume, came a concomitant heightening of their feelings of professional identity. These intertwined developments are the focus of this chapter, our last before leaving the ancient Roman fasces and turning to their later reception.

The story starts in earnest in the fourth and early third centuries BCE, which witnessed a wholesale reimagining of *imperium*. This is seen especially in the invention of the praetorship (367 BCE), the introduction of prorogation (i.e., extensions of commands beyond the year of the magistracy, first in 327 BCE), and the idea that consuls could personally delegate *imperium* (attested by 295 BCE). These developments decisively untethered the Romans from their regal-era archetype, that a dozen lictors with fasces expressed the sum of legitimate power.

Furthermore, the sustained military emergency of the Second Punic War (218–201 BCE) stimulated creative minds in the Senate to devise other extraordinary ways to give out the fasces as a symbol of *imperium*. These included special grants to private citizens at the consular level, seen especially

The Fasces. T. Corey Brennan, Oxford University Press. © Oxford University Press 2023.
DOI: 10.1093/oso/9780197644881.003.0006

to wage war in the Spanish theater. In 197 BCE, when the Romans decided to divide the Iberian peninsula into two regular praetorian provinces, they kept making these grants of enhanced *imperium*—giving each of the praetors setting out to that theater not the expected six but twelve fasces—and indeed later generalized the practice when creating other distant provinces in the second century BCE.

A real inflection point in the proliferation of the fasces came with Lucius Cornelius Sulla's comprehensive administrative reforms of 81/80 BCE. As we have seen, Sulla as dictator appeared in public even within the city proceeded by twenty-four lictors, the first individual ever to do so. That was just the start of it. He increased the number of praetors from six to eight, expected that consuls and praetors take up a territorial province only as prorogued magistrates after a year in the city, and generalized grants of consular *imperium* (long seen in the Spains, and later Macedonia, Asia, and Cilicia) to all provincial commanders.

What that meant was in principle almost 200 new fasces-bearing lictors would now be required each year. There were twenty-four for the two consuls, and notionally forty-eight for the praetors. In addition, the Sullan system needed 120 lictors for the ex-consuls and ex-praetors of the previous year, who henceforth were slated to depart from the city for provincial commands. And to that sum must be added, from the territorial provinces, senior magistrates with *imperium* from previous years. So when Plutarch and Appian report that in late 56 BCE a colloquy at Luca in Etruria between Julius Caesar, Crassus, and Pompey drew more than 200 senators as well as commanders from far-flung provinces accompanied by "120 lictors," it is probably not an exaggeration but rather a reflection of the effects of the post-Sullan system.[1]

The late Republic saw a related development, which was commanders handing lictors and fasces to individuals without delegating them *imperium*. By the mid-40s BCE, senior members of a governor's staff seem positively to have expected a grant of fasces, even when technical considerations argued against it. The standard allotment of fasces in these cases appears to have been two, at least to judge from early imperial practice.[2]

What is even more significant is that by the 40s BCE the Senate apparently aggrandized to itself the right of bestowing the fasces, without the confirmation of a popular vote. For early January 43 BCE, the Greek historian Appian relates how "the soldiers of Octavian furnished him lictors provided with fasces and urged him to assume the title of praetorian commander . . . he thanked them for the honor, but referred the matter to the Senate . . . believing that the Senate would vote these things to him voluntarily." It does seem that body was sufficient as a source, to judge from Cicero himself, who boasted of his role in getting Octavian his *imperium* but says nothing of subsequent confirmation in an assembly.[3]

Very soon the Senate started handing out fasces even where no *imperium* was involved. In narrating events of early 42 BCE, the imperial-era historian Cassius Dio details the extravagant honors that the triumvirs Antony, Lepidus, and Octavian had the Senate vote to the deceased and now deified Julius Caesar. He continues with a remarkable notice: "they also allowed the Vestal Virgins to employ one lictor each, because one of them, not being recognized, had been insulted while returning home from dinner toward evening." Again, there is no mention of a popular vote to ratify the arrangement.

The full college of Vestals at this time consisted of six virgin priestesses; we have no further information on which one of them was "insulted," where, and in what way. Given the distinctive appearance of these priestesses, it is amazing that the incident happened at all, even in low light. However, the upshot was that the Vestals as a group now received the full praetorian complement of fasces, evidently for the times when they left their precinct in Rome's Forum. In practice, probably no more than four lictors were needed, since a minimum of two Vestals seem always to have remained at the Temple of Vesta to tend the sacred, perpetual fire that burned within. The Vestals' right to lictors persisted at least into the second century CE, for Plutarch in listing their attributes mentions first that "when they appear in public, the fasces are carried before them." Apparently they were not always walking, for Plutarch adds that "he who passes under the litter on which they are borne, is put to death"—though probably after a trial, and not on the spot by a Vestal's lictor.[4]

The most vivid meditation on what the Vestals and their lictors might encounter in the streets of Rome belongs to the early first century CE, from a rhetorical exercise presented by the elder Seneca. The question in the composition is how one should select a generic "priestess." An argument we get is that the woman should be worthy specifically of the fasces. How so? For one thing, we are told that Rome's magistrates (here, praetors and consuls) were in the habit of lowering their own fasces when encountering a Vestal. This basic show of deference has ample parallels, and for the Vestals, may well be true. Then the elder Seneca offers an argument based on the premise that a Vestal's lictor will have to exercise coercion in the same way as a consul's. "Will the lictor ahead of her remove the crowd from this woman's path?," it is asked. Conversely, "will any practicing whore have to flee your sight?" The priestess's path should be an obscenity-free zone, extending also (it is implied) to the mere presence of questionable professions. "It is not without reason that a lictor attends a priestess: he removes a prostitute from her way."[5]

Other classes of priests also accrued fasces. Rome's *flamines*, at least the three major ones (devoted to Jupiter, Mars, and Quirinus, i.e., the deified Romulus), at some point gained a single lictor. Our earliest source for the privilege is the late Augustan period, and one imagines that it was granted on the analogy of the Vestals. In the municipalities of the Empire, individual lictors preceded members of the Augustales, an institution devoted to the imperial cult, dominated by freedpersons. In the mid-first century CE, Petronius in his *Satyricon* describes how the obscenely wealthy freedman Trimalchio decorated the door posts of his dining room with the insignia of the office, characterized as "rods and axes" in the plural. The image is absurd, and surely is meant to characterize Trimalchio as inflating his entitlement.[6]

FIGURE 6.1. Relief, probably early second century CE, from Iulia Concordia depicting three magistrate's attendants, a *victimarius* with axe, and two lictors bearing axe-less fasces. National Museum of Concordia, Portogruaro, Inv. no. 181.

Credit: Carole Raddato/Creative Commons.

Eventually Rome's empresses, or at least some of them, joined the ranks of priests. That is how a lictor came to Livia, in 14 CE, after her husband's death and divinization, and the accession of her son Tiberius. As Cassius Dio describes it, the Romans (i.e., the Senate) then "made Livia, who was already called Julia Augusta, his priestess." He continues: "they also permitted her to employ a lictor when she exercised her sacred office." Now, Tacitus states flatly that Tiberius "declined to allow [Livia] even the use of a lictor." But he also narrates that when the Senate next deified an emperor, namely Claudius in 54 CE, it made his widow Agrippina his priestess, with two lictors. What seems probable is that Livia got her lictor through a compromise between Senate and emperor, limited (as Dio quite precisely tells us) to her performance of the imperial cult. Whether women of the imperial household subsequent to Livia and Agrippina received lictors, even with limitations, is an open question. At any rate, after Livia and Agrippina, in the next century and a half at most four empresses would seem to have met the apparent technical qualifications—i.e., surviving a deified spouse and becoming priestess in his cult.[7]

Granting fasces to priesthoods and otherwise steadily expanding their number in the political system does not seem to have diluted their impact. Our sources for the late Republic are emphatic on this point. In 63 BCE, Cicero as consul successfully defeated a proposed measure that would have created a wide-ranging panel of ten agrarian commissioners, each with praetorian *imperium*. One of his (many) arguments against these decemvirs was the "terror" that their fasces would inspire in the public. Julius Caesar in his autobiographical *Civil Wars* criticizes a senatorial opponent for multiplying use of the fasces while wintering (49/48 BCE) in the province of Asia, to pave the way for his harsh exactions. The commander there "put individuals with *imperium* in charge not only of cities but practically of individual villages and outposts... the province was full of lictors and *imperia*, bursting with prefects and tax collectors." However, once Caesar established himself in firm control of Rome, he steeply raised the number of regular magistrates with *imperium* by doubling the number of praetors to sixteen.[8]

Multiplication of fasces only accelerated under the early Empire. In 27 BCE, Augustus established a new arrangement for the appointment of governors for the military important provinces. Those he combined into a large super-province, that he would hold with consular *imperium*. The Senate continued to administer the remaining provinces as before, through promagistrates. To do the actual work of governing his overseas territories, Augustus dispatched lieutenants endowed with praetorian *imperium* (in Latin, *legati Augusti pro praetore*). These individuals had five lictors, to show the delegated nature of their authority. This symbolic system persisted at least into the fifth century CE, and was familiar enough that such officials are sometimes termed simply *quinquefascales*, or "five fasces men."[9]

Indeed, Augustus's reign greatly increased the range of public officials receiving grants of fasces. Consider the "curators of the regions" in Rome, created in 7 BCE. There were fourteen Augustan regions, and each division received two officers charged with maintaining order. They were "allowed to use the official dress and two lictors," explains the historian Cassius Dio, "but only in the regions under their administration and on certain days." Still in principle, this added twenty-eight new fasces to the annual urban total. Another six came in 6 CE, when Augustus created a special military treasury, under the charge of three ex-praetors, with two lictors apiece.[10] We can readily trace how Augustus introduced upwards of a dozen additional lictors into the Roman political system.[11]

A final observation on the arithmetic of the fasces before turning our attention to the men who carried them. The inexorable rise in the number of officials who had lictors and fasces at their disposal inevitably raised some practical problems. Protocol puzzles were rife, some with consequences that could risk Roman lives. In the Republican era, if a prorogued consul and a man holding a special grant of consular *imperium*, each in the possession of a dozen fasces, met in the field, who would have precedence? There is no reason to think the consular "turn" was applicable here. So how to determine who had the right of initiative?[12]

Augustus and his successors tightened up the whole system, at least at the top, to remove ambiguities in the chain of command. The notion of a grade of *imperium* that was always "greater" (Latin *maius*) against the consular type was an innovation of Augustus, one that can specifically be dated to the year 23 BCE. Combined with the aggrandizement of militarily important provincial commands (in 27 BCE) and the assumption of tribunician power (also in the year 23), it formed the basis of his formal powers, and those of all of his successors as Princeps. In effect, what we see here is the originally unitary kingly *imperium* now split into multiple levels. In the early empire, the creation of the position of Princeps, and with it, a nebulous "imperial family" (*domus Augusta*) put new, quite unprecedented strains on the system. Consular *imperium* remains the base, but our evidence shows that the Romans could conceive of, and enshrine in a law, two additional situation-based levels of "greater" *imperium*. It was like the invention of the praetorship, but going in the opposite direction.[13]

Lictors in the Republican Era

Our survey here has led us to a rudimentary but still vital conclusion: that by the age of Augustus, at any given time, fasces-bearing lictors numbered in the hundreds. A few basic questions on these formidable persons immediately beg themselves. How did one become a lictor? What was their personal background? How were they organized? What was their status in relation to other public servants (in Latin, *apparitores*)? How much were they paid? What were their chances of advancing themselves further?

Let us start this inquiry with a story that Plutarch tells of the year 66 BCE, relating how Pompey speedily proceeded north into central Anatolia to replace Lucius Licinius Lucullus (consul 73 BCE) in his command against the Pontic king Mithridates VI—and while en route aggressively undid many of his predecessor's arrangements. To smooth the transition, we are told, their mutual friends set up a conference between the two in Galatia. Here we catch a rare glimpse of the dynamics between two teams of lictors. "Fasces wreathed with laurel were carried before both commanders in token of their victories, and since Pompey had made a long march through waterless and arid regions, the laurel which wreathed his fasces was withered. When the lictors of Lucullus noticed this, they considerately gave Pompey's lictors some of their own laurel, which was fresh and green." Yet despite this auspicious start, says Plutarch, the colloquium left the two commanders "still more estranged from one another."[14]

The anecdote suggests that the two groups of attendants had a natural solidarity that transcended the tension between their respective commanders. Indeed, there is (slight) evidence that lictors had formed a professional association already by this time. For two years later, the consuls of the year 64 BCE passed legislation to make the trade unions known as *collegia* illegal, with the exception of "a few certain ones which public utility had required, such as those of the carpenters," says the first-century CE historical writer Asconius, "and lictors"—if we follow a commonly accepted emendation of his text.[15]

And that is the sum of our Republican-era evidence for the internal history of lictors as a class. In general, our literary sources tend to take lictors for granted, and rarely focus on them as individuals, except largely to remark on egregious examples of cruelty or brutality. Cicero and the century CE Greek historian Appian are the only authors to identify Republican lictors by name, for a total of just three. Two of these come up in Cicero's prosecution speech of Gaius Verres. There is the Cornelius who served Verres as legate in 80–79 BCE in the Greek east, said to have been killed during a scuffle in the city of Lampsacus on the southern shore of the Hellespont, when he tried to kidnap for his superior a local noblewoman. Another is found with Verres in Sicily during his praetorian command of the years 73–71 BCE, and characterized as "the doorkeeper of the prison, the praetor's executioner, the death and terror of the allies and citizens of Rome, lictor Sextius." Add to this pair a certain Postumius, a lictor of the consul Marcus Cornelius Bibulus in 59 BCE, accused of providing the dagger for a supposed assassination attempt on Pompey and Bibulus's colleague Caesar in 59 BCE. As we can see, in none of these (scathing) descriptions do we get a lictor's full name.

Of these named lictors, Sextius receives the fullest character sketch. While ostensibly serving Verres in Sicily, he is said to have monetized his position by soliciting bribes from the families of the condemned. The lictor put a price on everything connected to his disciplinary duties, alleges Cicero: delivery of food and clothing to the imprisoned, decapitation by a single stroke of the axe as opposed to repeated blows, even permission to bury the executed. At least some of these victims were wholly innocent, Cicero stresses. These sensational allegations must have had a certain ring of plausibility to contemporaries. One notes that Cicero a decade later warns his brother Quintus, then governor of Asia, not to allow his lictor too much latitude in administering punishment. "Let your lictor be the servant of your clemency, not of his own," advises Cicero; "let the rods and axes bear before you insignia of rank rather than power."[16]

The Proximate Lictor

Though not especially interested in lictors' names, our literary sources do show sporadic interest in their basic organization. Cicero takes care to note that the savage Sextius was "nearest" or *proximus* lictor to Verres in Sicily. That was the senior member of the team, and as the title implies, the one meant to remain physically closest to the official. This lictor naturally would be the commander's most trusted attendant. Cicero reports a dream in which as an exile he encountered the seven-time consul Gaius Marius "with his fasces wreathed in laurel," and found himself escorted by his proximate lictor to safety. Tellingly, Sallust in his *Jugurthine War* calls the subordinate whom the Numidian king Jugurtha considered his "dear and trusted confidant" a "*proximus lictor*"—perhaps pointedly, the only mention of a lictor or fasces in this acidic work, highly critical of the Roman noble class of politicians.[17] But on the whole, our literary sources do not bother to mention a given lictor's title, even where his position suggests he was the "proximus."[18]

That said, we do catch occasional glimpses of certified Roman proximate lictors in action. Cicero implies that it was this lictor who had the chief responsibility for maintaining order in a praetor's provincial court. Appian terms this figure the "leader of the lictors," and tells how even at sea Antony's proximate took a prominent position in the bow and gave orders to the others on his squad. Indeed, the crucial role of the proximate lictor was to serve as his superior's most trusted bodyguard. It is no surprise to see reports that an attack on an official resulted in the death of specifically the proximate lictor.[19]

In his prosecution of Verres, Cicero paints what must be a topsy-turvy portrait of how a Roman official should manage his ensemble of lictors, including the proximate.[20] The location is the forum at Lilybaeum, in western Sicily, where Verres for a time had established his governor's tribunal, probably in the year 73 BCE. Cicero alleges that there the governor tried to force an elderly critic, Gaius Servilius of Panormus (a different judicial district), into a wager at law "with his own lictor," as a prelude to a proceeding on a capital charge.

As Servilius protested, "he was surrounded by six lictors, muscular fellows who had had plenty of practice in assaulting and flogging people, and who now proceeded to beat him savagely with rods; till finally the senior lictor Sextius . . . took the butt end of his stick, and began to strike the poor man violently across the eyes, so that he fell helpless to the ground, his face and eyes streaming with blood." Cicero emphasizes that all this took place in public view, near Verres's tribunal; specifically, Servilius "was beaten with rods before your judgment-seat till he fell to the ground at your feet." Yet "even then his assailants continued to rain blows on his prostrate body. . . ." Eventually, "he consented to accept the challenge." However, soon after this savage beating, Servilius died.

Cicero himself underlines some of the formal anomalies in this disturbing story of official violence. As a Roman citizen, Servilius should have been exempt from corporal punishment. But Verres, we are told, was so indifferent to the status of his victims "that before long his lictors were in the habit of actually laying hands upon the persons of Roman citizens without so much as waiting for his orders." Indeed, that is what Cicero implies happened in the case of Servilius. That fully six lictors initiated the beating must be another anomaly; the number surely is meant to seem gratuitously high, even putting aside the age of the victim.

How was this "nearest" lictor positioned when on the move? All our evidence, both visual and textual, for both the Republic and Empire, suggests that when lictors walked in procession, typically they did so in single file before their superior.[21] The proximate lictor came last in this formation of attendants, and it seems that the space between this lictor and his superior had a special distinction. In his collection of moralizing historical examples, the early first-century CE author Valerius Maximus describes how "our ancestors maintained with the utmost care the custom that no man should interpose himself between a consul and his *proximus* lictor, even though walking with the consul in the course of duty." Valerius continues, "only a son, and a boy at that, had the right to walk in front of his father, the consul." Yet the examples Valerius then provides of what he considers strictly proper practice imply that in general, commanders were not so fastidious in this respect.[22]

What does seem to have been a firm requirement of protocol is that officials entitled to lictors were expected to keep them close when appearing in public. In Rome, this practice extended beyond the streets of the city. Lictors stood close by magistrates when they performed duties such as presiding over the Senate, hearing cases at law, and addressing the Roman people in formal or informal assembly. The practice stretched into the late Empire.[23]

Lictors in the "Apparitorial" System

For the professional organization and social experience of magistrates' attendants (*apparitores*) in general, most of the evidence is epigraphic, and largely from the high Empire. The apparitorial system is a vast and complicated topic, that encompasses—in addition to lictors—scribes (*scribae*), messengers (*viatores*), and heralds (*praecones*). We can limit ourselves here to a few basic observations. Slaves were excluded from serving in these roles, but freed slaves were not. These several grades of attendants each had membership in their own corporate bodies called *decuries*—in the developed system, there were three such panels for lictors—and they expected to receive their assignments by lot. The central treasury paid their salaries, and so these jobs carried a certain measure of prestige. For some, the positions also provided the opportunity for a certain degree of social mobility. We find ample instances of ex-lictors explicitly honored (in Rome, but also as far afield as Ephesus) for substantial patronage. Indeed, the funerary monuments of even some less exalted lictors in Rome emphasized their special status to the point of pomposity.[24]

In a fundamental 1983 study on *apparitores*, Nicholas Purcell collected eighty-seven inscriptions on lictors, almost all imperial in date. From these he offered a sketch of their backgrounds (he found that fully three-quarters were freedmen, largely recruited from Rome), basic duties, and organization.

Scribes had greater distinction than lictors, messengers about the same; indeed, outside Rome the hybrid office of "lictor viator" is sometimes found. Heralds were a cut below the lictors, and still further down came junior apparitorial grades such as porters and keepers of sacred chickens used for augury. The personal assistants of magistrates (*accensi*) stood somewhat outside the system, in that they received their assignment by appointment, not by allotment. The relative status of magistrates' attendants in the late Republic was surely the same. In the Empire, at least, all these roles had their own decuries or panels, in which membership clearly mattered. It is consistently trumpeted in the imperial-era inscriptions, and we occasionally see the apparitorial decuries acting as corporate bodies.

Members of the "III decuriae" of lictors attended Rome's emperors, consuls, and praetors, as well as a variety of urban officials. Here the post of "nearest" or *proximus* lictor was chief (as we have seen from the literary evidence); but there was also a further honored status, namely that of *decemprimus* (literally, "one of ten seniors"). Outside the three decuries of lictors, "curiate" lictors (in Rome, organized in divisions called *curiae*) served the priests; and "popular" lictors (sometimes called *denuntiatores*, literally, "announcers") attended the assemblies. The geographical spread of relevant inscriptions is not enormous, though we find evidence of lictors in service in Sardinia, Africa, Asia, and Galatia, and "retired" in Gallia Lugdunensis, Aquitania, Hispania Citerior, even Bithynia (Nicomedia). Lictors for both magistrates and for priests are found in colonies, most notably Ostia and Puteoli, where their organizational structure loosely imitates that of Rome. Numismatic evidence suggests that Paestum (a Roman colony since 273 BCE) had lictors too.[25]

The Romans seemed largely content with the apparitorial system, and we hear of no serious attempt to refine or otherwise change it. That said, Suetonius does report that the Senate passed a decree enhancing the number and status of attendants who would accompany Domitian (reigned 81–96 CE) whenever he held one of the two consular posts, an office he occupied ten times as emperor. Suetonius mentions the measure while explaining Domitian's extreme fear of assassination; it was for this reason, we are told, that he refused this novel honor. The summary of the Senate's decree for Domitian strikes one as an example of extreme adulation, rather than a thoroughgoing reform. When consul, says Suetonius, "Roman knights selected by lot should precede him among his lictors and attendants, clad in the *trabea* [i.e., a purple-bordered robe that marked members of the equestrian order] and bearing lances." In other words, the Senate here sought to introduce simultaneously an increase in the number of a consul's attendants, a dramatic enhancement of the group's social status, and additional insignia of office to supplement the fasces.

The Senate's rationale in mixing together Roman knights and lictors presumably was to distinguish the emperor from his colleague in the consulship. Yet it must have been the mention of the lances that spooked the paranoid Domitian. His (uncharacteristic) refusal of this new distinction shows that he apparently trusted the traditional complement of lictors, and was suspicious of getting too close to Roman knights chosen through sortition and given even ceremonial arms. Cassius Dio suggests that Domitian did accept a different privilege voted him by the Senate, "of employing twenty-four lictors and of wearing the triumphal garb whenever he entered the Senate house." Again, the presumed point of the measure was to signal the emperor's precedence in Rome, whatever the arrangement of consuls.

In the event, as Suetonius emphasizes in the same context as describing the proposal to enhance the emperor's entourage, Domitian lost his life at the hands of close associates, in a conspiracy formed by his wife, his friends, and his favorite freedpersons. Domitian's demise also seems to have marked the end to the emperor's (limited) display of twenty-four lictors in the city—at least for a time. When the emperor Anthemius (reigned 467–472 CE) assumed the consulship at Rome on January 1, 468, he used the cumulative total of two dozen fasces, combining those of his principate and his magistracy.[26]

Social Status and Economic Mobility of Lictors

Thanks both to the digital revolution and a few new epigraphic discoveries, the corpus of material relevant to the apparitorial grades has expanded somewhat since Purcell published his article; I count more than 125 inscriptions in which lictors appear, an increase of almost 30 percent. Yet this additional evidence does not fundamentally change his basic findings. Unfortunately, the vast majority of these items, including the recent additions, do not admit close dating.[27] So it is doubly welcome that from a startlingly late year (558 CE) and an unlikely location, we have a funerary monument at Atripalda (near Avellino) in Campania for a lictor who succumbed "at approximately age thirteen." The deceased's age certainly comes as a surprise. But the inscription confirms the testimony of the statesperson Cassiodorus, that this occupation still existed in the West in the mid-sixth century CE, more than a millennium after we are told it was first introduced at Rome.[28]

Here I will restrict myself to brief discussion of just five individual items, one quite new, that I feel add further nuance to Purcell's picture of the professional life of lictors. To start, we have two inscriptions which we can confidently ascribe to lictors active in Rome during the Republican era. Purcell chose not to mention these texts. Yet they seem important, for they are the only ones extant from this era that name individual lictors, and each offers insight into the social status of these attendants as it stood before the principate. The first of the pair comes from an inscribed funerary monument, probably of the mid-first century BCE, found in Rome's Tor Pignattara neighborhood. A freedwoman set up this memorial for herself and two other manumitted slaves of one Marcus Vergilius. Named in first position is a freedman Marcus Vergilius Sphaerus, who is given the title lictor; then the dedicator, and finally a third freedman without title. What is notable here is Sphaerus's freedperson status, the fact that he receives the title of his occupation as an honorific, and with it, first position in the list of names.

Our second inscription, also funerary, does not in itself admit close dating, but is generally regarded as belonging to the Republican era. It commemorates two freedmen, each proudly termed "lictor," apparently freed by two different owners of the (large) senatorial Cornelia family. The last line of the inscription offers a surprising item: a freeborn "Pompilia, daughter of Gaius" is named as the wife of this second lictor. In general, freedmen marry women of their same social status, and even unions between ex-slaves and freeborn daughters of freedmen are extremely rare. Indeed, for the Republic, this inscription seems unique. What is more, Pompilia is a tony name, that evokes especially memories of Rome's second king Numa Pompilius. As chance has it, the Ciceronian *Handbook on Electioneering*, in a discussion of electoral conditions for 63 BCE, identifies as one of the renegade Catiline's closest associates from the equestrian order a certain Pompilius. Given the rarity of the name—it is otherwise unattested for the entire middle and late Republic—and the baleful fate of the Catilinarian conspirators, we may have here a case of father and daughter, and evidence from the nature of her marriage that the family had fallen on hard times. Whatever the precise background to this inscription, what is certain is that it shows a lictor's capacity for impressive social mobility by the time of the late Republic.[29]

Third, the epigraphic foundation charter of the colonia Iulia Genetiva, a settlement established at Urso in southern Spain in 44 BCE, offers a glimpse of relative status among apparitorial grades. In the copy that we have—which dates to the later first century CE, from the Flavian era—we find it ordained that each of the two annual chief magistrates of the colony—known as *duumvirs*—should employ from among the inhabitants "two lictors, an aide (*accensus*), two scribes, two messengers, a copyist, a herald," plus a soothsayer and a flutist.

For our purposes, the most valuable aspect of the inscription is the part that describes how all these apparitorial posts entailed exemption from the military during the year of service, and received salaries on a gradated scale. Of those attached to the duumvirs, "for each clerk, 1,200 sesterces; for each aide, 700 sesterces; for each lictor, 600 sesterces; for each messenger, 400 sesterces; for each copyist, 300 sesterces; for each soothsayer 500 sesterces; for a herald, 300 sesterces."[30]

So a hierarchy for the sub-clerical grades clearly emerges from this colonial charter, with the lictors just below the *accensi* and somewhat above the messengers. In terms of net income, a lictor in Urso probably earned more than a Roman legionary, who in the later Republic and earlier Empire received 900 sesterces a year, yet from that sum was liable for a range of mandatory expenditures, including equipment and food. Moreover, it is likely that salaries were lower for the *apparitores* based in Urso than those in Rome.

Our fourth item is in fact literary. Just six years after the establishment of the colony at Urso, in 38 BCE, we are told that a law was passed in Rome barring slaves from serving as lictors. One can see how the lictors as a group will have wanted to protect their standing and also keep enslaved individuals from doing the work for free. Yet what most immediately must have prompted the measure was the chaotic political situation of precisely that year. Fully sixty-seven individuals are said to have held the praetorship in 38 BCE; at that point, a normal college would have totaled sixteen. It is conceivable that the decuries could not supply enough authorized lictors to go around, and so the task of carrying the fasces for the dozens of unexpected praetors fell to slaves. The legislation demanding free or freed status for lictors surely responded to this unusual set of circumstances, and seems to have stuck, for otherwise we find no enslaved lictors in our record for any era.[31]

We can now turn to our fifth brief case study: a bilingual honorary inscription—found in eight fragments in 2012 and first published in 2018—that sheds spectacular new light on the size, organization, patronage, and prestige of those urban decuries. The text was carved on two matching limestone slabs, originally mounted on a base for a statue group. The ensemble was set up at Patara, a prosperous port city on the southwestern coast of Lycia in Anatolia.

The honorands are named: the ex-praetor Lucius Luscius Ocra, now a legate with praetorian *imperium* of the emperor Vespasian, along with his homonymous son and his wife Iulia Severina. The inscription dates to

Ocra's governorship (74–76 CE) of the newly formed province of Lycia and Pamphylia; there is every indication that Patara was the seat of his provincial government.

What interests us here is the group that dedicates this monument honoring the imperial legate, a rank informally known as the "five fasces man" (*quinquefascalis*): "the lictors who attend him, Gnaeus Cornelius Fructus, Aulus Lucretius Capra, Tuccius Ephebus, Gaius Popillius Carpimus, (and) Gnaeus Cornelius Potitus." So with these five names we have, uniquely, a record of all the lictors in an individual unit. Popillius Carpimus, listed fourth in the lictors' group, is said to have managed the execution of the monument.[32]

What further catches our attention is the stated reason for the dedication. The lictors are honoring Ocra, along with his son and wife, not simply because he is their superior, whom they (necessarily) closely attend. The reason stated is "that he generously rewarded them from his own salary, (as) patron of the III decuries of 370 lictors who attend emperors, and consuls, and praetors, and other magistrates."

There is a lot here to unpack. For a start, it emerges that Ocra was the patron of the organization of lictors at Rome. Patronage of associations of lictors is otherwise attested, but all the secure instances come from Ostia. So this unambiguous notice is quite new. In addition, Ocra supplemented his own lictors' official pay with monetary gifts—evidently at a high level, since this group had the capability to erect a large pedestal with inscription supporting three statues. It seems quite possible that the elaborate Patara monument would have outstripped the regular annual income of all five lictors put together. Put another way, the imperial legate must have indirectly paid for his own family monument, and still left his lictors a tidy sum.[33]

Next, and of extreme interest, is the long formula that specifies the membership of the three decuries, expressed in terms quite unparalleled in lictors' inscriptions for Rome or elsewhere. That the panel of lictors at Rome consisted of a set number of members—as our text tells us, notionally 370, at least under the Flavians—is wholly new. Yet the large total hardly comes as a surprise, given the accumulation already by the late Republic of offices entitled to fasces, which Augustus only further multiplied. How the 370 lictors were divided between the three decuries meant to serve "emperors, consuls, praetors, and other magistrates" is anyone's guess; at any rate, the three panels cannot have been of equal size. What matters is the equation of these decuries with a fixed number of members, which in turn connotes prestige.

This recent find from Patara offers us the first example of a team of lictors honoring their assigned magistrate in their province.[34] Elsewhere, lictors as donors of honorary monuments are attested only acting as individuals. Also, the explicit testimony we find here of monetary gifts from a governor from his salary to his support staff is unique, as is the item that the lictors used part of this money to finance the monument in honor of the imperial legate and his family. What emerges most clearly from this inscription, however, is the lictors' pride in their privileged status, and their interest in commemorating not just their generous patron but, by extension, themselves.

Later evidence for a positive personal bond between an individual commander and his lictors is not plentiful. Prudentius in his *Against Symmachus* (402 CE) stands practically alone when he speaks of four noble Roman magistrates of the fourth century CE who converted to Christianity along with the lictors on their staff.[35] What is not in doubt is the persistence of the professional organization of these attendants. Lictors as well as scribes maintain their corporate existence into the sixth century CE, in Rome, in the provinces, and eventually at Constantinople. In the West, they are found petitioning for confirmation of their privileges and salaries five separate times under the emperors Theodosius I (reigned 379–395) and his son Honorius (395–423), each time with success. We have seen the survival of these attendants under the Ostrogothic kingdom in the sixth century CE, with the death of the boy lictor reported for 558 CE. It is with some justice that we can regard them as "the last remnant of the ancient civil service of the Roman Republic."[36]

Roman Fasces in the Medieval and Renaissance Eras

Knowledge of the Fasces at the Turn of the Millennium

After the definitive dissolution of Rome's Western Empire, we have to look hard to find contexts of reception for the fasces. Our first instance may come from the very start of the millennium, in pre-Norman England, with the illustrators of the Junius Manuscript at Oxford's Bodleian Library (datable to the first half of the eleventh century). This is one of the four most significant surviving manuscripts of Old English verse, and contains versions of parts of Genesis, Exodus, and Daniel, illustrated with Anglo-Saxon drawings.

In eight of these drawings, by two different artists, the figure of God holds (usually) in his left hand and against his left shoulder a rod bound by two or more bands, which is generally interpreted as a sealed scroll or a type of scepter. This feature is best seen in one partially painted illustration of God quashing a rebellion by Lucifer, which accompanies a bipartite poem on Genesis (Figure 7.1). The illustration fills a full page, and is divided into four registers. In the uppermost portion, Lucifer—not yet fallen—grasps a slender scepter. In contrast, the third register of the drawing portrays God holding a scroll-like object that looks remarkably like an axe-less fasces in his left arm, while casting with his right a bunch of three spears down toward Lucifer and his angels, now massed in the bottom register.

What source did this illustrator draw on for this arresting multi-tiered image of power and authority? The composition of a sealed scroll resting on God's left shoulder is essentially unparalleled among English artists of this era. Scholars have argued for Carolingian influence on the iconography, specifically that the insignia of Lucifer amid the fallen angels has close parallels

The Fasces. T. Corey Brennan, Oxford University Press. © Oxford University Press 2023.
DOI: 10.1093/oso/9780197644881.003.0007

FIGURE 7.1. Detail from illustration in the Junius Manuscript (eleventh century CE, Oxford, Bodleian Library MS. Junius 11). This illustration, which accompanies a poem on Genesis, shows God bearing an (axe-less) fasces in his left arm while throwing spears with his right downward at Hell.

Credit: Bodleian Libraries, University of Oxford, https://digital.bodleian.ox.ac.uk/objects/d5e3a9fc-abaa-4649-ae48-be207ce8da15/.

with imperial art of the mid-ninth century. The argument has been refined to posit specifically the Carolingian-era Utrecht Psalter, which had reached Canterbury by the year 1000, as the source for the multi-tiered illustration.

Yet here the length and thickness of God's "scroll," the rendering of the object as a bundle (none of the other seven instances in the Junius MS have the cylinder shape bisected by a vertical line), the detail of its binding (a spiral rather than parallel rings), and the emphatic manner in which it is rested on his left shoulder all call for comment. The image seems closely modeled on the lictor bearing his fasces—so closely that the inspiration may have come, via Carolingian channels, ultimately from observation of Roman-era relief sculpture.[1]

The word "fasces" never fully fell out of Latin use in the medieval period. Though its primary technical meaning seems to have been forgotten, there was a general understanding that it somehow connoted "supreme power" or "official honors." Yet the actual object was so foreign to Western artists by the early medieval period that they did not reproduce it even when found in works they copied. The word "lictor" fared somewhat better in the post-antique period, perhaps because—unlike the fasces—this institution was mentioned in scripture. So in the late fourteenth-century Wycliffite translation of Acts 16:35–38, when Roman magistrates at the colony of Philippi sent lictors to free Paul and Silas from prison, we find "littoures" accurately glossed as "that ben mynistris of ponysching."[2]

But let us return to the Junius illustration. Even if the identification is accepted, in this Anglo-Saxon Lucifer scene the fasces of God stands completely in isolation, even within its own manuscript, as a distant and unexpected echo of a much earlier era. We lack significant visual representations of the symbol for the rest of the medieval period, and indeed for much of the Renaissance.

Renaissance Humanists and the Fasces

In the fifteenth century even some well-read humanists did not fully understand the nature and significance of the fasces that they found mentioned in classical texts. Take, for example, Jean de Rovroy, a translator (ca. 1439) of a Latin treatise of the second century CE, Frontinus's *Stratagems*. In setting out a confident exposition of the meaning of the word "fasces," de Rovroy seems led astray by the Old French cognate *faisse* (from Latin *fascia*, a "strip of cloth"). "These imperial signs called fasces were ribbons of purple or gold which Roman Princes tied around their heads," he says. "The Consul or Judge was thus recognizable by virtue of these ribbons . . . and by the axe that they bore in front of them, in the same way the Prince carries a sword in front of him as a sign of office." The misconception about headbands was an old one, dating back at least to the *Elementarium* of the eleventh-century Italian lexicographer Papias (1053, first published in print 1476).[3]

In contrast, some contemporary fifteenth-century humanists in Italy demonstrate an easy familiarity with the Romans' display of the insignia.

Writing around 1425, "Lucius Fenestella"—the pseudonym of the Florentine lawyer and papal secretary Andreas Flocchus (1400–1452)—in a treatise on Roman magistracies demonstrably read Livy closely, and gave short shrift to the medieval exegetical tradition. So he knows that there were "twelve lictors who carried before each of the consuls an axe bound up in bundles (fasces) or rods." He is aware that the emblem was said to have an Etruscan origin, but seems to prefer the tradition that Romulus introduced it to Rome. The work was first published in print ca. 1475, and saw dozens of reprints into the mid-sixteenth century. Flavio Biondo (1392–1463), for works such as his *Italy Illuminated* (1453) and *Rome in Triumph* (1459), consulted still more widely, in both Greek and Latin sources. He is superbly informed not just on the expected antiquarian traditions on the fasces, but also on finer technical points, such as their prohibition in the free city of Alexandria.[4]

In the next generation, Niccolò Machiavelli in his *Discourses on Livy* (written ca. 1517, published 1531) speaks not of fasces but of lictors. He comprehends that Rome's kings received a dozen of the attendants, thinks that the consuls of the Republic (somehow) shared the same number, and points out how the decemvirs, after a promising start, grotesquely violated this principle (25.1, 40.3). More fulsome on the fasces proper is Machiavelli's contemporary, Caelius Rhodiginus (= Lodovico Ricchieri of Rovigo, 1469–1525), in the course of an 800-plus-page antiquarian miscellany published in 1516 by the Venetian Aldine press. Drawing on multiple sources in both Greek and Latin, Rhodiginus sets out a learned explanation of the origin and rationale of several Republican customs involving the fasces, which he terms "an invidious mark of the magistracy." These include the removal of axes within the city, the practice of dipping the rods before the people, as well as the rotation of the fasces among the consuls. A later, even more authoritative exposition by the French humanist Guillaume Budé (1526) further cemented a proper understanding of the institution.[5]

Indeed, by the first decade of the sixteenth century, the fame of the Roman fasces was sufficiently established that we find learned Italians applying the term to contemporary situations. In 1510 the papal secretary Paolo Cortesi (1471–1510) pictures the pope as a holder of *imperium*, who wields the terror of his fasces to keep in check a hostile and even dangerous public. In 1529, the Italian legal scholar Andrea Alciato (1492–1550) produced an even more erudite reference after the French king Francis I attended one of his lectures at Bourges. Alciato remarked, with more than a hint of grandiosity, that "the royal majesty in person has appeared to lower the fasces, the ensigns of his power, in honor of myself, while sitting on the throne of jurisprudence." All the same, when Alciato composed his book of what he called "emblems"—symbolic images paired with a Latin motto, all with a moralizing explanatory text—fasces did not make the cut. A first edition appeared in 1531 with 104 emblems; the next century and a half would see the publication of over 170 more editions in various languages, with massive expansions, but none including the fasces.[6]

The Fasces in Italian Art of the Renaissance

Yet it is already in the last quarter of the fifteenth century that we start to find sporadically in the arts prominent depictions of fasces, as a symbol of authority and the administration of justice (loosely construed). At Verona in the Piazza dei Signori, a set of four axe-less fasces in relief decorates the pedestal to a central column of the Loggia del Consiglio, constructed in the years 1476–1493 as the meeting place of the patrician city council. The tops of each bundle are shown burning small flames in stone, as if the object were a torch. The painter Filippino Lippi used a similar motif in Rome at Santa Maria sopra Minerva, in the Carafa Chapel (1488–1493). On the chapel's right wall, the *Dispute of St. Thomas Aquinas* shows the saint seated at the center of a complicated allegorical scene, within a vaulted pavilion in a Roman landscape, crushing a heretic with his foot. Into the pavilion side walls are set six tall axe-less fasces, three on each side of Aquinas, that all are depicted issuing flames.

In his native Florence, Filippino Lippi provides an even more emphatic depiction of the fasces, this time as functioning Roman insignia, wielded by lictors. In the church of Santa Maria Novella, for the burial chapel of Filippo Strozzi in the east transept, Lippi started a fresco cycle in 1487, which after a lengthy diversion to Rome for the Carafa commission, and the death of Strozzi himself (in 1490), he completed in 1502. The cycle is devoted to scenes from the lives of St. Philip and St. John the Evangelist. A lunette on the upper left wall of the chapel shows St. John withstanding torture in a vat of boiling oil. The setting is Rome (as a banner with the legend "SPQR" makes clear), and the evangelist's persecutor is none other than the emperor Domitian, who is patently enraged at his victim's survival. This is the version of the story found in Jacobus de Voragine's *Golden Legend* (1275). Among the emperor's companions and attendants are two lictors, who stand at the extreme left and near the far right of the frame—not especially close to the emperor—in fabulous adaptations of Roman military dress. Their fasces are fantastically tall, with their axe blades looming well above the heads of each attendant.[7]

Of crucial importance is Raphael's design for *The Conversion of the Proconsul* (preparatory drawing and cartoon ca. 1514–1516) (Figure 7.2). The design was later woven as a large tapestry (4.95 m × 7.77 m), to form part of his Acts of the Apostles series (1519) for the walls of the Sistine Chapel. This scene is based on an episode in Acts 13:6–12, which takes place on Cyprian Paphos in the mid-40s CE. There St. Paul foils a Jewish pseudo-prophet who tries to use his influence with Sergius Paullus, a Roman governor (in the Greek text of Acts, termed *anthupatos*, which is the proper translation of his official Latin title "proconsul"), to block him from learning about the Christian faith.

Toward the center in Raphael's composition is depicted a laureate Paullus, trying to control a frenetic scene from a magistrate's "curule" chair, set in an ornate classical interior with columns, pilasters, and arches. The scowling governor sits at the head of a virtual triangle whose base is formed by saints Barnabas and Paul standing on one side, and Elymas, who staggers from the

FIGURE 7.2. Design of Raphael (1483–1520) for *The Conversion of the Proconsul.* One of a series of cartoons for tapestries, commissioned by Pope Leo X for the Sistine Chapel. Body color on paper mounted onto canvas, ca. 1515–1516.

Credit: Victoria & Albert Museum (London), inv. Royal Loans.8. Image ID 2006AT3622.

other, temporarily blinded by Paul. A dynamic group of thirteen ancillary figures observes the miracle, four from the side of the Christians, the rest from that of Elymas.

The Roman elements of the picture offer a mix of realism, grandeur, and decline. The feet of Paullus's chair are noticeably dirty, and are placed on a short podium that bears an explanatory inscription in Latin, showing his name and title as "L. SERGIUS PAVLLVS / ASIAE PROCOS" ("Lucius Sergius Paullus, proconsul of Asia"), and noting that this was the moment of his conversion by Paul's preaching. It is the only one of Raphael's designs for the Sistine Chapel tapestries (eventually, ten in all) that has an inscription. It is correct as to the man's rank and its abbreviation, plus adds "Lucius" as a first name (not found in Acts) and enhances the importance of his province. Two sets of steps flank the governor's podium. The face of each displays a design, as if carved in shallow relief, of military spoils in a heap; a fasces can be spotted amid both. Poised on the steps at the governor's side, above most others in the assemblage, stand two lictors, each balancing a short but thick axe-bearing fasces on a different shoulder.

Of the many ancillary figures, the lictors are among the most integral to the scene. The fully extended arm of a gesturing St. Paul bisects their bodies, and their two heads and that of the Roman governor form another triangle, with that of the lictor nearest Paullus at its peak. What also grabs notice is the proximate lictor's fasces, which in the entire busy tableau is the object on the highest plane. It is rendered in detail and essentially in full, down to a stabilizing handle at its base that the lictor grips, directly under the hand of Paul himself in the foreground. On the actual tapestry—as opposed to the preparatory drawings—the axe-head is woven at the precise top center of the pictorial frame. For both fasces, the blades of the axes, inserted laterally at top, extend fully one-third the length of the rods, whose binding is colored a vivid red. The lictor nearest Paullus rests his head suggestively on the middle section of his fasces, just beneath its menacingly long blade, and his gaze follows and reinforces that of Paullus.

The original passage in Acts has nothing to say about Paullus's lictors, and so their prominent presence in *The Conversion of the Proconsul* is wholly the contribution of Raphael. Indeed, their appearance on the steps of the governor's podium and the treatment of their fasces suggests Raphael's characteristic concern for historical accuracy, based in part on personal study of monuments and coins. What is their function in the composition? The lictors and their fasces define and accentuate the position of the governor Sergius Paullus, but in a way that goes beyond the merely antiquarian or decorative.

One notes Paul's dramatic gesture with his left arm (on the tapestry), which places his hand in the visual field as if poised to take the fasces from the proximate lictor—a Christian supplanting the authority of the Roman state.

Whatever the precise interpretation of the piece, the lictors' eye-catching position in Raphael's Sistine Chapel commission, and the great artist's attention to the particulars of their (then unfamiliar) equipment, guaranteed an iconographic future for the fasces.

In fact, the kit soon appears again in one of Raphael's designs, in the Hall of Constantine of the Vatican Apostolic Palace, completed by members of his workshop following the artist's tragically sudden death (April 1520). Its context is a faux bronze frieze panel devoted to the "Magnanimity of Constantine," placed below the center of the epic *Battle of the Milvian Bridge* on the south wall of the Hall. In this battle (306 CE), Constantine removed his rival Maxentius, and so—as the large painting's Latin caption tells us—firmed up the position of Christians, during his long subsequent reign as emperor (306–337 CE).

This frieze shows the seated emperor pardoning a pair of bound captives after the Milvian battle. A winged Victory hovers behind Constantine, while a lictor stands at his left, amid a scene of both carnage and hope. The attendant holds a large axed fasces, and looks toward the emperor, seemingly awaiting a command to execute the prisoners of war. Here again, as in the Sistine Chapel tapestry, a lictor with a historically accurate fasces plays a crucial role in the dramatic narrative. Indeed, there is good evidence that Raphael's own intention was to render this composition on one of the main walls of the Hall, rather than at the secondary level it now holds.[8]

The Fasces as a Symbol of Justice

In the second quarter of the sixteenth century, the fasces came to acquire some symbolic meanings unimportant or even unknown to the Romans, as the insignia found their way into central positions in allegorical compositions. It would seem that the devastating attack on Rome (May 1527) by mutinous troops of the Holy Roman Emperor Charles V was a prime impetus for this development. Put briefly, the reigning pope, Clement VII de' Medici (1523–1534), sought to regain control of the city following its sack by assertively emphasizing his powers to direct the system of justice, especially against the competing claims of the Roman nobility. Paul III Farnese (1534–1549) followed Clement in this—indeed, with more success. In these decades, the administration of law took on an enhanced ideological role in the politics of the papal court, and a new practical importance in larger society. And the Roman fasces, which by the mid-sixteenth century could be understood without explanation as a sign of justice, ultimately and perhaps inevitably figured in iconographic expressions of these developments.

In this context, the year 1543 marked a red-letter date for representations of the fasces. To celebrate Paul III's success in monopolizing the right to administer justice in Rome, his nephew, Cardinal Alessandro Farnese, commissioned from the artist Giorgio Vasari a large oil on canvas painting with an allegory of "Farnese Justice." The cardinal aimed to display it in the main hall of his residence in Rome, the palace of the Cancellaria.

Vasari's composition proved highly complex, and original to the point of obscurity. To speak only of the principal images, a half-naked Justice— or, as Vasari sometimes identifies her in correspondence, the justice-goddess Astraea—in partial Greco-Roman dress embraces with one arm an ostrich (considered a symbol of patience and even-handedness in the law), while she places an oak wreath with the other on Truth, who has been introduced to her by Father Time. Putti fly over Justice's right shoulder, bringing her new armor and weapons. To the belt of Justice are chained seven personified Vices, two of whom—Corruption and Ignorance—sit vanquished on a tiled floor with a pile of treasure and a pair of axed fasces at their feet. The fasces do not look especially imposing: Vasari has taken care to show that they each consist of just five rods, and are held together not by a leather strap, but rather a rich-looking pink ribbon. It is the treasure rather than the fasces that captures the gaze of Corruption; Ignorance has her eyes covered.

In a letter dated January 20, 1543, Vasari himself explained in some detail the elaborate symbolism of his work to Cardinal Farnese, including the item that "the putti with arms as well as dictator's fasces, located between the legs of the vices, truly demonstrate what occurred while in their service." It is hard not to take these debased and somewhat dandified "fasci dei dittatori" as referring to justice as formerly administered by members of the Roman nobility, some of whom based their status on supposed family origins in the Roman Republic. Here the Farnese version of Justice does not use ancient fasces, but a panoply of new, different arms and resources. We are lucky that we have Vasari explaining to his patron the meaning of the symbolic aspects of his challenging work. The traditional image of the Roman fasces had not yet appeared in emblem books, neither in that of Alciato nor in those of his immediate followers. Through Vasari, it may be that the device finally entered emblematic language.

Vasari was demonstrably interested in the symbolic potential of the fasces. He had painted the kit just the previous year, in 1542, on a wooden panel depicting Justice, as part of a series on the Virtues executed for the ceiling of the Cornaro Palace (= Ca' Corner Spinelli) in Venice. There Lady Justice, gazing upward at the heavens, her back toward the viewer, is joined on her right by a crowned male with scepter, and at her left is attended by two additional male figures with bowed heads. In most un-Roman manner, together they shoulder a single fasces with axe. The rods of the fasces are bound not with a cord but rather with a fine fabric, whose loose end at the top flutters in the wind.

We find a similarly decorative approach to axed fasces in a 1544 depiction of *Justice*, attributed to Battista Dossi of Ferrara. Here Lady Justice raises with her left hand her most familiar traditional emblem, the scales (a symbol of equity), and she holds her head high, ignoring three jars in gold and silver that spill coins at her feet. With her right arm, she balances a long fasces that is set on the ground; its rods are tall enough that the top of the axe-head extends to the height of her nose. Yet the fact that the fasces' rods are tied with a wide, delicate ribbon certainly diminishes the ferocity of the emblem, which seems to be the goal in this and similar representations.[9]

The combination of the scales and fasces as attributes of a standing Lady Justice soon becomes practically expected. And the presence of Justice among the four Cardinal Virtues—traditionally listed after Prudence, and before Fortitude and Temperance—guaranteed her frequent depiction also in non-legal settings. In Pierio Valeriano's wildly influential *Hieroglyphica*, first published in Basel in 1556, one finds an illustration of Justice with scales in her left hand and a short (axe-less) fasces resting on her right shoulder; the text explains the rods as a token of her "severity and rigor," the functional equivalent of a sword. In another widely consulted text, Vincenzo Cartari's *Images of the Gods of the Ancients* (first published 1556), Lady Justice is depicted holding the scales with her right hand and a column-like axed fasces with her left as she approaches a female Injustice cudgeling a suppliant youth with a rough stick. When Justice wields the fasces, she typically does so in combination with the scales or a sword, rarely both.

Representations of Justice with fasces but without either one of those major markers are rare, and are largely confined to funerary art. A sterling sixteenth-century example is the tomb of Pope Paul III Farnese, whose determination in controlling the administration of law at Rome we have seen. Guglielmo della Porta executed this work in the years 1549–1575 in the nave of St. Peter's; within sixty years of its completion it was twice dismantled and moved to other spots within the Basilica. Before the main pedestal of the monument, with a bronze seated statue of the pope, is a pair of recumbent figures, Justice (finished by April 1554) and Prudence. The former—originally a nude reclining on drapery, but covered in 1593—rests a miniature axed fasces in the crook of her left arm, and in a feature that is easily missed, she cradles a small flame (a traditional symbol of charity, or communion with the divine) in her right hand.

What seems especially noteworthy here is that in the course of about seventy-five years the fasces could progress from antiquarian curiosity to a central feature of a papal tomb. This is all the more remarkable since at this time its significance was purely secular—in the medieval and Renaissance periods, there was not even a tradition of assigning fasces to the images of saints as a symbol of their martyrdom. Still, the tombs of three later Popes incorporate fasces into their iconography, all as signifiers of justice: Urban VIII Barberini (r. 1623–1644, with monument designed by Bernini ca. 1627–1647); Innocent X Pamphili (r. 1644–1655, with tomb completed 1730); and Innocent XII Pignatelli (r. 1691–1700, finally commemorated in 1746).

Indeed, Bernini's work for Urban VIII is directly inspired by della Porta's for Paul III, with the twist that he presents Justice and Charity as the main personified virtues, and with much more dynamism and elaboration, partly achieved by introducing putti as supporting characters. Justice here gets a balance as a sign of her impartiality, and three additional emblems: a sword, the fasces, and a book. "Cumulative justice, individual to individual, is symbolized by the sword," argues Irving Lavin, "distributive justice, society to the individual, by the fasces; legal justice, the individual to society, by the book." To underline that divine justice is meted out only reluctantly, Lavin points out that in Bernini's creation the putti visibly show squeamishness about employing their implements, with the fasces-bearer even turning away from Justice, seemingly to hide behind her back.[10]

The Fasces as a Symbol of Concord

We have been getting ahead of ourselves here. In the first half of the sixteenth century, alongside the ever-increasing interest in the Roman-style fasces, there is lingering fascination with the Aesopic story of the father who educates his quarrelsome sons by urging them to break sticks in a bundle, and then individually. We have seen that in the Low Countries, the tale had reached textbook status by the first decades of the 1500s, providing an illustration of Sallust's moralizing observation in the *Jugurthine War* that "with harmony small matters grow, with discord great ones are ruined."

The fable demonstrably had an impact on the artist Giorgio Vasari—as we have seen, a trailblazer in depicting the fasces as a tool of Justice. In 1544–1545, in a decorative cycle painted for a ceiling in the Refectory of Monteoliveto in Naples (today, the Sacristy of Sant'Anna dei Lombardi), Vasari introduced allegorical female figures of Virtue (i.e., chastity), Modesty, Peace, and Concord. The last of these is shown seated, with head lowered and eyes averted from the viewer, embracing with both arms a stocky bundle of longish rods bound with cord at a single point. The assemblage rests on her left shoulder; she gazes at a pair of broken sticks that rest under her right foot. In 1548 Vasari painted these same four personified Christian virtues on the ceiling of the "Chamber of Abraham" in his own home, in Arezzo. Here again, a thick set of similarly bound rods is the attribute he chose for the figure of Concord. She holds her right hand to the assemblage; there are broken rods, too, now placed prominently in Concord's left hand, an even more assertive statement of the perils of disunity.[11]

The idea of the axed fasces as a symbol of concord also comes into view around this time, however obliquely, in Claude Paradin's *Devises heroïques* (1551, second expanded edition 1557). This French book was the first publication of decorative "devices"—symbolic images, usually joined with a Latin motto, that aristocratic families used as quasi-heraldic expressions of identity. Under the motto HOC LATIO RESTARE CANUNT ("such destiny, they prophesy, awaits Latium," from Vergil's *Aeneid*) is pictured a pair of fasces chained together, each with a laurel wreath dangling from the beak of its halberd-style blade that tops the center of the bundle. Paradin tells us that these items, "carried in antiquity before the Roman Consuls . . . sufficiently represented the power, domination and authority that the triumphant Italy formerly claimed to have over everyone, however through concord, public order, and love of the Republic." But now, it is explained, Italy's civil divisions and political factions have figuratively imprisoned these rods and axes. Paradin's work found an English translator before the end of the century, who elaborated that the spectacle of crowned lictors carrying the fasces signaled "the triumphes of . . . Italie, and the whole gouernment of the world, and also that the Romaines by their great wisedome, peace, and affection to the common wealc, purchased to themselues no litle praise and dignitie." Notable here is also the application of the fasces to allegorize contemporary politics— a precocious instance of what would become a common phenomenon.[12]

8

Early Modern and Neoclassical
Fasces

Cesare Ripa's Figurative Handbook and Its Influence

A decisive moment in the image of Concord as portrayed specifically by
Vasari came some four decades after his works in Naples and Arezzo, when it
entered into a fundamental allegorical handbook. That is the *Nova Iconologia*
of Cesare Ripa (1555–1622), a seemingly comprehensive compilation of
emblems, first published in Rome in 1593, with an expanded illustrated edition appearing in 1603. Its attractive alphabetical organization and straight-
forward elucidation of visualized concepts won it many reprintings—four
in Italy alone between 1613 and 1625. A French translation was published in
1636; by the mid-eighteenth century there had appeared ten further foreign
editions in three additional languages. In short, Cesare Ripa's highly acces-
sible work effectively eclipsed its predecessors in the symbol-book genre. It
also stimulated further inquiry into allegorical representations, so much so
that we can speak of a "Ripa tradition" not just of figurative handbooks, but
of works of art.

Ripa's illustrated 1603 volume offers a dozen different personified forms
of Concord for the reader to consider; in the compendium, only Peace and
Victory get more variants. Here Ripa offers as one guise of Concord "a woman
who holds in her hand a bundle of rods (*fascio di verghe*), tightly fastened . . . of
which each by itself is weak, but all together are strong and hard." He further
explains that in human affairs it is "through union that greater strength is
achieved," quoting Sallust to amplify his point, perhaps at second hand from
a text of Dorpius's Aesop.

The Fasces. T. Corey Brennan, Oxford University Press. © Oxford University Press 2023.
DOI: 10.1093/oso/9780197644881.003.0008

Ripa in his iconological treatise sought to disengage also the resonances of the rods with axe, which he does not conflate with the *fascio di verghe* of Concord, but carefully distinguishes as "consular fasces." One of his versions of Lady Justice is a "woman dressed in white, her eyes bandaged; in her right hand she holds a bundle of rods with an axe tied together with them, in the left a flame of fire, and beside her you will have an ostrich"—one thinks here especially of Vasari's depiction of Farnese Justice—"or she holds the sword and the scales. This is the kind of Justice that judges and secular executors exercise in the Courts."

As is his practice, Ripa then explains each of the elements of the personification that he has described. The blindfold, which we have not yet seen Justice combine with the fasces, is said to ward off temptation. Of the bundle of rods with the axe, he says this device was "carried by the ancient Roman lictors before the consuls and the Tribune of the People"—an error, perhaps for the early experimental office of consular tribune—"to show that one must not linger in castigation, where Justice demands it, nor be precipitous, but have time to ripen judgment while unbinding the rods that cover the axe."

Two other personifications get the consular fasces in Ripa's *Nova Iconologia*. The symbol of Jurisdiction is a "man dressed in purple, who in his right hand holds a scepter . . . and in the other the consular fasces," both tokens, we learn, of "natural jurisdiction." And in one version of Clemency, there is described a woman who has thrown down her arms, and leans against an olive tree (associated with peace) on which consular fasces are suspended. The sense is that she does not want to exert force against the guilty, even though strict justice has entitled her to do so.

So the concept of justice is central to each of the three appearances of the fasces proper in Cesare Ripa's work. Previous emblem books had rarely highlighted the insignia, and so its presence in several sections of Ripa is significant. He casts the emblem in a positive light, offering the observation that unbinding the kit for use in itself promotes thoughtful deliberation. The author is careful to define what constituted the Roman "consular" emblem, which he differentiates from a mere bundle of sticks.[1]

However, the fact that Cesare Ripa uses the same phrase—*fascio delle verghe*—of the attributes of both Justice and Concord practically assured their later syncretism. Indeed, we soon find that development in later versions of Ripa's own work. In an expanded 1630 edition printed by the Paduan publisher Donato Pasquardi, the seated figure of Aristocracy (a new addition to the corpus) holds in her right arm a slender bunch of long rods bound together, adorned near the top with a laurel garland; an axe lays on the floor below. The significance of the bundle, we learn, is "that the Republic ought to be united for its preservation and the public benefit." The now-familiar Micipsa quote from Sallust on *concordia* follows, with comments on the laurel (a reward for benefactions) and the discarded axe (a symbol of punishment).

Thirteen years later, in the French translation of Ripa by Jean Baudoin (1643), the conflation is complete. A laureate Concord is shown standing, raising up a heart in her right hand, and nestling a squat fasces with double axe-head in her left arm (Figure 8.1). The accompanying explanation is straight from the Aesopic textbook tradition: "she is represented by the bundle of rods (*le faisceau de verghes*), each of which is thin, but all together are immensely strong," again with the Sallust citation. There is no good reason, of course, that along with the rods Concord should get an axe, even a two-headed one. However, once illustrated, this personification discernably took on a life of its own.[2]

FIGURE 8.1. Concord with a double-axed fasces, in French translation of Cesare Ripa, *Nova Iconologia* (1603) by J. Baudoin, *Iconologie où les principales choses qui peuvent tomber dans la pensée touchant les vices sont représentées* (Paris 1643), 36 fig. xxvii.
Credit: Google Books.

An additional result of the runaway success of Cesare Ripa's *Nova Iconologia* is that it greatly expanded the market for other emblematic studies. During Ripa's own lifetime, the Antwerp-based artist and humanist Otto van Veen (1556–1629, also known as Vaenius) published three such works in quick succession, *Emblems of the Roman Poet Horace* (1607), *Emblems of Cupids* (1608), and *Emblems of Divine Love* (1615). The first of the series saw more than twenty editions, with translations into multiple vernacular languages. In 1646 the French poet and novelist Marin le Roi de Gomberville (1600–1674) simply took the collection as his own, erasing all mention of Vaenius, and published it as a moral instruction manual for the young Louis XIV (born 1638, and reigned 1643–1715). The plagiarizing volume, which contains a dual dedication to the queen regent of France, Anne of Austria, and first minister and de facto head of state Cardinal Jules Mazarin, somewhat amazingly generated its own series of editions, including in English (first in 1721).

The format of Vaenius's original Horace book is highly attractive: on the left-hand page, short excerpts from the Roman poet and other authors, as well as the compiler's own reflections, ostensibly comment on large-format allegorical engravings that fill the right. In addition to the ancient texts he has selected, there is deep but unspoken reliance on St. Thomas Aquinas's *Summa Theologica*, especially his treatment of ambition and vainglory (*Questions*, 131–132). The highly intricate and well-informed classicizing illustrations in this work total 103, fully ten of which feature the fasces, including (significantly) the first and last of the collection. Vaenius's primary aim here was not to create an encyclopedia of symbols, but rather to put to work a preexisting visual vocabulary for a larger didactic purpose. Basic interpretation of the engravings, however, is often difficult, since the imagery of these moralizing compositions is so dense that they often outstrip the corresponding text.

What is unambiguous is that Vaenius in this collection puts the fasces at the center of his iconographic universe. For his very first emblem, "Virtue Unshaken," he opens by citing Horace (*Odes* 3.2.17–20) on the mark of true virtue, that "neither takes up nor lays aside / the axes at the fickle mob's behest." He then adds some lines of his own, on how virtue is its own reward, and despises honor and wealth. The corresponding image? An armed Virtue, surrounded by six personified attributes of her "unshakenness," crushing with her left foot a female Fortune, who fearfully clutches her traditional symbol of a rudder. On the ground beneath the supine Fortune are scattered an overturned metal vase, a trumpet, wreaths, a crown, a scepter, coins, and an axed fasces. The final emblem in the collection, which illustrates death as the last material limit, and virtue as the sole quality able to survive it, shows the same items (but now two fasces) assembled with evident care next to a skeleton. Another engraving, meant to illustrate literally a figure of Horace (*Odes* 2.26.9–12), shows the (obvious) inability of lictors with fasces to clear nightmarish ideation from a disarranged mind. Here and throughout Vaenius's Horace collection, the recurring figure of the fasces seems designed to prompt a meditation on the desire for honor and glory, and its concomitant ills.

Vaenius in this work is much more expansive on the meaning of the fasces than what we find in Ripa, but also deeply skeptical as to their value. For the emblem titled "Immortal Virtue," the engraving shows a wreathed male figure with axed fasces and book, representing Jurisdiction or the Law, who works with a warrior to lift Virtue to heaven; the funeral of a Roman emperor can be seen on earth below, underlining the political context of the scene. But that is the sole positive portrayal of the insignia in the book. Elsewhere Vaenius presents the rods and axe not as an accessory of Lady Justice, but of her one-legged daughter Nemesis, who savagely punishes with a lash while cradling a

FIGURE 8.2. "Inquietude of Mind," in Otto van Veen (= Vaenius), *Quinti Horatii Flacci emblemata* (Antwerp 1607, reprinted 1612) pp. 91–92, no. 43.

Credit: Google Books.

fasces. Aspirants to true wisdom and virtue refuse them when offered, along with other flashy props.[3]

The Fasces of Cardinal Mazarin

Given this largely hostile presentation of the fasces in Vaenius, one wonders what the Italian cardinal Jules Mazarin (1602–1661) made of the illustrations when he received de Gomberville's pirated French edition of the emblem book. As a woodcut on the dedication page of de Gomberville's book shows, the cardinal's coat of arms in fact featured a fasces of thick rods topped with an axe; across its center runs a broad horizontal stripe, charged with three gold stars. This armorial was absolutely central to Mazarin's self-presentation as a Roman (he was in fact from Abruzzo), a spiritual descendant of Julius Caesar, and the living embodiment of the virtue of Justice. There is no evidence that this was an ancient emblem of his Mazzarino family. The fasces crest first appears in 1638, the year he was nominated as cardinal, and one suspects that he simply made it up. Two recent popes had shown the way that one could leverage and diffuse an evocative family emblem: Gregory XIII (1572–1585) with his Boncompagni family dragon, and the reigning pontiff Urban VIII (1623–1644) with his Barberini bees. Similarly, Mazarin used his fasces as a personal brand—the first individual in the modern era to do so.

Mazarin's personality and power in the years 1642–1661 ensured that his fasces coat of arms became practically ubiquitous, thanks especially to eager artists and encomiasts who essentially created a praise industry for the cardinal and statesman. In Paris, the insignia adorned Mazarin's palace (now the Bibliothèque Nationale de France), his foundations such as the Collège des Quatre-Nations, the Louvre summer apartment of Anne of Austria, and eventually the decoration of his catafalque, and ultimately (1689–1693) his mausoleum. In Rome, Mazarin's arms can be spotted most conspicuously on the façade of SS Vincenzo e Anastasio (built 1646–1650) near the Trevi Fountain. Engraved frontispieces of the many books dedicated to Mazarin was just one medium for amplifying the image further.[4]

Among much else, this fervid era of meditation on and propagation of the Mazarin fasces definitively crystallized the notion that the rods and axes symbolize unity. In June 1659 the royal chaplain P. du Fayot wrote to the cardinal that he drew new assurances of political peace between France and Spain (established later that year by the Treaty of the Pyrenees) from his reflection on "your Consular Fasces and on this assemblage of several rods, separate in themselves, but united with the application of a strong bond." More expansive is court historian André Félibien's description of an ephemeral monumental arch that the artist Charles Le Brun designed in the Place Dauphine, along the processional route by which the newlyweds Louis XIV and Maria Theresa of Spain entered Paris on August 26, 1660. There the presence of the fasces was interpreted as a "symbol of union and harmony, representing this great Cardinal establishing the concord and Peace between France and Spain." The author continues that "the axe which is in the middle of the bundle and which signifies Justice and Power, represents the strength of his spirit and the justice of his actions, by which . . . he became the arbiter of a Peace of which all of Europe today feels the advantages."[5]

The audacity of the encomia of Mazarin and his armorial is well seen in an allegory of the Peace of the Pyrenees of 1659, apparently designed by Charles Le Brun, and known to us from a contemporary Dutch engraving. Three monarchies, portrayed as classical gods, are shown hunting a lion, a symbol of Spain. Two attack with the spear-like points of their halberd-style axed fasces. At the center of the composition is France, in the person of young Louis XIV represented as Jupiter, with a fasces-spear and an eagle tendering him a lightning bolt. From his right, the Habsburg empire charges as Mars with his fasces; on his left, England arrives in the guise of Neptune astride a sea-chariot, brandishing a fasces-*cum*-trident. The multiple fasces, the depiction of three stars shooting toward heaven, and an accompanying Latin inscription with praise of "Julus" confirms that it is Mazarin who is the true honorand, as the architect of the alliance.[6]

Proliferation of Figurative Fasces in Europe (ca. 1600–1789)

A colossal effort would be needed to process contemporary interpretations of just Cardinal Mazarin's fasces in his two decades as chief minister of France (1642–1661). For one thing, the sheer volume of material shows the immediate impact on seventeenth-century European culture of the iconographers Cesare Ripa (1593 and 1603) and Vaenius (1607), amplified by their many followers, emulators, and plagiarists. The case of Mazarin also raises fears that a sketch, even in outline, of developments after 1600 in Baroque and Neoclassical allegorical representations of the fasces is impossible. Indeed, it might have been, were it not for the fact that Antje Middeldorf-Kosegarten in the *Reallexikon zur Deutschen Kunstgeschichte* has provided such a study, in the form of a detailed and highly informative short survey of the fate of the figurative fasces up through ca. 1825.

As one might expect, Middeldorf-Kosegarten charts for the post-Ripa period a proliferation of the fasces as symbol across almost every conceivable visual medium, from architectural sculpture to decorative arts, in paintings of every type, on monuments that range from honorific arches to tombs, as well as in medallic art and engravings, especially in Italy, France, the Low Countries, Germany, and Austria.

Yet by the time the fasces reach the mid-eighteenth century, one observes that a finite range of basic meanings prevail. Writing in 1756, the French jurist and encyclopedist Honoré Lacombe de Prézel (1725–1790) devotes only a few sentences to the emblem. "They are given as an attribute to Justice and to Authority. The bundle of rods in the hands of Concord is a symbol of the strength of peoples united together. Holland has a fasces of seven arrows, to denote the seven United Provinces." In 1793, an extended German edition of de Prézel's handbook adds a little more. The fasces symbolizes "the dignity and power of the supreme leadership, of justice, and of the unity of peoples." Further, fasces can serve as "allegorical images of empires, states and republics," as well as signify an individual "who is a member of such an assembly which has the highest power in a state."

One item immediately leaps to the eye. A bunch of seven arrows was indeed a symbol of the Dutch Republic (1588–1795), and remains a component of the modern coat of arms of the Netherlands. As such, it is frequently seen on its coins and medals, but not arranged in a close bundle, but rather loosely, all crossed in saltire. Yet the motto of the old United States of the Netherlands was taken from Micipsa's quote in Sallust ("Concordia res parvae crescunt"), which by now was also inextricably linked to the fasces proper. So occasionally we do find the unification of seven provinces symbolized by the fasces in allegorical representations.[7]

Otherwise, the actual evidence of the period 1600–1750 corresponds tolerably well to Lacombe de Prézel's categories. First, Lady Justice. When this figure holds a fasces, we find her regularly joining it with scales, or a sword, or both; or sometimes further combining a book, scepter, or (very occasionally) a blindfold. Of course, she can shed any of these attributes (a sign of Clemency) or lose them. In the Neapolitan Luca Giordano's painting *Justice Disarmed* (ca. 1670), an allegory of the Turks taking Crete from Venice, it is Vasari's "Farnese Justice" in reverse, as it were. Though Lady Justice still holds a sword in her hand, Cupid steals the scales from her, and at her feet lie her fasces (with rods pointedly loosened) and a dead ostrich.

The early Baroque period, however, offers a prominent exception to the standard presentation of Lady Justice, not considered by Middeldorf-Kosegarten. It comes in the imposing ceiling fresco of Pietro da Cortona, the *Allegory of Divine Providence and Barberini Power* (1633–1639), in Rome's Palazzo Barberini. In one of the side panels of the ceiling, Hercules fights off the Harpies at the urging of Justice behind to his left, who strides balancing a large axed fasces on her left shoulder but with no other accoutrements. Joined by Plenty (with cornucopia), Justice comes to the aid of beggars ranged below.

This juxtaposition of fasces and cornucopia, which has its roots in the imperial largesse scenes of the second-century CE Roman coinage, becomes common by the last quarter of the seventeenth century as a signifier of the prosperity derived from the proper application of power. A pioneer in this regard was the Habsburg king Charles II of Spain (1674–1700), in his role also as king (since 1664) of Naples and Sicily. In the mid-1680s he minted a stunning silver coin issue where the reverse depicted a crown resting on a large cornucopia and fasces crossed in saltire, themselves set upon a globe showing the Mediterranean area. The legend highlights the two symbols: HIS VICI ET REGNO ("with these I have conquered and with these I reign.") This design is all the more remarkable since, before the French Revolution, money that features the fasces is exquisitely rare.[8]

Perhaps it was bound to happen that mythological figures other than Justice (or her alter ego, the star-maiden Astraea) should lay claim to the fasces. In the earliest seventeenth century we find a representation of Minerva with the kit, and thereafter sporadically; Mars is found with the fasces by the mid-nineteenth century. Personifications of virtues adjacent to Justice (such as Fortitude and Temperance) get it, too. As a symbol of unity and harmony, the fasces also comes to stand for the inviolability of true friendship, as early as the 1650s.

What offers an actual surprise is the Alsatian church of St. Léger in Guebwiller, where the Austro-French architect Gabriel Ignaz Ritter provided among six painted medallions in the wooden choir stalls (1775–1779) a portrait of Moses holding the Ten Commandments, a fasces resting on his left shoulder. In images of Christian martyrs, representations of the fasces are rare, and seem to signify that a given saint was condemned under Roman law. In Christian iconography more generally, fasces appear only in representations of one of the seven gifts of the Holy Spirit—the Spirit of Counsel. Yet her attributes in this regard are not an original invention, but rather derived from those of Lady Justice.[9]

So it is ironic that among monarchies, it was the papacy, starting especially
with Paul III Farnese (1534–1549), that first embraced the fasces as a symbol
of its authority and (ideally) thoughtful application of justice. The emblem is
not widely associated with the personal presentation of secular sovereigns—
even the Holy Roman emperor—in the seventeenth and first three quarters
of the eighteenth century. As noted, Charles II of Naples and Sicily seems to
be the only ruler in this period to place the fasces on his currency, in a limited series of the years 1684–1687. Somewhat surprisingly, kings and emperors
use the emblem sparingly in medallic art as well. A notable exception are the
rulers of Great Britain, where two specimens neatly show the development of
the image. The reverse of a silver medal of 1660 that commemorates the restoration of the Stuart monarchy and the entrance of Charles II into London
shows among its figures Lady Justice, with fasces and scales, extending an olive
branch to a seated personification of Britannia. On the official Royal Mint
medal for the 1727 coronation of George II, Britannia herself leans upon an
axe-less fasces and cradles a cornucopia as she crowns the seated king.[10]

The Fasces of Louis XIV (1689)

One especially significant example of royal fasces art is found in Paris, in the
courtyard of the Musée Carnavalet. It is a bronze full-length portrait statue
(Figure 8.3) on a decorated pedestal, that the French monarch Louis XIV
(born 1638, reigned 1643–1715) commissioned in 1687 from the sculptor
Antoine Coysevox (1640–1720). Coysevox's statue was dedicated on July 14,
1689—100 years to the day before the fall of the Bastille, as scholars have often
noted. The occasion was graced by a grand civic procession; the erection of a
large, ephemeral, octogonal "Temple of Honor" decorated with an extensive
allegorical program glorifying the king; and a fireworks display. Amazingly,
it escaped the systematic destruction of bronze public statues ordered by the
revolutionary Legislative Assembly in August 1792.

For this statue, the king, rendered slightly over life-size, wears a tall contemporary periwig, but is otherwise clothed in the military dress of a Roman
emperor, complete with a muscular cuirass and the field cloak known as a
paludamentum. He is standing, his right hand forward and open, while his left
arm rests on a helmet surmounting an axe-less fasces. Discarded armor, mixed
with music sheets and fruits from a cornucopia, is heaped at his feet, mostly to
his sides and behind. Laurel and palm branches run up the rods of the fasces.

The Roman dress is striking, but not in itself unexpected for the Sun
King. Representations of the monarch in the 1660s and 1670s offer plenty of

FIGURE 8.3. Statue (1687–1689) of Louis XIV of France, by Antoine Coysevox (1640–1720), in the courtyard of the Musée Carnavalet, Paris.

Credit: Lionel Allorge/Creative Commons.

parallels, which cumulatively come off as a heavy-handed effort to communicate imperial achievement.[11] Here there is a marked effort to emphasize specifically the warrior signaling the cessation of conflict, and the fruits of peace. Indeed, a Latin dedicatory inscription on the base addresses him as VICTORI PERPETVO, SEMPER PACIFICO ("perpetual victor, ever peaceful").

Why the addition of the fasces? To be sure, the rods topped with a helmet but without an axe, entwined with foliage, convey the more pacific aspects of the king's justice and authority. But the fasces also surely summons up a concrete historical allusion. The occasion of the sculptor Coysevox's commissioned work was to mark the king's official reconciliation with the city of Paris over the civil unrest of his minority, when Cardinal Mazarin had to face down a series of violent uprisings over the years 1648–1653. This anti-absolutist movement was known as the "Fronde"—French for "sling"—because of the Parisians who protested by slinging rocks through the windows of Mazarin's supporters. No one who knew of these events could disassociate the Fronde from Mazarin, or Mazarin from the fasces. As we have seen, the Roman emblem was an essential and near-ubiquitous element of the cardinal's "brand," culminating with the catafalque at his funeral in 1661. So the decision by Coysevox to reintroduce the fasces in this form, and as an armrest for the king, strikes an effective balance between dominance and generosity, justice and clemency, and an old and new era of governance.

Coysevox was certainly sympathetic to Cardinal Mazarin. After the dedication of his Louis XIV statue, the sculptor turned to realizing Mazarin's mausoleum (1689–1693) in the chapel of the Collège des Quatre Nations (Figure 8.4). The final composition has two kneeling figures in marble at its summit: Mazarin, and, slightly behind him to his left, a putto shouldering the cardinal's trademark fasces, its axe rising above the winged infant's head.[12]

FIGURE 8.4. Statue group for mausoleum (1689–1693) of Cardinal Jules Mazarin, by Antoine Coysevox (1640–1720), in the chapel of the Collège des Quatre Nations, Paris. Musée du Louvre, inv. no. 552.

Though other monarchs proved somewhat reticent about putting too much emphasis on the fasces in the years 1600–1775, numerous lesser political figures in Europe showed no such hesitation. For instance, the Spanish diplomat Diego de Saavedra Fajardo (1584–1648) in his anti-Machiavellian emblem book *Political Maxims: Idea of a Christian Political Prince* (first published in 1640, and dedicated to an eleven-year-old son of King Philip IV) used the fasces to emblematize intergenerational renovation of political elites. Under the motto EX FASCIBUS FASCES ("from the fasces, [more] fasces"), Saavedra depicted a row of four young trees growing in a field where lie unbundled rods with an axe. The rods of the fasces, "the emblem of magistracy," it is explained, when planted, sprout and reproduce.

Dilution of the Fasces as Emblem

In truth, by the mid-seventeenth century, we find the fasces well established throughout Europe as a catch-all symbol for stable and competent governance. There is lavish evidence for the allure that the fasces had on public officials at every level in this era: from ministers of state to mayors and city councilors, especially in Holland and German-speaking zones. These persons incorporated the fasces in various forms and collocations into their portraits and tombs, the buildings in which they officiated (both the exteriors and interiors), even their furniture. By extension, the device was used to commemorate individual laws or legal reforms, treaties, or the concept of administration of government—whether at the local, regional, or national level, in eras present or past.

One might add that eventually the fasces came to symbolize the skillful administration of corporations. In 1749, for example, the Danish Asiatic Company issued a large (42 mm) and heavy (30 g) silver medal to commemorate the 300th anniversary of the royal house of Oldenberg, in the person of Frederik V, king of Denmark and Norway (1746–1766), whose portrait appears on the obverse. Centered on the medal's reverse is an extravagantly crowned "DAC" monogram, set on a triply crossed ensemble of a fasces, a winged caduceus, and a cornucopia, all decorated with floral chain. The power and prosperity of state and commerce here merge as one. Significantly, in the era before the French Revolution, fasces seem entirely absent from actual civic coats of arms, flags, and the like.[13]

By the mid-eighteenth century, iconographic handbooks seem determined to push the fasces' range of reference ever further. Here the French architect and decorator Jean-Charles Delafosse (1734–1789) set a standard of sorts. In 1767 he described, in the preface to his *New Historical Iconology*, his aim to illustrate through imaginative engravings with commentary "the most memorable events from the creation of the world to the present, following the major epochs in both sacred and profane history." But Delafosse goes beyond even that grandiose plan, and supplies images for continents and present-day nations, as well as for concepts, in the Ripa tradition.

The result is an ambitious and original hybrid, a high-concept artists' emblem book, but for interior decorators. Fasces or fasces-like assemblages can be spotted in more than a dozen of the images gathered over seventy-seven plates. That number includes those devoted to Africa (the rationale is that Rome's lictors brought the insignia there when the city waged war on Carthage), and seven different countries, including Portugal (where a wolf is shown dismembering the rods, explained as an allusion to its civil strife in the thirteenth century), but not Holland (despite its contemporary coat of arms with the seven arrows).

Sometimes in Delafosse's work the fasces appears in wildly incongruous contexts, and gets correspondingly tendentious glosses. The Bronze Age? The author explains that they represent the weapons by which man harms himself. Thrace? The reference, we are told, is to the fifth-century BCE king Teres, the region's first lawgiver. The depiction of the elastic topic of "Various Fame"? The fasces here denote "heroes and illustrious sages."

Any educated person will have recognized these as fantasies. Now, alongside the eruption in iconological activity in the early modern period, there was sustained work on the antiquarian aspects of the fasces. Let us note here just two conscientious examples in medallic art, almost two hundred years apart. The impulse to recreate authentic Roman insignia is seen in perhaps its purest form in Renaissance Padua, in the work of engraver Giovanni da Cavino (1500–1570), specifically in his many imitative medals based on Roman coins—among them a Julius Caesar reverse type of the year 44 BCE, with crossed caduceus and axe-less fasces. That, of course, was wholly derivative. However, an astounding original effort to imagine the historical fasces came in 1743, when Jean Dassier, chief engraver to the Republic of Geneva, with his son Jacques-Antoine, produced a series of sixty bronze medals (accompanied by a printed guide) that presented dramatic highlights of Roman history from Romulus to Augustus. Fasces appear in eleven of their scenes from the Republic, with most falling in the period down to the end of the Hannibalic War in 201 BCE. The Dassiers are unusual in their insistence on imagining the fasces in action, with lictors inflicting decapitations on the reverse of the sixth medal of the set (the brutal judgement of Brutus over his sons in 509 BCE) and the obverse of the fifteenth (the execution of Manlius's son, with date given as 339 BCE).

Jean-Charles Delafosse in his pattern book was not the first to plonk down the fasces in patently ahistorical contexts. Already in the earliest sixteenth century—indeed, with Raphael no less—one finds fasces integrated into scenes of trophies or spoils, an image which has no precedent in the visual art of the ancient Romans. Indeed, how would it, unless such a scene were imagined from the perspective of a foreign enemy, or combatants in a civil war? (Interestingly, the Dassiers indulge in precisely that thought experiment, on two of their medals, viewing Roman losses from, respectively, Carthaginian and Parthian perspectives.)

In Raphael, as I have argued, such inconcinnity has a purpose, namely to point up the ephemeral nature of Roman imperial rule. Despite the fact that the image of fasces-as-spoils intrinsically makes no real sense, artists in especially the seventeenth and eighteenth centuries then invoked it again and again, largely in reliefs and ornamental engravings, with no discernible effect on overall meaning. One suspects that the designers did not know or especially care about their inclusion of the rods or axes with other weapons for trophy ensembles. What Delafosse does is arguably worse, precisely because of his strained attempts at elucidating his design choices. Overall his volume attenuates the symbiology of the fasces to the point that in some places they disintegrate into mere decorative objects, void of meaning other than connoting "the antique." It would seem that with the 1760s the fasces had come to the end of its journey as a living emblem.[14]

Popular and Revolutionary Fasces

Fasces on the London Stage (Seventeenth Century)

In August 1747, an anonymous reviewer for the Jesuit *Journal de Trévoux* was cooly picking apart Ben Jonson's *Catiline* (1611), recently abridged and translated into French by Pierre Antoine la Place. One aspect of the tragedy he especially faults is the portrayal of Cicero, whom he says cuts an unimpressive and at times "ridiculous" figure. "In Act III Scene xv. when the conspirators come to stab him, he shows himself at the window and from there makes a harangue. . . . Does a Consul have to throw in his lot with scoundrels? Does he not have lictors who can arrest them?"

The reviewer here is not criticizing Jonson's classical learning (which he considers superior to Shakespeare's), but rather his dramaturgical choices. Indeed, a pair of lictors already had appeared as actual characters in Jonson's comical satire *Poetaster* (1601), handling fasces that show the influence of contemporary English weaponry. At a pivotal point in the plot (IV.2), the magistrate Asinius Lupus is informed that Augustus's daughter Julia, Ovid, and others are staging a mock Olympian banquet at the emperor's court. In response, Lupus gives his attendants the order "Come, / your *Fasces, Lictors*: The half Pikes and the Halberds, / take them down from the *Lares* [i.e., shrine of the household gods], there," to quash this apparent act of treason. Eventually, on order of Caesar himself, they turn on Asinius Lupus, and fit him (appropriately enough, considering his name) with ears of an ass. Lictors took the stage once again in Jonson's *Sejanus His Fall* (1603), where after a trial in the Senate (III.1), a praetor tells them to "resume [i.e., take up] the *fasces*." Since Jonson clearly knew about lictors and their powers of coercion and arrest, the reviewer implies, why not use them in the *Catiline*?

The Fasces. T. Corey Brennan, Oxford University Press. © Oxford University Press 2023.
DOI: 10.1093/oso/9780197644881.003.0009

Looking back at the original London performances of the *Poetaster* and *Sejanus*, it is hard not to ask how those lictors were costumed and equipped. In the *Poetaster*, despite its Roman setting, it seems some characters wore Elizabethan clothing. Were the Lictors among them? Perhaps—contemporary audiences do not seem to have been overly sensitive to anachronisms of this type. But the important thing for our purposes is that Roman-inspired "fasces" (constructed with more emphasis on the blade than the rods, to judge from Jonson's gloss) figured among the stage properties in this play, as well as in the later *Sejanus*, which debuted at the Globe Theater. A year or so later, George Chapman—famed for his translations of Homer—aimed at authenticity in the fasces he prescribed for his *Caesar and Pompey: A Roman Tragedy*. "Enter some bearing Axes, bundles of rods, bare; before two Consuls, Caesar and Metellus," instructs a stage direction (I.1) in the first published (1631) version of the historical tragedy.

Shakespeare alludes to both lictors and their rods in his *Antony and Cleopatra* (ca. 1607). In his *Coriolanus* (between 1605 and 1608) the playwright brought lictors—and one assumes fasces—onto the stage. The rods and axe may have found other public venues, too, at this time. The emblematic figure of Astraea appeared in full costume in one of the street-corner "tableux vivants" organized around the triumphal entry of James I into London in March 1604. Did she hold her characteristic fasces? The dramatist Thomas Dekker is irritatingly coy. "Having tolde you that her name was Justice, I hope you will not put me to describe what properties she held in her hands, sithence every painted cloath can informe you."

One can state with full confidence that when our anonymous French Jesuit reviewer was reading Jonson in the mid-eighteenth century, lictors were an established theatrical convention in historical dramas—and not just those on Roman themes. In 1750, an advertisement for a performance at Aylsham (near Norwich) of Nathaniel Lee's *The Rival Queens* (1677), a play about Alexander the Great, promised that the king's entry into Babylon would feature a grand procession "adorn'd with Drums, Trumpets, Lictors with their Fasces, Trophies, Standard-Bearers, Prisoners of War, and all other pompous Solemnities suitable to the Occasion."

Revivals of *Coriolanus* were particularly loaded with fasces. Thomas Sheridan in his 1754 production at London's Covent Garden conjured up for Coriolanus's return from the field (II.1.156–171, where the First Folio directions describe as attendants only "Captaines, and Souldiers, and a Herauld") a huge triumphal procession that adds lictors, incense-bearers, musicians, and standard-bearers. This most un-Shakespearean spectacle

paved the way for further bloated adaptations. In 1788, a Philadelphia newspaper touted a "Grand Pageant, as performed at London ninety-nine nights
successfully, exhibiting the principal characters of Shakespear." Opening
the event at the Southwark Theatre would be a sequence that included
"ROMAN SOLDIERS—BANNER—FASCES—TROPHIES, S.P.Q.R.,
&c.—CORIOLANUS—[and his mother and wife] Veturia and Volumnia."
The spectacle must have been a most familiar one by the end of the eighteenth
century. In 1795, an anonymous critic pointed up a "strange blunder" in John
Philip Kemble's long-running production of *Coriolanus* at London's Drury
Lane theatre: not the character of the triumphal procession, but the introduc-
tion of "Roman *fasces* in the suite of the Volsian General," i.e., Tullus Aufidius.
To be fair, this error in the story of Coriolanus has ancient authority.[1]

   So we can trace two distinct strands in the reception of the fasces as we
arrive at the crucial date 1789, the year that saw both the United States' new
Constitution take effect (March 4) and in France the opening volley of its
Revolution (July 14). There is, first and foremost, an antiquarian interest in
the "authentic" Roman fasces, which thrived under Renaissance classicism
and naturally found new life under the recent (since ca. 1760) Neoclassicism
movement. Then there is the emblematic tradition, seen most famously in the
Nova Iconologia of Cesare Ripa, which especially in its later manifestations
projected onto the rods and axe a kaleidoscopic range of secondary symbolic meanings quite unknown to the Romans, especially that of unity
and concord. In the seventeenth and eighteenth centuries, western elite
and non-elite persons alike had the opportunity to develop a good visual
sense of both the literal and figurative conceptions of the fasces, thanks
in part to popular entertainments and spectacles, as well as public art (including ephemeral constructions). The role of the theater was especially
powerful in communicating the basic nature and functions of the lictors'
dress and insignia, as living persons wore the historic costumes and carried
the properties and acted the roles, sometimes as speaking characters. Public
art was the main mechanism for disseminating the more complex nuances
of fasces as emblem, though street performances and pageants surely also
played a part.[2]

Fasces and the Young United States

It is primarily through the emblem tradition that the fasces made its way into
the political life of the United States. At first glance, the symbol seems ill-
suited for the independence movement of the thirteen colonies of British

America. We have noted how the personified Britannia had officially acquired a fasces by 1727, the year George II came to the throne. In November 1762 his grandson and successor George III rode to open Parliament in a new state coach adorned with a large gilded Triton at each of its four corners, the two at the rear bearing fasces crowned with tridents, a celebration of British sea power.

To represent an independent America, Thomas Jefferson originally had in mind not the fasces, but the bundle of rods specifically as it featured in Aesopic fable. "A proper device (instead of arms) for the American states would be the Father presenting the bundle of rods to his sons," he wrote in his account book in an entry under the year 1774 (but probably penned in 1776). A proper device required a motto, and here Jefferson suggested "Insuperabiles si inseparabiles" ("insuperable if inseparable"), adapting a phrase from the jurist Sir Edward Coke (1552–1664), his admonition to the British Houses of Parliament to work together. However, others were thinking specifically of the Roman fasces. In the opening weeks of the Second Continental Congress (convened May 10, 1775 in Philadelphia), John Dickinson of Pennsylvania mooted as symbols an "Olive Branch in an armd [*sic*] Hand / Caduceus not on a Wand / but a Roman Fasces."

On July 4, 1776, the Second Continental Congress appointed Jefferson, John Adams, and Benjamin Franklin to design a seal for the new United States. When the committee submitted its report six weeks later, it recommended a different Latin motto on the same theme—*e pluribus unum* ("out of many, one")—to accompany a design in which a main element was a circle of thirteen linked shields representing the states. The Philadelphia artist Pierre Eugène du Simitière (1737–1784) appears to have led the committee to its choice of motto. The direct source was not a classical author (which often has been supposed), but rather a popular British monthly, *The Gentleman's Magazine*, which for decades had used "e pluribus unum" as a catchphrase on its title page, matched with the image of a nosegay of flowers, itself borrowing the idea from a seventeenth-century French publication. But it took some political vicissitudes and significant iconographic revisions for the Congress of the young United States finally, on June 20, 1782, to adopt a definitive national seal. Its obverse design shows, among other elements, an eagle with wings outstretched, clutching in its beak a scroll with the motto "e pluribus unum."[3]

Since at least the publication of the *Nova Iconologia* of Cesare Ripa in 1593, the fasces had been firmly established as a symbol of strength through unity. And so this selection of "e pluribus unum" as the national motto cinched the fasces' future in the United States, notwithstanding its simultaneous exploitation in the United Kingdom.

As the American people fought for and won their independence, two contemporary French artists more or less independently had chosen the fasces as a symbol for the union of thirteen former colonies. When Benjamin Franklin arrived in France in December 1776 as commissioner for the United States, the artist Jean-Honoré Fragonard (1732–1806) honored him with an allegorical drawing titled "To the Genius of Franklin" (1778), which represented the statesman and inventor as an angry Jupiter, with America as a Greek-style civic goddess seated close to his right, her right hand resting on an axe-less fasces lying horizontally on the ground.

And immediately after the Revolutionary War, in 1784 the Virginia General Assembly in Richmond commissioned the Neoclassical sculptor Jean-Antoine Houdon (1741–1828) to create a life-size statue of the state's native son, George Washington (1732–1799), commander in chief of the Continental Army. Houdon began the piece in 1785 (visiting the United States to have Washington model for him), signed it in 1788, finished it in 1791 or 1792, and delivered it from Paris in 1796. In the completed version, Washington wears an American Revolutionary military uniform, but the other attributes of Houdon's work emphasize his return to civil life. He is hatless, and rests his right hand on a walking stick and his left on his general's cloak draped over a tall bundle of thirteen rods forming a fasces, on which also hangs a sword. A plowshare, evoking both the story of the Roman Republican hero Cincinnatus (and with it, Washington's presidency of the Society of Cincinnati, a postwar American officers' club) and the general's occupation as a Virginia planter, rounds out the composition. Yet again, the position of Washington's hand on the fasces, which in this age is first and foremost an emblem of civic authority, ultimately draws inspiration from the 1689 statue of Louis XIV at the Musée Carnavalet in Paris, which also commemorates a leader's triumphant resolution of conflict.[4]

The first prominent appearance in public life of an American fasces well preceded the completion and delivery of Houdon's work. On April 14, 1789, the House of Representatives, just two weeks after achieving its first quorum, adopted a device to be carried by its sergeant-at-arms—specifically a mace (Figure 9.1), patently modeled on the long silver ones used in the British Houses of Commons and Lords since the time of Charles II, and those in several colonial legislative bodies.

The American version was in some respects an expression in three dimensions of the obverse of the new seal, with strong Roman coloring. In

FIGURE 9.1. Mace of the United States House of Representatives. Harris & Ewing, photographer, 1914.

Credit: Harris & Ewing photograph collection, Library of Congress no. 2016866217.

its present incarnation—the British destroyed the original mace when they burned the Capitol in 1814, and a proper replacement came only in 1842—it consists of a bundle of thirteen ebony rods, bound by a silver band that patently emulates the lacing of the Roman fasces. A silver globe is set at the top of the bundle, itself surmounted by a silver eagle with wings half-extended; from the bottom of the rods protrudes a handle, another feature taken from the Roman insignia. This "Mace of the Republic" (as it is sometimes called), about 46 inches in length and 13 pounds in weight, usually stands on a pedestal to the right of the desk of the Speaker of the House. But it has a disciplinary function, too. There have been perhaps a dozen occasions when the Speaker has issued the chilling order for the sergeant-at-arms to pick up and shoulder the mace to restore order among legislators. Almost all these instances belong to the nineteenth century, with none (at time of writing) since 1917. Its effectiveness can be seen from the fact that no sergeant-at-arms yet has had to use it in its essential form, which is that of a club.[5]

French Revolutionary Fasces

A little more than two months after the First Congress of the United States passed its resolution to create a fasces-like mace, France's ancient national assembly of the Estates-General was thrown into tumult. On June 20, 1789, representatives of its (non-privileged) Third Estate took an oath at Versailles not to disband until they had given France a written constitution. This soon led to the recasting (on July 9, 1789) of the national assembly as the Constituent Assembly, whose delegates now effectively took on the governance of the state.

Resistance to the French crown rapidly escalated. In Paris on July 14, 1789, about a thousand insurrectionists stormed and captured the Bastille, a centuries-old royal fortress and prison that stood as a towering symbol of the tyranny of the Old Regime. Two days later, Britain's ambassador to France famously characterized the event "as the greatest revolution that we know anything of," reporting in a dispatch to London that "from this moment we may consider France as a free country, the King a very limited monarch, and the nobility as reduced to a level with the rest of the nation."

Following these almost unthinkable developments, artists quickly developed a new range of emblems to trumpet revolutionary ideals. In the iconological process, the fasces managed to win a privileged place among these revolutionary symbols. As we have seen, in the early modern era the fasces had become increasingly associated with concord and unity. So in late December 1789, when the Constituent Assembly decided to divide France into eighty-three "Departments," it was not much of a conceptual leap to represent the ideal of separate but (ideally) cohesive administrative units as the bundle of a fasces. Another factor in pushing forward the fasces in the sense of cohesion and solidarity must have been the ubiquity of the political slogan "Liberté, Égalité, Fraternité," coined by Robespierre in December 1790. In the subsequent personification of this phrase in the arts, its three elements took the guise of women. In typical representations, Liberty wielded a pike topped with a red "Phrygian cap" that loosely adapted the *pileus*, a symbol of manumission in ancient Rome, while Equality held a level, and Fraternity a fasces.[6]

Yet alongside this distinctly post-classical interpretation of the fasces, the revolutionaries simultaneously will have understood the Roman insignia in its core ancient function, as how ancient magistrates with *imperium* cleared, coerced, punished, and executed, subject only to the popular sovereignty that accorded them this status and its signs. In sum, the Roman fasces recommended itself to the Revolution as the symbol par excellence both of state power and of an indivisible community, of strength and unity.

Indeed, over the decade of the Revolution, the fasces achieved and maintained real iconographic centrality, through the rest of the Constituent Assembly (which issued its Constitution in September 1791), and then the spans of the Legislative Assembly (October 1791–August 1792), the National Convention elected to rewrite the Constitution (September 1792–1795), and the resulting Directory (1795–1799), and indeed into the Consulate (1799–1804) and the Empire of Napoleon I (1804–1815). Over this time, the fasces rapidly developed from a sign of legitimate power and solidarity to a general symbol of the united French people. Significantly, for the first time in the history of any nation, in 1792 the fasces figured in the (provisional but widely circulated) seal of the sovereign state itself.

One did not have to look hard to find fasces in the period of the French Revolution. The political messaging was relentless, across an unprecedented expanse of media. In addition to public art in the form of architectural embellishments, paintings, statues, banners, engravings, and spectacles, says James A. Leith, "the citizen would also come across republican scenes and symbols in books, newspapers, letterheads, ladies' fans, snuff-boxes, playing cards, crockery, and even furniture. Patriotic beds appeared with the posts carved in the shape of fasces or pikes topped with liberty bonnets." Obviously there were consumers for these products, which extended also to calendars, clothes, dishes, and even wallpaper with repeated fasces.

In the visual arts, the French revolutionary fasces can be depicted either with or without an axe. But when the axe is found, it usually protrudes from the top of the bundle of rods. In its developed form, this axe takes the shape of a halberd, with the blade indifferently turned to the left (as in the coat of arms of Mazarin) or right. In contemporary polychrome depictions, the rods or the cords that bind the rods sometime show the new French tricolor combination—blue, white, red—even before it was officially adopted for a new national flag on October 21, 1790. An early and important example of such a colored fasces is the one that divides the two tablets in the official printing of the "Declaration of the Rights of Man," adopted by the Constituent Assembly on August 26, 1789.

Yet many other symbols concurrently entered the Revolution's visual vocabulary, as Leith explains: "the Level, token of equality; the bonnet, indi-
cator of Liberty; the Cockade, emblem of the nation; the pike, weapon of
the free man; the Club, instrument of popular will ... the Oak, mark of re-
birth and social virtue; and the eye, symbol of divinity and watchfulness." In
addition to these signs, one finds a whole range of female personifications
of political concepts: Liberty (enormously important and popular), but also
Reason, Nature, Truth, Virtue, Probity, Force, Union, and Victory, each with
their own attributes. Starting in August 1793, a male figure well known from
mythology encroaches on this coterie of abstractions—Hercules, represented
as the embodiment of strong and forceful popular power.

What is more, all these symbols can be mixed and matched—with no
discernible change in the meaning of the fasces when combined with other
elements. It is especially common to find its top surmounted by the "Phrygian
cap" or red bonnet. The assemblage of fasces plus cap powerfully invoked the
imagined spirit of the early Roman Republic, in its assertion of ideals of liberty and justice against tyranny. But there are many more modifications to
the fasces in this era. A pike, or several, can be tied to its rods, and then ad-
ditionally be topped by a cap. The "hand of justice"—formerly an insignia of
royal power—or one or more spears can replace the axe or pike. Oak leaves,
or laurel, or both, can surround the bundle. Sometimes the Gallic rooster sits
on top of the fasces. Nor does this preclude the introduction of still other
elements into a composition with the fasces, such as law tablets, a cornucopia,
or even a snake (a symbol of sagacity or, when devouring its tail, eternity).
And the fasces can be imagined as a two-dimensional object, e.g., as a device
on a pillar or on a shield.

To complicate matters still further, the revolutionary personifications also
appear with our shapeshifting emblem. Here the most important is Liberty,
standing or seated, in Roman dress, who has as common attributes a staff
surmounted by the Phrygian cap and the fasces. It is this figure which, after
the monarchy is definitively brought down on August 10, 1792, wins pride of
place on the seal of the first French Republic. Yet many other allegorical figures
interact with the fasces in revolutionary iconography, such as Justice (unsur-
prisingly), Reason, the Constitution, Victory, Peace, or (on the state coinage)
the winged Genius of France. One constant, however, is that depictions of
any figure shouldering the fasces are rare. The Revolutionaries do not seem to
have had much interest in the lictors or their functions.[7]

Given these variables, it would take considerable effort to disengage all
the nuances of how the fasces were employed and what they were supposed

to represent in the Revolutionary era—as past meticulous investigations of the Gallic rooster or on the figure of "Marianne" (i.e., the female figure of Liberty) demonstrate. For the fasces, it does seem that the real turning point was the declaration of the Republic on September 22, 1792, and with it, the decision to eliminate any reference to the traditional emblems of the Bourbon dynasty—and indeed, physically to destroy the old state seal that pictured the king, as well as the royal scepter and the crown. Among the first debates in the new National Convention was what new seal to use for its archives. The solution, as many scholars have discussed in detail, was a "feminine civic allegory." In its definitive rendering, the seal shows a woman—widely known as "Marianne"—standing with a pike topped with a cap in her right hand, her left hand resting on a Roman fasces with a lateral axe, a rudder at her feet, with the legend "Au nom de la République Française" ("in the name of the French Republic").

To be sure, the presence of specifically the Roman fasces here is somewhat paradoxical, since the Old Regime extensively used this classical symbol before the Revolution. Indeed, the pose of the woman on the seal, resting her left hand on the fasces, reminds one of the 1689 bronze portrait statue of Louis XIV by sculptor Antoine Coysevox in the courtyard of the Musée Carnavalet. So this symbol of Marianne as Liberty looks both backward and forward, toward the classicizing iconographic tradition of the monarchy, but marking a clear discontinuity with its power structures. Though never officially approved to serve as a national emblem, this seal rapidly found use in all branches of state administration (including in territories occupied by France) and many venues in wider public life. But it also launched an intense debate, sparked in part by some evident unease about the figure's gender.

Immediately after establishing revolutionary government on October 10, 1793, the National Convention made a U-turn on the "Marianne" archival seal it had introduced a year previous. It now decreed that the fasces—"symbol of the union of all the French"—was to find a prominent place alongside the sacred ark of the (July 1793) Constitution on a new national seal and currency. The decision was not implemented. A month later, the Convention changed its mind again, and decreed that the seal should bear the image of a (male) "colossus," the Greek mythological hero Hercules, a symbol of the power of the French people. It then reaffirmed that decision in both February and April 1794. But even that came to nothing, and the essentials of the "feminine civic allegory," including the fasces, persevered, with various vicissitudes, to the present day. It became official in 1848, when Jacques-Jean Barre (1793–1855) engraved a Great Seal for the Second Republic, showing a seated Liberty with radiate crown holding a spear-topped fasces, among other attributes, which is still used. And since 1905, an axed fasces set on branches of oak and laurel has formed the central element of the French Republic's national coat of arms. So in the end, perhaps simply by virtue of its evocative Roman history and general familiarity in France, the fasces won out.[8]

The Fasces on French Coinage of the Revolutionary Era

A truly comprehensive study of the development of the fasces as emblem in this period would involve writing a good bit of the cultural, political, and even military history of the French Revolution. For the essentials, it may be enough to focus our inquiry on a single high-profile context, the dissemination of the fasces in the mass medium of French state coinage. The coins readily show how quickly the fasces claimed an especially commanding place in the Republican imaginary. The coinage, like the debate over the seal, also underlines the instability of the fasces as a symbol in this era, amid so many competing emblems in a tumultuous political culture. Another reason this material is worth special examination is that some of the allegorical types with fasces inspired minters elsewhere, including outside of Europe, and in France saw periodic revivals until the introduction of the euro in 2000. Hence the (unavoidably dry) descriptions I offer here.

For the years 1789 into 1792, the royal mints (there were fully seventeen of them) continued to issue coins with a traditional design of the regime: a portrait bust of Louis XVI on the obverse and a crowned coat of arms of France (or France and Navarre) on the reverse. But in the year 1791, two new basic "Revolutionary" reverse types appear, each somewhat jarringly paired with an obverse portrait of the king, who still was formally head of state.

The origin of the first of the new reverses, for denominations in gold and silver, can be traced to a decree by the National Assembly of January 11, 1791. The resulting competition was won by Augustin Dupré (1748–1833), already noted for his American medal designs commissioned by Benjamin Franklin and Thomas Jefferson, and soon (July 1791) to be appointed France's engraver general of currency. The iconography Dupré chose for the new French reverse is quite involved. Under the legend (in French) "Reign of the Law," the winged Genius of France stands right, inscribing a tablet set on a draped column with the word "Constitution"; she does her carving with a scepter, at the tip of which is an open eye, a symbol of Reason. A diminutive fasces, surmounted by the liberty cap, is set to the Genius's left; and to the figure's right is a small Gallic rooster. The revolutionary date fills the exergue, i.e., the small space beneath the central design. The second of these reverses (decreed May 17–20, 1791), reserved for denominations in copper, has a large axe-less fasces with pike crowned by a Phrygian cap, within an oak wreath; the legend (in French) is "the Nation, the Law, the King," combined with the relevant date of the Revolutionary era. It is noteworthy that Dupré felt compelled to integrate mention of the monarchy in the reverse design.

In the year 1792, coins all show Louis XVI on the obverse, and one of four reverses—two royal (a crowned shield or shields), and two "Revolutionary" (either "au Génie" or the fasces). And though the National Convention abolished the monarchy on September 21, 1792, declared the Republic on the following day, and condemned the king to beheading on January 21, 1793, minting continued of the Louis XVI obverse paired with revolutionary reverses bearing the date "1793 / Year 5 of Liberty." Some of these coins were verifiably struck after the execution of the king.

The times certainly called for a review of the coinage, and a reshuffle came on February 5, 1793, in which the role of the fasces was significantly diminished. On the gold and silver, a simple wreath of oak leaves with the legend "French Republic" now replaced the king's portrait; the Genius of France design (with the small fasces at left) was retained for its reverse. For the copper, the large fasces reverse, with its reference to "the king," was wholly retired. In its place came a new Dupré composition, pointedly stamped on heavy bronze flans manufactured from confiscated church bells. The obverse showed an inscribed tablet with radiant eye above, flanked by grapes and grain-ears; the reverse emphasized justice and equity, in the form of a wreathed scale crowned with Phrygian cap.

These issues were short-lived. The application of the decimal system to currency (set in motion by decrees of August 24 and October 8, 1793) necessitated still another reform, that occasioned the minting of all new designs—including a composition of Dupré that would become his most famous, namely Hercules uniting figures of Liberty and Equality (for the silver 5-franc piece), as well as his head of Liberty in Phrygian cap (for denominations in copper).

There again the decision was made to downplay the fasces. On the actual decimal coinage of the Directory era, the emblem makes just one brief and easily missed appearance, on test strikes for a low-denomination copper piece, dated to the year 1795. This is somewhat puzzling, since the emblem remains popular on contemporary medals, e.g., one celebrating Napoleon's victory in his Italian campaign (1796, with fasces on the shield of Minerva), or another marking the opening of the third session of the Corps-Législatif on May 20, 1798 (with a huge fasces on a podium surmounted by a Phrygian cap, surrounded by attributes of peace and prosperity).

One factor for the Directory in limiting display of the fasces on actual coins may have been that the device had developed an unwelcome association with some Revolutionary financial crisis measures. It probably did not matter much that it appeared in 1791–1792 on several of the *monnaies de confiance*, i.e., unofficial currency privately issued during an urgent coin shortage, only to be outlawed in August 1792. More seriously and immediately, the fasces was memorably engraved on some of the now essentially worthless *assignat* notes. These were first introduced in December 1789 as a type of government bond, but soon functioned as a (continually depreciating) paper currency, printed in mind-boggling volumes. By the time of their suppression in 1797, it is estimated that a total of 1.2 billion notes had been printed (not including counterfeits). On the 400 livres *assignat*, a double-axed fasces with staff and cap positively grabs attention as the central part of the stunning design, which has an eagle as supporting figure. The 50-livres *assignat* features paired double-axed fasces mounted on the face of a large podium for a figurative group. If indeed the fasces was tainted in this way, the Revolution obviously had a large repertoire of patriotic symbols and personifications to serve as substitutes on its coins.

To return to the one trial appearance of the fasces on coinage of the Directory, this is another Augustin Dupré design, for a copper 10-centimes piece. The obverse is dated to Year 3 of the new Revolutionary calendar (i.e., September 22, 1794–September 21, 1795). Here the legend REPUBLIQUE FRANÇAISE encircles a snake, which wraps itself around a club and a bundled fasces, its head appearing at the top of the rods. Its meaning? On this experimental issue, the fasces is most naturally taken as representing union, the club—a hallmark of Hercules—force, and the snake prudence. But what is the source of this unprecedented and rather esoteric concoction?[9]

The story may start with the *monnaies de confiance* of 1791 and 1792. In response to the severe shortfall of low-denomination coins in France, the Brothers Monneron, an enterprising Parisian family firm, minted in England at Birmingham tokens in copper marked with middling monetary values, for re-import to their country. Three of the Monneron brothers were deputies to the National Constituent Assembly, which lent a quasi-formal air to their private initiative.

Two of the Monneron issues, minted in 1792 before the National Assembly finally (on September 3) prohibited the importation and use of tokens, would seem to show a crucial advance in the Revolutionary iconography of the fasces. The obverse for a 5-sol token, based most immediately on a design by state engraver Augustin Dupré, sets an elaborate scene (Figure 9.2). Hercules is pictured on a seashore, with ships in the distance, seated right on the skin of the Nemean lion, struggling to break a set of (axe-less) fasces over his knee. His trademark club is propped by his side, a statue base is seen behind. The legend reads LES FRANÇAIS UNIS SONT INVINCIBLES ("the united French are invincible"), and (in French) "Year IV of Liberty" in the exergue. A lower value (2-sol) token has the same basic composition, but Hercules successfully splintering a scepter with the legend LA SAGESSE GUIDE LA FORCE ("wisdom guides force"), and (in French) "the end of despotism" in the exergue.

To the casual eye, these paired tokens offer a startlingly assertive Revolutionary message, on the power of popular unity, and the superiority of the fasces to the royal emblems of the Old Regime. The connections of the Monneron brothers, and their use of a Dupré design in this durable medium, suggests a major moment in the organized political communication of the Revolutionary era. The choice of Hercules as the central figure would seem to anticipate by at least a full year his rise to prominence in the symbological apparatus of the Republic.

So what is the meaning of the seashore and ships? As it turns out, the Hercules type with the bundle of rods is completely derivative, and dates back to the reign of Louis XIV. As early as 1662 and up to the late 1780s,

FIGURE 9.2. Bronze 5-sol token, Brothers Monneron, 1792 (Hennin 435). On obverse, Hercules with club and lion skin behind, makes futile efforts to break a bundle of rods.
Credit: Bertolami Fine Arts Auction 9, Lot 2129 (April 29, 2014).

the Six Corps of Merchants—a Parisian society of merchants' guilds established in the Middle Ages—had used for the reverse of its jetons precisely
this depiction of Hercules with the Latin motto VINCIT CONCORDIA
FRATRUM ("the unity of brothers prevails"). A portrait bust of the reigning
king adorned the obverse. Well before the French Revolution—apparently
in 1776—the Corps had contracted with the engraver Dupré to update the
reverse image, but evidently it was never produced. The Monneron Brothers
simply bought the die from Dupré, and worked with the Birmingham mint
of Matthew Boulton to tweak the design for the revolutionary market. In
Britain, the Hercules pattern later (1820) found its way even onto a test strike
by the Royal Mint during the transition between George III and IV.

Despite its distinctly regal roots, the rebranded Hercules-with-rods seems
to have fired French political imaginations. On August 10, 1793—the first anniversary of the fall of the monarchy—the artist Jacques-Louis David (1748–
1825) masterminded a street festival with four "stations" meant to illustrate
the progress so far of the Revolution. The fourth and culminating station involved a colossal ephemeral statue of Hercules on the Esplanade des Invalides.
A contemporary engraving by Paillard de Villeneuve (1751–1828) pictures this
creation, with the caption "The French People Overwhelming the Hydra of
Federalism"—an elastic term, but essentially denoting all those who opposed
the sovereignty of the Departments. The colossal figure (said to have topped
seven meters) stands on a mound, where he rests his left arm on an axe-less
fasces; with his right he raises a club over a half-human, half-serpent monster,
lying vanquished at his feet. The monster's right arm pathetically clutches at
the transverse binding of the rods.

Fortunately, we have David's own description to the Club of Jacobins
from July 19, 1793, of the sculpture as he planned it, which serves as a salu-
tary reminder of the difficulties in interpreting Revolutionary iconography
from visual appearances alone. "In the middle of the square" of the Place des
Invalides, explains David, "on the top of a mountain, the French People will be
represented in sculpture by a colossal figure, with its vigorous arms bringing
together the Departmental fasces; ambitious Federalism rises from its muddy
marsh, with one hand pushing aside reeds, with the other forcing itself to de-
tach some portion [sc. of the bundle of rods]. The French people see it, take its
club, strike it, and force it back into its stagnant waters, never to re-emerge."

This "fourth station," when executed, certainly caused a sensation. On
November 17, 1793, the Convention resolved that David sculpt in bronze a
permanent colossus twice that size for the Pont-Neuf, and voted to enshrine
its image as a new state seal. Dupré prepared a sketch for the seal, which shows

an enormous Hercules, resting on his club, and holding both Marianne and a personified Justice in miniature, standing close together in his giant right hand. None of this saw realization. Nor did Dupré's 1794–1795 coin design pairing Hercules's club with the fasces make it into circulation.

Of course, Hercules had no real connection with either the Aesopic bundle of sticks or the Roman fasces. So it seems worth suggesting that the traditional Six Corps jeton, via its repurposing in 1792 by a Birmingham mint, at least partially inspired David's 1793 allegory on the collective power and indivisible unity of the French people. No other image of the idiosyncratic pairing of Hercules with the fasces was so immediately before the eyes. In David's sculpture, the gesture of the colossus's right hand, which rests on the fasces, derives directly from the pose of Liberty on the seal of 1792—which in turn, as we have seen, draws inspiration from a 1689 grand public statue in Paris of Louis XIV.[10]

Despite the efforts of David and Dupré, the Hercules type does not seem to have found much of an export market. When the revolutionary governments of Italy in 1797–1804—the various "Republics" that sprung up in Naples, Rome, the Piedmont region, and Venice—chose the iconography of their flags and coins, they consistently returned to the French freestanding fasces. Here the reverse type of the fasces surmounted by a Phrygian cap, in use on copper coinage in the years 1791–1793, and on the military flags of France's Demibrigades since 1796, proved particularly influential.

The Impact of French Revolutionary Fasces

Naturally there were adaptations of the French archetypes. Most striking is a design found on the money of the fleeting first Roman Republic (February 15, 1798–September 30, 1799). There the obverse shows an eagle with outstretched wings, within an oak wreath, standing on an axed fasces which is placed horizontally on an altar, behind which are flags crossed in saltire. The altar bears reliefs of a dagger and liberty cap, images derived directly from the reverse of Brutus's famous "Ides of March" denarius of 42 BCE. The short-lived Roman Republic of 1849 also made much of the basic wreathed eagle with fasces motif in its struggle against the rule of the Papal States, as did the coalition that fought for the unification of Italy (fully achieved in 1870).[11]

In the New World, starting in 1791 the official coinage of the French colony of Saint-Domingue on the Caribbean island of Hispaniola had mirrored the copper Revolutionary fasces reverse types. But the fasces could also signify revolution against the Republic. In 1802, in the Haitian War of Independence against Napoleonic France, the government of Toussaint Louverture introduced on the obverse of its coinage a standing Liberty whose right hand rested on an axed fasces, and left held a pike with cap. This came in the year after the promulgation of a new Constitution and shortly before Louverture's arrest and death. Henri Christophe (1767–1820) continued this basic type when he formed the independent northern State of Haiti in 1807. As president, in 1807 and 1808 he minted at Cap Haitien coins featuring a haunting Liberty with the same attributes of fasces and pike, but in the opposite hands, and tipping the bundle as if to ready it for deployment. The reverse of this issue featured Christophe's monogram at center, a precocious indication of his autocratic style (in 1811 he would be proclaimed as king of Haiti). A more conventional (axed) fasces capped with a liberty hat appeared on Haitian coins of its First Republic period (1825–1849).

The spirit of the revolutionary types with fasces also had a certain influence in the Americas beyond France's colonies in the New World, finding a place on the coinage of Mexico (in its First Republic period, 1823–1863) and Ecuador (soon after its Republic was declared in 1830). Consider also Chile, which asserted its full independence from Spanish rule in 1818. The medal that celebrated its "liberal" Constitution of 1828 showed on its obverse an anchor with its shank rendered as the bound rods of a fasces, a clever and original symbol conveying, as the legend in Spanish tells us, UNION SEGURIDAD FUERZA ("unity, security, force")—aspirations for stability

FIGURE 9.3. Low-denomination bronze coin (2 baiocchi) of Roman Republic of 1798–1799. Obverse shows fasces surmounted by a Phrygian or liberty cap (Latin *pileus*), borrowing French revolutionary iconography.

Credit: Bertolami Fine Arts E-Auction 32, Lot 1081 (November 1, 2016).

dashed by the civil war of 1829–1830. On the gold coins of Chile during the subsequent Republican era (1831–1891), the predominant image after 1839 was that of a personified Liberty (with attributes of Minerva) with one hand on an (axe-less) fasces arranged with cornucopia, and the other on the country's Constitution of 1833. The accompanying legend reads IGUALIDAD ANTE LA LEY ("equality before the law"). It is noteworthy that, despite two Liberal revolutions against the ruling autocratic Conservative faction (1851, 1859), followed by the Liberals themselves decisively gaining the upper hand in 1861, this iconography stayed the same until the civil war of 1891 brought this period of the Republic to a close.[12]

Napoleon and the Fasces

But to return to France, the odd tale of the Republican Hercules and his fasces gets an epilogue of sorts, under Napoleon Bonaparte. Napoleon's coup of November 9–10, 1799 (18 Brumaire of Year VIII in the Revolutionary calendar) overthrew the Directory, and ushered in a new form of government, known as the Consulate. What followed needs only a quick summary. A new Constitution adopted on December 13, 1799 (22 Frimaire) handed over the government to three consuls, of whom Napoleon as first consul held all effective power. A plebiscite of February 7, 1800, legitimated the Brumaire coup; subsequent legislation provided that the three consuls received their positions for life (August 4, 1802). But soon the system of the Consulate was abolished (May 18, 1804) to make way for the Empire, formally inaugurated with Napoleon's coronation on December 25, 1804. And so France became an authoritarian state—and in its official iconography, Napoleon ended up decentering all the allegorical figures of the Revolutionary era, including those representing the French people themselves.

One would think that the government of the "Consulate" would exploit the Roman insignia of rods and axe. Sure enough, a fasces framed by laurel decorated the cover of contemporary printed versions of the new 1799 Constitution. And in the weeks following the 18 Brumaire coup, the painter Antoine-Francois Callet (1741–1823), formerly an official portraitist of Louis XVI, started a grand work, *Allegorical Painting of 18 Brumaire year VIII or France Is Saved*, in which Hercules appears with the sort of tall and thick axe-less fasces that in Republican iconography typically symbolizes the Departments. Callet exhibited a sketch of the composition in Paris at the Salon of 1800, and—almost certainly with the encouragement of the new consuls—a finished version at the Salon of the following year. Thankfully, the

Salon catalog of 1801 (no. 49) offers an explanation of the complex imagery of Callet's large painting.

The work is divided into two registers, light and dark, portraying how "Discord flees at the first rays of a new dawn," according to the catalog entry. Above, bathed in brilliant light, the victorious female figure of France (with facial features of Napoleon Bonaparte) holds aloft an olive branch of peace. She is supported by a dynamic cluster of figures that stand for the fifteen armies of the Republic. Close to her side stands, apart from all the others, a pharaonic figure symbolizing the Army of Egypt, which Napoleon commanded in 1798–1799. The scene in the lower register is hard to make out, due to Callet's aggressively dark tones. The Salon catalog identifies a ship loaded with cultural plunder from Italy and captured enemy military banners as "the vessel of state arriving in port." To the right, a huge Hercules stands on a rock, embracing a bundle that extends almost his full height. He represents the government of the Consulate, we are told, crushing with his feet and his club monsters who are the enemies of order and of peace, which include a leopard symbolizing Great Britain.

For all of Hercules's heroic efforts, it is Napoleon who dominates the composition—indeed, completely. Jérémie Benoît argues that in Callet's painting, "the lower register [is] that of reality, in contrast to the upper level reserved for power or ideas. Hercules, the image of the people in revolutionary discourse, thus has become the executor of the great works of France. He no longer has power. . . . The political overthrow is complete."

Yet the contemporary reception of Callet's allegorical work on the coup was almost uniformly negative, ranging from puzzled incomprehension to hostile dismissal. One critic termed its ambitious allegory an "omlette soufflée." Callet in his painting on Napoleon's alleged salvation of France undoubtedly aimed to assign Hercules and his fasces to a second order of importance. What happened is that under the remainder of the Consulate and the First Empire, allegorical painting fell out of official favor altogether.[13]

Certainly, the Republican-style fasces did not altogether fade under Napoleon. Fasces with laurel, accompanied by the initials "R. F." (= République Française), figure on a revamped flag for the infantry introduced in March 1803. The fasces on the medals of the Napoleonic era are also common enough. But they hardly ever occur in contexts that refer directly to his deeds as first consul or emperor, with just a few such significant appearances of the emblem on the more than 900 types known for the years 1799–1809. Probably the most significant expression of the fasces in the First Empire came in the decorative arts. Gilt fasces-legged console tables designed by Pierre-Louis-Arnulphe Duguers de Montrosier (1758–1806) mark an early expression of a fashion where in Empire style the Republican political symbol par excellence is transmuted into one design element among many.[14] Nor do fasces figure much in France for three decades after Napoleon, under the Bourbon Restoration (1814–1830) or the Orleans Monarchy (1830–1848). Against this background, the decision by the Second Republic of 1848 to make the fasces a central symbol of the nation seems designed to broadcast a revival of original Revolutionary ideals, akin to its adoption of "Liberty, Equality, Fraternity" as an official motto.

IO

American Fasces

Prologue: Fasces and the Lincoln Memorial (1922)

It would be "the greatest and costliest monument ever erected by any Republic to the memory of one man," wrote poet Dallas Williams in 1920, of the Lincoln Memorial, then nearing completion in Washington, DC. The idea had been long in the works. Not quite two years after the assassination of the sixteenth US president (April 14, 1865), Congress established a Lincoln Monument Association for the creation of a grand sculptural group. But its hasty choice of a complicated design by the unpopular sculptor Clark Mills (1815–1883), and failure to procure the necessary funds, eventually doomed the original project. Efforts, however, continued, which led most importantly to the identification (1901) of a plausible site, in Potomac Park, on the western axis of the National Mall, looking east toward the Washington Monument and the Capitol building. In February 1911, Congress formed a new Lincoln Memorial Commission, and granted it a $2 million budget, with a mandate to decide on a plan and start construction immediately.

It still took more than a decade (and an additional million dollars) to complete the temple-like monument designed by the selected architect, Henry Bacon (1866–1924). On its dedication on Memorial Day (May 30) 1922—fifty-seven years after Lincoln's death—the Commission chair, Chief Justice and former US President William Howard Taft, termed it "the culmination of the highest art of which America is capable." Not all critics agreed. Harvard architecture dean Joseph Hudnut later opined that the structure, "coldly cribbed from the Parthenon, canopying ... an enormous statue of Lincoln, is a curious ornament for a French garden," i.e., the urban vision of the L'Enfant Plan (1791) for the heart of the nation's capital.

The Fasces. T. Corey Brennan, Oxford University Press. © Oxford University Press 2023.
DOI: 10.1093/oso/9780197644881.003.0010

What there is no denying is the lasting popular appeal of the monument. The white marble Memorial, with its ascending series of platforms, tall fluted Doric exterior columns, broad façade, and distinctive recessed attic, is one of the most instantly recognizable architectural works of the twentieth or any century. It also perennially has ranked among the ten most-frequented monuments in the world, with close to eight million annual visitors in the years 2015–2019. The currency of the United States has played a crucial role in disseminating the image of the monument. Since 1929, the Lincoln Memorial has been pictured on the back of the five-dollar bill. Between 1959 and 2008, it featured also on the reverse of the one-cent piece, with the legend "E Pluribus Unum" placed above.[1]

The Lincoln Memorial is on the whole an austere affair, with the bulk of the exterior decoration found high up, above the colonnade, on the friezes and cornices, the work of sculptor Ernest C. Bairstow (1876–1962). So it is all the more striking that in the approach from the main plaza to the entrance, up a series of stairs and platforms, the first and only architectural sculpture that the visitor encounters at eye level is an enormous pair of axed fasces. They are carved in low relief, more than 3 meters in height, one on each of the eastern faces of the huge cheek walls that frame the base of the final sequence of stairs. These are clearly Americanized fasces. Each shows thirteen rods in a binding, suggesting the union of the thirteen original states. And atop each of the axeheads that extend inward from the upper side of their bundles is the head of a bald eagle. Huge tripods surmount each of the staircase walls; they are matched to the size of the fasces and serve to accentuate them further.

The interior of the Lincoln Memorial is divided into three chambers— north, south, and central, separated by tall Ionic columns, with a ceiling 60 feet (18.3 meters) in height. Here the fasces appear explicitly or implicitly many more times. On the main wall of the north chamber one finds the inscribed text of Lincoln's Second Inaugural Address (March 4, 1865), set in three tall columns of thirty-five lines. A bundle of thirteen rods in low relief, an eagle at its base, stands at either side of the inscription, carved by Evelyn Beatrice Longman (1874–1954) to run the full height of the lettering.

Above the Address is a long (18.3 m × 3.6 m) canvas mural painted by Jules Guerin (1866–1946) entitled "Unity," an allegorical composition that at its center shows, among many figures, the "Angel of Truth" reconciling representations of the American North and South. Punctuating the scene are about a dozen and a half slender, gnarled trunks of cypress trees, suggesting again and again the shape of an axed fasces as they appear and disappear amid stylized foliage.

On the opposite wall in the south chamber, a second Guerin mural, "Emancipation," tops another engraved Lincoln text, the Gettysburg Address (July 3, 1863). In this painting, the focus is on the "Angel of Truth" freeing enslaved Blacks, amid a similarly large number of fasces-trees. On the left side of the "Emancipation" mural, a wreathed female figure with sword and scroll—the personification of Justice—sits on a wide throne for which an axe-less fasces forms the front of each armrest.

The central chamber of the Memorial displays the centerpiece of this secular temple, the famed sculpture (1918–1922) of a seated Abraham Lincoln designed by Daniel Chester French, imposing in size (5.8 m in height), and itself set on a 3-meter-high pedestal. The president's tall (3.8 m), wide chair closely resembles that of Justice in Guerin's mural, with each arm composed of a fasces. Lincoln's clenched left hand hangs over the top of one axe-less bundle, while his right hand rests in an open gesture directly on top of the other fasces, conveying (it is often remarked) simultaneously determination and compassion.

"Repeated throughout the memorial, the fasces reveal the higher meaning of the Lincoln Memorial and the way the memorial's designers meant to honor Abraham Lincoln. It is the 'theme of the memorial.'" The source of this bold, overarching interpretation? The official website of the United States National Park Service (NPS). Indeed, the NPS makes the case that "the Lincoln Memorial's symbolic use of fasces" is "the unifying feature of the memorial," one that "emphasizes the importance of the union of the states and Lincoln's role in preserving that union."

And that is not the end of the claims by the NPS. "The implication" of the collocation on the US penny of E PLURIBUS UNUM with the façade of the Memorial "is that the entire structure is a representation of the fasces, a representation of strength through unity, a monument not only to Lincoln but to the Union itself." Ironically, it is noted that "this symbol is so overlooked that, even when pointed out, many observers will not recognize it."

More is the pity. For as the NPS further explains, the image of the fasces "symbolizes the very idea of our nation: that many states bound together form one nation, and out of many people come one nation. Each wooden rod is breakable individually, but bound together they are strong. Each state is weaker individually, but bound together by the Constitution, they are stronger."[2]

Fasces and George Washington

We have seen that this theme of the fasces representing unity was quite unknown to the ancient Romans. But it was current among the elite political class in the young United States in the 1770s and 1780s, as our discussion of the relationship of the fasces to Jefferson, Franklin, Washington, and the first sergeant-at-arms of the House of Representatives demonstrates. So how then did American artists of the early twentieth century come to take this understanding of the symbol not just as a valid interpretation of the fasces— alongside autonomy, justice, and the rule of law—but indeed the predominant one?

One factor that must have facilitated public awareness of the fasces as a political symbol was its prominence in the cult of America's first president, George Washington. Here Jean-Antoine Houdon's sculptural portrait (signed 1788) of a relaxed Washington with a shoulder-height fasces was decisive for other artists' depictions of the war hero and statesman during his two terms of office (1789–1797). Examples are numerous, across a range of media, and almost all emphasize Washington's role as civilian leader.

In a 1793 design for the United States Capitol, architect Stephen Hallet sketched a pediment for the central portico that syncretized the Roman dictator Cincinnatus with Washington, seated with the fasces at his feet. In Gilbert Stuart's 1796 full-length portrait of Washington (known as the Landsdowne portrait, after its first owner), the president is shown in contemporary dress but gesturing in the manner of a Roman orator, his right hand extended over a table whose one visible leg is formed of an axe-less bundle of rods topped by an eagle. Later, the reverse of English engraver Thomas Halliday's "Presidency Relinquished" medal for Washington—dated "1797" but struck in 1816—displays a sheathed sword, an axed fasces, and a branch of oak arranged on a draped pedestal bearing a United States shield.

Such pacific and polite representations of the fasces were in fact the norm in memorials to George Washington after his death in 1799. In an 1806 engraving for the Society of Cincinnati, John Eckstein depicted Washington in uniform, standing upon a pedestal; at the president's side is a fasces leaning against a tree trunk on which hangs his officer's hat. Quite different in approach is the French architect Joseph-Jacques Ramée's unsuccessful design (1813) for a Washington monument in Baltimore, which took the form of a triumphal arch with the fasces shown high up on its façade in twin trophy tableaus.[3]

Fasces and the Military of the Early United States

None of this is likely to have generated much actual passion for the fasces as a political symbol. A different matter was the early decision to import contemporary French Revolutionary iconography, including the fasces, into the American military sphere. Crucial for this development was the Naval Act of March 1794, that commissioned the building of the nation's first six frigates—to be named the *Chesapeake, Constitution, President, United States, Congress,* and *Constellation.* The *Constitution*—launched 1797, and soon winning fame as "Old Ironsides"—boasted a figurehead on its stern described by its designer, sculptor William Rush (1756–1833) of Philadelphia, as "an Herculean figure standing on the firm rock of Independence resting one hand on the fasces, which was bound by the Genius of America and the other hand presenting . . . the Constitution of America . . . the foundation of Legislation." As we have seen, the odd collocation of Hercules and the fasces entered the visual vocabulary of French politics in 1792, and then took root. A watercolor depiction of the frigate *Constitution* at sea ca. 1803 by painter Michele Felice Corné (1752–1845) provides enough detail for us to see that Hercules rested his left hand on the fasces, in the now-expected manner.

Another of these first frigates, the *President* (launched 1800), sported fasces ornaments at both head and stern, perhaps also by Rush. A contemporary account describes the head as bearing "the Bust of our late President Washington, supported by two female figures, Truth and Justice, standing on a Rock . . . the figure of Truth holding in her right hand the mirror of Prudence, and the left resting on the fasces, the emblem of Union; on her head a wreath of palm." Elsewhere in the composition, the "American Eagle" darted "thunder and lightning at the Hydra, the emblem of anarchy and confusion," as we have amply seen in French allegorical art of the mid-1790s. On the stern, in an equally elaborate scene, was depicted "the figure of America . . . at her feet the American fasces, erect, supported by the standards of the army and navy." The personified America was flanked by figures of Wisdom and Strength, the latter shown with her left hand "resting on a Herculean club." So already one could claim to pick out "the American fasces" from such a crowded (and derivative) ensemble of images.

Not all, however, found this French-influenced iconographic program compelling. In November 1799 the final details of another frigate, the USS *City of Philadelphia,* constructed by private funds, with carving again by William Rush, prompted a puzzled reaction by one newspaper journalist. "Her head which is an Hercules with his attendant emblems, has lately been put up," remarked the report, "a very handsome piece of sculpture; though we question the legitimacy of one of the emblems, which is the Roman fasces in the left hand of the figure, intended to represent the American union."

It is a pity that we cannot view these early artistic representations of the fasces for ourselves. During the First Barbary War (1801–1805), the *USS Philadelphia* was captured by Tripolitans off the North African shore (October 1803), only to be reboarded and deliberately torched by Americans (February 1804). Though the *Constitution* is still very much extant and moored in Boston, its original Hercules figurehead was smashed to bits in September 1804, when the ship collided with the *USS President* while on patrol off Tripoli. The *President* itself fell into British hands in 1815 and was broken up in 1818.

In the summer of 1807 the *Constitution*, now looking toward the end of its service in the Mediterranean, made call at Livorno in Italy, where it picked up 51 crates weighing 15 tons, filled with elements in Carrara marble of what would be the first military memorial in the United States. This was the work of Tuscan sculptor Giovanni Carlo Micali (died 1821), who was privately commissioned by US Navy Commodore David Porter to commemorate six naval officers killed in the First Barbary War. When assembled, the parts of the Tripoli Monument would form a 9-meter-tall Roman "rostral" column displaying ship rams, topped by an American eagle (armed with a shield and decked in a scroll inscribed E PLURIBUS UNUM), surrounded by allegorical figures. Among the personifications is an America, represented by a partially naked Native American woman accompanied by two cherubic male children, one of whom is bearing a small axe-less fasces. In 1814, this part of the monument came in for savage criticism by the famed architect Benjamin Henry Latrobe (1764–1820): "this is a badly imagined and executed figure, and has nothing of the native American character or costume." This particular iconographic experiment of pairing a Native American (since the sixteenth century a traditional symbol of America) with the fasces would not be repeated.

In its first decades, the Tripoli Monument found little love. On its arrival in the United States, Congress refused even to waive port duties for the marble creation, and furthermore declined to allocate funds for its erection. It was set up in 1808 at the Washington Navy Yard, very much as a stopgap. There it was vandalized during the War of 1812. Matters improved starting in 1831, when the large memorial migrated to the west terrace of the US Capitol, facing the Mall. Finally in 1860 it was moved to the US Naval Academy in Annapolis, where it stands today.[4]

A more consequential and indeed exciting reification of the American fasces came in the year 1815, with a competition to design the first public war monument in the United States. The object was to memorialize the thirty-nine citizens of Baltimore who died in the defense of Fort McHenry against the British on September 12–14, 1814—the same battle that Francis Scott Key immortalized in his patriotic anthem "Star-Spangled Banner." The French-born artist and self-taught architect Maximilian Godefroy (1765–1840) submitted three designs to a committee headed by the mayor of Baltimore. On March 25, this group chose Godefroy's most allegorical submission, a plan for what he termed a "Fascial Monument," with its base standing 39 feet (11.9 meters) tall to support a colossal female statue (Figure 10.1).

The French Revolutionary and even Napoleonic influences on this communal monument are striking. The base, a tall cenotaph in an Egyptianizing style—a first for the United States—supports a thick axe-less bundle of many rods, reminiscent of representations of the eighty-three Departments of France in Revolutionary art. A neoclassical statue at top, by Canova's student Antonio Capellano (1780–1840), would personify a victorious Lady

FIGURE 10.1. Battle Monument (1815–1825) by Maximilian Godefroy (1765–1838), Monument Square, North Calvert Street between Fayette and Lexington Streets, Baltimore, as seen in 1846. Photographed by John Plumbe (1809–1857).

Credit: Daguerrotype collection, Library of Congress, no. 2004664424.

Baltimore holding a wreath. In the end the memorial would cost $60,000—over twenty times the budget for the earlier Tripoli Monument—drawing on both public and private funds.

The first printed description of the architect Godefroy's eclectic design, published in the news press just a few days after the committee's decision, praises it as a "classical and dignified commemoration." But it also suggests that the "ingenious" architect's choice of a giant fasces as the "principal and characteristic part of the monument" was exciting because it was so unfamiliar, at least on this scale. "A circular Fasus [*sic*], in marble, 18 feet high, will rise . . . as a symbol of the Union," we are told. The column's top register was ornamented with wreaths of laurel and cypress, signs of glory and mourning. Godefroy had employed fasces as architectural decoration on previous work in Baltimore. But this choice of introducing a giant-sized fasces—at that point surely the largest ever rendered—to symbolize the United States was precisely what made Godefroy's Battle Monument so original.

The newspaper report notes a further crucial aspect. "On the fillets of the Fasus will be inscribed the names of those men [whom] valor and gratitude have thus immortalized." The listing of both enlisted men and (above their names, between the wreaths) three officers on a war memorial was democratic and new. "Because of their glorious death," reads an inscription on the actual monument, "they strengthened the bonds of the union."

Unlike the Tripoli Monument, imported from Italy to mark a far-off conflict against Libyan pirates, Godefroy's "Fascial Monument" commemorating the valor of Baltimoreans against the British instantly caught the imaginations of the public. On the Battle's first anniversary, September 12, 1815, a procession of dignitaries paraded a model of the "Fascial" creation through the streets before laying the monument's cornerstone in a central square, next to the city's new (1809) courthouse. An 1816 engraving of the design received nationwide circulation; American, British, and French critics alike later would chime in with their (mostly favorable) impressions of Godefroy's work. The Battle Monument was dedicated on September 12, 1822, and finally completed in 1825. Two years later, the city chose the image of the Lady Baltimore statue for its municipal seal.[5]

Fasces and the United States Capitol

About this time, the fasces reached the very center of the US Capitol. The building was begun in 1793, was burned by the British in 1814, and after 1818 was entering a new phase of construction. A heroic sculpture group in plaster by young Italian-born artist Enrico Causici (1790–1833), *Genius of the Constitution*, executed in the years 1817–1819, was placed in a niche on the south wall of what is now the National Statuary Hall, but what was then the chamber of the House of Representatives. The female Genius (commonly misidentified as "Liberty") stands with the scroll of the Constitution in her right hand, an American eagle to her right. To her left is an ingenious and perhaps wholly original creation: a bundle of rods in which a rattlesnake— in the American context, a symbol of fierce independence—serves as the cord that binds the fasces. It was also decided that long axe-less fasces would form the vertical moldings of frames of the monumental paintings for the new Rotunda; the first four of these, by John Trumball (1756–1843), por- tray the signing of the Declaration of Independence and high points of the Revolutionary War (commissioned 1817, realized 1819–1824).

Capitol architect Charles Bulfinch (1763–1844) planned to use the motif still more extensively for the ornamentation of the Rotunda, on a relief sculp- ture above the door, and also for the main (east) pediment. But in each in- stance, he hit snags. The diary of the sixth president of the United States, John Quincy Adams (who served 1825–1829), sheds valuable light on this process of give-and-take in the design of a "Genius of America" sculptural group for the pediment—and his support of growing resistance to the emblematic tra- dition and the iconography of the French Revolution.

For May 31, 1825, Adams records a meeting with Bulfinch and sculptor Luigi Persico (1791–1860), who in a competition for the pediment had submitted what was evidently the least objectionable proposal of more than thirty submissions. Persico's rendering showed "a personification of the United States standing on a throne, leaning upon the Roman fasces, surmounted with the cap of Liberty, with Justice at her right hand, blindfolded, holding the sus- pended balance, and in the other hand an open scroll, and Hercules at her left, seated on a corner of the throne, embracing the fasces, and emblematic of strength." Representations of Plenty and Peace rounded out the composition.

Adams had a superior knowledge of the arts, and he was eager to settle on a final design for the Capitol pediment, for which a crowded competition had not yielded a satisfactory solution. Yet the president in response merely substituted his own allegorical scheme, albeit one that foregrounded reli- gious and literal political elements over classical allusions. He advised that Plenty and Peace "should be discarded, as well the Roman fasces and the cap of Liberty." Instead of Hercules ("too much of the heathen mythology for my taste"), Adams suggested "a figure of Hope, with an anchor—a Scriptural image." Then, in place of the fasces, Adams proposed a pedestal inscribed with the dates of the signing of the Declaration of Independence (July 4, 1776) and the first day of government under the Constitution (March 4, 1789).

The resulting sense? "The American Union" established by these founding documents, "supported by Justice in the 12–14 past, and relying upon Hope in Providence for the future." Adams was well aware of the difficulties his trio might cause for interpretation, and so advised an accompanying inscription to "explain the meaning and moral to dull comprehensions." In actualizing the group over the next three years, Persico closely followed Adams's instructions, flanking the Genius with Justice (without blindfold) and Hope, and not a fasces in sight. The explanatory text was never added.[6]

Though the fasces narrowly failed to find a spot on the east pediment of the Capitol (completed 1828), the emblem soon became inescapable in more quotidian political contexts. For example, in the run-up to the 1840 presidential election, the Whig party of the successful candidate, William Henry Harrison, leveraged the fasces on campaign broadsides and ribbons to illustrate its new slogan "union for the sake of the Union." The phrase was coined on July 4, 1839, by Virginia congressman Henry Wise (1806–1876) in an appeal to the party to close ranks behind a single candidate, and (as it was soon interpreted) to put aside internal differences on questions of a national bank, Masonry, and even abolitionism. Harrison died after just one month in office, in early April 1841. But the motto stuck, as did the iconography: in 1844, at the Whig National Convention in Baltimore, a banner promoting the party's candidate Henry Clay (1777–1852) and his commitment to a strong Union was suspended by a fasces. But by the mid-1840s, nativist groups were using the fasces, too, to symbolize their conception of unity—against immigrants.[7]

As the question of abolition of slavery became more pressing, and anxieties about the stability of the Union grew, the fasces proliferated. The neoclassical sculptor Hiram Powers (1805–1873), born in Vermont but since 1837 based in Florence, played a crucial role in associating the fasces with the abolitionist cause. Powers had gained international celebrity—and admiration in the abolitionist movement—for an 1843 life-sized nude female sculpture, *The Greek Slave*, which generated $100,000 in ticket sales when it toured the United States in the 1840s. Powers's central ambition, however, was to place an allegorical work in the US Capitol building—or on top of it, crowning the new dome that was then planned, and to be constructed in the years 1856–1866.

In the fervid revolutionary year 1848, Hiram started without a commission a new life-sized sculpture, a clever hybrid of the Venus de Milo and the Prima Porta Augustus, which he titled "America" (with a brief interlude as "Liberty"). Writing in September 1848 to a Cincinnati patron, Powers explained his conception of the work: "She stands as if addressing a multi-tude and she holds the symbol cap [i.e., of Liberty] upon her fingers ends [*sic*] high above her head. This is the prize. Beneath her foot, and directly under the cap, she is crushing a crown. This is the danger. The support for the statue is a bundle of sticks, which she touches significantly with her right hand. This symbol represents unity or the means. She will be draped lightly to just above the knees, and her arms will be exposed. Her expression will be that of triumph."

In November 1849 the artist changed a few of the attributes in his plaster model for the work, including a laurel wreath on the thirteen rods of the fasces—in his words, "to show that union is always triumphant"—and (conse-quentially) broken chains under the figure's left foot. Instead of the cap in left hand, the figure's fingers were configured "so that they pointed to Heaven." His private correspondence at the time shows that these modifications re-flected his anxieties about American national cohesion in the context of the slavery question.

Not long after Powers started carving *America* in marble, newspaper journalists in Britain and the United States breathlessly shared details of the statue. "The figure finds her support on the fasces," reported the *Home News for India, China and the Colonies* in September 1850, "indicative, it is said, of the fact, that justice is the true foundation of a free commonwealth." Also, "the destination of the statue is reported to be Washington." Meanwhile, through powerful friends, Powers lobbied, indeed at the highest levels, for a US Capitol commission for his *America*. After many vicissitudes, on March 13, 1855, Congress in fact committed to purchase "some work of art executed or to be executed by him, and suitable for the ornament of the Capitol." Yet President Franklin Pierce (who held office 1853–1857) refused to commit on the question of whether that work should be *America*, evidently fearing in-terpretation of the sculpture as an anti-slavery statement. Pierce's successor James Buchanan (1857–1861) in essence sought to buy off Powers by ordering, instead of *America*, life-size portrait statues of Jefferson and Franklin for the House wing of the Capitol. As for the original of Powers's *America*, it made it no further to Washington than the docks of Brooklyn, where in 1865 it was totally destroyed in a warehouse fire.[8]

Already in 1853, Captain Montgomery Meigs (1816–1892), the military engineer who supervised ongoing construction of the Capitol, could not con-vince a distinctly frustrated Powers to submit designs for a projected new com-mission, sculptures for the extension's north pediment and the cornice above the Senate door. However, rival sculptor Thomas Crawford (1813–1857), an

American based in Rome, was pleased to oblige. He suggested for the cornice reclining personifications of Liberty with a freedom cap, and Justice with fasces, pen, and palm branch.

What would seem to be an antiseptic design proved too radical for Secretary of War Jefferson Davis (1808–1889), later president of the Confederate States during the Civil War years (1861–1865). He was the cabinet member who oversaw the Capitol Extension work and as such, in April 1854, reviewed Thomas Crawford's proposal. Davis's objections to the cap, which was now associated in the South with the abolitionist cause, prompted Crawford wholly to recast the Liberty figure as "History." For Justice, Davis joined by Meigs persuaded Crawford to add a set of scales to the figure, suggesting that he join it to her fasces or replace it altogether. Crawford did the latter, and revised her other attributes to imply wider global ambitions for American justice. Jefferson Davis stated a reason for faulting the fasces. In his view, the "lictors rods" still carried the original Roman meaning of corporal punishment. And that would intrude on the now-accepted general understanding of the symbol—as Davis and Meigs phrased it, "in union is strength."

One gets the sense that aesthetic considerations were not driving the war secretary and the army engineer to micromanage the sculptor Crawford, but rather reluctance to antagonize Southern political sensibilities. Yet Meigs and Davis clearly were pleased with Crawford's work and responsiveness to criticism, for in 1855 they commissioned the artist to create a colossal statue of Liberty to top the newly authorized cast-iron dome of the Capitol.

On October 18, 1855, Crawford sent to Meigs from Rome a revised design for the dome statue, his second of what would be three versions. "It is quite possible," wrote Crawford in an accompanying letter, "that Mr. Jefferson Davis may, as upon a former occasion, object to the Cap of Liberty," a new addition to the original design, "and the fasces" that he now placed in a series on the base of the figure. "I can only say, in reply, that the work is for the people, and they must be addressed in language they understand, and which has become unalterable for the masses. The emblems I allude to can never be replaced by any invention of the artist."

Crawford seems correct in his assessment of the fasces as a broadly intelligible American political symbol at this moment. In the 1856 US political election, the Republicans (and their candidate John C. Frémont) and nativist Know Nothings (represented by former US president Millard Fillmore) each illustrated their campaign materials with the emblem. In 1857 a pair of decorative axed fasces wrapped in laurel branches found a place on the wall behind the Speaker's Podium in the House of Representatives chamber, designed by Capitol architect Thomas U. Walter (1804–1887). And in 1859 French-German engraver Anthony C. Paquet (1814–1882) introduced a seated Liberty motif to the obverse of experimental half-dollar and twenty-dollar United States coins, in which her left hand rests atop an American shield, while her outstretched right hand stabilizes an upright fasces by gripping the axe-head that protrudes from the top. An olive sprig and three arrows are placed at the base of the shield, and (on the $20 coin) an eagle stands behind; a border of thirteen stars completes the design. The Roman emblem, in its original form, could hardly be more integral to this expression of American values in peace and war.[9]

But here again, Jefferson Davis pushed Thomas Crawford on the details and spirit of his statue design for the Capitol dome, most consequentially persuading him to substitute a helmet for the traditional Phrygian cap of Liberty. The fasces, which occupied a subsidiary position, stayed. What happened next could not have been foreseen. Crawford finished a plaster cast of the sculpture in his Rome studio, but died in October 1857 before shipping it to the United States. The Republican Abraham Lincoln assumed the American presidency on March 4, 1861; five weeks later, open war broke out between the American North and South, with Davis heading a Confederate States of America. The dome structurally was not able to receive the work until late 1863, as the Civil War still raged.

So Crawford's *Statue of Freedom* or *Armed Freedom* really straddles two eras, divided by the critical year 1861. It is an odd composite, that conflates traditional attributes of America (including elements of Indigenous dress), Liberty, and—at the insistence of Jefferson Davis—Minerva. Overall the statue offers, as Vivien Green Fryd has forcefully argued, a militaristic expression of Manifest Destiny. The bellicose figure (almost 6 meters tall) stands in a triumphant posture on a globe marked E PLURIBUS UNUM, whose curvilinear base is surrounded by thirteen upright spear-tipped axe-less fasces and, below, wreaths—an ensemble which Crawford had termed to Meigs as "emblems of Justice triumphant." Fryd demonstrates how the lag between the statue's design (1856–1857) and its final realization (1863) powerfully shaped its reception. The year of its installation saw Lincoln's Emancipation Proclamation (January 1, in which he ordered the freeing of "all persons held as slaves") and the Battle of Gettysburg (July 1–3), which shifted momentum in the war decisively to the Union. As a result, for Northerners, the statue radiated a message of national unity, as well as support for those recently emancipated in the Confederate states.[10]

Crawford's dome statue for the Capitol offers one element that seems wholly original: the rendering of the thirteen fasces as bending along its base. Now, the very presence of fasces in this supreme position marks a final stage in their ascent as the symbol par excellence of the union of the states. As we have seen, Crawford feared Jefferson Davis would veto their inclusion. But their curving aspect is extraordinary. This has a direct visual link with the French Revolutionary token of the Monneron Brothers, which shows Hercules failing to snap a bundle of rods with his knee. Given the strain on the American Union in the 1850s, we are entitled to see here a loud topical reference.

Fasces in the American Civil War and Aftermath

The heated presidential election of 1860, fought amid the unswerving descent of the United States into disunion, brought with it a dramatic escalation of fasces imagery, in both political rhetoric and in visual media. It is especially pronounced in the campaign ephemera of the presidential candidate of the Constitutional Union Party, John Bell (1796–1869) of Tennessee, a self-styled centrist who had as his running mate former senator Edward Everett (1794–1865) of Massachusetts. Supporters of the Republican candidate Abraham Lincoln employed the symbol, too, in one instance simply recycling the precise fasces iconography that the Know-Nothing candidate Millard Fillmore had used in 1856.

The fasces only accelerated on this trajectory during the war. In June 1861 a writer for a Virginia newspaper opined that for the new Southern Union of eleven breakaway states "the fasces may still stand as an emblem upon our coat of arms." That hope did not materialize, since the Union states jealously guarded and assertively promoted the symbol. One consequential development came on December 21, 1861, when President Lincoln signed a bill allowing the creation of America's first post-Revolutionary military decoration, a Medal of Valor for the Navy. That was soon (in July 1862) amalgamated into a single Medal of Honor for Navy and Army personnel, with appropriate variants. The dynamic central design of the medal—used by the Army until 1903, and by the Navy to the present—strongly resonated with the contemporary fight against secession. It shows within a gold five-pointed star the goddess Minerva, standing with her left hand resting on fasces and right hand holding an American shield, driving off Discord in the form of snakes.[11]

As tensions between North and South were rapidly reaching a breaking point, some tried to monetize the moment. Two of the most enterprising—indeed unscrupulous—were the brothers Eli A. (1827–1898) and Charles D. (1831–1881) Benson. These were Vermonters who owned music stores and published sheet music simultaneously in Chicago, Nashville, and Memphis—so on both sides of the rapidly widening territorial divide. In September 1860 there appeared in their stores printed music—"respectfully dedicated to all lovers of OUR GLORIOUS UNION"—for a "Prize Banner Polka" attributed to a "Sanderson." E. A. Benson in Chicago is listed as primary publisher. A contemporary newspaper report reveals that the composer was in fact Eli Benson himself, and that he vigorously (and somewhat surprisingly) promoted the piece in Tennessee in the summer of 1860 before its release; he also copyrighted it there in 1861.

The colorful cover of the sheet music for the "Prize Banner Polka" depicts, as one would expect, a painted patriotic banner of a type then awarded in large group competitions. Despite the date and publishing details, the artwork broadcasts blatant boosterism for the Union cause. The illustration squeezes in a remarkable number of established American patriotic tropes. The central image features a Liberty wearing a Phrygian cap, who stands on a fortress rampart near a smoking cannon, holding the pole of an American flag and resting her hand on an American shield; with her left foot she stomps on a crown. Scattered on the ground near stacked cannonballs are an axed fasces and an olive branch, and further away, a snapped scepter and—provocatively, as we have seen from Hiram Powers's *America*—broken shackles. Before Liberty, a crossed sword and scroll (the Constitution) occupy a privileged space. But what demands the attention of the viewer is the frame for the picture, its vertical portions composed of two strikingly tall axed fasces almost twice the height of the female figure, which bear shields of the thirteen original states.

Clearly the Bensons thought this fasces-heavy assemblage of images would stir up passions and sell music. And to hedge bets, that same year Charles Benson in Nashville copyrighted a "Confederate Prize Banner Polka" penned by a "Saunderson," publishing it with a mundane cover in 1861. One can say with certainty that the true composer was his Chicago-based elder brother, for the musical notation reveals that the two polkas are exactly the same song. The brothers continued to churn out heavily patriotic numbers for both sides, with complicated publication details, for the rest of the war.[12]

The efforts of these charlatans show that by 1860, the fasces was the expected symbol of the Union. And the emblem only grew in power and poignancy with Abraham Lincoln's successful leadership in the war. For March 4, 1865, the date of Lincoln's second swearing-in as president, the fasces struck a celebratory tone. Treasury draftsperson J. Goldsborough Bruff (1804–1889) prepared a large-format invitation to the National Inaugural Ball where a pair of sturdy axe-less fasces topped by eagles formed the dominant image, framing much smaller half-portraits of Lincoln and his vice president, Andrew Johnson. On one of the fasces is entwined a thin banner inscribed E PLURIBUS UNUM—WE ARE ONE AND INDISSOLUBLE. On April 9, the surrender of the Army of Northern Virginia at Appomattox confirmed that motto as a statement of fact.

The president's shocking assassination just five days later, on April 14, 1865, forever affirmed Lincoln's fame as the martyred savior of George Washington's Union. The next week, as the corpse of the slain president lay in state in the center of the Capitol Rotunda (April 19–21), it is related that "all the pictures on the rotunda walls were covered with black and the statues were completely draped, except the statue of Washington, which wore a black scarf." Stylized fasces re-emphasized the message of Lincoln's achievement, second only to that of the first president. On the catafalque hastily designed by Commissioner of Public Buildings Benjamin Brown French (1800–1870), "at each corner of the dais," reported one Washington newspaper, "is a sloping union column, representing bundles of fasces tied with silver lace." Another paper described how "at each corner [sc. of the bier] was a group of fasces, bound with silver bands, and on each side was a collection of muskets, carbines, and swords" arranged as trophies. No flag was displayed in the Rotunda, making the statue of George Washington (a plaster copy of Houdon's portrait with the thirteen rods) and the fasces—now dubbed "union columns"—the only symbols of the nation in this sepulchral setting.[13]

From this point, the United States saw a torrent of fasces in public art, which would last for several generations to come. There is no need here to chronicle the proliferation of the emblem on war memorials, commemorative statues (including those for slavery advocate John C. Calhoun [1782–1850] and Lincoln's political opponent Stephen A. Douglas [1831–1861]), administrative buildings and courthouses, campaign banners and posters, patriotic medallions, and prints and postcards. Three official uses of the emblem do demand special notice: the first appearance of fasces on United States postage stamps (the Official Stamps, a series printed from 1873–1884 for government use, in high denominations ranging from $2 to $20); on a state seal (that of Colorado, adopted in 1876, and used on its flag 1907–1911); and on regular currency (the so-called Indian Head Gold Eagle $10 coins in gold, minted 1907–1933, where on the reverse an eagle perches on a horizontal axe-less fasces).

For Abraham Lincoln himself, the emblem is eye-catching, especially on two monuments each completed in 1874, his Tomb in Springfield Illinois, designed by Larkin G. Mead (1835–1910), and the Emancipation Memorial in Washington, DC, the work of Thomas Ball (1819–1911). For Springfield, the sculptural centerpiece of the mammoth structure—its base 72 feet square, with a double stairs leading to a terrace from which rises a 117 foot (35.6 m) obelisk—is a standing statue of Lincoln signing the Emancipation Proclamation that Mead had started to design even before the assassination. "It is of heroic proportions," said one newspaper the day of the monument's inauguration by President Ulysses S. Grant (served 1869–1877), describing how "as a symbol of the Union to which he devoted his life, the banner of the republic is thrown in bas-relief upon the fasces near the statue, at the foot of which is a crown of laurels." In Ball's Emancipation group (dated 1874, erected 1876, and now attracting understandable scrutiny), Lincoln extends his left hand symbolically to grant freedom to a crouching Black freedperson, while resting his right on a podium bearing symbols of the Union carved in low relief, including fasces (indeed four, at each of the corners) and a medallic portrait of Washington. Beyond doubt, the fasces was now an expected attribute in portrayals of Lincoln. The designers of the early twentieth-century Lincoln Memorial in Washington focused on this convention, but created a wholly original monument by choosing to foreground the emblem and magnify it on a grand scale.[14]

Fasces in the United States during the Rise of Fascism

As luck would have it, precisely five months after the dedication on May 30, 1922, of the Lincoln Memorial in Washington, DC, about thirty thousand armed supporters of the Italian Fascist movement staged a "March on Rome." As we shall soon see, this was a nationwide demonstration that, through the threat of violence, effected a largely bloodless transfer of the country's political power to their leader Benito Mussolini (1883–1945), ratified on October 30, 1922. Within weeks, the newly empowered Fascists then set in motion plans to make their party symbol, the Roman rods and axe, ubiquitous in Italy. By the first anniversary of the coup, Mussolini's movement can fairly be said to have achieved its goal. Surely this development, widely reported in the world press, including that of the United States, caused deep embarrassment about the focus on the fasces in the US capital's costly memorial to Lincoln?

Far from it—at this time in the United States, the notion of the rods bound with an axe as a universal signifier of unity was firmly entrenched. To illustrate how slow these events in Italy were to impact American perceptions of the fasces, let us turn to a case study from the mid-1920s that played out 7,400 kilometers distant from Mussolini's Rome, in Cleveland, Ohio.

In the April 1925 issue of the American monthly professional journal *The School Review* there appeared a short article with the intriguing title "The Story of the Fasces at Central High School." The author was Helen M. Chesnutt (1880–1969), one of the first African American graduates of Smith College (AB, 1901), and then a Latin teacher at this Cleveland public school, which she herself had attended. What the reader finds is not a tale of controversy, conflict, or resistance to the newly emerged Italian political symbol, but rather a lightly written and engaging description of a class project on recreating the Roman fasces that kept on expanding.[15]

"The whole thing started last year," explains Chesnutt, who then narrates a sequence of events that seem to belong to the fall of 1924. Her class was reading a speech of Cicero's that mentioned a Roman commander's fasces with their axes falling into the hands of pirates. In the discussion that followed, one student pointed out that the fasces were represented "on the reverse side of the new dime."

The reference is to a United States 10-cent piece, introduced in 1916 and struck for each of the next twenty-nine years, a coin commonly (from especially the mid-1930s) but erroneously called the "Mercury dime." The obverse in fact shows a personification of Liberty with a Phrygian cap that is (unexpectedly) winged; the reverse has a fasces with olive branch. To resolve the question why an American coin should feature a Roman fasces, one of Chesnutt's students volunteered to write directly to the US Treasury Department.

The Latin student's instincts were sound. Indeed, the 1916 *Annual Report of the Director of the Mint* to the secretary of the Treasury had succinctly explained the intent of the design. "The obverse shows a head of Liberty with winged cap. The head is firm and simple in form, the profile forceful. The reverse shows a design of the bundle of rods, with battle-ax, known as 'Fasces,' and symbolical of unity, wherein lies the Nation's strength. Surrounding the fasces is a full-foilaged [*sic*] branch of olive, symbolical of peace."[16]

As it happened, a Treasury official, in reply to Chesnutt's class, offered none of this published information but instead "suggested that the designer of the coin . . . might be able to help us." That was the German-born artist Adolph Alexander Weinman (1870–1952), who achieved equal fame as a

FIGURE 10.2. United States "Mercury" dime (struck from late 1916 to 1945), here 1944 (Denver mint). Obverse shows personification of Liberty with winged Phrygian cap; reverse has fasces with olive branch.

Credit: Stack's Bowers Galleries, May 2021, Collector's Choice (US) Auction, Lot 92175 (May 19, 2021).

medalist and architectural sculptor in the neoclassical idiom. So Chesnutt's students sent an inquiry to his New York City address. To the class's delight, Weinman responded and helpfully set out in a "charming letter . . . in his own handwriting" his rationale for choosing the fasces.

"He had had in mind," as Chesnutt paraphrases Weinman's note, "the story of the father who gave each of his sons in turn a bundle of sticks and bade them break them. None was able to do this until he unbound the bundle and showed them how easily they could be broken when separated. The fact, then, that 'in union there is strength' is clearly symbolized by the Roman fasces." As for the other elements of the dime's reverse, Weinman held that "the battle ax represents preparedness for war, and the olive branch about the fasces represents the blessedness and beauty of peace." What Helen Chesnutt does not explain, but simply presumes the educated reader to know, is that Weinman in his reference to the sticks was summarizing an ancient moralizing tale in which an old man taught a lesson on unity to his quarrelsome sons by demonstrating that it was easy to break rods one at a time, but not when bound in a bundle. We have seen that this story found a place in Aesop's collection of *Fables*, and attracted a ready audience in the Renaissance and beyond.

Adolph Weinman's generous letter to the Latin students of Cleveland's Central High School confirms what we otherwise would have expected from the actual coin. For his design of the dime, he clearly was interested in the Roman fasces primarily as a living symbol. In historical terms, there is no close connection between the ancient Roman fasces and the Aesop fable of the old man and his sons, other than the attractive coincidence that each involves a bundle of sticks. The axe placed in the bundle was for the Romans an instrument of justice, rather than of combat, as Weinman considered it. And, as we have seen, the olive branch is unrelated to the ancient fasces, both in its material aspect and in its iconography.

All the same, the letter from the famous sculptor fired the imagination of Chesnutt's students. She relates that the school's Latin club formed a committee "to get all of the information possible about the fasces—to find out of what it was made and to get together the material for making a 'life-sized' one to suspend from the wall of the Latin room." The school's manual training department helped by making polished wooden rods, and a local hardware store provided an axe-head to the students, one of whom attached a broomstick to serve as its handle. The most difficult challenge was finding suitable strips of red leather to bind the bundle, which eventually had to be imported from Pittsburgh. Once all the parts were ready, with borrowed gilt paint, wire, and some glue, Chesnutt wrote, "we made the fasces and proudly hung it on the wall."

Nor was that the end of the story of the fasces at this Cleveland high school. Chesnutt tells how her students went on to make miniature fasces from twigs, cardboard, and string—just two-and-a-half-inches long—as a badge for members of the Latin club. The project proved such a success that the school's principal suggested that the club make 200 more, for attendees of the third annual Ohio Latin Conference, which was to assemble at Oberlin College in three weeks' time (November 17, 1924). The students just barely accomplished that additional task, but took great satisfaction in doing so.

There is one conspicuous gap in Helen Chesnutt's narrative of her students' production of a fasces model and badge: acknowledgment of the symbol's use in contemporary Italian politics. The omission must have been deliberate. Indeed, in the United States following the dedication of the Lincoln Memorial in 1922—and, that same year, the Fascist coup in Italy—the fasces, if anything, took on a new life as a design element, not least in public architecture.

During the 1930s in particular, numerous prominent examples of the fasces spring up in Washington, DC, including the Arlington National Bridge (completed 1932), Commerce Building (1932, now Herbert C. Hoover Building), Department of the Post Office Building (1934), National Archives,

Department of Labor, Department of Justice, and Supreme Court Buildings (each completed 1935). Outside Washington, fasces form an important motif in public buildings that cover a wide geographical span, again mostly dating to the 1930s. Consider (almost at random) the exterior of the Hartford Connecticut US Post Office, Courthouse, and Federal Building (constructed 1931–1933, renamed William R. Cotter Federal Building in 1982), which offers a typical example. A series of twenty-nine aluminum spandrel panels with stylized "Federal Eagle" and paired fasces separate the second and third floors on three of the building's four elevations, essentially wrapping the structure.

One common element in these instances of American public art is that the fasces either appear by themselves, or accompany allegorical personifications. Hardly ever do figures in any medium pick up the kit. And no one in the United States seemed to be interested in the role of the lictor—with the notable exception of Pittsburgh artist Charles Bradley Warren (1903–1967), with a granite statue he created for the Justice Building (1939) of Raleigh, North Carolina. For a ledge on the principal façade of the building, Warren created an enigmatic 4-meter-tall bearded and robed sculptural figure entitled "Justice," his right hand resting on a standing axed fasces. Soon after its installation, in the summer of 1940, a Raleigh newspaper reported that "some curious visitors inquired as to what the statue represented and were told it was a Roman lictor." On that explanation, reactions turned sour. "In view of the lictor's place in history, tenants of the new 'Law and Justice' building prefer to call the front statue 'Moses.'" Today it is widely (and just as implausibly) known as "Solon," after the early sixth century BCE Athenian lawgiver.[17]

One gigantic question immediately presents itself. What were these planners, architects, and sculptors thinking? Given the sharp rise in the 1920s and 1930s of an alarming brand of nationalism in Europe, it seems an odd time simultaneously to be doubling down on the fasces in America by incorporating the emblem into so many high-profile public designs. From our vantage point, the troubling character of Italy's Fascist regime seems fully revealed by January 3, 1925, when Mussolini in a speech to the Chamber of Deputies took responsibility for his followers' violence, and grimly promised that Fascism would assure "tranquility" to Italy in any manner it thought necessary. The speech is widely considered the beginning of true dictatorship in Italy, and indeed its significance was recognized in the United States press even at the time.

An obvious explanation is that these American architects and artists were assertively claiming or even reclaiming a symbol that was part and parcel of their own national iconography since at least 1789. But the legal scholar

Eugene Kontorovich has raised an alternate, disturbing possibility: that these government projects were formed when many Americans still admired Mussolini and considered him an effective reformer. Kontorovich details the personal links of some of the relevant architects with Mussolini's Italy, or their publicly stated enthusiasm for his political program. In at least some cases, the deployment of fasces may have been by way of tribute.

To be sure, Italy's invasion of Ethiopia in October 1935, with sanctions by the League of Nations to follow the next month, marked a hardening of the regime and an international revulsion of feeling against Mussolini. However, even that did not signal the stop of provocative fasces designs, as the sculptural decoration of the 1939 Raleigh Justice Building shows. Compounding the edginess of the bearded lictor on that edifice was a decision by the North Carolina–based architectural firm of Northup and O'Brien to use as an exterior decorative scheme on the building the so-called Greek key pattern. What made it eye-popping both at the time and now is that the meander in stone distinctly resembles a repeated Nazi swastika. No easy answers present themselves for these bizarre choices. But it is to discussion of Mussolini's discovery, radical reinterpretation, and exaltation of the fasces, and subsequent attempts to eradicate the symbol, that we shall now turn.[18]

Constructing Fasces in Mussolini's Italy

The "Fascio" in Italy before 1922

In November 1914, when Benito Mussolini, then prominent as a revolutionary socialist, tried to mobilize popular opinion for Italy to intervene in World War I, he gave the name "Autonomous *Fasci* of Revolutionary Action" to his disparate supporters. The term *fascio* (plural, *fasci*) was then common in Italy, but in its core meaning of "bundle." Long before, already in the mid-1880s, it had entered that country's political lexicon to denote a loosely organized group with a shared ideology. Soon, the workers' movement in Sicily of the mid-1890s firmly cemented the word *fascio* into common use. At the time, the press even sometimes tagged members of the Sicilian *Fasci* as "fascisti." Two decades later, especially after Italy entered the war in May 1915, activist groups with "fascio" in their name would number in the dozens, ranging from the ultra-left *Fascio comunista anarchico* to the *Fascio nazionale femminile*, a home-front women's association.

What about the actual emblem of the Roman fasces in Italy in this era? Indeed, it took on a new life as a symbol of unity after Vittorio Emanuele II comprehensively unified the country in 1870, and then reigned as its first king until his death (aged just fifty-seven) in 1878. Memorials to the monarch after his death—both mooted and realized—demonstrate that well. For example, an 1879 exhibition in Torino of proposed designs included one that had among its sculptural figures a personified "Unity that holds as her emblem the Roman fasces." Another artist in the show had much grander things in mind. He submitted a study for a tomb monument in the form of a 50-meter column, shaped like a fasces, capped by a statue of the monarch.

The Fasces. T. Corey Brennan, Oxford University Press. © Oxford University Press 2023.
DOI: 10.1093/oso/9780197644881.003.0011

A Latin motto drilled the message home: VIS UNITA FORTIOR ("force united is stronger").

In the event, the memorials constructed for Vittorio Emanuele II that featured fasces did so on a somewhat more conventional scale, but still in a way that demands attention. At Modena in Emilia-Romagna, a monument to the king inaugurated in 1890 features as the most conspicuous feature of its pedestal a large sculptural figure of a seated Italia holding in her right arm a long fasces, while her left hand rests on a rock inscribed "STATUTO" (i.e., the written law). In 1891 the city of Sassari in Sardinia set up a similar commemoration of the king, but at its base a male figure rests somewhat incongruously on a lion, gripping the top of a protruding fasces with his right hand and the impressive staff of an Italian flag in his left. And in Rome, as one approaches the grand staircase of the Vittoriano (begun 1885, inaugurated 1911, completed 1935), high up to the right is the dynamic bronze sculptural group *Action* (1911) by Francesco Jerace (1853–1937). Here an enigmatic kneeling female figure in unmistakable Masonic headdress—generally regarded as a personification of the "Young Italy" unification movement, founded in 1831 by Giuseppe Mazzini—dominates the rear of the composition. A picture of resolution, she stabilizes an axed fasces with her left hand, and brandishes in her right a baton tipped with the head of a lion.[1]

Yet it was only after the conclusion of World War I that one of the political *fasci* used the Roman fasces to express its identity, and had its members proudly laid claim to the somewhat pejorative moniker "fascisti." The take-off point was Milan's Piazza San Sepolcro on March 23, 1919, when Benito Mussolini relaunched his war movement as a paramilitary group, the "Italian *Fasci* of Combat." The educator Regina Terruzzi (1862–1951)—just one of nine women present at the occasion—allegedly predicted then to her friend Mussolini that "you will be consul of Italy." It is said that the charismatic "poet-soldier" Gabriele D'Annunzio (1863–1938) had urged Mussolini to adopt the Roman fasces as the emblem of his new party.

What is certain is that it took some months for Mussolini to vigorously promote the symbol. The catalyst seems to have been the Italian general election scheduled for November 16, 1919, in the midst of the fraught "Red Biennium" (1919–1920), during which an economically distressed Italy seemed ripe for revolution. Three weeks before the vote, the Milan newspaper *Il Popolo d'Italia*—which Mussolini had founded in 1914—consistently began to tell its readers to check electoral ballots for the stamped emblem of a fasces (illustrated and annotated as "a bundle of rods with an axe in the middle") that would denote candidates of the "Fascist Bloc" (Figure 11.1) The

FIGURE 11.1. Detail of *Il Popolo d'Italia*, October 25, 1919, p. 1. In this issue the newspaper's editor, Benito Mussolini, first introduced the fasces as a way to mark candidates from his party in the forthcoming Italian general elections, to be held November 16 of that year. Credit: digiteca.bsmc.it.

headline that kicked off the campaign on October 25 screamed: "The Fascist emblem signifies unity, force and justice!" One novel feature: here the cords on the fasces appear loosened at the base of the bundle, and their ends flow to the left and right of the rods. The clear implication is that the kit is in the process of being readied for punitive use. Starting in 1920, the fasces adorned the membership cards of the movement—initially with loose cords, later without. Those cards were printed in huge numbers, and circulated through all Italy. By the end of the next year, the group had swelled reportedly to more than 300,000 members. On November 21, 1921, it was reconstituted as the National Fascist Party (*Partito Nazionale Fascista*, or PNF).[2]

The most visible and familiar sign of the paramilitary wing of Mussolini's party was a shiny black-collared shirt, evocative of both anarchists and the "Arditi," Italy's elite hand-to-hand fighters who tried to break the stalemate of trench warfare in World War I. Yet it quickly appeared that the Roman emblem of the fasces gave a veneer of legitimacy even to the Fascist *squadrismo* (i.e., political violence) which mushroomed especially from the spring of 1920. 'ITALY'S MODERN LICTORS' is how an admiring *New York Times* article (March 20, 1921) described such members of Mussolini's postwar *Fasci Italiani del Combattimento* and their readiness to use violence to achieve its goals. Under Rome's kings, it is explained, the attendants known as lictors personally executed the laws. But later under the Republic (trad. 509–31 BCE) and Empire, "marching before the magistrates with their fasces . . . borne on their left shoulder" they had become mere symbols of "the attributes of law as well as the potential power of the people, the law's origin." What Mussolini had done, it is argued, was nothing short of reviving the original form of the institution. "The Lictor of today is anything but symbolic, the mighty fasces have become mere metal emblems worn in coat buttonholes"—such badges had emerged alongside the cards as a public marker of group identity—"but he attempts to assert the majesty of the law as well as respect for the long-suffering middle class by military means."[3] The creation of the PNF in November 1921 served to institutionalize the Fascist irregulars still further.

The Fasces in Mussolini's "March on Rome"

One novelty of Mussolini's movement is that it insisted on the fasces as a living symbol which animated practical action. This is well seen in the newspaper *Il Popolo d'Italia* of August 2, 1922, where the journalist and propagandist Gaetano Polverelli (1885–1960) penned a fiery article entitled "The Law or the Axe." There he argued that the Fascist movement was "compelled" to correct the state's alleged failure to maintain the rule of law and hold "red gang leaders" to account. "If the State shows itself weak and cowardly . . . dictatorship will become necessary . . . the rods and axe, which are the symbol of the fasces, will return into action as in the healthy and great days of Rome."

To be sure, Italy had been long in tumult, with just the previous six months seeing three different governments, rampant inflation, militant assaults on authority, labor action of all sorts, and a sharp uptick in Blackshirt squad violence directed against both institutions (city councils, union offices, newspapers) and individuals. Polverelli's call to arms appeared just the day after Prime Minister Luigi Facta (1861–1930) had formed a new government, and while an anti-Fascist "legalitarian" general strike was in its second day, with bloody consequences in several of Italy's major cities. The very day of the article's publication, armed Fascists took full control of Ancona and forced the Socialist city council to resign.

As it happens, "The Law or the Axe" marks just the beginning of a series of essays in Mussolini's newspaper, stretching into mid-October, that urged civil war, a takeover of the state, or a "dictatorship" to resolve the ongoing political crisis. Not two weeks later, planning for a Fascist "March on Rome"—its character deliberately left vague in public pronouncements—began in earnest at an August 13 meeting of the National Council of the PNF. The arc of the story is well known. On October 24, during a mass gathering of Fascists for a party congress in Naples, Mussolini openly threatened to take Italy's government by force. But the relatively disciplined behavior of Blackshirts at the various assemblies and on parade in the city caused politicians in Rome to relax their guard. Then, in a well-coordinated effort that spanned the days October 27–30, 1922, Mussolini's paramilitary squads seized key transport and communication points throughout the country. Simultaneously, 25,000–30,000 of his Blackshirt followers—armed with a wide variety of weapons, including sport rifles, revolvers, knives, and clubs—converged on Rome. On the morning of October 28, to the shock of Prime Minister Facta, Vittorio Emanuele III (1869–1947, king of Italy since 1900) refused to declare a "state of siege" (i.e., martial law). Facta resigned, and despite the presence of close to 30,000 government troops within the city, on October 30 the king facilitated the formation of a new government, with Mussolini replacing Facta as its head. This coup took on enormous symbolic importance for the Fascists, who later (starting in 1926) even officially reckoned October 28, 1922, as the first day of a new calendrical "Fascist Era."[4]

Our focus here in examining this toxic train of events is, as always, on the development of the fasces as symbol. For that, we have an unusually revealing source: forty-three minutes of documentary footage of the "March on Rome," as compiled and edited by Umberto Paradisi (1878–1933) for a speedily produced feature film. The first screening of his finished product—with the title *A Noi* (literally, "to us," a war cry of the Arditi)—took place on November 7, 1922, only eight days after the Mussolini government had assumed power. Indeed, the PNF had immediately (November 3) adopted Paradisi's work as the official film of the March, and had seen to its prompt distribution in theaters. That detail of course should give us pause. The film effectively promotes the Fascist narrative, for it demonstrably tries to shape historical memory of the events by eliding the timeline, omitting key details—such as that Mussolini was in Milan for two of the three crucial days of the March—and suppressing all incidents of violence, most notably, a Fascist attack on the San Lorenzo district on the morning of October 31 that left 13 dead and over 200 wounded. However, Paradisi's eagerness to convey the size and range of participation in the big takeover offers an unselfconscious glimpse of Fascist iconology as it stood at this still early stage.

A correspondent for the London *Observer* registered his impressions of the film on seeing its premiere in Florence in mid-December 1922. "The shifting scenes showed a whole world of Fascists," he reflected. "It is the story of 'the conquest of Rome,' by the youth of Italy, and is divided into three periods: The Naples Congress, October 24; the march on Rome of 52,000 Fascists from every part of Italy, infantry and cavalry, together with their allies, the Nationalists, a few days later; and finally, the triumphal march through Rome of Mussolini, under the windows of the Quirinal [i.e., the royal palace], and the homage paid by the Fascist army to the 'Unknown Warrior' [i.e., at the Vittoriano]." The reviewer's main takeaways? "I saw Mussolini smile . . . and best of all"—and this is a telling detail for the political climate of the period—"for the first time I saw an Italian audience rise to its feet when the king appeared on the film, and was deafened by their cheers."[5]

What matters for us in this film is the representation of the fasces. It comes as some surprise that in the sequence of over 200 scenes the symbol is hard to discern. At just one point in the footage does the emblem receive the full focus of the camera. That comes just short of the six-minute mark, in a five-second segment at the Naples congress where one spots a fasces design at the center of a large floral wreath on a stand. Elsewhere, the keen-eyed will spot crude fasces scrawled in chalk on a requisitioned train, or on the occasional vehicle. One car conveying helmeted Blackshirts through the streets of Rome sports on its hood a black flag with a large fasces. Throughout the film, many Blackshirts carry flags of the old Fasci Italiani del Combattimento, where the central design is either an eagle on the wing with the fasces, or the rods and axe alone, but it receives no real visual emphasis in the film. A truly close examination of close-up scenes shows some Fascists wearing an enameled fasces badge.

The title cards of Paradisi's film, however, more than made up for the comparative dearth of fasces visible in footage of the actual March. Each one of the cards—and there are more than six dozen in all—presents a large axed fasces with unfurling cords before a radiant star. It comes off as a branding effort, one that imposes coherence and meaning on the dizzying flurry of events that flit across the screen. The week after the release of the film, a front-page cartoon in *Il Popolo d'Italia* aimed for the same effect in still starker terms. With the caption "16 November 1922—the new government is presented to the Camera" (i.e., of Deputies), there is depicted on a daïs in the assembly's chamber a giant fasces, its axe head positioned as if both addressing and menacing the body.[6]

The "March on Rome" of October 1922 prompted the American press to report closely (and, on the whole, favorably) on the fortunes of Mussolini and his Fascisti. Journalists were quick to explain to readers the Roman origins of his party's name, sometimes using the reverse of the current US dime as a visual aid. The rods and axe, such as those depicted on the US coin, "represented the power of chastisement, the might of government and the law," related one widely syndicated column a few days (November 2, 1922) after Mussolini had seized power. Another journalist (November 21, 1922) underlined that they "signified the authority of a united nation, governed on principles of law, order and impartial justice." A third syndicated account (December 7, 1922) was more expansive on the meaning of the fasces. "They were emblems of law, order and justice, and signified the power of united strength—the strength and majesty of Rome. And now it is this old ensign that is being used to band together in unity the youth of a new Italy—to rally them to the old ideals."[7]

Mass Marketing the Fasces in Early Fascist Italy

Not two months after his Fascists had come to political power in the October 1922 March, Mussolini, now as prime minister, launched an official effort to recover the "authentic" form of the Roman fasces, to feature on a new issue of coins. Already in December 1922, Finance Minister Alberto De Stefani (1879–1969) can be seen closely managing the project, an obvious attempt to insert a central Fascist image into Italian everyday life.

The representation was to appear on 1- and 2-lire denominations in nickel. These coins had been in development, with obverse and reverse based on more conventional designs, even before the Fascist coup. The aim of this new coinage, as announced on December 27, 1922, on the front page of *Il Popolo d'Italia*, was to highlight "the emblem of ancient Rome and of the new Italy."

A few days later (January 1, 1923), on the proposal of Mussolini himself, Italy's Council of Ministers formally resolved that the newly minted coins display on one side the portrait of the reigning king, Vittorio Emanuele III, and on the other the fasces. A royal decree of January 21, 1923 solemnized the intention of memorializing the fasces in this conspicuous and durable way. However, the announcement already had generated much attention, including prominently voiced concern that the design of the fasces meets the highest artistic standards, given its crucial importance for the new regime's propaganda.[8]

To be sure, the task was vexed, and vexing. No Roman fasces—not even verifiable parts of fasces—are known to have survived from antiquity. Nor does any ancient author fully describe the fasces for their own sake. Representations on Roman-era coins and historical reliefs, though plentiful, hardly offered a congruent picture, and in the early 1920s no modern reference work on the ancient design was at hand. Indeed we have seen that, starting already in the sixteenth century, a whole series of attempts to render the fasces for a range of artistic and political purposes had introduced still more variation, as well as deliberately ahistorical additions. To meet these challenges, Finance Minister De Stefani turned to the most distinguished Italian archaeologist of his day. This was Giacomo Boni (1859–1925), chief excavator of the Roman Forum and the Palatine, champion of revitalizing Roman antiquity, member of the Fascist National Party, and (from March 1, 1923) a senator of the Kingdom of Italy.[9]

Boni's idea was physically to reconstruct the fasces with meticulous attention to the ancient evidence, and to complete the task by April 21, the traditional date of Rome's foundation by Romulus. For that was the day he chose to invite Italy's chief ministers to the Antiquarium of the Roman Forum, where he would show them a "true model" of the fasces and deliver a disquisition on the significance of its parts and the whole.

As it happened, the Italian public caught a glimpse of Boni's efforts weeks before that event. On April 4, 1923, a little more than three months after its initial notice of the coin rebranding, *Il Popolo d'Italia* published Boni's results, with a detailed account of how he reached them, and a preliminary image of how they would be rendered on the 2-lire piece. In what seemed to be obverse position was a tall vertical fasces, with an axe blade protruding not from the top of the bundle of bound rods, as in official Fascist representations up to this point, but from the middle of its right side. A small decorative lion's head topped the axe handle.

Boni, it was explained in the article, working from ancient historical reliefs, had decided to prepare his model of "the *fascio littorio* that the Romans really used" with the technical help of one of his Palatine excavators. Both the minister of finance and Prime Minister Mussolini himself had seen and approved the reproduction. Boni's conclusion was that the historical fasces, made of birch rods "bound with red leather straps" and displaying an "axe attached externally along the beam," stood "almost two meters high." This of course meant they stood as tall, if not taller, than the lictors who carried the assemblage. In Boni's view, after "quite exacting work on the form and symbolic meaning of the fasces," the device was not just "a symbol of strength and dominion." It also carried "a profound religious significance," the reader is told, without further elaboration.[10]

Here we can turn for further explanation to Boni's student and biographer Eva Tea (1886–1971), who in 1932 presented Boni's reconstruction of the fasces as a major episode in his later career. She reports that Boni characterized the fasces as "a very serious thing, which makes us shudder, especially when, with the help of this instrument—the inseparable emblem of the highest Roman judiciary—within we see the unsuspected very human depths of primitive Italic law."[11]

It is clear from Tea's account that Boni expended enormous effort on getting his model of this tool of justice precisely right. Boni was expert in botany, and a pioneer in the study of paleobotany. So once he decided that the rods must be composed of white birch (*betula alba*)—then exceedingly rare in central Italy—he put a premium on finding a proper specimen of the wood, and considered sources as far distant as Russia. "It would be strange," he is said to have joked, "if I had to end up making the Fascist emblem out of rods grown in Bolshevik territory." Fortunately, the region of Lazio yielded birch that was suitable, found east of Rome on the banks of the Aniene river. The task of coloring the leather straps in an authentically Roman shade was simpler, for here Boni, as Tea relates, turned to a common plant widely used in antiquity to make red dye, rose madder (*rubia tinctorum*).

Boni waived all compensation for his experimental research, privately requesting in a letter of April 20 that the money the Treasury had allotted for his efforts be used to make glass and enameled copper models of the emblem to mark the upcoming first anniversary of the Fascist revolution (October 28, 1923). On that occasion, when the fasces-bearing coins would be in circulation, he planned to offer another presentation on "the historical-legal interpretation of the fasces as a symbol of supreme Roman courts."[12]

In the year 1923, in the countdown to October 28—the first anniversary of the Fascist coup—Mussolini's regime energetically promoted the symbol, in an open effort to have the "lictor's fasces" (Italian *fascio littorio*) permeate every corner of Italian society. Most important of course was Italy's new nickel coinage, minted that summer, the product of Boni's high-level scholarly work on the form of the "definitive" fasces. For the first anniversary, the regime also introduced the fasces on new postage stamps, six in all, by three different artists; the lower denominations (10, 30, and 50 *centesimi*) clearly invoke Boni's recreation of the fasces. Even the state's cigarette monopoly had a role to play. "It is clear that Premier Mussolini, Italy's big man of the hour, knows the value of publicity," noted *The Buffalo Times* on March 9, 1923. "He is fixing things so

FIGURE 11.2. Kingdom of Italy, gold 100-lire coin (1923). The head of King Vittorio Emanuele III is on obverse (with name of engraver Attilio Silvio Motti below); fasces on reverse, with commemorative dates OTTOBRE 1922 Δ–1923. Minted to celebrate the first anniversary of the Fascist March on Rome (October 28, 1928).

Credit: Bertolami Fine Arts. Auction 9, Lot 1346 (April 29, 2014).

that every Italian who smokes a cigarette will see on its wrapper a reminder of the Fasces of ancient Rome." The fasces-branded cigarettes indeed were rolled out that year. Called Eja!, from a Fascist battle cry, its carton prominently featured a fasces, with axe-head protruding not laterally (as in Boni's model) but from the top of the bundle, centered in an Italian tricolor field.[13]

By the time of the first anniversary of the March on Rome, commercial concerns even outside Italy are found making a shameless bid to profit financially from the political moment. Readers of *Il Popolo d'Italia* for October 28, 1923, opened their papers to a prominent advertisement by the perfume house Arys of Paris announcing its new fragrance FASCIO. The ad depicted a fasces (again, with an axe-head at top) and offered a pitch that drew directly from the Fascist party lexicon, "Il profumo dell'ardire e della giovinezza— IRRESISTIBILE." (A literal translation—"the scent of daring and youth"— does not convey the political sloganeering of the tagline.)[14]

A Gift of "Mystical" Fasces to Mussolini

Touches of whimsy such as fasces-branded cigarettes and perfume should not distract us from the fact that in the months following the Fascist coup, some members of the Italian public embraced the symbol with a startling intensity that resembled religious fanaticism. A particularly revealing case study comes from a most unlikely source—a women's rights march in the historic center of

Rome on the morning of May 19, 1923. It featured over one thousand women from some forty nations who had come to the city as delegates to the Ninth Congress of the International Woman Suffrage Alliance (IWSA), which soon was set to adjourn.

The background to this march? Six days earlier, Mussolini as prime minister had opened the IWSA Congress with an address that apparently stunned all in the audience. He stated that he would not oppose women's voting rights in his country, at least in limited form. Now, in the months since Mussolini's Fascist Party had staged its coup d'état in late October 1922, it was widely thought he was resolved on the continued exclusion of Italy's women from participation in politics. So as the Suffrage Alliance meeting entered its final day, the delegates decided to make Mussolini confirm his openness to reform. They slowly paraded en masse from their meeting venue on the Via Nazionale to the prime minister's offices at the Viminal Palace, just 600 meters distant. Their aim was to hand the Congress's chief demands to Benito Mussolini in person.

The Italian newspaper *Il Messaggero* characterized the women's demonstration as "impromptu." However, its own reporting suggests that the event was well choreographed. Each nation's contingent was grouped together, under its own flag, in two divisions, each arranged alphabetically. Delegates from the twenty-five countries that had so far granted voting rights to women headed the procession; those from the eighteen that yet had not walked behind them, including a massive showing from members of Italy's *Federazione Pro Suffragio*. And on the marchers' arrival at the Viminal Palace at 9:30 a.m., Mussolini was there to greet them, flanked by two top ministers. In actual fact, he had agreed already in January 1923 to host the deputation, following a planned parade.[15]

For what followed on the Viminal, multiple contemporary accounts highlight the role of the Milanese educator Regina Terruzzi—lifelong socialist, precocious supporter of Mussolini at the San Sepolcro rally of 1919, and now Italy's head delegate to the Congress. In Italian reports, it seems she single-handedly managed to shape the large, spirited gathering into something approaching a formal reception by the prime minister. The resolutions of the Congress passed into Mussolini's hands, and indeed he pledged again soon to extend the vote to Italy's women, albeit in an incremental way. (As it turned out, Italian women gained the right to vote in local elections two and half years later, on November 22, 1925, shortly before such elections were wholly eliminated.) The way this high-stakes confrontation on the Viminal proceeded so smoothly dazzled even the international press. "MUSSOLINI

INVADED BY HOST OF WOMEN," screamed a headline later that same day on the front page of the *Saskatoon Daily Star*. "Italian Premier Voices Warm Welcome When 1,000 Descend on His Offices with Alliance Resolutions; Call for Votes in All States."[16]

The morning produced one surprise. Toward the end of a long series of introductions, Terruzzi brought forward a young Italian scholar, Cesarina Ribulsi (1892–1963), a recent (1915) laureate of the University of Rome. She offered to Mussolini a full-size replica of the fasces. *Il Messaggero* observes this *fascio littorio* was "composed of freshly-cut rods," and characterizes it as "a symbol of authority and justice," adding that Ribulsi had composed a dedication in Latin for the occasion. Mussolini, for his part, "greatly appreciated this kind homage."

On the whole, Italy's newspapers—which in their reporting did not give special prominence to the suffragists' demonstration—merely note Ribulsi and her gesture in a long list of women presented to Mussolini. However, Rome's *Il Piccolo* wrote up this incident in a stand-alone article, removing all mention of the context of the Congress, as if the gift of the fasces were an independent event of some importance. Some details were changed, and new ones were added. The article offers an unsettling glimpse into fasces fervor, even at this early stage of Mussolini's regime, and so deserves close attention.[17]

Here we are told that Cesarina Ribulsi was based "in the Fascist Popular University" (no mention is made of the city) where she "fervently carries out the work of propagating living Romanism (*romanità*)." She had "exactly reconstructed the fasces according to historical and iconographic evidence" and added her Latin inscription specifically as "a good omen" to mark the anniversary of May 24, 1915, the date that Italy entered World War I, and by extension, it is said, the start of Mussolini's "organic work of reconstructing the values of our lineage."

The article in *Il Piccolo* then describes fully the various components of Ribulsi's fasces. "The bronze axe comes from a 2000-year-old Etruscan tomb"—we are left to imagine whether it was authentic, a forgery, or a replica—"and has a sacred shape, with a hole for attachment to the handle; similar ones are preserved in our Kircher Museum" housed in the Collegio Romano in Rome's center. It continues: "Twelve rods of birch, according to ritual prescription, are tied with strips of red leather that form a noose at the top to hang the bundle, as in the bas-relief at the staircase of the Palazzo Capitolino dei Conservatori." (The reference seems to be to a panel that shows the emperor Hadrian's arrival in Rome.)

Much is made of the color of the creation. "The expressive roughness of the fasces is softened by the contrast between the green of the bronze patina"—here compared to that of the door of the Temple of Romulus in the Roman Forum—"and the red of the leather." Ribulsi evidently had an opportunity to explain her aims, for we are told that when Mussolini accepted the gift, he "remarked in a joking tone, 'You have given me a history lesson.'"

Why joke? By this point, Mussolini must have felt he was fully expert in the form and meaning of the Roman fasces. Indeed, given the flurry of official activity and public engagement that surrounded the quest to reconstruct the "authentic" Roman fasces in the first four months of 1923, it is hard to determine what Cesarina Ribulsi had in mind on May 19 when she filed into the Viminal Palace with the IWSA delegates and presented her own reconstruction of the fasces to the "Duce." By that point, all of Italy knew that Giacomo Boni had completed his model, and that the mint's chosen sculptor had rendered it, awaiting only formal confirmation (which would come June 14). Can Ribulsi seriously have imagined that Mussolini would embrace her model as an alternative?

The details that can be disengaged of Cesarina Ribulsi's life and career offer few clues of what she aimed to accomplish with her fasces.[18] Born in Torino and educated in Rome, in the early 1920s her main public association was with the study of modern Italian history, especially the political program of the Italian revolutionary Giuseppe Mazzini (1805–1872). As seen, the *Il Piccolo* article adds the item that she was teaching, from a Fascist perspective, Roman studies in the Italian "popular university" system of adult education. She also presumably knew the head Congress delegate Regina Terruzzi, a strong Mazzinian practically from birth, and at the time the president of the Popular University of Milan. What does offer a promising lead is her Rome address. In 1921 Ribulsi listed her domicile as the Palazzina Calzone, a magnificent art nouveau mansion recently constructed on the Via del Collegio Romano. That was the home of two immensely rich natives of Torino, the printing magnate Ettore Calzone (1848–1932) and his wife Camilla Calzone Mongenet (1861–1944). The latter was a prominent Theosophist and one of the chief adherents of the Italian philosopher, hermeticist, and alchemist Giuliano Kremmerz (1861–1930). At the time, Ribulsi apparently worked as her secretary.[19]

It is a pity that we have no image of Cesarina Ribulsi's version of the fasces, to see whether it ran the risk of seeming derivative of Boni's, or—considering the government's stake in his project—undesirably divergent. On the facts we know, the most distinctive attribute of Ribulsi's model was the aged (or artificially distressed) axe-head, which was described to Mussolini as Etruscan, thus evoking the most distant origins of the fasces. (One wonders whether it really came from an Etruscan tomb, or rather had some connection to the Kircher Museum, cited in *Il Piccolo* as holding analogous items, which was across the street from her home.) It is also striking that Ribulsi had found white birch for her rods, whereas Boni had so much trouble, despite his high official position and passion for botany.

Indeed, Ribulsi's use of the ancient-looking blade with those "freshly cut" sticks introduced an innovation: the green patina of the axe-head, the white of the birch rods, and the red leather straps corresponded precisely to the colors of Italy's contemporary flag. One remembers that when Cesarina Ribulsi delivered her fasces to Mussolini, she specifically connected them with a patriotic anniversary that would be observed six days hence, on May 24, that of Italy's 1915 intervention in the First World War. Perhaps she even hoped Mussolini would display her tricolor device on his official duties that day; he was scheduled to inaugurate a major military cemetery near Gorizia (northeastern Italy), the nation's first large-scale memorial to its war dead.

But what are we to make of the context of Cesarina Ribulsi's presentation, a women's march on the Viminal Palace to demand universal voting rights? The occasion of course offered Ribulsi a chance to show Mussolini a very tangible example of her contribution to his ideological project. But that does not explain how she came to be included among the delegates whom Mussolini received. She appears nowhere in the voluminous official Report of the Rome Congress, not even as an alternate delegate.[20]

Indeed, the notion of Ribulsi carrying a full-scale fasces among the many distinguished members of the IWSU deputation strikes one as highly provocative—and not just for the blatant political message. It must be remembered that in the popular imagination of the era, axes and hatchets were closely associated with temperance women and suffragists.[21] The IWSA had a long reputation as a mainstream, nonviolent organization, and served as a large umbrella for a wide variety of national suffrage associations. Nor did "suffrage militancy" have a footing in Italy, either before or after the war. But the phenomenon was abundantly familiar to Italians, thanks to breathless, highly negative coverage in the national press of especially key British incidents in the pre-war period. Whether she intended it or not, Cesarina Ribulsi's act of handing over a fasces with its axe to Mussolini in the precise context of an international suffrage demonstration strikes one as a gesture *seppellire l'ascia di guerra*, "to bury the hatchet"—a symbolic repudiation by

Italian women of combative tactics and a pledge of deference to his regime in the matter of voting rights.

Support from this interpretation comes from the one additional detail we have of this incident, that Cesarina Ribulsi came to the Viminal to meet Mussolini clothed in red—the traditional color of anti-suffragists. For this item, we have to turn to an offbeat source, the esoteric journal *Krur* for 1929. This was a low-circulation periodical issued by a recently established occultist, neo-pagan clique called the Ur Group. The editor of *Krur* was the nativist, anti-Semitic, anti-Christian conspiracy theorist and philosopher Julius Evola (1898–1974). All of the articles in the year's output of *Krur* have symbolic pseudonyms in their bylines, or are unsigned, such as a disquisition on Giuliano Kremmerz.

The year's output of the journal was reprinted as a single volume, where several pieces are grouped under the category "Experiences," including a short article in quasi-oracular style by one "Ekatlos" entitled "The 'Great Trail': The Stage and the Wings," originally printed in December 1929.[22] Here the writer offers an impressionistic sketch of five episodes in the life of a secret group, based in Rome, and bound by an archaic ritual initiated sixteen years previous. "Ekatlos" makes the eye-opening claim that the powers this group, unlocked first in 1913 through the private excavation of a tomb outside the city, somehow were responsible for Italy's ultimate victory in the First World War, and since then have been shaping the successes of Fascism.

Two of these episodes, both from the postwar period, are instantly identifiable, and each is relevant to our story. First, "Ekatlos" says that in 1919, "by 'chance,' by the same forces, through the same people," Mussolini heard a pronouncement that he would be "consul of Italy" and at the same time received an "Etruscan ritual formula of purification." The group member in question clearly is Mussolini's friend Regina Terruzzi, who, as we have seen, was reputed to have made the "consul" prediction in Milan at the formation of the *Fasci Italiani del Combattimento* on March 23, 1919.

"Ekatlos" then continues: "Later. After the March on Rome. An insignificant fact, an even more insignificant occasion." That is how the writer describes the 1923 IWSU Congress in Rome and the participation of Cesarina Ribulsi. "Among the people who pay homage to the Head of Government, one, dressed in red, steps forward and gives him a fasces. *The same forces wanted this*: and they wanted the exact number of rods, and the way they were cut and the ritual interweaving of the red ribbon; and they still wanted—again—the 'chance' that the axe for that fasces was an archaic Etruscan axe, to which equally mysterious paths led us."

The author then breaks with the deliberately cryptic style to offer a foot-note on the matter, in which the published description of Ribulsi's fasces in *Il Piccolo* is cited at length, without mentioning Ribulsi's name. "Ekatlos" closes this note by saying the newspaper misunderstood the significance of the model. "Of course, in all this—for those on the stage—it is not simply a 'historical-archaeological' reconstruction."

The takeaway is downright creepy. If we are to believe "Ekatlos," the oc-cult group had found a genuinely Etruscan axe-head, forces awakened by the members' ceremonies had guided its incorporation into a ritually correct fasces, and its pagan energy had been transmitted to Mussolini and the Fascist movement. In short, they had outdone the officially sanctioned fasces created by the archaeologist Giacomo Boni, which was simply an antiquarian model.

Starting in the mid-1950s, Evola saw to the reprinting of the collected writings of the Ur Group, including this essay, which within the field of eso-teric studies stimulated sustained interest and speculation, that continues to the present moment. Who is "Ekatlos"? Who were the initiates in his or her group—other than (apparently) Regina Terruzzi and Cesarina Ribulsi? Who were their intellectual influences, and what was the precise nature of their ac-tivities? What is the relationship of that group to the later Ur Group? How did the "Ekatlos" manuscript make its way to Evola? What role did this all play in the development of "mystic fascism," soon (1930) institutionalized in its own state-supported school in Milan?[23]

It would take considerable effort just to collect all the (largely inconclu-sive) views on these larger problems, never mind to resolve them satisfactorily through fresh archival work. Of course, additional questions present them-selves, including a basic one: What happened to Cesarina Ribulsi's model of the fasces that she presented to Mussolini at the Palazzo Viminale?

Perhaps it did not travel very far. On September 24, 1925, the English writer Harold Begbie published in London's *Daily Mail* an encomiastic sketch of Mussolini and his political reforms, based on an interview held in his office on the Viminal. "On the central table in [Mussolini's] room," Begbie informs his readers, "lies a full-size model of the fasces carried by lictors be-fore the emperors and consuls of ancient Rome—an axe surrounded by close-banded rods. He laid his hand upon it and said: 'A symbol! Unity by means of authority.' "[24] Could this facsimile of the fasces be the one created by Ribulsi? Or was it that of Boni, or the effort of someone else? Unfortunately, answers are just guesswork. What is more important here is Mussolini's reported dec-laration, already in 1925, that the fasces represents "unity," which is a claim that Boni (who had died in July of that year) does not appear to have made.

Amplification of the Fasces under Mussolini

So our discussion of fasces model-making in Italy underlines how the Fascist regime, almost immediately after seizing power in October 1922, invested enormous resources into forcing the party symbol into every crevice of Italian public and private life. And it shows that some of Mussolini's most fervent admirers saw a remarkable range of meanings residing in the fasces, far beyond its conventional associations as a Roman instrument of justice and sign of rank, to include even mystical properties. For his part, Mussolini in September 1925 succinctly described the fasces model displayed in his office as a sign of "unity by means of authority"—which turns the American ideal of "strength through unity" on its head.

In a little more than year's time, by decree of December 12, 1926, the fasces would be made the official emblem of the Italian state. This marked not the end of the campaign to propagate the ancient image, but rather a new and deeply unsettling beginning. The decree institutionalized the fasces as the emblem of the state and tried to regularize its presentation in a strict visual identity system. The newly official status of the fasces offered a ready-made way to express support of Mussolini's regime.[25]

Scholarly study of the Roman lictors and their fasces quickly became a crowded subfield, with about a dozen books and substantial articles on this rather specialized subject appearing in Italy in the years 1927–1936. The era saw numerous investigations of the Roman use of the fasces, aimed at a wide range of audiences, from school libraries (e.g., P. Ducati's 1927 *Origins and Attributes of the Fasces*) to adherents of the emerging occultist school of Fascist mysticism. The most authoritative definition of the fasces would seem to be the one philosopher Giovanni Gentile (1875–1944) ghost-wrote for Mussolini to appear in the article "Fascism" (1932) for the *Enciclopedia Italiana*, namely a "symbol of unity, of force and of justice." This formulation in turn was cribbed from the October 25, 1919, issue of *Il Popolo d'Italia* that first introduced the fasces as a logo to Mussolini's political adherents.

The one thing almost all discussions of the fasces of this era have in common—whether popular, esoteric, or scholarly—is a desire to trace a straight historical line from "authentic" Roman practices to contemporary Fascist representations. For instance, the archaeologist Giulio Quirino Giglioli (1886–1957), in a highly tendentious introduction to A. M. Colini's 1933 *The Fasces of Rome Researched in the Ancient Monuments* (itself a valuable compendium of the textual and visual sources), considers the invocation of the symbol during the French Revolution as "inexact," and that in the Roman

Republic of 1849 a "transient revival." Giglioli asserts that it is only the will of a "Duce romano" [*sic*] that has caused true renewal of the fasces and has allowed Italy, under that symbol, to repossess ancient Rome's "glorious mission."[26] The political context of Mussolini's regime militated against thinking about reception of the ancient Roman fasces in global terms.

In the arts and architecture, there was massive propagation of the image in Italy. Indeed from December 1, 1925, there was a requirement that ministerial buildings had to display the fasces, extended in the next year to all governmental buildings. Its incorporation on a grand scale in public building initiatives became inevitable. An early conspicuous example is the Bolzano Victory Monument, dedicated July 12, 1928. It was designed by architect Marcello Piacentini (1881–1960), and erected on land in South Tyrol annexed from Austria after World War I (indeed on the very spot of an Austrian monument demolished in 1926–1927). The Victory Monument is notable for its assertive display of fasces and provocative Latin inscription championing ancient Rome's imperialism.

"Architects and building engineers found the shape and proportions of the *fascio littorio* a significant element to add value," observes Daniele Vadalà in a concise survey of the sign's manifestations "from the allusively symbolic to the rhetorically bombastic" under Fascist rule.[27] It would take many years of work to register all the significant appearances of the fasces in Italian public building and visual and graphic art under Mussolini's regime. Such an effort properly would take in not just all of civic and military life in Italy, but also the country's colonies in Africa, and pieces it exported elsewhere (including the United States), e.g., for exhibitions and fairs. Such a catalog would also have to encompass permanent constructions, temporary features on preexisting structures, and wholly ephemeral items that featured the fasces. For the latter two categories, our knowledge has exploded in just the last dozen or so years, thanks to the digital publication of a major chunk of the film and photo archives of Istituto LUCE (acronym of "L'Unione Cinematografica Educativa" = "The Educational Film Union," established 1924).

But let us look past these complexities for the moment. One indisputable red-letter date for the Fascist fasces was the "Decennale," the tenth anniversary of the March on Rome, celebrated throughout the year 1932—and indeed beyond. At the very center of the celebrations was the "Exhibit of the Fascist Revolution," that opened on October 29, 1932, on Rome's Via Nazionale in the Palazzo delle Esposizioni. The façade of the Palazzo (built 1882) was rendered almost unrecognizable, thanks to the addition of four enormous aluminum columns in the form of stylized fasces, each standing 30 meters high. Though originally scheduled to run for no more than six months, the Exhibit was considered so electrifying that it remained open for two years, and drew nearly four million visitors.[28]

Another key event was the 1934 architectural competition to build a huge Fascist party headquarters in Rome next to the Colosseum, on the newly realized (1932) Via dell' Impero (today's Via dei Fori Imperiali). Thankfully the scheme never was realized. For one thing, two separate designs—that of Adalberto Libera (1903–1963), and also Saul Bravetti (1907–1971) with Gianluigi Giordani (1909–1979)—offered a tower shaped as a fasces taller than the height of the ancient amphitheater (Figure 11.3). In both those entries for the competition, the gigantic fasces before the headquarters seems to have incorporated a podium for Mussolini to deliver mass harangues.[29]

Indeed, in this epoch, vigorous promotion of the fasces as symbol was to permeate public and private life. In Italian, the Roman bundle of rods with axes is known—notwithstanding slight Latin authority for the phrase—as a *fascio littorio* (plural, *fasci littori*). Mussolini's regime soon seized upon the second element of this formulation to make *littorio* (roughly, "the lictors' activity") a synonym for *fascismo*. In the 1934 competition for the new Fascist Party headquarters, the structure was accordingly called the "Palazzo del Littorio."

Indeed, though (as we have seen) many cultures starting in the early modern era had tried to leverage the symbol of the fasces for one reason or other, it was a special innovation of Mussolini's regime to idealize the humble lictor and raise him to prominence. The not-so-subtle suggestion was that all

Sopra: Prospettiva verso il Colosseo.   *Sotto:* Il plastico visto anteriormente

FIGURE 11.3. Contribution of architects Saul Bravetti and Luigi Giordani to the 1934 design competition for the Palazzo del Littorio (Fascist Party headquarters), to be constructed on the newly realized (1932) Via dell' Impero (= Via dei Fori Imperiali) in Rome.

From *Architettura: Rivista del Sindicato Nazionale Fascista Architetti*. Special number 1934 (p. 113). Milan and Rome: Fratelli Treves.

elements of Italian society should model their behavior on that of the lictor, and selflessly and energetically carry forward the standard of *fascismo*.

By the early 1930s, strained extensions of the *littorio* concept made their way seemingly everywhere in Mussolini's Italy. A "Ponte Littorio" bridge was built to cross the Tiber, joining the Vatican area with that of Flaminio (1929). A new town was founded in the newly reclaimed Pontine marshes as Littoria (1932). "Littoriali" denoted competitions in sports (1933) and soon also in culture and art (1934). An Italian national airline was introduced as Ala Littoria (1934). The largest youth organization was renamed "Italian Youth of the *Littorio*" (1937).[30]

Yet Mussolini seems only once to have appeared in public preceded by actual fasces, on horseback in a grandiose ceremony in Tripoli—acceptance of the so-called sword of Islam—on March 20, 1937. A contemporary image shows a pair of native Libyans playing the part of lictors, bearing fasces with axes, each on different shoulders, posed before Mussolini. The experiment was not repeated. Even for the dictator, there proved to be limits to promotion of his regime's main symbol.[31]

Eradication of Fasces and Epilogue

American Resistance to the Fasces in the Era of World War II

It took thirty-six months of feverish construction, but finally on Monday, August 12, 1940, a splendid new federal building and post office opened its doors to the citizens of the California city of Fresno. The US Treasury Department Section of Fine Arts had commissioned six artists to embellish the exterior and interior of the $600,000 structure (almost $12 million in 2021 US dollars), which combined minimalist modern design with monumental classicizing elements.

One of the most imposing spaces in the structure was the large room for the US District Court on the second floor, with tall cork-lined walls 22 feet (6.7 m) high. "In the background over the judge's podium," reported the *Fresno Bee* the day before the grand opening, "will be seen several square feet of highly-polished walnut paneling, in the center of which is inscribed Justice By Law—Law By Order" (Figure 12.1). As a decorative element, "also inscribed upon the paneling is the ancient Roman fasces, also outlined in gold leaf." The emblem was placed high up on this polished curvilinear wall, just below the (novel) motto.

Some six weeks later came a shocker. "'No! No!' Say Judges; Dictator Symbol Rouses Jurists' Ire," read the headline in the *Bee*. Federal judge Léon René Yankwich (1888–1975) refused to open the fall session of the court if the inscribed paneling remained; in this he was backed by two of his colleagues on the bench. As a short-term remedy, Judge Yankwich ordered an American flag to cover the offending legend and symbol. The Fresno postmaster started the administrative process to get the design chiseled out.

The Fasces. T. Corey Brennan, Oxford University Press. © Oxford University Press 2023.
DOI: 10.1093/oso/9780197644881.003.0012

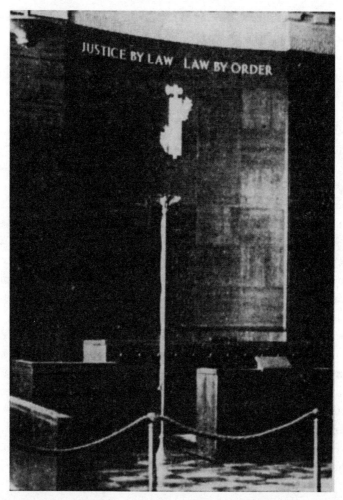

FIGURE 12.1. News photo from *The Fresno Bee—The Republican* (October 3, 1940, p. 17), illustrating Federal judges' protest regarding decoration of new courtroom with perceived Fascist motifs.

Credit: The Fresno Bee/PARS International Corporation.

Oddly, the placement of the axe-head on top of the bundle—rather than inserted laterally, as on the US "Mercury" dime and for that matter in contemporary Italian Fascist practice—was one of the attributes that excited Judge Yankwich's suspicion and criticism. "As far as I know," he is reported to have said, "the symbol on our dimes may mean unity." But in contrast to the 10-cent piece, on the courtroom wall "the sheaves are missing, and the axe is in a different place." No artist stepped forward to defend the design;

explained the *Bee*, "the fault seems to rest on the shoulders of an unidentified architect in Washington, DC."

Yankwich, who had studied Classics in his native Romania and at the Sorbonne before emigrating to the United States, voiced a thoroughgoing criticism of the courtroom decoration. The letter he wrote to the Fresno postmaster offers a detailed and well-informed rationale of why he insisted on its removal, citing both the symbol and the accompanying quotation.[1]

"The fasces is an emblem of power and not at all coincident with the American concept of the limitation of power through law. Our ideal is justice through law. The other is the ideal of the totalitarian state where the dictator is the source of law and order."

The judge continues: "With us, law is the source of power, and as the supreme power, also limits the power of everyone, even the executives. We emphasize law and justice, not order. We are not policeman, and the fasces is an emblem of authority. In dealing with justice we must stress an orderly process, the ideal of equal justice, trial in open court by a jury of our peers. Law by order, as contained in the motto, is the antithesis of our creed."

One suspects as a working hypothesis that the sculptor William Zorach (1889–1966), then employed by the US Treasury Section of Fine Arts, had a hand in the composition. His wife Marguerite Zorach (1887–1968) had been commissioned to paint two large panels for this same Fresno courtroom, which in January 1941 surprisingly were rejected upon delivery by two of the federal judges in Fresno; later, in 1960, William Zorach himself created a limestone relief sculpture for the exterior of the New York Civil Court building with the title "Justice through Law and Order," a small variation on the Fresno motto, otherwise seemingly unparalleled in the English language.

Whatever the identity and motives of the designer, the federal judges' protest was widely reported and seems to have struck a patriotic chord nationwide. In an extreme reaction, a religious newsletter flat out represented the new Fresno federal building as an extension of Mussolini's regime. "Traveling a bit too fast, the Fascist designers . . . not only worked fasces into the panels of the courtroom but had the audacity to inscribe therein the Fascist motto 'Justice by law, law by order.'" The notion that the inscription was borrowed directly from Mussolini's regime is erroneous but understandable, given its similarity to the Fascist mantra "Ordine, Autorità, Giustizia" ("Order, Authority, Justice").[2]

The Fresno incident does not stand in isolation. Well before the United States entered World War II, pressure mounted to change the reverse of the 10-cent coin itself. A Washington newspaper in June 1931 reports "numerous letters" to the director of the US Mint objecting to the design. But it dismissed the reaction as ill-informed and alarmist, since the emblem in its developed form "came to represent the principle that the power was in the people." The design of the dime should be of no concern, the column continues. "If that which they fear now as a sign of fascism is significant at all, it is of the principle upon which the American republic was founded, and on which it exists today."

A decade later, in late April 1941, US Secretary of the Treasury Henry Morgenthau Jr. (1891–1967) received a letter from the women's division of the New York–based Committee of Americans, a group focused on national war preparedness that claimed a membership of more than a million, insisting on a stop to "further minting of dimes with the emblem of fascism on them." By law, after twenty-five years the Treasury on its own authority could change a coin design. For the "Mercury" (i.e., Liberty with winged cap) dime, designed by Alexander Weinman and introduced in 1916, that period had now elapsed. Though the demand was widely reported, it found little support in the press. A New Jersey newspaper argued that, despite Mussolini's appropriation of the fasces, they "still stand for an ancient Rome, with honor unimpaired . . . as well as to the union of American states." A college paper in North Carolina characterized the petition to the Treasury as "ridiculous."

After the United States joined the Allied cause in December 1941, feelings naturally intensified, as well as confusion. In May 1943, some citizens of Danbury, Connecticut, boiled over in anger when they saw a carved wooden fasces surmount a war honor roll set up in a public park. A rabbi even refused to take part in the inauguration ceremony, where he was scheduled to offer the closing benediction. To complicate matters, it was revealed that the headpiece was the work of an Italian-American woodworker—who at the time had three sons in the US armed services. The mayor of Danbury removed the fasces but then soon restored the carving, pending guidance from Washington on whether the symbol was indeed un-American.

A local newspaper tried to downplay the affair. The artist "took the design from the back of a dime and thought it appropriate as symbolical of unity of purpose and of labor," it was explained. "It doesn't seem very serious," concluded the report. "The dime is good American." Another newspaper agreed that the fasces reverse symbolized "the strength that comes from unity," and at any rate this dime had been introduced in 1916, "three years before Mussolini's rise to power."[3]

However, just ten days after the Allied victory in Europe, on May 17, 1945, Henry Morgenthau Jr. announced that the Treasury would be replacing the dime that it had used for the last twenty-nine years. Henceforth it would bear a likeness of President Franklin D. Roosevelt, who had died the previous month. On January 30, 1946, the Treasury introduced its new type, with a stunning bust of the deceased president on the obverse. The coin's reverse showed a reworking of the fasces as a "liberty torch" flanked by branches of olive and oak, said to represent peace and strength. Since its introduction, this coin has circulated essentially unchanged to the present.

Few made a public case for keeping the old reverse design, which now was understood as tainted by Italy's recent history. "The fasces have been an embarrassment ever since Mussolini adopted them as symbol for his Fascists," opined the *Honolulu Advertiser* in July 1946, "and while they are both gone now, the old Roman symbol of authority suited him better than it ever did us anyway—the bundle of sticks to beat people with, and the ax to chop off their heads!"[4]

Italian Fasces under Nazi Control

As it happened, the Italian Fascist government had collapsed on July 25, 1943, and it was announced on September 8 that the Kingdom of Italy would cease military operations against the Allies. However, within days, the Germans rapidly managed to take control of most of peninsular Italy, occupy Rome, free Mussolini from his detention at a mountain resort in Abruzzo, and set him up as head of a collaborationist regime.

Mussolini, for his new Fascist Republican Party (PFR) and, by the end of the year, Italian Social Republic (RSI), decided on a new emblem—one that featured a fasces with an axe now inserted in the top. Mussolini deliberately borrowed this from the iconography of his pre-1921 "Italian *Fasci* of Combat," and ultimately, from that of the French-inspired revolutionary movements of late eighteenth- and mid-nineteenth-century Italy. It is extraordinary that he adopted this "Republican" form of the fasces. For in effect he was discarding the iconographic and conceptual imaginarium that he had so relentlessly constructed over the previous two decades.

The goal here evidently was both to repudiate Italy's monarchy, and to evoke "Sansepolcrismo," the spirit of the rally at Milan's Piazza San Sepolcro (March 23, 1919), where Mussolini first set out his revolutionary program. In actual fact, the government that Mussolini formed had little contact with the principles set out at San Sepolcro. Rather, the RSI was a Nazi puppet-state confined largely to the German-occupied north of the country, with its headquarters at Salò (near Brescia, on Lake Garda). Mussolini's German patrons established him at nearby Gargnano, essentially under house arrest.

Mussolini based his new governmental coat of arms closely on one that the Kingdom of Italy had used for about two years (1927–1929) to showcase its partnership with the Fascists.[5] There the Savoia royal crest was paired with the *tricolore* flag of Italy in the form of a shield; a thick vertical fasces occupied the field's central white band. An eagle with spread wings, rendered in gold in the supposed manner of Roman imperial standards, surmounted the shield. The RSI update naturally dumped the Savoia portion of the design altogether. The new-look Fascist shield had its colors reversed, i.e., now with red on the left and green on the right, presumably to emphasize Mussolini's break with King Vittorio Emanuele III. The axe-head was rendered as that of a halberd, and moved to the top of the bundle. As in the original "Fascist Bloc" seal of 1919, the cords are shown coming loose.

The RSI indulged in other heavy-handed visual statements. Most notable is the final combat flag that the puppet government adopted in early May 1944. The field is a conventional *tricolore*, where the center white stripe presents an eagle in black, standing on a horizontal Republican fasces, its wings extending into (re-reversed) green and red fields. The English-language press widely supposed that Mussolini himself had designed the banner as a new national emblem. So the replacement of the Savoia arms, which had stood on the Kingdom of Italy's flag since 1861, attracted special attention in newspaper reports. With the fall of Rome imminent, journalists also savagely ridiculed the new flag as pointless. ("It would be appropriate to run it up to half-staff right now," was a characteristic comment.) The eagle-on-fasces itself was of course entirely derivative. The coinage of the Roman Republic of 1798–1799 had used precisely this composition. It is found even in the general run of earlier Fascist iconography, but with the fasces' axe-head in medial position, not at the top of the bundle.[6]

The German surrender at Caserta in Campania (April 29, 1945) formalized the end of fighting in Italy, and total Axis capitulation in Europe followed shortly afterward (V-E Day, May 8, 1945). Yet Italians already had obliterated some of the most conspicuous symbols of fascism, much in the space of a single day. The announcement on state radio at 10:45 p.m. on Sunday, July 25, 1943, that King Vittorio Emanuele III had accepted the "resignation" of Mussolini and had appointed Marshal Pietro Badoglio (1871–1956) to his governmental posts triggered widespread jubilation. The morning that followed brought a frenzy of hammer and chisel work on public buildings, monuments, and even street signs throughout Italy, before Badoglio effectively imposed stern martial law measures on the entire nation.

One of the earliest targets of anti-Fascist sentiment in Rome was Palazzo Venezia, where Mussolini had established his office in September 1929. What was specifically detestable was the pair of giant fasces that famously framed the balcony adjoining Mussolini's quarters, from which he used to harangue "oceanic" crowds in the enormous piazza below. Photographs from July 26, 1943, show these fasces, which stood more than 3 meters high, already removed. Other images from the day show the spontaneous work of destruction of sculptural fasces, in Rome, Milan, and Genova. In a typical scene, a man in street clothes works high on a ladder, hacking away at sculptural elements, with an approving crowd below.[7]

But such impromptu, uncoordinated efforts could hardly alter the propaganda landscape in any comprehensive way. They also will have ground to a halt by mid-September 1943 under German occupation. So when the Allied forces first entered Rome, on June 4, 1944, they found most of the major expressions of Fascist ideology in the urban fabric more or less intact.

The Fate of the Fasces in Rome's Foro Mussolini

By far the largest and most boisterous of the physical expressions of Fascism in Rome, and indeed in all Italy, was the Foro Mussolini, 2 kilometers north of the Vatican, also on the west side of the Tiber river. Originally planned and executed as a city of physical education and sport by the architect Enrico Del Debbio (1891–1973, working in the years 1927–1933), with important later contributions especially by Luigi Moretti (1907–1973), it straddled more than 80 hectares beneath Monte Mario. Its stylish facilities included "Palazzo H," containing the core of a Fascist Academy of Physical Education, two large stadiums (one aspiring to a capacity of 100,000, the other seating 20,000), a magnificent indoor pool complex (housing also a personal gymnasium for the "Duce"), Luigi Moretti's landmark school for fencing, and much else.

One of the Foro's most familiar features was its smaller "Stadium of the Statues" ("Stadio dei Marmi"), completed in 1932. That was a heavy, Hellenized outdoor arena for which sixty Italian towns or cities each had contributed a monumental male nude statue in a different athletic pose. The new town of Littoria (founded 1932) appropriately gifted the statue of a lictor, sculpted by Aroldo Bellini (1902–1984), portrayed at ease with his left hand resting on a tall fasces on the ground.

The fundamental purpose of the Foro Mussolini was to serve as the premier laboratory for a new generation of physical education instructors, schooled also in military practices and Fascist party thought. But the regime intended the expansive grounds and lavish facilities to function on a much larger scale, as an arena of exemplarity. "The great athletic center is a symbol as well as a practical instrument" for a thoroughgoing remodeling of the Italian people under Fascism, as one American educator observed in 1935, with a mixture of horror and admiration. Mussolini's "program of education, training enthusiasms, and social pressure is focused at this spot," he acutely observed, "and from here is to radiate to all Italians, both at home and abroad."[8]

The best-known monument of the Foro Mussolini complex stood at its principal entrance as one crossed the Tiber: a brilliant white obelisk of Carrara marble, 40 meters tall, that even without its huge lateral pieces and base totaled 380 tons in weight. Plainly visible even from the other bank of the river was its Latin inscription MVSSOLINI DVX ("Mussolini the leader"), inscribed vertically in massive letters. A tall stylized fasces, carved deep into the stone, flanked the lower part of the obelisk's inscription.

The very existence of a Mussolini obelisk at that site was meant to amaze, and the regime worked hard to ensure that it ranked among Rome's top landmarks. Indeed, the LUCE news image company had devoted at least two dozen newsreels to the dramatic events that brought the monolith from excavation in Tuscany at Carrara to erection at the new Forum, a process that took four full years. After its dedication on October 28, 1932 (i.e., the first day of "Year 10" of the Fascist era), depictions of the obelisk were practically ubiquitous on youth organization medals, membership cards, certificates, awards, and even school report cards for almost a dozen years.

The rear of this imposing and indeed immovable monument looked northwest over the Piazzale dell'Impero ("Empire Plaza"). This was a majestic pedestrian boulevard formed by a series of multilevel platforms designed by Luigi Moretti (Figure 12.2). The space was executed in 1937, to celebrate Italy's armed annexation of the kingdom of Ethiopia in the previous year. A vast monochromatic Roman-style mosaic surface—some 7,000 square meters, the work of the artist Gino Severini (1883–1966) and others—paved the Piazzale, which linked the obelisk to the Fountain of the Sphere (1932), almost 200 meters distant, and then the main stadium of the Forum.

The Piazzale consists of a long and broad rectangular walkway (ca. 122 m × 50 m), with a narrower (ca. 10 m) undecorated platform running up its middle, that led to a circular piazza (ca. 92 m in diameter), with the marble sphere-fountain at center. Near the outer boundaries of the walkway, Moretti

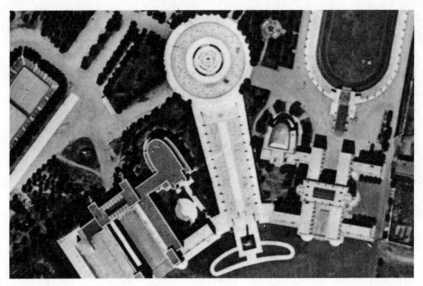

FIGURE 12.2. Luigi Moretti's Piazzale dell'Impero in the Foro Mussolini, as photographed by a British RAF reconnaissance plane on May 27, 1944.

Credit: Aerofototeca Nazionale inv. RAF 1944, 150 421 276229 0.

artfully positioned twenty-four large marble slabs, twelve on each side, whose inscriptions were meant to mark landmark dates in Fascist history. The mosaic designs that covered much of the lower portions of the multilevel pavement are set out in distinct scenes, with divisions for ten on each side of the raised central platform. Sixteen scenes (alternating between large and small) run around the fountain. Within the main scenes of the walkway are further subdivisions, where the unpredictable orientation of figures lends an unusually dynamic quality to these vignettes in pebbled stone.

Throughout the Piazzale mosaics, there is much blending of the Roman past with the Fascist present, with emphasis especially on athleticism, but also agriculture, construction, the arts, and (prominently centered) contemporary military conquest. A map showing the general area of the ancient Forum Boarium in Rome (the alleged spot of the suckling of Romulus and Remus) is twinned with one setting out the plan of the Foro Mussolini, including yet-unbuilt portions. The mosaics use Fascist emblems and even slogans as decorative elements on a massive scale, and amplify their message with persistent repetition. (The title DUCE has been counted 264 times in the Piazzale.) A focal point of the elaborate composition comes in the transitional space from walkway to piazza, with the figure of a personified Italia, pointedly depicted as a young male, positioned above the Capitoline Wolf. He balances a large stylized fasces with his right hand, and is surrounded by allegorical representations of the arts.

Almost 240 fasces in all figure as elements in the mosaic pavement, and are integrated into the decorative program in such a way that one could not eradicate them without destroying the Piazzale. One enters the space from the obelisk walking either past or over large mosaic fasces, arranged in paired rows of seven. The two mosaic strips of the walkway each have as their inner borders a repeating pattern of smaller upside-down fasces, a total of 112 on either side. Each sequence of fasces extends along the space for an individual pictorial scene; transitions are marked by a distinctive fasces incongruously topped with an eagle's head, combined with a monogram M, and flanked by laurel and oak branches. The scheme of decorative fasces continues, with variations, beyond the main platform of the Piazzale, around the monumental Fountain of the Sphere. There one finds another 112 fasces arranged in an intricate circular design.

An obvious artistic source for this ambitious production is the imperial Roman (second century CE) Plaza of Corporations in Ostia. There an open forum is bounded by a long series of small rooms with mosaic floors, many with inscriptions, that depict industries relating to maritime trade. Yet it seems worth suggesting that the arrangement of the Mussolini Forum mosaics shows even more strongly a contemporary influence, that of motion picture technology. The two monochrome mosaic rows of the walkway resemble 35-mm film strips, then quite established as the standard gauge for cinema projection. Each row gives the impression of ten "frames," separated by strong black frame lines. On the inner edge, where one would expect the thin line of the film's optical soundtrack (Italian *colonna sonora*), is the border of fasces. It does appear as though pedestrians in the Piazzale were meant to experience a rapid mosaic montage of ancient and modern Imperial history.

One difference between the mosaics and actual film stock: in the Piazzale, each "frame image" is oriented sideways, toward the central platform, for ease of viewing. From this perspective, the frame on average measures (on a rough-and-ready reckoning) 8.5 m wide and 6.1 m tall (i.e., 1.4:1). This proportion is very close to the standard film ratio (1.375:1) prevalent after 1930, and its use may be deliberate—though comprehensive measurements of the Piazzale would be needed to press this argument. The important point for our purposes is that it is the "Duce" and the fasces that are meant to lend cohesion to this sprawling, eclectic tableau of energized activity.[9]

From the upper sections of the Piazzale, one could see to the right, beyond the Stadio dei Marmi, the outlines of Enrico Del Debbio's planned headquarters for the Fascist Party, designed in 1937 to be the largest building in Italy. That was inaugurated only in 1956, as the seat of Italy's Ministry of Foreign Affairs. The Foro Mussolini might have been even bigger. Planned for this general area, but never realized, was an architecturally innovative square that Moretti had designed for the mass armed mobilizations of Fascist party members called *adunate* ("musterings"). Capacity was meant to be 400,000, in answer to the elliptical piazza at St. Peter's designed by Gian Lorenzo Bernini (1598–1680). What caused the Vatican actual alarm was the plan for a 120-meter colossus figure in a geometric loincloth representing Fascism (but looking distinctly like Mussolini). Announced in May 1936, the work of casting actually started, but was waylaid by international sanctions against Italy for its invasion of Ethiopia, and then the world war.

Indeed, the site had developed such a practical and symbolic importance that early Allied planning (November 1940) had contemplated bombing the Foro Mussolini, along with several other strategic sites in Rome, such as its main train station. So what was to be done with this modernistic monument to megalomania now that Rome was liberated? In the event, the United States military converted Foro Mussolini into the Fifth Army Rest Center on June 19, 1944, just fourteen days after Allied troops had entered the city. The Rest Center for the remainder of 1944 and for much of 1945 housed ca. 2,500 soldiers at a time, most staying for just a few days before redeployment.

After July 25, 1943, the complex had shed Mussolini from its name, to be known variously as "Foro della Farnesina," "Foro d'Italia," and eventually (by 1948) as "Foro Italico." Many tens of thousands of especially American, British, and French soldiers will have experienced the site before war's end. *LIFE* magazine archival images taken in June 1944 by staff photographer Carl Mydans (1907–2004), and illustrated US Army souvenir guides for the former Foro Mussolini (1944 and 1945) provide a remarkable record of the buildings and spaces designed by Luigi Moretti, Ernesto del Debbio, and others, and how the GIs used them in this period, inside and out.

In a word, the Allies kept the Foro Mussolini site essentially intact— interiors and exteriors—especially since its aim was to continue its athletic and instructional focus, but now for soldiers in the North African and Italian zones. As such, the Rest Center would host any number of morale-building events, ranging from the Inter-Allied Boxing Championship in Moretti's iconic fencing school (now renamed "Building B"), to a women's beauty pageant (June 2, 1945) on the Piazzale dell'Impero. To judge from contemporary souvenir books, photographs, and newsreels, permanent physical interventions at the Foro seem minimal. The façade of the indoor swim complex lost its pair of fasces. The *Foresteria Nord* ("north guesthouse") was ceded to the Italian Communist Party, and the "Shrine of the Fascist Martyrs" located there was thoroughly dismantled. Otherwise, the Allies seemed content to recreate the Foro Mussolini as a dramatic, indeed ironic setting for their own wartime morale and propaganda purposes.[10]

The policy of the US Army—here and elsewhere in Italy—was to delegate responsibility for removing Fascist monuments and artworks to the Italians, and rather to focus on the larger military challenges of the still-raging war. But here there was a proverbial "Catch-22": so long as the Americans occupied the Foro (which they did until 1948), it remained beyond the reach of Italian authorities. In any case, Italy never developed a master plan to dismantle the material remains of the Fascist era. Nor did the ruling party of the postwar era, the Christian Democrats (DC), have much interest in implementing actual eradication—perhaps (it has been argued) for fear of alienating the core of their own political constituency. Cost was of course the main factor. The ubiquity of propaganda art in every conceivable medium, at every imaginable scale, and the integration of emblems such as the fasces into the very urban fabric, made erasure costly and difficult in this cash-starved era of reconstruction. In the circumstances, the simple act of appropriating and repurposing Fascist structures, so it seems, had to suffice in itself.[11]

In the early postwar era, even demolition decisions might betray a concern for economy. For example, in Lucca, just outside the city's eastern gate of Porta Elisa, there had been dedicated in 1931 a monumental "Fontana

FIGURE 12.3. Fasces borne by winged Victory (1940) in the Piazza Augusto Imperatore, Rome, on the wall of what today is the Istituto Nazionale di Previdenza Sociale, facing the Mausoleum of the emperor Augustus from the north (detail).

Credit: Anthony Majanlahti/Creative Commons.

Littoria" ("Fascist Fountain"), with four huge water-spouting fasces. The fountain was designed by the local sculptor Francesco Petroni (1877–1960), to mark Mussolini's visit to the city in the previous year. When war was concluded, the decision to dismantle the fountain came slowly, probably only in 1949. Yet in 2011, the monument's elements were reported intact, carefully stored in an underground passageway near Porta Elisa, within the city's famed sixteenth-century walls.

In Rome, even in 1959—a full fourteen years after the conclusion of World War II, and eleven years after the departure of the last American troops—the former Foro Mussolini complex remained in its essentials completely untouched, except for costly enhancements to the main stadium. Indeed, just about a year before the start of the 1960 Rome Summer Olympics, in the fall of 1959, the government of Italian prime minister Antonio Segni (1891–1972) found itself defending the very propriety of using the intact Foro as the main site of the Games. The Piazzale is what especially angered the left-wing opponents of Segni's Christian Democrats in the parliamentary debates over the Olympic venues—or more specifically, the "Fascist writings" on the obelisk, in the mosaics, and on Luigi Moretti's commemorative slabs.

Segni's government, which defended the vestiges of the former Foro Mussolini, was not long to last into 1960. In fact, in the six months leading up to the August 25 opening ceremony of the Rome Olympics, Italy saw three different prime ministers. The ubiquity of the fasces and associated Fascist images across an extraordinary spectrum of media at the Olympic sites, coupled with oscillations in the political will needed to tackle the project, made it seem like nothing would happen. It was only under the government of Amintore Fanfani (1908–1999)—just two and a half weeks before the start of the 1960 Games—that a small number of workers appeared on the Piazzale dell'Impero to start chiseling off inscriptions glorifying Mussolini.

The first text to go was inscribed in mosaic, in eight lines of equal length, toward the center of the northern part of the walkway. An English translation of the Italian text reads: "I SWEAR TO EXECUTE WITHOUT DISCUSSION THE ORDERS OF THE DUCE AND TO SERVE WITH ALL MY STRENGTH AND, IF NECESSARY, MY BLOOD THE CAUSE OF THE FASCIST REVOLUTION." This had been (since 1927) the oath of the Fascist National Party—and doubly provocative, since it omitted the opening words in use after 1933, "In the name of God and of Italy. . . ." The workmen, in eradicating the writing, created a bare patch roughly 2.25 m × 1.5 m, yet evidently saw no problem leaving in place a large fasces a few centimeters to the left of the offensive oath.

Over the course of the following week, the extreme right in Rome retaliated with pro-Mussolini graffiti that they painted on the Tiber embankments and other conspicuous places night after night. Clean-up crews could hardly cope. Soon the eradication of symbols in the Foro Italico halted, for simple want of time and (surely) to keep memories of Mussolini contained in the received media of marble and mosaic and not also throughout the city's historical center in fresh paint.[12]

"The contribution of Mussolini to the 1960 Olympics is significant," noted *New York Times* foreign staff reporter Robert Daley (born 1930) already in late March 1959, adding that few of the two million spectators expected to attend the Games will be unaware of that fact. What Daley did not mention or anticipate was that the 1960 Summer Games would the first, through the relatively new medium of television, to draw an additional audience of tens of millions, in twenty-one countries. Was the Fascist origin of the main sport centers cause for concern? Not in the least, based on the impression Daley gained from a tour of the facilities. "If all goes well," he predicted, "the most splendid Olympic games in history will be enacted here between Aug. 25 and Sept. 11 next year." Rather than critiquing the survival of Fascist statues in the Stadio dei Marmi—which Daley said look quite beautiful, so long as one does not examine them too closely—the correspondent chose to accentuate the organizers' planned display of "the glories of ancient, Renaissance and modern Rome."

As it happened, this was the first Olympics that prompted the host city to re-evaluate entirely its public face, and as a result initiate a massive intervention in its urban and regional environment. It helped that many of the giants of Italian modern architecture who had made their name before the war were active, available, and committed to the mission of the 1960 Olympics. These included the brilliant engineer-architect Pier Luigi Nervi (1891–1979), as well as Enrico del Debbio and Luigi Moretti, the master planners of the former Foro Mussolini, who each received high-profile commissions for the Rome Games.

What especially captivated the *New York Times* correspondent was two of Nervi's contributions, the Small Palace of Sport in the Flaminio district in the north of Rome, and, in the south of the city, the Palace of Sport on the Valchetta hill overlooking the Fascist-planned EUR district (an important secondary site for the Rome Games). The journalist counted these two structures, "both of which have seemingly unsupported dome roofs," as "the most impressive" of the venues that he toured. Further, Robert Daley noted with breathless excitement the prospect of ancient monuments as venues for the athletic events—which one notes was a solution devised out of practical necessity, only after Rome had won its bid—and of the staging of Renaissance-era athletic spectacles as part of the Olympic festival.

Put simply, against the twenty-three years of the Fascist regime, the Olympic organizers aimed to marshal twenty-seven centuries of Italy's history, the nation's leading lights of contemporary design, plus the Vatican and the popular Pope John XXIII (born 1881, reigned 1958–1963), all to emphasize contemporary Rome's continuity with its antique past, and to reshape painful memories of Mussolini and war. The Rome committee also carefully filtered the visuals for mass media, as the sumptuous official film *The Great Olympiad* (1961) amply shows: other than a short segment on field hockey in the Stadio dei Marmi, viewers get little sense of obvious Mussolini-era constructions in the city. The strategy worked. The dispute in Italy over Fascist iconography hardly mattered to the international audience, and indeed the relics of the ex-Foro Mussolini failed to become a major factor in the world's assessment of the 1960 Rome Games.[13]

The Fasces in Contemporary Cityscapes

Today, as any attentive visitor to Italy can attest, the task of eradication of the supreme Fascist symbol still remains very much incomplete. In Rome, the face of a 1933 fountain built into a wall on the Via di San Gregorio—175 meters south of the Colosseum, and directly across from the entrance gate to the Palatine Hill—displays two large marble plaques; on each the outlines of three fasces remain so clear that one wonders what the point was of removing them. A kilometer to the northwest, a plaque with three wholly intact fasces, bearing the date "Year 7" of the Fascist era (1929), is readily spotted, mounted on a modern support wall of the Theater of Marcellus that faces a main avenue. From there, less than 2 kilometers due north, one can view the nervy dedicatory inscription (1940) to the Piazza Augusto Imperatore, set on a building exterior wall, and flanked by twin winged "Geniuses," who converge on the text bearing reversed fasces. These examples are practically at random; a full roster of legible Mussolini-era fasces just in the historic center of Rome would make for a sizable list. For instance, a comprehensive catalog would have to include an astonishing array of manhole covers with fasces (some quite elaborate) by various manufacturers. These heavy cast street *tombolini* are in no way restricted to Rome, but can be found still in use throughout many urban areas in Italy.

What one is hard pressed to find after World War II, in Italy and indeed the rest of the world, is the creation of new works of public art that represent the fasces in a non-ironic sense. Just a single example comes to mind, the work of Alexander Stoddart (born 1959), since 2008 the Queen's Sculptor in Ordinary in Scotland. Indeed, the work in question is two identical casts in bronze of a heroic statue of John Knox Witherspoon (1723–1794), each dedicated in 2001.

Witherspoon was a dynamic Scottish Presbyterian cleric; an eminent educator, who served for twenty-six years as president of Princeton University; and a significant figure in the politics of revolutionary America and the young United States. He is especially known as the only clergyman and only college president to sign the Declaration of Independence in 1776. In the following year, he was one of four dozen signatories to the Articles of Confederation. An attribute of Witherspoon that has drawn increased attention in recent years is his complex (but essentially anti-abolitionist) public stance on slavery, and the fact that he himself owned slaves in New Jersey, which passed a gradual emancipation law only a decade after his death.

One of Stoddart's 10-foot statues was placed at the entrance of the campus of the University of the West of Scotland in Paisley, a town where Witherspoon once lived as a church pastor, and the location of the sculptor's studio. It was Paisley which initiated the project. The other statue was positioned prominently on the campus of Princeton University, just east of the East Pyne building (the home of several humanities departments, including Classics), facing across an open space toward the main library and chapel (Figure 12.4). On its tall masonry plinth topped by a short stone base, the Princeton cast rises to a height of almost five and a half meters.

On three sides of the pedestal, designed by Princeton architect T. Jeffery Clarke (born 1954), metal plaques explain John Witherspoon's various identities as "Preacher," "President," and "Patriot." Stoddart's monumental work effectively conveys all three roles without seeming too contrived. Witherspoon is portrayed as a powerful and authoritative figure, his posture erect, and his stern gaze fixed on the horizon as he preaches. Over his eighteenth-century period dress, he wears an open academic gown with wide billowing sleeves; his left foot is set forward, its buckle shoe partially protruding from the statue's base. Witherspoon partially raises his right arm, and his hand gestures with two fingers toward the sky. He lifts his left arm still higher, above a tall eagle-style lectern, to turn the page of a Bible that lies open on the eagle's outstretched wings, as its talons clutch a small globe.

FIGURE 12.4. Statue of John Witherspoon (2001), by sculptor Alexander Stoddart (born 1959), Princeton University campus.

Credit: T. C. Brennan.

The rendering of Witherspoon's arms and claw-like hands in his gown, when viewed against this eagle, make it seem as if he is about to take off into flight.

The eagle lectern, a symbol of the evangelist St. John, is still a familiar sight in Anglican (especially) and Presbyterian churches. However, the main body of the lectern is novel, and especially demands our attention. For the lectern's thick shaft is formed from an axe-less fasces, the bundle of sturdy rods bound with two horizontal bands. It is set on a double base, to the rear of which a stack of five books is propped, four of which show their spines—on the top, more than double the thickness of the rest, and differently positioned, a volume titled "Cicero," then "Principia" (i.e., of Isaac Newton), "Locke," and "Hume." The statue offers an unexpected (and unnoticed) visual trick. if one stands a little to the left of the eagle's head as it peers down from the top of the lectern, the "Cicero" volume appears against the fasces as if an axe-head.

"This is my heart's desire," explained Alexander Stoddart of his Witherspoon statue more than a year before its twin dedications. "Clean of satire, heroic realism with rhetorical content. It is a noble idiom." At the Princeton location, one could understandably mistake the monument for an installation of the mid-nineteenth rather than early twenty-first century. That is at least partly the point. "My heresy," said Stoddart in the same interview, "is that I don't exist in a chronologically controlled way. I keep diplomatic channels open with the past."

Indeed, Stoddart's Witherspoon monument represents a jarring and, in the contemporary context, seemingly isolated effort to reappropriate the pre-Fascist fasces as a symbol of legitimate authority. Without addressing this specific point, Stoddart implied as much when interviewed in the year 2000. "Modernism is inherently lazy and individualistic so it is happy to leave neo-classicism to Hitler. I feel an obligation not to leave well-made art in the grubby hands of Benito Mussolini."[14]

So far, Stoddart has been successful, to a degree, in this daring exercise in atavism. "The fasces represents Witherspoon's activities as a statesman," specified a matter-of-fact Princeton University press release just before the November 2001 US dedication. No one seems to have voiced protest at the time about this integral aspect of Stoddart's composition, nor (as of July 2021) written about it since, in Scotland or in the United States—with the exception of a single query cross-posted on two social media platforms which received no replies. It seems fair to say the emblem has grown largely unfamiliar, and as such has been ignored.[15]

What first sparked serious criticism of the monument was the findings of the Princeton & Slavery Project (established 2013, website launched 2017), which showed that Princeton's first nine presidents, including Witherspoon, all owned enslaved individuals. It soon was noted that the didactic plaques on the Witherspoon pedestal omitted that fact. Eventually, an open letter of July 2000, signed by over 350 Princeton faculty members, from thirty-four of the university's thirty-six departments, urged administrators to turn their attention to the statue. Among four dozen demands in a wide-ranging document: "commit fully to anti-racist campus iconography, beginning with the removal of the John Witherspoon statue (erected in 2001) near Firestone

Library." If the fasces itself was regarded as inflammatory, it was not stated. At the time of writing, the twin John Witherspoon statues are both still in place, and in Princeton the original plaques remain unrevised.[16]

Epilogue

So today it seems the fasces can hide in plain sight, even when prominently portrayed on university campuses in Britain and the United States. Our story clearly has taken a new direction. The first phase of the tale stretches an astounding two millennia, from the Etruscans of the seventh century BCE, then through the Romans under all their forms of government, indeed down to the last Byzantine dynasty, which fell only in 1453 CE. There the device of the fasces shows remarkable stability, as a horrid symbol of authority. The second phase starts in the later Renaissance, when an old didactic tale from Aesop, illustrating how sticks are stronger once bundled, is extended to the (unrelated) historical fasces. Over the course of the sixteenth through the early twentieth centuries, the Roman emblem is found representing not just expected concepts such as power, punishment, and justice, but—thanks to this fable—now also strength, unity, and liberty against tyranny.

The rise of Benito Mussolini in Italy introduces a third phase, that begins in 1919 but accelerates wildly after his seizure of power in Italy in October 1922. His movement purported to revive the ancient Roman resonances of the emblem. But it in fact retained aspects of the modern reimagining of the fasces, and introduced still further novelties, such as glorification of the lowly attendants who carried the fasces in antiquity. The fourth and present phase followed upon the fall of Italian fascism and the defeat of the Axis powers in World War II. In this era, the fasces has seen uneven backlash and unsystematic eradication, but in the context of a public that has grown progressively unconversant with the symbol. It is precisely the fasces' long history, with all its twists and turns into present-day unfamiliarity, that has given an opening to right-wing extremists searching for a symbol that is potent, but not widely provocative at first glance.

For a succinct summary of the current situation of the fasces as symbol, especially in the United States, it is hard to better a reference entry on the website of the ADL (founded in Chicago in 1913 as the Anti-Defamation League of B'nai B'rith). In 350 words, under the heading "General Hate Symbols," a clear and well-informed article scrupulously takes the reader from ancient Rome, "whose leaders used it as a symbol of authority and power," to the present moment.[17] The main point of the article is to explain how the fasces earned its invidious designation, over and above Mussolini's adoption of the device. "In the decades after World War II," the ADL author explains, "many Nazi symbols were adopted by American neo-Nazis, but the fasces did not experience the same popularity. . . ." However, the ADL site identifies (and illustrates) the logos of five separate American white supremacist groups that currently display the fasces. "Beginning in the late 2000s," we are told, "more American white supremacists turned to the fasces as a symbol, possibly because it did not have the strong negative connotations of the swastika and because extremists could defend their use of the fasces by pointing to its role in the symbology of the U.S. government." My hope is that this book, which has surveyed the meaning and interpretation of the fasces across a period of almost 2,700 years, shows that we are now a full century past the point where one can argue that the primary associations of the symbol are benign.

Abbreviations and Note on Translations

THE ABBREVIATIONS BELOW for modern works depend on those, when available, of the *Oxford Classical Dictionary* (4th edition), ed. S. Hornblower, A. Spawforth, and E. Eidinow (Oxford: Oxford University Press, 2012). Ancient works are identified by their abbreviations in the *Oxford Classical Dictionary* (except that *HA*, not *SHA* = *Historia Augusta*), supplemented by those of *A Greek-English Lexicon* (9th edition with revised supplement), ed. H. G. Liddell, R. Scott, H. S. Jones, and R. McKenzie (Oxford and New York: Oxford University Press, 1996).

AE = *L'Année Épigraphique*, published in *Revue Archéologique* and separately (1888–).

BMCRE = *British Museum Catalogue of Coins of the Roman Empire* (1923–).

CCCA = M. J. Vermaseren, Corpus cultus Cybelae Attidisque (1977–1987).

CIL = Corpus Inscriptionum Latinarum (1863–).

ELOstia = M. Cébeillac-Gervasoni, M. L. Caldelli, and F. Zevi, *Epigrafia Latina Ostia. Cento iscrizioni in contesto* (2010).

ICUR = Inscriptiones christianae urbis Romae (1922–).

IK = *Inschriften griechischer Städte aus Kleinasien* (1972–).

ILCV = Inscriptiones Latinae Christianae Veteres, ed. E. Diehl (1925–1967).

ILLRP = Inscriptiones Latinae Liberae Rei Republicae, ed. A. Degrassi, I² (1965) and II (1963).

ILLRP Supp. = "Inscriptiones Latinae Liberae Rei Publicae," ed. S. Gentili and G. Vergantini, in *Epigrafia. Actes du colloque international d' Épigraphie latine en mémoire de Attilio Degrassi pour le centenaire de sa naissance (27–28 mai 1988)* (1991) 241–491.

ILS = Inscriptiones Latinae Selectae, ed. H. Dessau (1892–1916).

Inscr. Ital. = Inscriptiones Italiae (1931–).

MRR = T. R. S. Broughton, *Magistrates of the Roman Republic* I–III (1951–1986).

NS = *Notizie degli scavi di antichità* (1884–1929).

RE = *Real-Encyclopädie der klassischen Altertumswissenschaft*, ed. A. Pauly, G. Wissowa, and W. Kroll (1893–1980).

RIC = H. Mattingly, E. A. Sydenham, and others, *Roman Imperial Coinage* (1923–1967); revised edition of vol. I only, ed. C. H. V. Sutherland and R. A. G. Carson (1984).

RPC = *Roman Provincial Coinage*, ed. A. M. Burnett, M. Amandry, and others (1992–). *Roman Provincial Coinage Online* (includes vols. I–IV, VII 1 and 2, VIII and IX) at http://rpc.ashmus.ox.ac.uk

RRC = *Roman Republican Coinage*, 2 vols., ed. M. H. Crawford (1974).

RS = *Roman Statues*, 2 vols., ed. M. H. Crawford (1996).

TLL = Thesaurus Linguae Latinae (1900–).

Translations of ancient Greek and Roman authors found in the text are adapted from the relevant, most current Loeb Classical Library editions, namely those of W. B. Anderson (Sid. Apoll. *Epist.*), J. W. Basore (Sen. *Constant.*), S. M. Braund (Juv.), E. Cary (Cass. Dio and Dion. Hal. *Ant. Rom.*), W. de Melo (Plautus), J. D. Duff (Sil. *Pun.*), H. R. Fairclough (Verg. *Aen.*), B. O. Foster (Liv. 1–10), J. H. Freese (Cic. *Leg. agr.*), L. H. G. Greenwood (Cic. *Verr.*), W. W. Keyes (Cic. *Rep.*), R. A. Kaster (Macrob.), C. Macdonald (Cic. *Cat.*), D. Magie (*HA Hadr.*), B. McGing (App. *BCiv., Mith., Pun.*), H. C. Moore (Tac. *Ann.* and *Hist.*), A. F. Norman (Lib. *Epist.*), S. D. Olson (Ath.), W. R. Paton (Polyb.), B. Perrin (Plut., *Cic., Crass., Luc., Num., Publ., Sull.*), B. Radice (Plin. *Pan.*), J. C. Rolfe (Suet. *Iul., Tib.,* and Gell. *NA*), A. C. Schlesinger (Liv. *Per.* and Obsequens), D. R. Shackleton Bailey (Cic. *Phil.* and Val. Max.), F. W. Shipley (Augustus *Res Gestae*), H. J. Thomson (Prudent. *Hamart.*), F. R. Walton (Diod.), N. H. Watts (Cic. *Pis.* and *Rab. Post.*), F. W. Wright (Jer. *Epist.*), and J. C. Yardley (Liv. 23–39). Translations of ancient non-literary texts (where not otherwise indicated) are my own. Throughout this book, I have taken the liberty of translating short quotations from works of modern scholarship in French, German, and Italian into English.

Notes

CHAPTER I

1. Cic. *Verr.* 2.5.39. For a sample of other passages describing the fasces as a tangible sign of office, see Liv. 2.54.4 (474/3 BCE), 10.25.5 (295 BCE); Cic. *Att.* 8.15.1 (March 3, 49 BCE); Plin. *Ep.* 1.24.6; cf. Pliny the Elder (*HN* 10.46), who states that the public auspices determine their movement.

2. For "fasces" as metonymy for "high office" in Rome, see, e.g., Cic. *Leg. agr.* 1.9; Prop. 2.16; Ov. *Fast.* 1.80 ("new"); Lucan 1.178, 5.389, 8.79, and 270; Sen. *Ben.* 4.31, *Brev. Vit.* 7.8, *Phaedr.* 983–984; [Sen.] *Octavia* 679; Manil. 1.795 and 2.146; Sil. *Pun.* 7.541 and 8.216; Stat. *Silv.* 2.2.123 (qualified as "unstable") and 4.4.32; Mart. *Epigr.* 8.71.6 ("annual") and 72.6; Amm. Marc. 21.10.8 (of the emperor Constantine allegedly advancing Germans to the consulship); Rut. Namat. 175–176. It is especially common in this sense in the fourth and fifth centuries CE, in the writings of Ausonius, Prudentius, Claudian, and Sidonius Apollinaris, and the usage extends to municipal offices (e.g., Apul. *Met.* 10.18) and the literature of Byzantium (see, e.g., *Anth. Gr.* 1.4.3 [after 463 CE] and 16.48.6 [between ca. 518–526 CE]). For fasces in a list of attributes of power, see, e.g., Cic. *Clu.* 154; *Rab. Post.* 16–17; *Pis.* 22–23.; Verg. *G.* 2.495; Sen. *Ben.* 1.5; Lucan 2.16–19; Stat. *Silv.* 3.3.115–117; Sil. *Pun.* 10.391–393; Juv. 10.35 and 79; Tert. *De Spect.* 12 [97v] (accentuating frivolous attributes of office); Min. Fel. *Oct.* 27.7–10; Cass. Dio 38.43.4 (of 58 BCE); Lib. *Or.* 33.5; Prudent. *Perist.* 10.143–145. In general, see *TLL* s.v. *fascis* coll. 304.57–306.19, with additional examples in the hundreds.

3. "Six fasces": for Greek, see esp. Polyb. 2.23.5, also 2.24.6, 3.40.9 and 11, 56.6, and 106.6; Diod. Sic. 29.26, 31.42, 33.2; App. *Syr.* 15.63. Latin "sexfascalis" occurs only in the epigraphy of Africa: *CIL* VIII 7015, 8324. The "twice six fasces" or "twelve fasces" as metonymy for "the consulship": Ov. *Tr.* 4.9; Val. Max. 3.4.4 (referring to 216 BCE); *Laus Pisonis* 70 (exhibited during a Senate meeting on the day of entering office); Sen. *Ira* 31 (of a suffect consul); Stat. *Silv.* 1.2.175–176 and 4.1.8–9; Mart. *Epigr.* 7.63.9–10, 8.66.3, 9.42.6.

4. Cic. *Verr.* 2.5.97; Val. Max. 2.7.7.

5. In general for this more expansive meaning of fasces, see *TLL* s.v. *fascis* col. 306.20–32. Magistrate unworthy of the fasces: Claud. *C. Eutrop.* 2.54–56, 130 (the insignia are "deformed" thanks to a eunuch's consulship) and 502–503 (cast down by horrified lictor). Alleged buying and selling of fasces: Cic. *Pis.* 49 (by the commander Aulus Gabinius in 55 BCE to the Egyptian king); Columella *Rust.* praef. (buying the insignia despite their inherent "honor [*decus*] and *imperium*"); Calp. *Ecl.* 1.69–71 (buying fasces makes them worthless). Civil war described as crushing the fatherland with its own fasces: Sen. *Brev. vit.* 5.15.

6. See Liv. 2.55.3 (reported speech of Volero Publilius in 473 BCE). The low birth of lictors was always taken as a given: see Plut. *Comp. Lys. Sull.* 4.4; Claud. *C. Eutrop.* 2.309–310. A lictor characterized as foolish: Pers. 5.175.

7. See Plaut. *Asin.* 554–577, esp. 564–565 and 574–575 with the commentary of Porter (2019) 127–128; Liban. *Ep.* 797.2 = N97.2.

8. Cic. *Leg. agr.* 1.9 *formidulosi* ("terrifying"); Hor. *Carm.* 1.2.35 *superbos* ("arrogant"), cf. Stat. *Silv.* 2.7.7, as well as 5.3.189 "pacifying"); Val. Max. 2.7.7 *imperiosissimi* ("most imperious"), cf. 6.4.1b "heavy" (i.e., in application, as a good thing).

9. See Lucr. 3.996 *fasces saevasque secures* ("fasces and cruel axes"), with its expansion by Verg. *Aen.* 6.818–819 (of Lucius Brutus, consul 509 BCE); in each the relevant phrase in the same metrical position at line's end.

10. Aesop, *Fables* Perry 53 = Babrius 47 in Gibbs (2002) no. 493 translation.

11. Plut. *Mor.* 174 E. For its wider dissemination, see Ratcliffe (2014a and 2014b).

12. On the genesis and wide dissemination of this text, the *Aesopus Dorpii*, see Thoen (1970), with the number of editions eventually topping 200. Consulted in Anon., *Fabularum quae hoc libro continentur*, etc. (Strasbourg 1515), published by Matthias Schurer, fol. VIII. On early printed editions of Aesop, starting with that of Ulm physician Heinrich Steinhöwel in 1476, see Dicke (1994). On the quotation from Sallust (*Iug.* 10.6) and its quasi-viral history in the Medieval and Renaissance periods, see Pedullà (2018) 10–26, esp. 15: "appearing in thirteenth-century French encyclopedias . . . in Italy it would be reiterated by a wide range of authors before migrating onto cartouches, building facades, majolica tiles, medals, coins, and tapestries."

13. See adl.org/education/references/hate-symbols/fasces (accessed on July 12, 2021), with images from five separate extremist organizations.

CHAPTER 2

1. For what follows, see Falchi (1898), 155–158.

2. Sil. *Pun.* 8.433–438, esp. 434–435 on the fasces.

3. On this, see especially Cass. Dio 48.43.3 (a reported edict of 38 BCE enforcing the citizenship requirement) with Mommsen (1887), 333 n. 1.

4. Dion. Hal. *Ant. Rom.* 3.61–62, with quotes from 61.2 and 62.1; Cic. *Rep.* 2.31–32. On the Etruscan origin of the fasces and other markers of Roman legitimate power,

see also in general Diod. Sic. 5.40; Sil. *Pun.* 8.484–487 (Vetulonia as source). For Tarquinius Priscus as the first to import these insignia into Rome, see Flor. 1.1.5 (implied); Strabo 5.2 C 220 (explicit).

5. See Liv. 1.8.2–3 (Romulus borrowed from Etruscans); Stat. *Silv.* 4.1 (Latium); Claud. *C. Eutrop.* 2.130 (Latium) and *Cons. VI Hon.* [396 CE] 1 (Romulus); Prudent. *C. Symm.* 1.556–557 (Ausonia); Macrob. *Sat.* 1.17.7 (Tullus Hostilius and the Etruscans).

6. See Becker (2013), 351–354.

7. Pokorny (1959), 111 s.v. *bhask-*; Verg. *Ecl.* 9.65.

8. Gell. *NA* 12.3; Cic. *Rab. Post.* 13; Plut. *Mor.* 280 B = *Quaest. Rom.* 67. "Licere": see Vittori (2006), 15.

9. Cf. Ar. *Pax* 734–735 for theater security. See also Hippias ap. Ath. 6.259D (Erythrae); Polyb. 15.29.13 (Alexandria); Dion. Hal. *Ant. Rom.* 8.44.3–4 and App. *Ital.* 3.8 (Volscians); Liv. 9.11.13 (Samnites); Sall. *Iug.* 12.3 (Numidians); Plin. *HN* 8.185 (Memphis).

10. The memorable formulation is that of Marshall (1984), 130.

11. Liv. 1.40–41.

12. On all this, see *MRR* I 2–3, with sources (to which add Verg. *Aen.* 6.817–821), esp. Liv. 2.1.7–11 and 5.8; Plut. *Publ.* 6.2–3; and Flor. 1.3.9 (accusing Brutus of cynically punishing his sons to burnish his public image). The conflicts in our (many) sources over particulars do not affect our basic arguments here.

13. *RRC* 443/1; cf. *RPC* I 1701.

14. See Claud. *Cons. Stil.* [400 CE] 2.322–325; Prudent. *C. Symm.* 1.556–557.

15. On the custom of lowering fasces attributed to Publicola, see Cic. *Rep.* 1.62 with 2.53 and 55; Liv. 2.7.7; Dion. Hal. *Ant. Rom.* 10.59.5–6; Plut. *Publ.* 10.5 with Val. Max. 4.1.1; Flor. 1.3.9 ("Horatius" Publicola); Quint. *Inst.* 3.7.18; Cass. Dio 3.13.2 = Zonar. 7.12.

16. See, e.g., Ausonius *Opusc.* I (*Praefatiunc.*) 1.37–38, speaking of his own priority as consul in 379 CE. Nice (2017) offers a thorough survey of ancient evidence and modern scholarship relating to the consular "turn," however, arguing unpersuasively that it is a late (post 79 BCE) innovation and that in the Republic, consular colleagues had no mechanism to differentiate their fasces.

17. On the Roman people as the source of the fasces, see, e.g., Cic. *Verr.* 2.5.163, on which cf. Gell. *NA* 10.3.11–13; Lucr. 3.996; Verg. *G.* 2.495; Hor. *Epist.* 1.16.33–34 (but cf. 6.53–54 allowing for personal influence as a factor); Sen. *Phaedr.* 983–984; [Sen.] *Octavia* 679; Sil. *Pun.* 7.541; cf. Juv. 10.79. Mode of punishment in 500 BCE: Dion. Hal. *Ant. Rom.* 5.57.4.

18. On the difficult chronology of Caesar's dictatorships (49, 48/7, 46/5, and 44 BCE), see *MRR* III 104. Lucan (5.389–390 and 663) singles out Caesar's (second) consulship of 48 BCE as an especially shameful appropriation of the fasces and axes: see the discussion of Matthews (2008), 239–240.

19. See Polyb. 3.87.7 (24 lictors of the dictator) and cf. 6.53.8 (noble funerals in Rome); Liv. *Per.* 89; and the discussion of Brennan (2000), 41–42. For an argument, based

on what seems to be an overconfident reading of Polybius, that all archaic dictators had twenty-four lictors, see Martin (2021), 199–201. Another wrinkle in our discussion of the dictator is introduced by Cass. Dio 43.48.1–2, for the year 48 BCE, who attests that six lictors also accompanied Caesar's master of the horse. However, there is good reason to think that this show of the fasces was not an original attribute of the dictator's attendant but perhaps an innovation introduced by Caesar himself: see Brennan (2000), 43–47, esp. 46–47.

20. On the axes, see Wilson (2021), 199–203.

21. On a dictator "sending away" a consul, see Liv. 22.11.5 (217 BCE), on which see Brennan (2000), 263 n. 80 for discussion. Our later Greek sources on the episode (Plut. *Fab.* 4.3 and App. *Hann.* 12.50) seem to imagine that the consul was reduced to a private citizen, which was demonstrably not the case. In general, for an attempt to delineate and explain the dictator's powers, see Brennan (2000), 39–43, to be read with the critiques of Konrad (2003) and Drogula (2015), 89–90 and 161–180 (each excellent in detail but to my mind not fully persuasive in the main argument); and Wilson (2021), 170–174 (essentially in agreement with the views presented here).

22. Cass. Dio 43.14.3 (the vote) and 19.3 (the quote).

23. Passages cited here (in order): Liv. 3.33.8 and 36.3–5; Dion. Hal. *Ant. Rom.* 10.59.3–5; Liv. 3.39.8 and 9.34.1–2. The experiment of the decemvirs, each with his own rods and axe, made a deep impression on the Roman historical imagination, surely under the influence of Caesar's display of seventy-two lictors for his triumph of 46 CE: see, e.g., in the early fifth century CE, the vivid description of Prud. *C. Symm.* 2.423–425. In general, on the fantasy of this constitutional crisis, see Brennan (2000), 53–54.

24. On all this, see Brennan (2000), 53–54 (consular tribunes, with discussion of Liv. 6.34.6–7, quoted here, on their lictors); 54–57 (censors).

25. Armstrong (2016), 86.

26. Stressed (indeed to an extreme) by Tassi Scandone (2001), 12 and 26.

27. On these later Etruscan lictors, see the comprehensive study of Tassi Scandone (2001). Roman-style fasces already appear in Capua for the year 63 BCE: Cic. *Leg. agr.* 2.92. On this development, see Schäfer (1989), 197–200.

CHAPTER 3

1. For the monument, see Schäfer (1989), no. 18 with tab. 38–39. Upside-down fasces: [Ov.] *Cons. ad Liviam* 141–142 (death of Drusus Nero); Tac. *Ann.* 3.2 (death of Germanicus).

2. Popillia: Cic. *De or.* 2.44. Iunia (died 91 BCE): Cic. *De or.* 2.225. Iulia: Suet. *Iul.* 6.1 and Plut. *Caes.* 5.1. Iunia (died 22 CE): Tac. *Ann.* 3.76.

3. Funeral of Sulla: App. *BCiv.* 1.105.493–106.500; Plut. *Sull.* 38.2. Lictors for organizers of funerals: Cic. *Leg.* 2.61. Silius Italicus in narrating Hannibal's cremation of the

fallen consul Lucius Aemilius Paullus following the battle of Cannae in 216 BCE has the Carthaginian general place on his pyre "the shield, the sword . . . the rods and axes taken in the battle, broken now but once a badge of power that all men feared" (*Pun.* 10.560–577, esp. 564–565). Silius is not describing a traditional Roman funeral, but rather a composite rite with copious epic borrowings: see Erasmo (2008), 75–76.

4. For a full description and discussion (with illustrations) of the Arieti tomb, see Giatti (2007).

5. For the practice in general, see Plin. *HN* 15.133 and the section of Cassius Dio Book VI summarized in Zonar. 7.21, each mentioning also that *imperatores* customarily sent a laurel-decorated dispatch to the Senate touting their accomplishments (for which see also Liv. 5.28.13 and 45.1.6; Cic. *Pis.* 39). Laureled fasces attributed to Gaius Marius (consul I 107, VII 86 BCE): Cic. *Div.* 1.50 and 2.36 (a dream). Attested for Pompey in 80 BCE: Front. *Str.* 4.5.1. Laurels maintained with difficulty: Plut. *Luc.* 36.2–4 and *Pomp.* 31.2–3 (same incident of 66 BCE). Gaius Antonius as prorogued consul in 62 BCE: Obsequens 61A. Reticence to decorate fasces in civil conflict: see Caes. *BCiv.* 3.71.3 and Dio 41.52.1 (Pompey in 48 BCE, noting however that he accepted the title "imperator").

6. On this, see Catalano (1978), 491–505; Linderski (1986), 2156–2158. The most extensive recent treatment of *imperium* is that of Drogula (2015), who unconvincingly interprets it as only encompassing military authority and expiring within the *pomerium*.

7. Liv. 24.9.1–2.

8. For discussion of the location of the *Porta Triumphalis* (uncertain and disputed), see Haselberger (2002), 200; Wiseman (2021), 30–32.

9. Gaius Piso returning from Macedonia: see esp. Cic. *Pis.* 53–55, 74, 97, with the discussion of Volk and Zetzel (2015), 208–211. Cicero himself returning from Cilicia with laureled fasces: see esp. Cic. *Att.* 8.3.5–6 (Feb. 18–19, 49), 9.1.3 (March 6, 49), *Fam.* 2.16.2 (May 3, 49 BCE, alleging that he found the custom already tedious), *Att.* 11.7.2 (December 1, 48 BCE, telling how he temporarily gave his lictors plain staves so as not to provoke hostile soldiers), and in general Zarecki (2014), 110 (including on Cicero's eventual dismissal of his lictors). A few years previous, the commander Gaius Pomptinus (praetor 63 BCE) had waited for five years outside Rome, surely with his lictors and their laurels, before he managed (with great difficulty) to triumph in 54 BCE: Brennan (2000), 579. Symbolism for soldiers: Front. *Str.* 4.5.1. Augustus: *Res Gestae* 4.

10. Pompey: Vell. Pat. 2.40.4 and Cass. Dio 37.21.3–4. Julius Caesar: see sources in *MRR* II 304 with Schäfer (1989), 201, and Koortbojian (2013), 119. Subsequent development is hard to trace, in part since Suetonius says little about lictors and fasces in his lives of the Julio-Claudians, and (frustratingly) nothing in that of Augustus. At Tac. *Ann.* 13.9 (55 CE), the emperor Nero is said to have added laurels to his fasces to mark his subordinates' successes, which suggests they were still usually unadorned. See Mart. *Epigr.* 10.10 (after late 95 CE) for a consul entering office on

January 1 with laureled fasces, also Claud. *Cons. IV Hon.* [398 CE] 1–17, esp. 14 ("laurel-crowned axes"). For an emperor explicitly said to have assumed laureled fasces on his accession in 238 CE, see Herodian 7.6.2 (cf. *HA II Maximin.* 14.4 and *III Gord.* 9.6).

11. Cass. Dio 59.3.5; Suet. *Calig.* 15.1.

12. Sil. 9.419–421.

13. On the garment, see Varr. *Ling.* 7.37, emphasizing its conspicuousness. On the Caudine episode, Liv. 9.5.13. Prohibition within the city: Cic. *Verr.* 5.13, Tac. *Hist.* 2.89; cf. *HA Gall.* 16.4. Ceremony of departure: Liv. 21.63.7–11 (criticism for omission); 31.14.1, 41.10.5 and 13 (177 BCE, had to be repeated), 42.49.2 (emphasizing spectacle), 45.39.11 (with explicit mention of lictors assuming the cloak); Suet. *Iul.* 71 (62 BCE, Caesar exploiting the pageantry of the occasion to smuggle a young Numidian noble out of Rome); Cic. *Fam.* 8.10.2 (51 BCE, a decree of the Senate as a necessary preliminary); Caes. *BCiv.* 1.6.6 (ex-praetors in 49 BCE depart for their provincial commands without a popular vote confirming their military *imperium*); and Varr. *Ling.* 7.37 (musical aspects); cf. Sil. *Pun.* 6.444 (spectacularity) and Suet. *Ner.* 43.2 (profaned). Ceremony at re-entry: cf. Cic. *Pis.* 55 (with the implication that the *sagum* was the appropriate garment for lictors to wear at a triumph). Still worn by lictors in later antiquity: Jer. *Ep.* 1.7 (in this instance, pinned by a gold fibula). In general, with further references, Kuttner (1995), 138–142.

14. On the many variant forms that the Roman fasces and its components would henceforth take, see the exhaustive treatment of Schäfer (1989), which removes the need for extended discussion in this work.

15. *RRC* 301/1 with Cic. *Rab. Post.* 12, 63 BCE.

16. App. *Pun.* 66.293–300, esp. 295. On the "virgae," see Schäfer (1989), 200–201.

17. Livy (45.35.4) is explicit that the commander in question, Lucius Anicius Gallus (praetor 168 BCE), had been allowed by a plebiscite to retain his *imperium* within the city on the day of his triumph. His (tactless) triumphal games as prorogued praetor in 167 (Polyb. 30.22.1–12; ignored by Livy) should have been held right after his triumph (see Brennan [2000], 337 n. 222), for which his lictors will have retained their axes.

18. *RRC* 357/1a and b. On Norbanus in Sicily, see Cic. *Verr.* 2.5.8 with Brennan (2000), 836 n. 32.

19. See *RRC* 372/2. In discussing this coin, Crawford rightly takes these images as an evocation of *imperium* in its civil and military forms. He may also be correct in thinking it was meant to commemorate a Lucius Postumius Albinus (praetor in 180) who triumphed from Further Spain in 178.

20. Here I exclude from discussion *RRC* 393/1a (82 BCE) and 405/5 (by 57 BCE). Though each of these coins has a fasces (with axe) on its obverse, the two relevant moneyers represent it in reduced form, to serve merely as one control mark among many (indeed, in the latter case, over 40 different objects) for prolific types.

21. *RRC* 403/1. *Pace* Schäfer (1989), 206 n. 68, who considers Rome to hold a spear, it seems at least partly because of his conviction that only lictors can be represented carrying fasces in Roman art.

22. *RRC* 414/1.

23. For Septimius's Ephesus issues, see Stumpf (1991), nos. 34–36.

24. Brutus: *RRC* 443/1. Buca: *RRC* 480/6; on the iconography of his reverse, cf. e.g., *RRC* 450/2, 48 BCE, where the reverse bears clasped hands actually holding a winged caduceus.

25. See *RRC* 434/2 (54 BCE, Quintus Pompeius Rufus) and 473/2 (45 BCE, Marcus Lollius Palicanus).

26. For the coin issues of Lucius Livineius Regulus discussed here, part of an even larger personal series, see *RRC* 494/26a and 26b and 494/27–28 (reverse with six fasces), 31 (reverse with two fasces, also with a legend revealing that the moneyer is a son of the praetor). On the vexed question of their interpretation, see the discussion in *MRR* III 124 with Welch (1990) on Caesar's experiment of 45 BCE with the urban prefecture. On the date of the praetorship, see Brennan (2000), 929 n. 493.

27. In 40 BCE, the curule chair between two axe-less fasces features on the reverse of a bronze coin issued by two magistrates ("duovirs for a five-year period") of the Roman colony of Dyme in the province of Achaea (*RPC* I 1284). In the years 34–31 BCE, the motif reappears across the Mediterranean, on two bronze denominations minted for the province of Cyrenaica and Crete. The commander Aulus Pupius Rufus, a quaestor with *imperium* at the praetorian grade, adapts the basic design by restoring axes to the fasces, and swapping the curule seat for a camp chair in the higher denomination (*RPC* I 919–920), and for a quaestor's seat (with additional marks of the rank) in the lower (921–922). In that same province, about a dozen years later under Augustus, the praetor Marcus Lollius Palicanus also used the camp seat between fasces as a numismatic reverse (*RPC* I 940). More remotely, coins of the duovirs of New Carthage under Augustus and Tiberius also have the fasces (in this case, axe-less) as a flanking device, but with a military standard at the center: see *RPC* I 178 (Augustan) and Álvarez Burgos (2008), 468 (Tiberian); cf. *RPC* I 484, from an uncertain city of Spain, with fasces flanking a rectangular object.

28. Koson: *RPC* I 1701, with Stein in *RE* IV.2 (1901) col. 1676 for the sources on Cotiso. Koson on his obverse drops the *accensus* found on the Roman prototype, and in his space adds a monogram (probably BA, denoting Greek "basileus" = "king"), and also substitutes his own name in Greek letters for the original "BRVTVS" legend. Crassus: *RPC* I 915 for the unique single fasces reverse; cf. 914 (with obverse crocodile, a symbol of Egypt; on reverse, a prow decorated with six stars and a dolphin). Rhoemetalces I: *RPC* I 1706 (single fasces); 1704–1705 (fasces with capricorn and globe).

29. Two famous examples suffice to make the point. On the twelve lictors (with axe-less fasces) preceding Augustus on both walls of the Ara Pacis frieze (dedicated 9 BCE),

see Torelli (1982), 44–46 and 59 n. 63; cf. 36, on the lictor who follows the Vestal Virgins. On the twelve lictors (mixed with female personifications) accompanying the emperor's triumphal chariot on the north inner bay of the Arch of Titus, see Östenberg (2021), 38.

30. Galba: *RIC* I 467 with Kraay (1956), 38, on the visual effect of this ensemble scene, adducing the panels of the Arch of Titus as a parallel.

31. On Trajan's restoration issues in general, see Komnick (2001). Restitution of Brutus *denarius*: *RIC* II 797. Acclamation issue: *RIC* II 265, 309 (gold); 656–658 (bronze). Cf. also *RIC* II 172 (silver) and 466 (bronze), dating to the period 103–111 CE, where a personified Arabia holds a bundle of what seem to be cinnamon sticks on the left shoulder, as if it were the rods of the fasces. For later derivative types, see, e.g., *RIC* IVa 800a for an issue of Septimius Severus (210 CE); and Leu Numismatik Auction 2, Lot 279 (May 11, 2018) for Geta in 210 CE (on whom cf. also *RIC* IVa 159b).

32. Cancellation of debts: see *HA Hadr.* 7.6 with *RIC* II 591 (with two citizens), 592 (three citizens), also 590 and 593 (lictor standing alone). Misidentification of the figure: see, e.g., S. W. Stevenson, C. R. Smith, and F. W. Madden, *A Dictionary of Roman Coins, Republican and Imperial* (London, 1889), 681. For descriptions of the relief sculptures, commonly known as the "Anaglypha Traiani," see Torelli (1982), 90–91 (arguing vociferously for a Trajanic date), and more cautiously, Boatwright (1987), 182–190.

33. Joint consuls in 140 CE: *RIC* III 92 (gold, with title COS III), 628 (bronze, no legend); cf. *BMCRE* II pl. 39, 9. The wand known as a *vindicta* was an instrument in a common type of manumission ceremony administered by lictors.

34. For one of a pair of lictors on the emperor's podium, see the (rare) sesterius (161 CE) of Lucius Verus (co-ruler 161–169) sold as Auktionshaus H. D. Rauch Auction 107, Lot 318 (November 12, 2018). For the pairing of a lictor with another attendant, see probably the sestertius *RIC* III 1370 (163–164 CE, Verus's crowning of Sohaemus of Armenia); in the design of the corresponding aureus (*RIC* III 512), the figure is much less certainly a lictor.

35. For some representative early LIBERALITAS types, see the coins connected to Hadrian's first and seventh (and last) largesses: *RIC* II 552 (118 CE, where Liberalitas stands on the emperor's daïs; a seated official hands out coins), 254 (an aureus of 138 CE, Liberalitas stands left and occupies the entire field, holding abacus and cornucopia), and 766 (138 CE, Liberalitas on podium, herself emptying a cornucopia into the fold of a citizen's toga). For the coin recording Antoninus's fourth largesse, see *RIC* III 774. For the revival of this type under Marcus Aurelius, see *RIC* III 914 (166 CE) and 1208 (177 CE); Commodus, see *RIC* III 300 (180 CE); 134 with 471a (186 CE), 564 (190 CE), and 591 (192 CE); under Septimius Severus, where his sons Geta and Caracalla are also squeezed onto the platform, *RIC* IVa 279 (209 CE). Postumus: *RIC* Va 27. On Liberalitas in general, see Manning (1985), esp. 74–82.

36. Liberalitas issue of 152–153 CE: *RIC* III 229. Of 161 CE: *RIC* III 311a. Lictor portrait of 161 CE: *RIC* III 1362.

37. Sestertius (minted under the authority of Caracalla) with new-model fasces: *RIC* IVa 422A. The Severan coinage also features a reverse scene where the emperor sacrifices at a tripod altar, accompanied by a flute-player and another attendant with a staff on his left shoulder, who is just possibly a lictor: see *RIC* IVa 308 and 309 (206 CE, Septimius Severus); 181 (207 CE, Caracalla).

38. See the basic treatment of Delbrück (1929), esp. 15, fig. 8, for the lictors on the Arcadius column; 154–156 N 35 (Aspar, w[estern] consul 434); 117–121 N 16 (Clementinus, e[astern] consul 513); 137–139 N 22 (Magnus, e. consul 518), 144–146 N 29 (Philoxenus, e. consul 525); also 95–99 N 4 (Astyrias, w. consul 449) and (for the Bourges diptych) Volbach (1976), no. 36, all with the general discussion of Cameron (2015), 268 (refuting the notion that the personified cities are serving the consuls), and cf. 278–280 on the Aspar silver plate (arguing for eastern manufacture).

39. On the fasces of later antiquity, see especially Delbrück (1929), 64–65 (with nn. 220 and 221 on the purple coloring), with Cameron (2015), 268 n. 99, on the so-called flags.

40. Lydus *Mag.* 32; cf. 19 (additional emphasis on axes) and 37 (paired rods). The translation is that of Bandy (1983).

41. Collection of the Decii: Cassiod. *Var.* 9.23.5 (533 CE). Cassiodorus on the fasces accorded to the consulship: *Var.* 3.5.5 (509–511); 2.1.4 and 2.3.7 (511). Prefect of the City: 1.42.3, and 1.43.1 and 5 (509–510, with Theoderic declaring himself to be their source); also 1.44.2 and 3.12.2 (510–511). *Praefectus praetorio*: 8.20.3 (527). Quaestor: 10.6.5 (534). Provincial governors in general: 6.1.5, 11.9.5, 12.1.4, 12.2.3. Fasces in general: 5.21.3 (523–526, with reference to their "dread-inspiring" psychological effect); 7.1.1. On late antique collections of insignia, see Sid. Apoll. *Epist.* 2.3.1 (cf. *Carm.* 7.156–157) and 8.8.2–3.

42. Corippus *Laud. Just.* 3.2.42 ("cruel axes" displayed in ceremonial at the Consistorium). For use in provinces, see further below, on Justinian I's arrangements for Cappadocia in 536.

43. *Rhabdouchoi*: see Anna Komemne, *Alexiad* 12.6.5 with the discussion of Bernard (2020), 49–50, also citing Christopher of Mytilene (eleventh century) Poem 1 on the low social status of these attendants. *Magglabitai*: see Haldon (1984), 464 (stressing the non-military origin of this office), with Jenkins (1962), 200, on the sources (calling these attendants "closely akin to, if not directly descended, from the *lictores* of Roman times"). Varangians: see Schrijver (2012), 219–234, with further bibliography. Ignatius of Smolensk: Majeska (1984), 106–109.

CHAPTER 4

1. "Greater" consul: Festus, *Gloss. Lat.* 154 L. Choice of dictator: Liv. 8.12.13.

2. On Caesar as consul 59 BCE and the "turn," see Suet. *Iul.* 20.3. Priority in election determining the fasces: Taylor and Broughton (1949), esp. 5 on the presiding

consul's influence on elections; also Taylor and Broughton (1968), incorporating revisions suggested by J. Linderski. Augustus's reform: Gell. *NA* 2.15.3–8.

3. For the principle, see Liv. 28.9.10 (207 BCE, suggesting a daily oscillation of precedence in the auspices); cf. 22.42.7–9 (216 BCE), where a consul—presumably not possessing the fasces—uses his auspices to block his colleague's attempt to engage the enemy.

4. For Polybius's references to "holders of six axes," see Brennan (2000), 663–664; there are eight such mentions in all, including one (Polyb. 33.1.6) of an urban praetor as president of the Senate, when that body received an embassy from Achaea. That meeting may indeed have been outside the *pomerium* (cf. Liv. 34.43.1–2 and 42.36.1–2 for the procedure in receiving embassies from states deemed hostile); if so, one expects the praetor's lictors in fact displayed axes in their fasces. Praetors for Spain in the mid-second century BCE were called "six-axed" despite their enhanced (i.e., consular) *imperium*: Diod. Sic. 29.26, 31.42, and (from Posidonius) 33.2.

5. Six fasces as standard grade: Joseph. *BJ* 2.365 (a speech); Rut. Namat. 579–580; and cf. Ulpian in *Dig.* 1.16.14 (early third century CE), defining six fasces as the limit for proconsuls—despite the clear exceptions of Africa and Asia. *Consularis*: *CTh* 9.26.4 (416 CE, defining his insignia, which included the fasces, as well as that of the *praeses*, which did not). For his formula, see Cassiod. *Var.* 6.20.1 with Foss (1983), 201 n. 19 and 211 and n. 61; the translation is that of Bjornlie (2019), 271. On the official known as the *magister officiorum* deciding when governors can assume their fasces, see Cassiod. *Var.* 6.6.5. Justinian's innovations: Just. *Nov.* 30.6 with Foss (1983), 207–208. Proconsulate: Symm. *Ep.* 1.1.4; on the twelve fasces of the governor for Africa, see also Cyprian *Ep.* 37. On the special prestige of the proconsulates of Africa and Asia, inherited from the Republic, see Jones (1964), 385–386.

6. On the properties of elm, cf. Theophr. *Hist. pl.* 5.3.5 (least likely to warp). I owe this reference to David Lewis (Edinburgh).

7. For detailed general discussion of the number of lictors of the urban praetor, see Brennan (2000), 663–667. Specifically, see Censorinus *DN* 24.3 (= *RS* II 44) on the tribunician *lex Plaetoria*; Plaut. *Epid.* 23–28 (although the setting of the relevant passage is at Athens, the coloring is Roman); Cic. *Leg. agr.* 2.93. Cf. also Lactant. *Div. inst.* 1.21 with Val. Max. 1.1.9, on the (undatable) praetorship of M. Furius Bibaculus, who seems likely to have received his cognomen ("two-staffed"), from introducing his lictors into the distinctive ritual procession of his priesthood, that of the Salii. Valerius Maximus says this Furius paraded with "six lictors," but here he seems to err, influenced by imperial practice, for which see Mart. *Epigr.* 11.98.15; cf. Cass. Dio 53.13.8.

8. Implied indispensability of fasces: Sen. *Constant.* 12.2. On these abdications, see Liv. 23.23.1 and 7 and Plut. *Fab.* 9.4 (Fabius Buteo in 216 BCE); App. *BCiv.* 1.65.298–66.300 (Cinna in 87); 104.484 (Sulla in 79).

9. On Julius Caesar as praetor in 62 BCE, see Suet. *Iul.* 16.1–2, with Brennan (2000), 473 and 832 n. 238. Caecina Alienus in 69 CE: Cass. Dio 64.14.4. For the illegal

retention of insignia, see Suet. *Tib.* 4.2–3 (the emperor Tiberius's father as a praetor in 42 BCE). For dismissal of lictors as a preliminary to flight, see Tac. *Hist.* 3.11 (Marcus Aponius Saturninus, consular governor of Moesia, in 69 CE).

10. Cass. Dio 78(77).4.3 (Xiph.), named as "Julianus Asper," with Scott (2018), 70, for short discussion; for a detailed treatment of Gaius Iulius Asper, his family and his career, see Dietz (1997), esp. 483–485 on the consulship of 212 CE and the probable city prefectship of that same year.

11. *Aen.* 7.173. On this, see Rosivach (1980), 148–149.

12. See *Inscr. Ital.* XIII 2 7 and 44 = *ILS* 8744a and 108 for Octavian (January 7); *Inscr. Ital.* XIII 2 43 for the ordinary consuls, all with the additional passages gathered at *TLL* s.v. fascis col. 305.4–7; also Auson. *Opusc.* III (*Domestica*) 5, with esp. lines 43 and 48.

13. See Sen. *QNat.* 4A.13 and Amm. Marc. 15.2.3 against Stat. *Silv.* 4.2.61, the image of a "new lictor" on January 1; cf. Sil. *Pun.* 8.216, describing the succession of consuls as "changed fasces." On Rogatianus, see Porph. *Plot.* 7.

14. Plut. *Publ.* 6.2–3. See too Liv. 2.5.8, also describing the details of the punishment that the lictors inflicted on the sons of Lucius Brutus, adding that he viewed it from a tribunal with his consular colleague, but omitting the binding of hands. Plutarch (*Publ.* 7.1–3) has Brutus follow up this execution with soon another; after a confused melée in which his lictors violently insert themselves into a crowd to make a misguided arrest, order is restored, a trial is held of the genuinely guilty, and on receiving the verdict Brutus beheads his colleague's conspiratorial cousins.

15. Liv. 1.8.2, 17.5–6, 26.6–8.

16. Appius Claudius and Verginia: Liv. 3.48.3. Titus Manlius Imperiosus Torquatus (consul III 340 BCE): Liv. 8.7.13–22, cf. 4.29.5–6 and Val. Max. 2.7.6, and see, in general, Lushkov (2015), 46–53; for the lasting proverbial force of "imperia Manliana," note, e.g., Gell. *NA* 1.13.7 and August. *De civ. D.* 5.18. A suspiciously similar story is told of the dictator Aulus Postumius Tubertus in 431 BCE (*MRR* I 63). The dictator Lucius Papirius Cursor and Master of the Horse Quintus Fabius Maximus Rullianus (325 BCE): Liv. 8.32.8; cf. Val. Max. 2.7.8, with rhetorical flourishes. For the incident involving Papirius Cursor at Praeneste (319 BCE), see Plin. *HN* 17.81–82 (incidentally revealing that *destringere* was a technical word used of a lictor drawing an axe out of a bundle of rods); Cass. Dio 8.24 = Zonar. 7.24; Amm. Marc. 30.5.5.

17. Liv. 26.15–17; cf. Val. Max. 3.8.1. For the tradition that Capua in the Hannibalic War had demanded a share in the Roman consulship and with it, one set of fasces, see esp. Sil. *Pun.* 11.60–62. Livy suggests that Capuan magistrates had their own lictors at this time: see 23.10.6.

18. For the power of (mere) commands to lictors, see esp. Liv. 36.28.6 with Polyb. 20.10.7–9 and 21.5.3 (191 BCE), with the analysis of Eckstein (1995), 272.

19. Liv. 4.49–51; cf. Flor. 1.17.22. For 89 BCE, see sources in *MRR* II 36.

20. Sen. *Ira* 1.18.3 with 19.3; cf. Juv. 3.128–130 (a praetor orders a lictor to quicken his pace so he can more quickly flatter wealthy acquaintances).

21. Silent authority of lictors: Sen. *Controv.* 2.8 (of the earlier Republican era in general). On the psychological terror caused by lictors and their fasces, see especially Marshall (1984).

22. Plaut. *Poen.* 4–6; cf. Polyb. 30.22.6–12 for an (extreme) example of a lictor of the presiding magistrate trying to ensure the success of the performance. See also Suet. *Iul.* 80.2 (45 BCE) for a lictor announcing the arrival of a consul in the theater, "in the usual manner."

23. Martial (*Epigr.* 11.98.15–16) is explicit on the noisiness of the lictor in this activity. For passages on lictors clearing a path in the city of Rome, see, e.g., Liv. 6.38.8 (368 BCE); Plut. *Aem.* 32.2 (during triumph of 167 BCE); Plut. *Pomp.* 22.5 (70 BCE); Plin. *Pan.* 23.3 (which supplies the quote); cf. 61.7–9 (verbal aspects of this task) with 76.8, and Sil. *Pun.* 10.638–639 (implying that silence on the part of the lictors when re-entering the city was unusual). For the imperial era, see esp. Tac. *Ann.* 2.69 (in 19 CE the Syrian governor Piso uses his lictors to disrupt religious festivities at Antioch); also Sen. *Ep.* 94.60 and Plin. *HN* 9.127 (general), and cf. Hor. *Carm.* 2.16.34–35 (metaphorical).

24. Guides: Plut. *Cat. Mai.* 8.5; cf. Polyb. 10.32.2 (208 BCE, lictors aid in reconnaissance). Path-clearing in the camp (often with the technical word *summovere* = "remove"): Liv. 3.48.3 (449 BCE, ejection from an assembly); 4.50.5 (414 BCE); 45.7.4 (168 BCE) and 29.2 (167 BCE, emphasizing terror); App. *BCiv.* 1.78, 84 BCE. For imperial practice, see Tac. *Hist.* 3.31 (Caecina in 69 CE). Determining access: Liv. 23.15.15 (216 BCE). Heralds: Dion. Hal. *Ant. Rom.* 9.8.4 (480 BCE, allegedly convening a military assembly). Messengers: Flor. 1.5 (458 BCE, a lictor summons Cincinnatus from his plow to assume his dictatorship in which he rescues a Roman army trapped by the Aequi; cf. also Ov. *Fast.* 3.780–781), characterizing it as an exchange of plow for fasces, and Pers. 1.75, imagining that the lictor was responsible for taking in the plow from the field); Liv. 8.9.9 (340 BCE, in a battle against the Latins at Veseris in Campania, the consul Publius Decius Mus tells his lictors to announce to his consular colleague that he will sacrifice himself in a ritual act of devotion). Charge to accompany letter-carriers: Cic. *Fam.* 2.19.2. In general, for the function of lictors in a military setting, see Plin. *HN* 11.54 (comparison from the world of bees).

25. For the Campanians in 216 BCE, see Liv. 23.6.7; cf. 22.58.9, a lictor's similar command to a Carthaginian envoy earlier that same year. Carthaginian envoys turned out in 149 BCE: App. *Pun.* 90.424.

26. Cic. *De or.* 3.2–4 with Val. Max. 6.2.2; on 59 BCE, Val. Max. 2.10.7.

27. Enforcement of order in a court: Liv. 1.40.6–7 (ineffective, leading to the assassination of Tarquinius Priscus); Liv. 3.45–46 and Dion. Hal. *Ant. Rom.* 11.32.1 (tribunal of the decemvir Ap. Claudius in 449 BCE); Cic. *QFr* 1.1.21 (court, apparently in Rome, of a praetor 61 BCE); Suet. *Gram. et rhet.* 6 (a criminal procedure in Milan

ca. 14 BCE, suppressing applause for an orator, which the speaker characterized as an act of tyranny).

28. On the arrangement of the tribunal, see Dion. Hal. *Ant. Rom.* 8.45.3 (the tale of Coriolanus in 491 BCE). On 42 BCE, see App. *BCiv.* 4.32.136–34.146, on which see esp. 4.34.135 for the lictors; cf. also Val. Max. 8.3.3 (confirming the outcome) and Quint. *Inst.* 1.1.6 (later readership of Hortensia's speech).

29. On the matrons, see Festus, *Gloss. Lat.* 143 L (I thank Lewis Webb for the reference) and Val. Max. 2.1.5. Though Festus's text is corrupt, the essentials are certain thanks to the later epitome of Paul the Deacon. On the lictors' differing treatment of prostitutes, see Sen. *Controv.* 6.8 with 1.3.

30. On the incident of the Fabia sisters in 377 BCE, see Liv. 6.34.6–11; cf. Cass. Dio 7 F 29.1–2 = Zonar. 7.24, with Brennan (2000), 59 and 271 n. 6.

31. Lictors as escort to and from a magistrate's home: Liv. 3.26.11, a dictator in 458 BCE—clearly anachronistic, but presumably the practice Livy himself witnessed in his own day; cf. also Petron. *Sat.* 65 (the lictor of a *sevir Augustalis* knocks on a dining-room door), and Claud. *Cons. IV Hon.* [398 CE] 415–417, describing the practice of lictors guarding a magistrate's door as of deep antiquity. Lictors escorting magistrates to the home of another: Plin. *HN* 7.112 (on Rhodes in 62 BCE, Pompey forbids his lictor to knock on the door of Posidonius); Stat. *Silv.* 1.233 (for a wedding); Juv. 3.128–130 (for the morning salutation).

32. On this and what follows, see Liv. 39.12.2.

33. Sen. *Controv.* 9.2.1–29. Charges: Votienus Montanus at 9.2.16. Brothel: Pompeius Silo at 9.2.17. Public axe: Florus at 9.2.24. Capito on proper provincial procedure: 9.2.9–10. Improvised tribunal and drunkenness of the principals: Porcius Latro: 9.2.3 and 24. The lictor's reluctance: Argentarius and Montanus each at 9.2.22. Subversion of formulae: Triarius at 9.2.21 and Argentarius at 9.2.22. Inherent terror of symbols of Roman *imperium*: Albucius Silus at 9.2.6 and 8.

34. See Liv. 28.26–29, esp. 29.9–12 and App. *Hisp.* 35.140–36.146, esp. 36.145–146; for the quote, Liv. 28.24.14.

35. *HA Avid. Cass.* 5.1–2, citing a nonexistent source for the item, for which the context seems to be Avidius's time as a legionary legate in a Danubian province in the late 150s. For lictors administering military justice in the imperial period, see also, e.g., Front. *Str.* 4.28 (in the latter half of the 50s CE, Domitius Corbulo in Armenia orders his lictors to strip a cowardly cavalry prefect, and leave him indefinitely in that state).

36. For the accusation of Verres's misuse of lictors in general, see Cic. *Verr.* 2.5.39. For the principle that public officials should not use lictors for private aims, see Caes. *BCiv.* 1.6.7 (his accusation against the consuls of 49 BCE); cf. Liv. 39.32.10 (185 BCE, a consul of the year sheds his lictors in the city when campaigning for his brother in the elections for 184).

37. On the Philodamus affair and the death of the lictor, see Cic. *Verr.* 2.1.63–86, esp. 63 (Verres's special embassy), 67 (Cornelius killed), 69–70 (Lampsacene attempt to

burn Verres alive), 73 (Dolabella leaves Cilicia for Asia, abandoning the war he was waging), 75–76 (execution of Philodamus and his son by decapitation). In general on the commanders for Asia and Cilicia at this time, and the chronology of Verres's movements, see Brennan (2000), 557 and 571–572.

38. Magistrates ordering arrest: Asc. p. 58 C (Gaius Calpurnius Piso, consul 67 BCE). Lictors depicted as active at Thessalian Hypata: Apul. *Met.* 3.2 and 9; 9.41; also 1.24–25 with Summers (1970), 521.

39. Caesar: *Iul.* 43.2. Declamation: [Quint.] *Declam.* 286.4.

40. Jer. *Ep.* 1.3–14. See also Prudent. *Perist.* 10.555 and 1108–1109 (in 303 or 304 CE, a lictor tortures Romanus of Caesarea, and then executes him by strangulation), cf. 3.96–97 and 175 (in 303 CE, a lictor tortures Eulalia of Mérida, and then aids in her burning); and cf. Sid. Apoll. *Pan. Anthem.* 2.300–304 (imagining that a "lictor" ca. 183 BCE was charged to strangle Hannibal in jail, obviously retrojecting from the practice of his own day).

CHAPTER 5

1. Orders to kings: Polyb. F 74 (context uncertain, perhaps Perseus in 168 BCE, for which see Polyb. 29.20.1 with Liv. 45.7.4); Plut. *Pomp.* 33.3 and Cass. Dio 36.52.3, cf. App. *Mith.* 104.490 (order to a king to dismount, 66 BCE). Lictors imprisoning kings: App. *Ill.* 9.27 (the Illyrian king Genthius in 168 BCE, after a praetor hosts him at dinner).

2. Orders to holders of *imperium*: Gell. *NA* 2.2.13 (command to dismount, 213 BCE, from the annalist Claudius Quadrigarius); App. *BCiv.* 5.55.233 (41 BCE, orders to lower a naval ensign).

3. Unorganized resistance by the Plebs: Liv. 2.27.12 (495 BCE, supporting an individual's appeal as lictors dragged him away); 2.29.2–4 (494 BCE, forcibly preventing an arrest). Creation of the tribunate: Liv. 2.33.1 and 3, 3.55.10 with Brennan (2018). Repercussions for striking a lictor: Liv. 2.29.12; Dion. Hal. *Ant. Rom.* 9.39.4.

4. On this, see Ogilvie (1965), 366.

5. Sources (many) in *MRR* I 27–30.

6. Liv. 2.55.3; Dion. Hal. *Ant. Rom.* 9.39.1–4; cf. also Flor. 1.17.22, and Zonar. 7.17 (summarizing Cassius Dio).

7. Liv. 2.56.6–16 and Dion. Hal. *Ant. Rom.* 9.48.1–3.

8. For the system working as it should, see Liv. 3.10–11, effective tribunician defense against consuls' lictors arresting plebeians during a levy of 461 BCE. For what follows, see Liv. 3.31.6–8 and Dion. Hal. *Ant. Rom.* 10.31–32.

9. See especially Liv. 3.45.7, 48.3, 49.3–4, 56.2, 57.2–3.

10. See, e.g., Liv. *Per. Oxy.* 54, an incident of 140 BCE, where the (corrupt) text establishes at a minimum that a consul, when the plebeian tribune Tiberius Claudius Asellus tried to block his departure from the city, "used a lictor and a threat of force to deter Asellus from enforcing his veto" (Astin [1967], 127).

11. Breaking rods in 133 BCE: App. *BCiv.* 1.15.65. 88 BCE: Plut. *Sull.* 9.2. 67 BCE: Cass. Dio 36.39.3; Asc. p. 58 C. 59 BCE: Cass. Dio 38.6.3; Plut. *Pomp.* 48.1 and *Cat. Min.* 32.2; App. *BCiv.* 2.11.38–39.

12. Cic. *Pis.* 28 (least hazy on the details, and the source for the quote); *Red. sen.* 7 and *Red. pop.* 14 (each alleging that the homes of magistrates were attacked and that also a plebeian tribune was wounded); also Cass. Dio 38.30.2, explicitly linking the disturbances to Pompey's decision that Cicero should be recalled from exile.

13. See, e.g., Lucan 7.427 (India "no longer dreads the fasces of Latium"); cf. Tert. *Apol.* 25.4 (Crete as a victim of Roman fasces); Claud. *Cons. VI Hon.* 337 (404 CE, a Scythian river encounters the fasces). For a twist on this topos, see Claudian, in a panegyrical dedication to Gennadius (prefect of Egypt in 396 CE), who implausibly says that Greece and Egypt both "dread and love your fasces" (*Carm. min.* 19 [43] line 4).

14. Calamities of 150–146 BCE: Polyb. 38.3.8–13. Imperial governors: Juv. 8.135–137 and Prudent. *Hamart.* 441–442.

15. Flamininus: Liv. 33.1.5–6. Pompey: Plut. *Pomp.* 49.6. Antony with Octavia in 39/38 BCE: App. *BCiv.* 5.76.322–324. Tiberius: Suet. *Tib.* 11.1. Germanicus: Tac. *Ann.* 2.53; Suet. *Calig.* 3.2.

16. See Caes. *BCiv.* 3.106.4; cf. Lucan 10.11. Alexandria said to be exempt from fasces as late as 262 CE: *HA Tyr. Trig.* 22.10–13, citing also a (fake) inscription to that effect.

17. On Hannibal, see Liv. 30.28.7 with Sil. *Pun.* 8.672–673, a soldier's prophecy before the disaster at Cannae of a "Carthaginian triumph"; cf. also 10.563–564, Hannibal's supposed reverence for Roman fasces. On Viriathus, Flor. 1.33.13. Oppius: App. *Mith.* 20.78–79 with Brennan (2000), 358–359.

18. See Plut. *Crass.* 31.1 (Crassus dispenses with his lictors for the parley), 32.1–3, 33.5; cf. 29.6 (Crassus lost seven of his twelve lictors even before his death). See also Flor. 2.30, who criticizes Augustus's general Publius Quinctilius Varus (killed 9 CE) for thinking that Germanic tribes would fear the trappings of his office for their own sake.

19. Asc. 33 C, cf. 31 C for the selection of the first *interrex* of 52 BCE. On the consular candidates for 52, see Broughton (1991), 22; on Pompey's location, Sumi (1997), 85. Esquiline as place of execution: Suet. *Claud.* 25.3. On the chronology of these events, Ramsey (2016).

20. Cic. *Sull.* 68, and cf. 11–13; Sall. *Cat.* 18.5–8 (specific that the plot involved the actual seizing of fasces on the Capitoline, and alleging that it was Autronius and Catiline who would appear as consuls); Liv. *Per.* 101 (general notice of plot); Cass. Dio 36.44.3–4 (adding the item that the new consuls received an additional bodyguard from the Senate); and in general, Drummond (1999). On the continued importance in the Empire of the new consuls' descent into the Forum, see Suet. *Claud.* 7.1 (37 CE).

21. Silver eagle: Cic. *Cat.* 1.24 and 2.13; Sall. *Cat.* 59.3 (provenance). Catiline's departure for Manlius's camp with insignia: Plut. *Cic.* 16.4 and Sall. *Cat.* 36.1. Catiline's role in final battle: Sall. *Cat.* 57.5–61.9.

22. For the date of Cicero's 14th *Philippic*, see *Phil.* 14.14. Dolabella: Vell. Pat. 2.58.3. Octavian: App. *BCiv.* 3.48.194 with *MRR* II 344. On the date of his assumption of the fasces, see *ILS* 108 with Plin. *HN* 11.190.

23. See Cic. *Phil.* 14.16 for the tribune's assembly, and 14.15 for the details of the alleged plot.

24. Gaius Gracchus: Plut. *Gaius Gracch.* 12.2 (the lictors engage in physical removal); cf. Gell. *NA* 10.3.11, quoting a speech of Gracchus which plainly describes a lictor publicly stripping and beating with his rods an allied citizen who has been tied to a stake. Theater: see Diod. Sic. 37.12.3, presumably at Asculum, on which see Rawson (1985), 98–99. Cf. the alleged Capuan demand during the Hannibalic War (211 BCE) for a share in the consulship at Rome, which Silius Italicus (*Pun.* 11.60–63) characterizes as a bid for the fasces and, with them, equal rights.

25. For the case of Vettius, see Diod. Sic. 36.2a. Note also Gaius Flavius Fimbria (App. *Mith.* 52.207–210, 86–85 BCE), who seized fasces at Byzantium, had a consular commander decapitated (presumably by lictors), and successfully fought battles before he chose death by suicide when it seemed his forces would desert him; and Marcus Marius (Plut. *Sert.* 24.3–4, 76 BCE), a pseudo-magistrate of Sertorius's renegade government in Spain who fought in Asia in concert with the Pontic king Mithridates VI, and entered the cities they captured "with fasces and axes."

26. Saturninus: Val. Max. 7.3.9, cf. Vell. Pat. 2.77.3 and App. *BCiv.* 5.52.139 for his probable protection, once he reached Sicily, by Sextus Pompey. Pomponius: App. *BCiv.* 4.45.194.

27. Agnellus, *The Book of Pontiffs of the Church of Ravenna* 106 (trans. Deliyannis [2004]).

28. For this, see Sid. Apoll. *Epist.* 1.11.6 (deeply critical) with Mathisen (1979), esp. 603–604 (dating the man's unofficial then official tenure of the post of *praefectus praetorio Galliarum* from early 457 to early 458). But despite Sidonius's grumbling, we learn that the governor did not face punishment but rather received his authorizing codicils toward the end of his projected term.

29. Liv. 25.15–17 (212 BCE, Carthaginians cut down all of a consul's lictors while he was bathing in a river, and then the commander himself); Liv. 27.27.8 and Plut. *Marc.* 29.9 (208 BCE).

30. Liv. 37.57.1–2 (189 BCE).

31. App. *BCiv.* 1.71.326–330 and 78.356–357.

32. On Varinius, see Plut. *Crass.* 9.4–5 with Brennan (2000) 431–432 on his status. On the booty, Front. *Str.* 2.34, citing Livy; also Liv. *Per.* 97 and cf. Flor. 2.8.

33. On 67 BCE, see esp. Plut. *Pomp.* 24.6 (revealing the names of the praetors) and Cic. *Leg. Man.* 32–33 (capture of twelve lictors) with Brennan (2000), 434. Munda: [Caes.] *BHisp.* 31.

34. Cic. *Phil.* 5.17.

35. For Sulla, see App. *BCiv.* 1.100.465 (noting twenty-four "axes" plus bodyguard) and 104.484 (description of his abdication of 79 BCE, differentiating his lictors and bodyguard). For later instances, see, e.g., Cass. Dio 36.39.3 (consuls of the year 67 BCE); 36.44.3–4 (consuls of 65 BCE); App. *BCiv.* 2.12.43 (Caesar as consul in 59 BCE); cf. Cic. *Phil.* 2.112 (the nature of Antony's armed guard in 44 BCE). A consular bodyguard is even found under Augustus: Cass. Dio 54.10.1 (voted to the consul Gaius Sentius in 19 BCE). For Caesar in 44 BCE, see App. *BCiv.* 2.109.455 and (for the quote) 118.498.

36. See App. *BCiv.* 5.41.173–174, where Lucius Antonius (consul 41) and the triumvir Octavian meet in a parley before Perugia in 40 BCE, each first voluntarily shedding their military dress and reducing their lictors to two (i.e., from the consular complement of twelve) to show their goodwill.

37. Tac. *Hist.* 2.29; Dio Cass. 63.15.3.

38. See Herodian 7.8.5, a speech attributed to Maximinus in 238 CE, characterizing the position of the African governor and claimant to the throne Gordian I at Carthage; Claud. *Cons. Stil.* 3.220–222.

CHAPTER 6

1. On the developments outlined here, see in general Brennan (2014), 26–30, 36–38. Luca: Plut. *Caes.* 21.2 and App. *BCiv.* 2.17.62. On this, see also Lucan 5.12–13, remarking on the large number of fasces with axes gathered as the Senate met on Epirus in late 49 BCE.

2. On this, see Cic. *Fam.* 12.21 and 30. Two lictors as default: Cass. Dio 54.10.2, 19 BCE.

3. On Octavian's initial grant of *imperium*, see App. *BC* 3.48.194; Cic. *Phil.* 11.20. See also Plut. *Cic.* 45.3, *Ant.* 17.1, and cf. [Cic.] *Ep. ad Octav.* 4.

4. Vestals granted lictor: Cass. Dio 47.19.1; cf. Plut. *Num.* 10.3 and Torelli (1982), 36, for a lictor accompanying the Vestals on the Augustan *Ara Pacis*. Two Vestals needed at shrine in actual practice: implied by Macrob. 3.13.10–11, that details participants at a August 70 BCE feast for the inauguration of a *flamen*, which four Vestals attended. The banqueting scene on the Julio-Claudian *Ara Pietatis* in the Museo dell'Ara Pacis (inv. 2391) that shows five (or possibly six) Vestals reclining together strikes one as a fantasy.

5. Sen. *Controv.* 1.2.3 (argument of Publius Vinicius, consul 2 CE). In general on lowering fasces as a signal mark of respect, see Dion. Hal. *Ant. Rom.* 8.44.3–4, commenting on the dubious tradition of the exiled fifth-century BCE patrician Coriolanus, at the head of a Volscian army no less, removing his axes and lowering his fasces in the presence of his mother; cf. here also App. *Ital.* 3.8 (lictors dismissed). It does seem that a commander might choose to lower his fasces even to a private citizen: note, e.g., Pompey and Posidonius in Plin. *HN* 7.112 (fulsome on the gesture in general). Provincial governors and Tiberius, before his accession: Vell.

Pat. 2.99.4. Late antiquity: Prudent. *C. Symm.* 1.556–557 with Barnes and Westall (1991), 52; cf. Auson. *Ordo nob. Urb.* 11.3 (metaphorical).

6. See Ov. *Fast.* 2.19–24 (8 CE, the *flamen's* lictor assisting in the ritual of sweeping out and purifying houses); also Plut. *Mor.* 291 B-C = *Quaest. Rom.* 113, and Gell. *NA* 10.15.4. Augustales: Petr. 30.1, cf. 65.3.

7. On Livia, see Cass. Dio 56.45.1 and Tac. *Ann.* 1.14 with Brennan (2018), 2–3; on Agrippina, Tac. *Ann.* 13.2. On their precedent, we might expect four additional empresses to receive the fasces through the Severans: Plotina (wife of Trajan, reigned 98–117 CE); Lucilla (wife of Lucius Verus, co-reigned 161–169 CE); Titia Flaviana (wife of Pertinax, who reigned briefly in 193 CE); and Julia Domna (wife of Septimius Severus, reigned 193–211). But none of these women, nor any other in the relevant period, is positively attested to have held the distinction.

8. Cic. *Leg. agr.* 1.9; Caes. *BCiv.* 3.32.4.

9. On the term *quinquefascalis*, see *CIL* VI 41134 (168 or 169 CE), and cf. Cass. Dio 57.17.7 (17 CE) and Sex. Emp. *Math.* 29. On the five fasces in actual practice, see, e.g., Caes. *BCiv.* 1.30.2 (Curio's appointment to Sicily with delegated *imperium*); Cic. *Att.* 10.4.9–10.

10. On this, see Suet. *Aug.* 30.1; Cass. Dio 55.8.7 (for the quote) and 25.2.

11. In general on the addition of lictors under Augustus, see Suet. *Aug.* 37.1. Commissioners for roads: Cass. Dio. 54.8.4 (institutionalized in 20 BCE, two in number, each with two lictors). Aqueducts: Front. *Aq.* 99 (11 BCE, three commissioners each with two lictors, but only outside the city). Grain supply: Cass. Dio 55.31.4 (7 BCE, two ex-consuls as commissioners, each probably with two lictors). Augustus's generous grants of lictors to commissioners and prefects did not all last, at least within the city. For instance, Cassius Dio (55.25.3) shows that by the early third century CE, the "prefects of the military treasury" had lost their right to the fasces.

12. For a description of precisely that situation for the year 75 BCE, see Plut. *Pomp.* 19.5 with Brennan (2000), 513.

13. On all this, see especially Brunt (1977), 96, who succinctly summarizes the chronology for Augustus's novel powers, their rationale, and their practical consequence for the city, during his reign and beyond. In particular on the fasces, Cassius Dio (54.10.5) cites legislation of 19 BCE which he erroneously asserts made Augustus "consul for life" (a point refuted by his actual titulature). Yet Dio must be correct on his "right to use the twelve rods always and everywhere and to sit in the curule chair between the two men who were at the time consuls." The combination of "greater" *imperium* and evident exemption from the rotation of consular fasces made it clear that Augustus had a permanent right of initiative.

14. Plut. *Luc.* 36.2–4; see *Pomp.* 31.2–3 for the same episode.

15. Legislation of 64 BCE: Asc. *In Cornel.* 8 C = p. 59 Stangl, with the emendation "lictorum" for "fictorum," on which see Marshall (1984), 30. Subsequent legislation

that outlawed *collegia* expressly spared those deemed of ancient foundation (Suet. *Iul.* 42.4 for 46 BCE and *Aug.* 32.3 for 22 BCE), but we lack further specifics.

16. The lictor Cornelius: Cic. *Verr.* 2.1.67, 71. Sextius: *Verr.* 2.5.118–119 with 156; cf. Quint. *Inst.* 8.4.27 and 11.1.39–40, praising Cicero's description of the man. Postumius: App. *BCiv.* 2.12.43. Cicero's advice to his brother: Cic. *QFr.* 1.1.13–14 (60 BCE).

17. Sextius: Cic. *Verr.* 2.5.142. Dream: Cic. *Div.* 1.50; cf. 2.136 and Val. Max. 1.7.5. Jugurtha's "proximate lictor": Sall. *Iug.* 12.3.

18. See, e.g., the reports of a pre-battle sacrifice at Philippi (42 BCE), where the ritual went awry when a lictor set a reversed laurel crown on his commander's head (Plut. *Brut.* 39.1–2; App. *BCiv.* 4.89.374 and 134.563; Cass. Dio 47.40.7, cf. 38.4; see also Obsequens 70 for a different version, in which "the lictor placed the laurel on the fasces when they were reversed"); also Suetonius's report (*Tib.* 72.3) that the emperor Tiberius in his last years at Capri customarily bid farewell to his dinner guests standing in the middle of the dining room with a lictor by his side, evidently fearing assassination should he chat too near the door.

19. Court: Cic. *QFr.* 1.1.21. Naval presence: App. *BCiv.* 5.55.233. Deaths of proximates: [Caes.] *BAlex.* 52.3; Tac. *Hist.* 3.80.

20. For what follows, see Cic. *Verr.* 2.5.140–142.

21. See Dion. Hal. *Ant. Rom.* 3.62.1 (Tarquinius Priscus); Liv. 3.26.11 (458 BCE); Polyb. 11.29.6 (from a speech); Cic. *Verr.* 2.5.22–23; Caes. *BCiv.* 3.106.4 (deemed an inappropriate display in the free city of Alexandria, and sparking a dangerous riot); Epictet. 4.57; Liban. *Or.* 49.6; *HA Sept. Sev.* 2.6–7; cf. Diod. Sic. 36.7 (Salvius "Tryphon" as leader of a Sicilian slave revolt in 104/3 BCE, affecting the attributes of Roman consuls). For an exception, relating to situations where two consuls found themselves together, see Suet. *Iul.* 20.3, discussed below.

22. Val. Max. 2.2.4a–b, citing examples from 292 and 213 BCE. On the episode of 292, see also Liv. *Per.* 11; on that of 213, Claudius Quadrigarius (first century BCE) ap. Gell. *NA* 2.2.13; also Liv. 24.44.9–10 and Plut. *Mor.* 196 A = *Apophtheg. Rom. Fab. Max.* 7. The convention of the proximate lictor creating an inviolable space seems to have persisted, at least in principle, into later antiquity. See *HA Sev.* 2.7, a suspect story of a breach involving a provincial legate, meant to explain why henceforth such officials rode in carriages.

23. Lictors said to be present in the Senate during a meeting: Liv. 3.41.4 (449 BCE, ordered by the presiding magistrate to arrest a senator so as to silence his opposition to the proceedings); 9.8.2 (320 BCE). Attending their superior during legal proceedings in Rome: Dion. Hal. *Ant. Rom.* 3.62.1 (Tarquinius Priscus); Cic. *Clu.* 147 (69 BCE). This extended to imperial-era trials in the Senate: Tac. *Ann.* 6.40 (36 CE) and 16.32 (66 CE), both instances where lictors needed quickly to intervene to control the defendants. For lictors on the rostra in Rome, next to the magistrate, as he addressed the people in the *comitium*: Liv. 23.23.7 (a dictator of 216 BCE). For late antique practices, see Claud. *Cons. VI Hon.* 643–648 (1 January 404 CE), where the

emperor is described as sitting in the Forum of Trajan in the midst of twelve lictors wielding laureled fasces equipped with axe-heads that flashed in the sun with the appearance of gold. Axes said to be within the city in 395 CE: Claudian, *Pan. Prob. et Olybr.* 230–233 (commenting on their sparkle visible even from afar); cf. his *Cons. Manl. Theodor.* (399 CE) 336–340, expressing the wish for a generational succession of fasces and axes within his honorand's family.

24. For instance, the children of an Aemilius Nicomedes pleonastically term their father "decurial of the consuls' lictorian *decuria* of the III *decuriae*," at the top of a list of other apparitorial posts he held: *CIL* VI 1869 (p 3820) = *ILS* 1908 (Nicomedes).

25. On all this, see Purcell (1983), esp. 127–128 and 171, on questions of social mobility for lictors. On relative status of magistrates' attendants, see especially Cic. *Leg. agr.* 2.32, listing (in descending order) "scribe, lictor, herald, sacred chicken keeper." On Paestum, see Crawford (1971), no. 30 = *HN Italy* 1247.

26. See Suet. *Dom.* 14.1 and 3 with Cass. Dio 67.4.3; Domitian's consulships date to 82–88, 90, 92, and 95 CE. On Anthemius, Sid. Apoll. *Pan. Anthem.* 2.5–6, cf. 1.1–2.

27. Though we have ample epigraphic documentation of lictors for the Imperial period, only about 20 percent of these inscriptions (24 of ca. 125) admit close dating: for the first century CE, see especially *CIL* VI 1879; 36910 (pp. 4301, 4352) (Julio-Claudian); *CIL* VI 1887 (pp. 3229, 3820) = *ILS* 1944 (Flavian). The Trajanic era (98–117 CE) offers seven inscriptions on lictors, three of which honor the same man, a patron of Ephesus and a probable participant in the slave trade: *IK* 13.646; *CIL* III 6078 (p. 1285) and 12254 = *ILS* 1925 = *IK* 15.1544 = *IK* 59.123; *AE* 1998, 1346. For a proximate lictor under Trajan who died in 117 CE, aged twenty-eight, at Selinus, just a few days after the emperor himself, see *CIL* VI 1884 (pp. 3229, 3820) = *ILS* 1792. The most telling of the (four) Hadrianic documents (117–138 CE) is a bilingual inscription from Ephesus from ca. 129–132 CE, in which we find Hadrian's grandnephew—not yet a senator, apparently not on an official mission in Asia, and indeed not yet twenty years of age—getting a lictor: *IK* 13.734 = *IK* 59.125. Just two datable inscriptions come from the reign of Antoninus Pius (138–161 CE), from Ostia and Puteoli, which show how organizations of lictors in these colonies attempted to mirror the types of associations they observed in Rome: *CIL* XIV 353 = *ILS* 6148 (p. 187) = Bergemann (1990), no. 32 (Ostia); *CIL* X 515 = *ILS* 340 (Puteoli). After the mid-second century CE, the chronologically anchored evidence becomes sparse indeed. Notable examples: *CIL* VI 1847 (pp. 3225, 3818) = *ILS* 1899 (patronage of lictors by Commodus); *CIL* VI 1872 (pp. 2879, 3820) = *ILS* 7266 (patronage by a lictor of Tiber fishermen); *CIL* VI 32295 = *ICUR* II 5860 (p. 373) (survival of the III decuries of lictors into the 380s).

28. *CIL* X 1193 = *ILCV* 3869.

29. The inscriptions: *ILLRP* Supp. 40, with the accompanying discussion of Gentili and Vergantini at pp. 280–282; and *CIL* I 1989 (p. 974) = VI 1899 (pp. 3229, 3820) = *ILLRP* 796 = *ILS* 1902, with Weaver (1972), 192–193, for remarks on the rarity of marriages between freed (even those of the imperial household)

and freeborn in general, and Treggiari (1969), 84, on the isolation of this inscription in the Republican record. On the equestrian Pompilius see Quintus Cicero, *Comment. Pet.* 10.

30. *ILS* 6087 = *RS* I no. 25 (offering text, English translation and commentary) cap. LXII lines 1–3 (attendants of duumvirs), 4–8 (staff of aediles, magistrates who were not entitled to a lictor or an *accensus*), 10–21 (military exemptions), 21–28 (relative pay of staff).

31. On the law and its context in the year 38 BCE, see Cass. Dio 48.43.2–3, cf. 43.51.4.

32. For the text, commentary, and discussion of the Pataras inscription, see Bonisch-Meyer (2018), esp. 381 for honors elsewhere to L. Luscius Ocra (Balboura, Oenoanda, Xanthos, Attaleia). The mention in the Patara inscription that Vespasian and Titus in their censorship (an office that ran from mid-73 to late 74 CE) had adlected Ocra among the patricians gives us a *terminus post quem* for our inscription. "Quinquefascalis": see *CIL* VI 41134. For a partial list of lictors serving together, see *CIL* III 7371 = *ILS* 4056 from 124 CE (three lictors from a larger set attending a proconsul and a legare with praetorian *imperium*, inducted into mysteries at Samothrace with their superiors but also with slaves on the staff).

33. For patronage of organizations of lictors at Ostia, see *CIL* XIV 353 = *ILS* 6148; *CIL* XIV 409 = *ILS* 6146; *NS* 1953 p241 = *ELOstia* p. 173 (all apparently from the second century CE); and *CCCA* III 388 = *ELOstia* p. 167. A quite fragmentary inscription from Rome (*CIL* VI 31818a with p. 4788) shows a dedication of lictors (and other apparitorial groups?) to an unnamed patron.

34. Thus Bonisch-Meyer (2018), 394.

35. Prudent. *C. Symm.* 1.555–565.

36. See Jones (1964), 601, for the later survival of the lictors (citing petitions in the years 386, 389, 404, 407, and 409 CE), including this quote.

CHAPTER 7

1. See Bodleian Library, Oxford, MS. Junius 11, with frontispiece, and pp. 2, 3 (the scene of the rebellion of Lucifer), 41, 74, 76, 82 (cylinder in right hand) and 84, with the discussion of the illustration at p. 3 by Karkov (2001), 50, underlining the contrast between Lucifer's and God's insignia; Raw (1976), 137–139, 143–146, arguing for Carolingian influence and adducing a loose parallel in a late tenth-century Boethius manuscript; and Broderick (1983), 165–169, adducing specifically the Utrecht Psalter as a source. The cylinder is identified as a fasces in the database of the Archive for Research on Archetypal Symbolism (aras.org, accessed July 20, 2021).

2. On the word "fasces": see Du Cange et al., *Glossarium mediae et infimae latinitatis* (1883–1887), III col. 418a, citing St. Rodulf (d. 866) of Bourges, who sees the fasces as a mark of "kingly greatness." See Middeldorf-Kosegarten (1975), 463, for "fasces" used in a figurative sense in an imperial diplomatic letter of 1238, and also on the failure in the eighth–tenth centuries to reproduce the (late antique-style) "fasces"

in copies of the Magnus diptych (518 CE), for which see Delbrück (1929), 137–141 n. 22–25. For "lictores" in the Latin Vulgate Bible (translating Greek *rhabdouchoi*), see Acts 16:35 and 38; cf. 1 Samuel 22:17, where "lictores" is used anachronistically of a king's bodyguards.

3. For the text of de Rovroy (*Stratagèmes* II, IV, 35, A, fol. 46b) and analysis, see Goodrich and Hayaert (2015), 16, who follow Bossuat (1960), 473. Papias: Middeldorf-Kosegarten (1975), 463.

4. See Fenestella, *De Sacerdotiis et Magistratibus Romanorum liber* (Milan 1477), in the section "De Consulibus," pp. 25–26, with Laureys (1995). For Flavio Biondo, *Opera* (Basel 1531), see *Italia Illustrata* 300F on the Etruscan origin of the insignia; *Roma Triumphans* 56A on Publicola removing axes from the fasces; and 71D on Alexandria. For more on fifteenth-century antiquarian treatments, see Middeldorf-Kosegarten (1975), 463–465.

5. Caelius Rhodiginus, *Antiquarum Lectionum* (Venice 1516), 317; G. Budé, *Annotationes in libros Pandectarum* (2nd ed., Paris 1526), lxxviii–lxxix; cf. also P. Apianus and B. Amantius, *Inscriptiones sacrosanctae vetustatis* (Ingolstadt 1534), 240, a succinct description of the fasces but with a detailed illustration.

6. For Machiavelli, see *Discourses on Livy* (1531), sections 25.1, 40.3. Rhodiginus: *Lectionum Antiquarum* (1516), XII 7 and 8, cf. further X 7 on the lictor. Metaphorical sense: see Weil-Garris and D'Amico (1980), 89 with 112 n. 92, on Paolo Cortesi's *De Cardinalatu* (1510); and Green (1872) 11–12, on Alciato. For a bio-bibliographical sketch of Alciato, see Abbondanza (1960).

7. Verona: Middeldorf-Kosegarten (1975), 462 fig. 1, 465. Lippi: the bibliography on these two famous fresco cycles is massive. In general, see the various contributions to Nuttall, Nuttall, and Kwakkelstein (2020), esp. 228–258 (Strozzi chapel), 208–227 (Carafa chapel). For the torture of "St. John before the Latin Gate" in *Golden Legend* 69, see the translation of Ryan (2012), 284. Lippi attracted attention even in the sixteenth century for his unusually inventive, if not bizarre, reception of classical design elements: see Shoemaker (1978).

8. Ambiguous depictions of fasces: see, e.g., an anonymous French translation in manuscript of Petrarch's *Triumphs* (BNF Fr 594 fol. 134v), illuminated in 1503 at Rouen for Louis XII, that shows Reason holding a long fasces-like column with sinuous binding—but against her right shoulder. On Raphael's *Proconsul*, see especially Clayton (1999), 108–110 no. 27 (arguing that the tapestry would be displayed on the wall behind the papal throne); for the Constantine "Magnanimity" frieze, see Fehl (1993), esp. 16 for the evidence on Raphael's original conception of the piece, and 17–49 on the artist's historical interests and methods. On the historical Sergius Paullus (*pro cos.* in Cyprus 46–48 CE), see Thomasson (2009), 123 no. 32:010.

9. Fasces as a sign of justice: see E. Vico, *Discorsi sopra le medaglie de gli antichi* (Venice 1558), 47–48, cited by Middeldorf-Kosegarten (1975), 476. On the Sack as a pivotal moment in the fierce struggle between papacy and nobility for control of justice in Rome, see Rebecchini (2013), 154–155, also discussing the Farnese commission

in this context. On the Farnese *Justice* (now Naples, Museum of Capodimonte inv. 84214) as iconographic turning-point, see Cheney (2003) (emphatic on Vasari as iconographic pioneer), esp. 301 for translation of Vasari's letter; Pierguidi (2007) on its sources and enthusiastic contemporary reception. Vasari's *Justice* in the Cornaro Palace at Venice (later in Rome in the collection of L. Amendola di Capua): Cheney (2003), 287 (with the suggestion that the pair sharing a single fasces symbolize military and civil power). For the *Justice* of Battista Dossi (Staatliche Kunstsammlungen, Dresden, Gemäldegalerie Alte Meister inv. 126), see Middeldorf-Kosegarten (1975), 466 fig. 4 and 476. For an ambitious and wide-ranging evaluation of representations of justice, from antiquity to the modern era, see Resnik and Curtis (2011), with 18–22 (starting with Babylonian and Egyptian iconography). On the figure of the fasces-bearing celestial virgin Astraea in Italian seventeenth-century art (rare specifically in this guise), see Wallace (1967), esp. 434 for her attributes of the crown, balance, sword, and fasces.

10. See P. Valeriano, *Hieroglyphica* (Basel 1556), 315; V. Cartari, *Imagines deorum, qui ab antiquis colebantur* (Venice 1556, consulted in 1581 edition, 311); and in general on these developments, Middeldorf-Kosegarten (1975), 475–476. Tomb of Paul III: Coppel (2012), 33–37, with further bibliography. On its form, see in general Minor (2006), 76–80, identifying (without explanation) the Justice figure as "Fidelity." For the flame of Justice, see Ripa (1593), 189 (a sign pointing toward heaven). The fasces on tombs of Popes: Middeldorf-Kosegarten (1975), 476, 479–480, with Lavin (2005), 131–137 on that of Urban VIII, with 132 for the quote.

11. Concord in the Monteoliveto Refectory and Casa Vasari: Cheney (1987), 365 and 367 (illustrated), 360–361, 373–374. On Vasari's fascination with this figure, see further Maffei (2012), 658 n. 4, citing Vasari's notice (in his *Life of Tintoretto*) that the Venetian artist Paolo Veronese (1528–1588) painted a Unity with a bundle of rods.

12. *Devises heroïques* (Lyons 1557), 60–61, with the translation (or rather paraphrase) of this passage by P. S. William Kearney, *The heroicall deuises of M. Claudius Paradin Canon of Beauieu* (London 1591), 72. For the Latin quotation, see Verg. *Aen.* 7.271.

CHAPTER 8

1. See Ripa (1603, here cited in the edition of Maffei [2012]), 81, no. 58.4, for Concord with a bundle of rods; cf. no. 58.7, Concord with a bundle of arrows. Justice: 188–189, no. 151.4; on her blindfold specifically, see Resnik and Curtis (2011), esp. 62–105. Jurisdiction: 187, no. 150. Clemency: 69–70, no. 53.2. Rarity of the fasces in sixteenth-century emblem books before Ripa: see Middeldorf-Kosegarten (1975), 472, on the important exception of Claude Paradin (1551), and also citing isolated examples in works of 1581 and 1589. On the personal background of Cesare Ripa and the early history of his editions, see Biferali (2016), with copious bibliography.

2. See Middeldorf-Kosegarten (1975), 477, with the Ripa editions *Della più che Novissima Iconologia* (Padova 1630), pp. 58–59, and *Iconologie où les principales*

choses qui peuvent tomber dans la pensée touchant les vices sont représentées, trans.
J. Baudoin (Paris 1643), 36 fig. xxvii (image) and 38 (text). The first English translation of Ripa, that of Pierce Tempest, *Iconologia or Moral Emblems by Caesar Ripa*
(London 1709), reproduces the Aristocracy type with rods (6 with fig. 23), but not
the Concord (14 with fig. 56). For an elaboration of the type, see Gravelot and
Cochin II (1791), 73, for Aristocracy holding a fasces (a "symbol of union") with
laurel garland, and a detached axe (indicating "that force resides in the courage and
affluence of the citizens").

3. The relevant works by Otto van Veen are *Quinti Horatii Flacci emblemata* (Antwerp
   1607, consulted here in its 1612 edition); *Amorum emblemata* (1608); and *Amoris
   divini emblemata* (1615). French edition: de Gomberville, *La doctrine des moeurs,
   tiree de la philosophie des Stoiques* (Paris 1646). On the publication history, nature, and didactic purpose of Vaenius's 1607 work, see especially Gerards-Nelissen
   (1971), esp. 20–29, 45–52; Enenkel (2019). The word *fasces* appears just once in
   Vaenius's commentary (pp. 48–49, no. 21), despite the prevalence of the device
   in the engravings. "Virtue Unshaken": pp. 8–9, no. 1. "Death as the Last Material
   Limit": pp. 212–213, no. 103. "Inquietude of Mind": pp. 91–92, no. 43. "Immortal
   Virtue": pp. 14–15, no. 4, with the exposition of Gerards-Nelissen (1971), 50.
   Nemesis: pp. 26–27, no. 10; pp. 180–181, no. 87. Fasces refused: pp. 48–49, no. 21;
   pp. 82–83, no. 38; pp. 136–137, no. 65.

4. On all this, see especially Loskoutoff (2001–2002), (2002a), (2002b), (2003a),
   (2003b), and above all (2007), 199–414, on Mazarin's fasces, esp. 209 on its first
   appearance, too cautiously raising the possibility he invented the armorial himself. On Mazarin's fasces, see in general Middeldorf-Kosegarten (1975), 468; on
   illustrations of the catafalque, see Anon., *Pompa funebre nell' esequie celebrate in
   Roma al Cardinal Mazarini nella Chiesa de SS. Vicenzo & Anastasio* (Rome 1661).

5. See du Fayot, "L'ange de Paix à Monseigneur le Cardinal, Presenté à son Éminence
   le 4 Iuin 1659" in *Le portrait de son Éminence fait par la Paix, Dedié à son Éminence*
   (Paris 1660), 91; Félibien, *Description de l'arc de la place Dauphine presentée à son
   Éminence* (Paris 1660), 13–14 = Anon., *L'entrée triomphante de leurs Majestez Louis
   XIV Roy de France et de Navarre et Marie Therese d'Austriche son espouse* (Paris
   1662), 27 (with illustrations of the arch in plates between pp. 24 and 25). On these
   quotes, see Loskoutoff (2002b), 74 (the peace), 77 (the arch).

6. See Montaner (2007), 296–298, with esp. 297 (reproducing the engraving by
   Petrus van Schuppen) and n. 34.

7. For this and what follows below, see Middeldorf-Kosegarten (1975), 485, with
   471 and fig. 7 on an allegorized image (ca. 1640–1650) of Dutch unification by
   Theodor van Thulden. For de Prézel's views, see his *Dictionnaire iconologique ou
   introduction a la connoissance des peintures* (Paris 1756), s.v. *faisceaux* pp. 112–113;
   and cf. the German edition *Ikonologisches Lexikon oder Anleitung zur Kenntnis
   allegorischer Bilder auf Gemälden* (Nürnberg 1793), s.v. *fasces* p. 112. Origins of the
   insignia of the Dutch Republic: de Vries (1995), 86–93.

8. Clemency lets fasces slip away: Gravelot and Cochin I (1791), 63. Luca Giordano: Szépmûvészeti Múzeum, Budapest, inv. 4229; on the interpretation of this work, see Resnick and Curtis (2011), 78–79. Barberini ceiling: for an engraved reproduction and explication of the scene, see Carlo Cesi, *Galeria dipinta nel palazzo del Prencipe Panfilio da Pietro Berrettini da Cortona vero originale* (Rome 1690), pl. VI. Coinage of Charles II (Tarì = 2 "carlini," minted 1684–1687): Pannuti and Riccio (1984), nos. 11–14.

9. A Minerva with fasces (and augur's staff) appears already in 1601 on a honorary medal for the Flemish humanist Justus Lipsius: Middeldorf-Kosegarten (1975), 467 fig. 6. Other virtues depicted with fasces: Middeldorf-Kosegarten (1975), 484. Friendship: Middeldorf-Kosegarten (1975), 484–485. Fasces in a martyrdom scene: see, e.g., Pietro da Cortona, "S. Martina Refuses to Adore the Idols" (1654–1660), Princeton University Art Museum, inv. 1998–38 (abjectly lying on the ground, next to instruments of martyrdom). For a representative example of the personified Counsel, see the engraving series of Adriaen Collaert (ca. 1580–1600, after Maarten de Vos, ca. 1570), *Die sieben Gaben des Heiligen Geistes*, plate 3 (scales with axeless fasces) = British Museum inv. 1930,0414.75.

10. Eimer (2010), nos. 212 [1660] and 510 [1727].

11. See de Marly (1975), 449, for the "veritable flood of representations of that king in the Roman military habit."

12. On the history of this statue and its pedestal (with two reliefs in bronze by Coysevox), see Keller-Dorian I (1920), 63–68, with De Marly (1975), 449, on the portrayal of Louis XIV in Roman dress; see also Frank (1993), 133–162, on the statue's predecessor on the site (Gilles Guérin, "Louis XIV Slaying the 'Fronde,'" 1653–1654), its removal, and details of the elaborate 1689 dedication. The regime did not avoid representing the fasces after Mazarin's death: see, e.g., Charles Le Brun's "Réformation de la Justice" (1667) at the Château de Versailles, a commemoration of the king's reform of civil procedure, where a standing Lady Justice, holding an axed fasces and scales, consorts with a seated Louis XIV. For further examples at Versailles from this reign, see Middeldorf-Kosegarten (1975) 483. Mazarin mausoleum: Keller-Dorian II (1920), 5–13 and fig. 57.

13. On the idea (seventeenth–eighteenth century) of the fasces symbolizing "good" government based on existing legal norms, with northern European examples, see Middeldorf-Kosegarten (1975), 465. *Ex fascibus*: Diego de Saavedra Fajardo, *Idea de un Principe Politico Christiano* (Amsterdam 1655), 523–534, with illustration on 523 and quote on 526; there were more than twenty editions of this book in the original Spanish, as well as translations into five languages. For the Danish medal, see Classical Numismatic Group auction Triton XVIII, Lot 1503 (January 6, 2015). For a roster of cities and countries which incorporated the fasces into their heraldry by the last quarter of the nineteenth century, see Rentsmann (1876), tab. 10, nos. 217–227 with Index, p. 22.

14. Jean-Charles Delafosse, *Nouvelle iconologie historique ou attributs hieroglyphiques* (Paris 1767), with p. 1 for the quote; see also p. 5 with pl. 10 (Africa), p. 6 with pl. 13 (Bronze Age), p. 16 with pl. 37 (Portugal), p. 21 with pl. 51 (Thrace), p. 31 with pl. 63 (heroes and sages). In general on this work, see Middeldorf-Kosegarten (1975), 475, cf. 483 fig. 18 (Delafosse) and 474–476 (trophies); Ahn (2014), 53–54 (with lucid remarks on the oddball genre). For the Paduan medal, see Lawrence (1883), 7, no. 2; on the Dassiers, see Weigel (1995).

CHAPTER 9

1. Jonson review: cited in Craig (1990), 417. Jonson's *Sejanus*: Cain (2014), pointing up early seventeenth-century tolerance of anachronism in stage dress. Shakespeare: *Ant.* IV.1.3 (Caesar complains that his messenger has been whipped by Antony's rods), V.2.210–211 (Cleopatra imagining sexual assault by Roman lictors on her capture). Dekker on Astraea: cited in Dutton (2019), 12. Covent Garden: Ripley (1987), 341–342. Aylsham performance: *The Ipswich Journal*, May 26, 1750, p. 3. Philadelphia pageant: *The Independent Gazetteer*, November 15, 1788, p. 3.

2. On this, cf. de Marly (1975), 448 (arguing a different but related point, how the theater made Roman habit acceptable to elite individuals as costume).

3. George III: Coutu (1996), 181; this royal coach is still in use, and has featured in the coronation of all British monarchs since George IV in 1820. Jefferson account book entry for 1774: Bear and Stanton I (1997), 367, with n. 3 for the probable date. For the original motto, see Coke, *The Fourth Part of the Institutes of the Laws of England* (London 1681), 35. Dickinson: Smith I (1976), 386, with n. 2 (marginalia from May 23–25, 1775; cf. 390 n. 4 for his possibly related marginal note from May 23, "Adhere with Roman Firmness"). Seal: see in general Patterson and Dougall (1976); also Deutsch (1923), with special attention to the source(s) of "e pluribus unum."

4. Fragonard: Sheriff (1983), esp. 189–190. Houdon: Hallam (1978); Wills (1984); in the portrait, Washington wears a badge of the Society of Cincinnati at the bottom of his waistcoat.

5. On the mace, see the treatment by Bedini (1997), esp. 24 on colonial antecedents.

6. Dispatch: John Sackville in Stewart (1951), 105–106. Departments as the rods of a fasces: see Maury (1904), 147–148 (with allegorical illustration) and 336. The new "female trinity" of symbols: Leith (1968), 40.

7. Symbols: Leith (1965), 108–109 (roster); (1968) 49–50 (variety of media); also Scuccimarra (1999), 243 with 249 n. 75. Hercules: Vovelle (2015), 334. Position of axes: Maury (1904), 336 (also discussing substitutes for the axe, such as the pike or "hand of justice," and the tricolor cord). Wallpaper: Vauxcelles et al. III (1922), 23. In general on the fasces in the iconography of the French Revolution, see Middeldorf-Kosegarten (1975), 487–492. For an overview of the symbol in its contemporary architecture, see Alexander (1974), 108 n. 62.

8. On Revolutionary symbols, see Maury (1904) on the rooster, Agulhon (1979) on Marianne, and Scuccimarra (1999) and (2010) on the fasces, especially Scuccimarra (1999), 232–233, 235, 242, whose analysis I follow here. On the unease with the "feminine civic allegory," see Landes (1988), 159–163. On the debate over the seal, and the (again unofficial) choice specifically of Hercules, see Hunt (1983), 95–99.

9. For an overview of the French coinage in this period, see Mazard I (1965). Representative types discussed in text: Mazard nos. 84, 89 ("Au Génie" reverse type); nos. 24–31 (large fasces reverse type); nos. 118, 127, 176–177 (tokens of 1792 with fasces). Medals with fasces of the Directory period: see Hennin (1826), nos. 766 (1796) and 845–846 (1798). *Assignat* notes with fasces: Lafaurie (1981), nos. 163 (400 livres) and 164 (50 livres). On the trial 10 centimes piece of 1794–1795, see Mazard no. 357 = Hennin no. 678 (with explanation of the symbolism); cf. Hennin's remarks on no. 673 for its non-circulation.

10. On the Hercules tokens of 1792, see Margolis (1988), esp. Plate 31, nos. 12 (5 sols), 13 (Dupré design for the traditional Six Corps jeton, with Forrer I [1904], 647 for the date), and 14 (2 sols). On earlier Hercules jetons of the Six Corps, see, e.g., for a Louis XIV obverse of 1662, CGB Numismatics Paris Internet Auction, July 2020, Lot 587965 (July 28, 2020); for an undated Louis XVI (1774–1792) obverse, Lugdunum GmbH Auction 14, Lot 53 (November 15, 2018). For the Royal Mint's adaptation of the type for a pattern Crown in 1820, see Bull (2020), nos. 2057–2060. On David's Hercules of 1793, see David (1880), 136 (for J.-L. David quote); Hunt (1983), 99–104, with 100 fig. 2 for Dupré's sketch of a Hercules seal, and 101 fig. 3 for the Villeneuve engraving; the author does not bring the tokens into discussion.

11. Rinaldi I (1954), no. 175, cf. *RRC* 508/3.

12. For representative coins of Saint-Domingue and Haiti, see Krause and Mishler (2019), s.v. Haiti, nos. 21–23 (1802, Louverture); 3, 6, 8 (1807–1808, Henri Christophe); nos. A21, 24, 25.1–2, A22, 26, 27.1–2, 29, 31–32 (Republic 1825–1849), cf. 35 and 37 (minted in 1850 under the Empire). Chile: Fonrobert and Weyl (1877), 9851 (1828); and for the coins, Krause and Mishler (2019), s.v. Chile nos. 103 (1839–1841), 104.1–2 (1839–1845), 105 (1846–1851), 122 (1851–1853), 123 (1851–1853), 130 (1854–1867), 131 (1854–1867), 132 (1856–1865), 143 (1867–1875), 144 (1867–1873), 145 (1867–1892, the upper range of the series, presumably an early strike).

13. Constitution: Middeldorf-Kosegarten (1975), 489. Callet: Musée de la Révolution Française inv. MRF 1995.37, analyzed by Benoît (1993), 78–79 (quoted here) and Dwyer (2013), 52–53, with contemporary critical reaction discussed in Knels (2019), 257–259.

14. Flags: Maury (1904), 305. Fasces on Napoleonic medals: see especially Bramsen I (1904), 534 (commemoration of the Confederation of the Rhine in 1806, where an axe-less fasces forms the focus of an oath scene) and 553 (SOUVERAINETÉS DONNÉES of 1806, where the reverse shows an eagle with outstretched wings perched on a lateral fasces, above a table loaded with signs of the extent of

Napoleon's sovereignty, and his imperial throne). Note also nos. 20 (Cambacérès, second consul in 1799); 26 (Corps legislatif) and 89 (Comptabilité nationale, 1800); 133 and 138 (German commemorations of the Peace of Lunéville of 1801); 140 (Cisalpine Republic); 151–153 (king and queen of Etruria); 175 (Liberty and war); 270 (Helvetian confederation); 286 (Chamber of Commerce of Bordeaux, 1805); 753–754 (Fonderies de Vaucluse, 1808); 842 (provincial legions); and cf. 255, 258, 511, 609–610, 616 and 833 (Masonic tokens). Furniture: Middeldorf-Kosegarten (1975), 489. Though there are fasces-like elements in the famous book of Empire style decorative schemes by C. Percier and P. F. L. Fontaine, *Recueil de décorations intérieures* (2nd edition, Paris, 1812), actual fasces seem generally to be avoided (see pl. 9 for a minor exception).

CHAPTER 10

1. For Archie Dallas Williams (1873–1932), see *The Muncie* (Indiana) *Sunday Star*, January 25, 1920, p. 9, compiling a valuable list of efforts to honor Abraham Lincoln in public art to that date. On the original design by Clark Mills (1810–1883) and the ill-considered location for the projected multi-tiered monument, see Thomas (2002), 5–6. Taft quote: *Pittsburgh Gazette Times*, May 31, 1922, p. 3. Hudnut: *House & Garden*, July 1940, p. 42. National Park Service visitor statistics, including Lincoln Memorial (1936–present): irma.nps.gov/STATS/ (accessed June 30, 2021). For an excellent succinct description of the Lincoln Memorial, which informs this discussion, see the WPA guide *Washington, City and Capital* (Washington, DC, 1937), 331–338.

2. See "Secret Symbol of the Lincoln Memorial," accessed at nps.gov/articles/ on June 30, 2021.

3. Hallet (1755–1825): Scott (1992), 160–162. Stuart (1755–1828): Van Horn (2017), 402–404. Halliday (ca. 1780–ca. 1854): Musante I (2016), GW-57. Eckstein (1735–1817): Fraunces Tavern Museum (New York, NY), inv. 1984.12.033 (and many other collections) with Stauffer (1907), no. 687. Ramée (1764–1842): Miller (1964), 20–21.

4. USS *Constitution*: see Martin (1980), 26, for the description, citing an April 30, 1795, letter from William Rush to naval architect Joshua Humphreys. Corné's watercolor: Navy Art Collection (Washington, DC), inv. 296.1. USS *President*: *Claypoole's American Daily Advertiser* (Philadelphia), April 14, 1800. USS *City of Philadelphia* (later renamed *Philadelphia*): *The Vergennes* (Vermont) *Gazette and Vermont and New-York Advertiser*, December 5, 1799, p. 2 (citing a November 8 report). In general for naval figurehead art in this period, see Pinckney (1940). Tripoli Monument: Martin (1980), 86. Criticism of Latrobe: cited in *The Analectic Magazine* 6 (1815): 462.

5. Description: *Virginia Argus* (Richmond), April 2, 1815 p. 2; cf. *The Green Mountain Gem* (Bradford, Vermont), January 2, 1848, p. 245 for additional details. In general, see Alexander (1974), 101–112.

6. For a general narrative of these design decisions at the Capitol, with quotes, see Scott (1995), 62–65, and (specifically on Persico) Fryd (1992), 180–183; and in more detail on Adams's background and contribution, Verheyen (1996). On Causici's work, see Fryd (1992), 187–188, properly identifying the columnar object with snake as a fasces.

7. See, e.g., the broadside "Westward the march of empire takes it flight" (1840), lithograph by A. E. Baker and B. O. Tyler (Albany, NY) = Library of Congress control no. 2003690762; the ribbon "Our country's hope. Harrison & reform 4th May" (1840), published by J. S. Horton (Baltimore, MD) = Library of Congress no. 2008661354; and "Grand National Whig prize banner badge" (ca. 1844), lithograph by Edward Weber & Co. (Baltimore, MD) = Library of Congress no. 2003690764. Origin of the phrase (originally "union of the Whigs for the sake of the union"): *The National Gazette* (Philadelphia), July 6, 1839, p. 2. Nativists: see, e.g., Reilly (1991), no. 1845-1848 (membership certificate ca. 1845 of Native American Republican Association of Philadelphia, with paired axed fasces aggressively framing the central text).

8. See Wunder (1974), 25–29; and especially Fryd (1986), with 58 and 65–66 for the relevant quotes; cf. *Home News for India, China and the Colonies*, September 24, 1850, p. 580.

9. Campaign of 1856 (won by the Democratic candidate James Buchanan): Reilly (1991), 1856-6 (Fillmore), 1856-19 (Frémont). Walters: for chronologoy, Rosenberger (1948/1950). Paquet seated Liberty: Judd (2008), nos. 216, 235, 247–250, 253, 257, 262.

10. On Crawford and the Extension, see Fryd (1992), 183–184 and 244 n. 16; also Fryd (1984), 81 n. 42, citing the relevant correspondence (April 27, 1854) in full. On *Armed Liberty*, see Fryd (1992), 190–200. The October 1855 letter from Crawford to Meigs is quoted in T. Hicks, *Eulogy on Thomas Crawford* (New York, 1865), 87–88.

11. Southern Union: *Staunton Spectator*, June 25, 1861, p. 1. Bell and Everitt: Reilly (1991), 1860-17 (sheet music), 1860-18 (print). Lincoln: 1860-13 (a banner or a large poster shown in a print, cf. 1856-6). Medal of Honor: Mears (2018), 9–26; this proved to be just the first of many instances where the United States incorporated the fasces into its military medals and unit insignia, though almost all of the more than four dozen examples belong to the twentieth century, following World War I.

12. Identity of composer: *Republican Banner* (Nashville, TN), September 18, 1860, p. 3. Sheet music: Reilly (1991), 1860-3 (Union polka); Abel (2011), no. 330, with *The Tennessean*, November 19, 1861 (Confederate polka).

13. Shrouding of Rotunda artwork: Shea (1865), 134 (with the quote). Catafalque: *Evening Star* (Washington, DC), April 20, 1865, p. 1; *National Intelligencer*, April 20, 1865, p. 1; for the draping and the lack of flag, *Cleveland Daily Leader*, April 22, 1865, p. 2.

14. On these two monuments in general, see Savage (2018), esp. 89–128. Description of the Springfield statue: *The Pittsburgh Daily Commercial*, October 27, 1874, p. 2.

15. For what follows, see Chesnutt (1925). On the figure of H. M. Chesnutt, see Ronnick (2021); she summarizes the 1925 article at 111.

16. On the misnomer "Mercury Dime," that appeared in the popular press almost immediately after minting of the new type started, see Lange (2005). A winged Phrygian cap is a common attribute of the mythological hero Perseus on (especially) Greek Hellenistic coins, but seems unprecedented in numismatic depictions of a personified Liberty. Other than the wings, Liberty's hat here has nothing in common with the broad-brimmed *petasus* familiar from depictions (ancient and modern) of the god Hermes/Mercury. For the quote, see *Annual Report of the Director of the Mint for the Fiscal Year Ended June 30 1916* (Washington, DC, 1916), 8.

17. "Moses": *The News and Observer* (Raleigh), June 17, 1940. "Solon": Department of the Interior, National Park Service, National Register of Historic Places inventory—nomination form for Raleigh Capitol Hill District (November 19, 1974), item no. 7, p. 5, accessed at rhdc.org, July 29, 2021.

18. Reaction to Mussolini's January 3, 1925, speech: L. R. Taylor (the noted Roman historian) in *The Current History Magazine* 21.5 (February 1925): 785–786. Possible Italian Fascist influence on US Hoover- and Roosevelt-era architecture: Kontorovich (2014). Decorative scheme of Raleigh Justice Building: *Goodnight Raleigh* blog (May 3, 2013), accessed July 30, 2021, at goodnightraleigh.com.

CHAPTER 11

1. For two authoritative treatments of these early developments (often narrated and discussed), see O'Brien (2004) for the period through 1918, and the papers collected in Gentile (2002); more succinctly, see Ben-Ghiat (2020), ch. 1. On the various pre-Fascist Italian *fasci*, see Majanlahti and Osti Guerrazzi (2014), ch. 5. For an early use of "fascisti" with reference to the Sicilian workers' movement, see, e.g., *Gazzetta Piemontese*, December 13–14, 1893, p. 344. Torino exhibition of 1879: *Roma artistica* 5.10 (March 16, 1879), p. 75, and 5.12 (March 31, 1879), p. 91. On Jerace's *L'azione*, see Finelli (2013), 56–57.

2. On Terruzzi, see Falchi (2008), esp. 155–165 for her participation in S. Sepolcro. On her alleged prediction of "Console d'Italia," see de Turris (2006), 126–128. For D'Annunzio's stated contribution, see Hughes-Hallett (2013), 19; he allegedly was inspired by the sight on battlefields in France in the winter of 1914/1915 of "dead soldiers bound upright, to stakes, in groups of ten," which reminded him of the Roman fasces, which in turn symbolized for him "the gathering of powerless individuals into a single powerful entity."

3. *New York Times*, March 20, 1921, p. E2.

4. G. Polverelli's August 2, 1922, article, "La legge o la scure" in *Il Popolo d'Italia*, is cited, translated and discussed in Albanese (2019), 51–52. Albanese's study offers a comprehensive treatment of the March's background, planning, promulgation,

execution, and later mythology (on which see p. xi, on the "Fascist Era"), with particular emphasis on the Fascists' reliance on violence as a political tool.

5. *The Observer* (London), December 17, 1922, p. 8.

6. For the 1922 documentary *A Noi*, see Istituto Nazionale Luce M016201. Cartoon: *Il Popolo d'Italia*, November 15, 1922, p. 1.

7. *The Capital Times* (Madison, Wisconsin), November 2, 1922, p. 12; *Fall River* (Massachusetts) *Daily Evening News*, November 21, 1922; *The Kansas City* (Missouri) *Time*s, December 7, 1922.

8. On these developments, see Salvatori (2008), with esp. 349 for the coin project as "the regime's first official act of appropriation of the material and daily life of the Italian people"; and *Il Popolo d'Italia*, December 27, 1922, p. 1, for the initial announcement.

9. For what follows, see Salvatori (2012).

10. *Il Popolo d'Italia*, April 4, 1923, p. 5.

11. Tea (1932), II 542, quoted by Salvatori (2012), 425.

12. Boni cited in Salvatori (2012), 426 n. 20.

13. *The Buffalo* (NY) *Times*, March 9, 1923, p. 22. Stamps: Follo (2013), 71 n. 242.

14. *Il Popolo d'Italia*, October 28, 1928, p. 6.

15. *Il Messaggero*, May 20, 1920, p. 6. For details of the march and meeting, see also *Il Popolo d'Italia*, May 20, 1923, p. 5; *La Stampa*, May 20, p. 3.

16. *Saskatoon* (Saskatchewan, Canada) *Daily Star*, May 19, 1923, p. 1. A selection of reports in the North American press: *New York Times*, May 20, 1923, p. 7, cf. p. 10; *Washington Post*, May 20, 1923, p. 16; also *Alton* (IL) *Evening Telegraph*, May 19, 1923, p. 2 (Associated Press report); *Arizona Daily* Star (Tuscon, AZ), May 19, 1923, p. 8 (editorial); *The Evening News* (Wilkes-Barre, PA), May 19, 1923 (editorial).

17. *Il Piccolo*, May 24, 1923, p. 2, with headline "Il fascio littorio a Mussolini."

18. Birth: Torino (Tribunale) *Atti di Nascità* 1892, p. 88, no. 774 (March 9), noting also death in Rome, May 3, 1963. Education: *Reale Università degli Studi di Roma. Annuario dell'Anno Scolastico 1915–1916* (Rome 1916), p. 12. Mazzini expertise: *Rivista popolare di politica, lettere e scienze sociali* 30 (1924), 33 and 47, cf. 72. A short biographical notice of Ribulsi in *Quaderni del Gruppo di Ur* 17 (2007), 43, contains some items (e.g., entry into a convent after 1925) that I could not verify.

19. Address: listed in a directory at *Rassegna storica del Risorgimento* 8 (1921), 302. On Camilla Calzone Mongenet and her husband, see de Turris (2006), 133.

20. *International Woman Suffrage Alliance. Report of Ninth Congress, Rome, Italy, May 12th to 19th, 1923* (Dresden 1923).

21. In the United States, from ca. 1900 the temperance movement was widely known as the "Hatchet Crusade." More immediately, the militancy of the Women's Social and Political Union (WSPU) in the United Kingdom, which sharply escalated in the years 1912–1914, offered some shockingly memorable instances of suffragists' political violence with these implements that went well beyond smashing shop windows. Only the outbreak of war in August 1914 put a halt to these "suffragette

outrages," to use a contemporary term. For an extensive discussion of such suffrage militancy in general, see Riddell (2018).

22. For what follows, see *Krur* Serie 1929 (Rome 1929), 353–355.

23. On this school of "Mistica Fascista" (1930–1943), see the ample treatment of Carini (2009).

24. H. Begbie, "Mussolini, the Man and his Miracle," reprinted in *The Windsor Star* (Ontario, Canada), September 24, 1925, p. 27.

25. On the decree of December 12, 1926 in context, see Salvatori (2008), 336. Definition: G. Gentile in *Enciclopedia Italiana* (1932), s.v. "Fascismo," I 13.

26. Giglioli in Colini (1933), xi–xiii, with quotes from xiii.

27. Vadalà (2016), 10.

28. On the façade, see Painter (2005), 26–27.

29. See the special number "Concorso per il Palazzo del Littorio" of *Architettura* (ed. M. Piacentini) 1934, that features 43 submissions to the (ultimately fruitless) architectural competition for this site, including that of Libera (illustrated at 49–51) and Bravetti/Giordani (112–113). On this competition, see Manson (2015).

30. Painter (2005), 12 (bridge), 48–49 (youth group), 85–90 (town of Littoria).

31. Lictors at Tripoli: cover of *L'Illustrazione Italiana*, vol. 64 no. 11, March 28, 1937.

CHAPTER 12

1. See *The Fresno Bee—The Republican*, August 11, 1940, p. 11; October 3, 1940, p. 17. On Yankwich, see his obituary in *New York Times*, February 12, 1975, p. 40.

2. *Consolation*, January 8, 1941, p. 25. It was Mussolini's speech "The Fascist regime is authority, order, and justice" (September 14, 1929) that gave rise to the rallying cry "Ordine, Autorità, Giustizia," which often adorned public buildings; e.g., the phrase was inscribed on a 4-meter marble slab in a main hall of Giuseppe Terragni's famed Casa del Fascio (1936) in Como. On this, see Lacchè (2019), 17 n. 55; Rifkind (2006), 161.

3. Early objections: *Evening Star* (Washington, DC), June 26, 1931, p. 8. Morgenthau: *New York Times*, April 28, 1941, p. 15, with the *Asbury Park Press*, May 2, 1941, p. 8, and *The Daily Tar-Heel*, May 29, 1941, p. 2. Danbury: *The Journal* (Meriden, CT), June 2, 1943, p. 6; *The Wisconsin Jewish Chronicle*, June 11, 1943, p. 8; *Star Tribune* (Minneapolis, MN), June 10, 1943, p. 4.

4. *Honolulu Advertiser*, July 1, 1946, p. 14; cf. *The Billings* (MT) *Gazette*, February 6, 1946, p. 3 (blaming the "new meaning given to the fasces and the words derived from that root by Mussolini and his fellow dictators." For a contrary (and distinctly minority view), see Mosher (1945).

5. *Regio Decreto* no. 1048 of March 27, 1927, replaced April 11, 1929.

6. New flag ridiculed: e.g., *Fort Collins Coloradoan*, May 28, 1944, p. 4. Derivative image: see, e.g., a medal presented in 1935 to historian and politician Pietro Fedele (1873–1943), which on the obverse shows a turreted head of Italia (now male!)

superimposed on a large fasces, and on the reverse the eagle standing, its wings spread, on fasces: London Ancient Coins Auction 58, Lot 399 (July 12, 2016).

7. Rome, Palazzo Venezia: LUCE photo A00150849. Process of destruction documented: A00150891 and A00150892 and cf. A00150893 (Milan); A00150950 and A00150951 (Genova). Cf. also for Rome A00150866 and A00150870 (each undated, but after July 25, 1943).

8. For the propagandistic purposes of the athletic center, see especially the Istituto Nazionale Luce film (D005905) of Vittorio Solito, *Atleti del Foro Mussolini* (ca. 1940). For the quotation, see Cox (1935), 270.

9. Piazzale dell' Impero: Tymkiw (2019), with further bibliography. On the male Italia, see Follo (2013), 45. Rendering of the mosaics as celluloid film stock: I gratefully thank composer Paul Rudy for this insight, though he is not responsible for how I have developed his suggestion.

10. Boxing (December 12–16, 1944): United News newsreel UNY 140 (1945, "Allied Bombers Strike on Two Fronts"), Part 4. Beauty pageant (June 2, 1945): LUCE RW 45301.

11. For an explication of the general policy as outlined here, see Carter and Martin (2017). Their study offers the best account of the postwar fate of the former Foro Mussolini, with analysis that is applicable to the situation of Fascist remains in Italy as a whole.

12. Oath eradicated by August 9, 1960: see Istituto Luce (Fondo Vedo) FV00107156. Efforts (seemingly futile) on the same date to remove the title DVCE from the Piazzale: FV00107142, FV00107157, FV00107196-7, FV00107200, FV00107212.

13. The general narrative and analysis here of the 1960 Rome Olympics depends on Brennan (2010), which provides full references for the events described. For Robert Daley's assessment of the Rome venues for these Games, see *New York Times*, March 29, 1959, p. S3.

14. Stoddart quotes from *The Herald* (Glasgow), June 28, 2000. Press release: Princeton University *Weekly Bulletin*, November 5, 2001.

15. "John Witherspoon's statue in Princeton features an Eagle perched upon a sphere, perched upon a fasce [*sic*]. What is being symbolized?," asked a sole voice on August 21, 2020, on Instagram and Twitter. "Somebody say 'fascist world domination' " was his follow-up post.

16. Princeton & Slavery Project: slavery.princeton.edu (accessed July 12, 2021). Omission noted on Witherspoon plaques: K. Gilbert et al., "The case for Princeton's reconstruction," *The Daily Princetonian*, November 28, 2018. Faculty group demands removal: M. Michaels, "In open letter, faculty call for anti-racist action, diversity in decision making," *The Daily Princetonian*, July 7, 2020. Also intact on the Princeton campus is a second, less noticed life-size statue of Witherspoon, lodged high up in a niche of the East Pyne tower, the work (1896) of Scottish-born sculptor John Massey Rhind (1860–1936).

17. See adl.org/education/references/hate-symbols/fasces (accessed on July 12, 2021).

Bibliography

Abbondanza, R. 1960. "Alciato (Alciati), Andrea." In *Dizionario biografico degli Italiani*, II 69–77. Rome: Istituto della Enciclopedia Italiana.

Abel, E. L. 2011. *Confederate Sheet Music*. Jefferson, NC: McFarland.

Aguhlon, M. 1979. *Marianne au Combat. L'imagerie et la symbolique républicaines de 1789 à 1880*. Paris: Flammarion.

Ahn, J. C. 2014. "The Ruins of *Iconologie*: Redefining Architecture in Jean-Charles Delafosse's *Desseins*." *Athanor* 23: 53–63.

Albanese, G. 2019. *The March on Rome: Violence and the Rise of Italian Fascism*. Trans. S. Knipe. Abingdon and New York: Routledge.

Alexander, R. L. 1974. *The Architecture of Maximilian Godefroy*. Baltimore, MD: Johns Hopkins University Press.

Álvarez Burgos, F. 2008. *La moneda hispánica desde sus orígenes hasta el Siglo V*. Madrid: Editorial Vico & Segarra.

Armstrong, J. 2016. *War and Society in Early Rome: From Warlords to Generals*. Cambridge: Cambridge University Press.

Arthurs, J. 2012. *Excavating Modernity: The Roman Past in Fascist Italy*. Ithaca, NY: Cornell University Press.

Astin, A. E. 1967. *Scipio Aemilianus*. Oxford: Oxford University Press.

Baldacci, A. 1933. *Il Littorio, dalla preistoria al regime fascista*. Bologna: Stabilimenti Poligrafici Riuniti.

Bandy, A. C. 1983. *Ioannes Lydus. On Powers or the Magistracies of the Roman State*. Philadelphia: American Philosophical Society.

Baranowski, M. 1929. *Il Fascio Littorio nella numismatica universale moderna*. Perugia: V. Bartelli.

Barnes, T. D., and R. W. Westall. 1991. "The Conversion of the Roman Aristocracy in Prudentius' Contra Symmachum." *Phoenix* 45: 50–61.

Bear, J. A., Jr., and L. C. Stanton, ed. 1997. *Jefferson's Memorandum Books: Accounts, with Legal Records and Miscellany, 1767–1826*. 2 vols. Princeton, NJ: Princeton University Press.

Becker, H. W. 2013. "Political Systems and Law." In *The Etruscan World*, ed. J. M. Turfa, 351–372. London and New York: Routledge.

Bedini, S. A. 1997. *The Mace and the Gavel: Symbols of Government in America.* Philadelphia: American Philosophical Society.

Ben-Ghiat, R. 2001. *Fascist Modernities: Italy, 1922–1945.* Berkeley and Los Angeles: University of California Press.

Ben-Ghiat, R. 2020. *Strongmen: Mussolini to the Present.* New York: W. W. Norton.

Benoît, J. 1993. "La peinture allégorique sous le Consulat: structure et politique." *Gazette des Beaux-Arts* 121: 77–92.

Bergemann, J. 1990. *Römische Reiterstatuen. Ehrendenkmäler im öffentlichen Bereich.* Mainz: P. von Zaber.

Bernard, F. 2020. "Laughter, Derision, and Abuse in Byzantine Verse." In *Satire in the Middle Byzantine Period*, ed. P. Marciniak and I. Nilsson, 49–50. Leiden and Boston: Brill.

Biferali, F. 2016. "Ripa, Cesare." In *Dizionario biografico degli Italiani*, LXXXVII: 639–643. Rome: Istituto della Enciclopedia Italiana.

Bjornlie, M. S., ed. 2019. *Cassiodorus. The Variae: The Complete Translation.* Oakland: University of California Press.

Boatwright, M. T. 1987. *Hadrian and the City of Rome.* Princeton, NJ: Princeton University Press.

Bond, S. 2016. *Trade and Taboo: Disreputable Professions in the Roman Mediterranean.* Ann Arbor: University of Michigan Press.

Bondanella, P. E. 1987. *The Eternal City: Roman Images in the Modern World.* Chapel Hill and London: University of North Carolina Press.

Bonisch-Meyer, S. 2018. "Neue Inschriften aus Patara IV: Liktoren und ihr legatus Augusti. Eine bilingue Ehrung für L. Luscius Ocra und seine Familie." *Chiron* 48: 375–400.

Bossuat, F. 1960. "Jean de Rovroy traducteur des *Stratagèmes* de Frontin." *Bibliothèque d'Humanisme et Renaissance* 22: 273–286, 469–489.

Bramsen, L. E. 1904–1913. *Le médaillier de Napoléon le Grand.* 3 vols. Paris and Copenhagen: A. Picard & fils and Gyldendalske boghandel Nordisk forlag.

Brennan, T. C. 2000. *The Praetorship in the Roman Republic.* 2 vols. New York: Oxford University Press.

Brennan, T. C. 2010. "The 1960 Rome Olympics: Spaces and spectacle." In *Rethinking Matters Olympic: Investigations into the Socio-cultural Study of the Modern Olympic Movement*, ed. R. K. Barney, J. Forsyth, and M. K. Heine, 17–29. London, ON: International Centre for Olympic Studies.

Brennan, T. C. 2014. "Power and Process under the Republican 'Constitution.'" In *The Cambridge Companion to the Roman Republic*, 2nd ed., ed. H. I. Flower, 19–53. Cambridge and New York: Cambridge University Press.

Brennan, T. C. 2018. *Sabina Augusta: An Imperial Journey.* New York: Oxford University Press.

Broderick, H. R. 1983. "Observations on the Method of Illustration in MS Junius 11 and the Relationship of the Drawings to the Text." *Scriptorium* 37: 161–177.

Broughton, T. R. S. 1991. *Candidates Defeated in Roman Elections: Some Ancient Roman "Also-Rans."* Philadelphia: American Philosophical Society.

Brunt, P. A. 1977. "Lex de Imperio Vespasiani." *Journal of Roman Studies* 67: 95–116.

Bull, M. 2020. *English Silver Coinage since 1649.* 7th ed. London: Spink.

Cain, T. 2014. "Sejanus His Fall: Stage History." In *The Cambridge Edition of the Works of Ben Jonson Online.* Accessed at universitypublishingonline.org/cambridge/benjonson/k/essays/stage_history_Sejanus/.

Cameron, A. 2015. "City Personifications and Consular Diptychs." *Journal of Roman Studies* 105: 250–287.

Carini, T. 2009. *Niccolò Giani e la scuola di mistica fascista: 1930–1945.* Milan: Mursia.

Carter, N., and S. Martin. 2017. "The Management and Memory of Fascist Monumental Art in Postwar and Contemporary Italy: The Case of Luigi Montanarini's *Apotheosis of Fascism.*" *Journal of Modern Italian Studies* 22: 338–364.

Catalano, P. 1978. "Aspetti spaziali del sistema giuridico-religioso romano." In *Aufstieg und Niedergang der römischen Welt* II 16.1, ed. H. Temporini and W. Haase, 440–553. Berlin and New York: Walter de Gruyter.

Chesnutt, H. M. 1925. "The Story of the Fasces at Central High School." *The School Review* 33: 303–306.

Clayton, M. 1999. *Raphael and His Circle: Drawings from Windsor Castle.* London: Merrell Holberton.

Cheney, L. D. G. 1987. "Vasari's Chamber of Abraham: A Religious Painted Ceiling in the Casa Vasari of Arezzo." *The Sixteenth Century Journal* 18: 355–380.

Cheney, L. D. G. 2003. "Giorgio Vasari's Astraea: A Symbol of Justice." *Visual Resources: An International Journal of Documentation* 19: 283–305.

Colini, A. M. 1933. *Il fascio littorio di Roma ricercato negli antichi monumenti.* Rome: Libreria dello Stato.

Coppel, R. 2012. *Guglielmo della Porta: A Counter-Reformation Sculptor.* Madrid: Coll & Cortés.

Coutu, J. M. 1996. "William Chambers and Joseph Wilton." In *William Chambers, Architect to George III*, ed. J. Harris and M. Snodin, 175–185. London and New Haven: Yale University Press.

Cox, P. W. L. 1935. "Opera Nazionale Balilla: An Aspect of Italian Education." *Junior-Senior High School Clearing House* 9: 267–270.

Craig, D. H. 1990. *Ben Jonson: The Critical Heritage, 1599–1798.* London and New York; Routledge.

Crawford, M. H. 1971. "Paestum and Rome: The Form and Function of a Subsidiary Coinage." In *La monetazione di bronzo do Poseidonia-Paestum: Atti del III Convegno*, 47–109. Naples: Centro internazionale di studi numismatici.

David, J. L. J. 1880. *Le Peintre Louis David, 1748–1825: Souvenirs & documents inédits.* Paris: Victor Havard.

De Libero, L. 2001. "Zerbrochene Rutenbündel, zerschlagene Amtsstühle. Römische Amtsinsignien im Spannungsfeld kollidierender *potestates*." In *Geschichte als Verpflichtung*, ed. M. Hundt, 1–30. Hamburg: Krämer.

De Marly, D. 1975. "The Establishment of Roman Dress in Seventeenth-Century Portraiture." *The Burlington Magazine* 117: 442–451.

De Sanctis, G. 1929. "I fasci littori e gli ordinamenti romani antichissimi." *Rivista di filologia* 57: 1–9.

De Turris, G., ed. 2006. *Esoterismo e fascismo: storia, interpretazioni, documenti.* Rome: Edizioni Mediterranee.

De Vries, H. 1995. *Wapens van de Nederlanden. De historische ontwikkeling van de heraldische symbolen van Nederland, België, hun provincies en Luxemburg.* Amsterdam: Jan Mets.

Delbrück, R. 1929. *Die Consulardiptychen und verwandte Denkmäler.* Berlin: De Gruyter.

Deliyannis, D. M. 2004. *Agnellus of Ravenna: The Book of Pontiffs of the Church of Ravenna.* Washington, DC: Catholic University of America Press.

Deutsch, M. E. 1923. "*E Pluribus Unum.*" *Classical Journal* 18: 387–407.

Di Legge, F. 2017. *L'aquila e il littorio. Direttive, strutture e strumenti della propaganda fascista negli Stati Uniti d'America (1922–1941).* Alessandria: Edizioni dell'Orso.

Dicke, G. 1994. *Heinrich Steinhöwels* Esopus *und seine Fortsetzer: Untersuchungen zu einem Bucherfolg der Frühdruckzeit.* Tübingen: Max Niemeyer Verlag.

Dietz, K. 1997. "Iulius Asper, Verteidiger der Provinzen unter Septimius Severus." *Chiron* 27: 483–524.

Doordan, D. P. 1997. "In the Shadow of the *Fasces*: Political Design in Fascist Italy." *Design Issues* 13: 39–52.

Drews, R. 1972. "Light from Anatolia on the Roman *Fasces*." *American Journal of Philology* 93: 40–51.

Drogula, F. K. 2015. *Commanders and Command in the Roman Republic and Early Empire.* Chapel Hill: University of North Carolina Press.

Drummond, A. 1999. "*Furorem incredibilem biennio ante conceptum* (Cicero, *Pro Sulla* 67)." *Rheinisches Museum* 142: 296–308.

Ducati, P. 1927. *Origini e attributi del fascio littorio.* Bologna: Stabilimenti Poligrafici Riuniti.

Dutton, R. 2019. *Jacobean Civic Pageants.* Edinburgh: Edinburgh University Press.

Dwyer, P. 2013. *Citizen Emperor: Napoleon in Power 1799–1815.* New Haven, CT: Yale University Press.

Eck, W., A. Caballos, and F. Fernández. 1996. *Das senatus consultum de Cn. Pisone patre.* Munich: C. H. Beck.

Eckstein, A. M. 1995. "Glabrio and the Aetolians: A Note on *Deditio*." *Transactions of the American Philological Association* 125: 271–289.

Eimer, C. 2010. *British Commemorative Medals and Their Values.* London: Spink.

Enenkel, K. A. E. 2019. *The Invention of the Emblem Book and Transmission of Knowledge, ca. 1510–1610*. Leiden and Boston: Brill.

Erasmo, M. 2008. *Reading Death in Ancient Rome*. Columbus: Ohio State University Press.

Falasca Zamponi, S. 1997. *Fascist Spectacle: The Aesthetics of Power in Mussolini's Italy*. Berkeley and Los Angeles: University of California Press.

Falchi, F. 2008. *L'itinerario politico di Regina Terruzzi: dal mazzinianesimo al fascismo*. Milan: F. Angeli.

Falchi, I. 1898. "Vetulonia: nuove scoperte nella necropoli." *Notizie degli Scavi* (April 1898): 141–163.

Fehl, P. P. 1993. "Raphael as a Historian: Poetry and Historical Accuracy in the Sala di Costantino." *Artibus et Historiae* 14: 9–76.

Ferrini, G. C. 1927. *I Tre Millenni di vita del fascio littorio*. Florence: Vallecchi.

Finelli, M. 2013. "I mazziniani ed i repubblicani e la costruzione del Vittoriano (1885–1911)." In *Cento anni del Vittoriano 1911–2011*, ed. R. Ugolini, 47–61. Rome: Gangemi Editore.

Follo, V. 2013. *The Power of Images in the Age of Mussolini*, diss. University of Pennsylvania.

Fonrobert, J., and A. Weyl. 1877. *Sammlung überseeischer Münzen und Medaillen*. Berlin: J. A. Stargardt.

Forrer, L. 1904. *Biographical Dictionary of Medallists, Coin, Gem, and Seal-Engravers, Mint-Masters, &c., Ancient and Modern*. Vol. I: *A–D*. London: Spink.

Foss, C. 1983. "Stephanus, Proconsul of Asia, and Related Statues." In Okeanos: *Essays Presented to Ihor Ševčenko on His Sixtieth Birthday by His Colleagues and Students*, ed. C. Mango and O. Pritsak, 196–219. Cambridge, MA: Harvard Ukrainian Research Institute.

Frank, C. D. 1993. *The Mechanics of Triumph: Public Ceremony and Civic Pageantry under Louis XIV*, diss. University of London, Warburg Institute.

Fryd, V. G. 1984. *Sculpture as History: Themes of Liberty, Unity and Manifest Destiny in American Sculpture, 1825–1865*, diss. University of Wisconsin-Madison.

Fryd, V. G. 1986. "Hiram Powers's *America*: 'Triumphant as Liberty and in Unity.'" *American Art Journal* 18: 54–75.

Fryd, V. G. 1992. *Art and Empire: The Politics of Ethnicity in the United States Capitol, 1815–1860*. Athens: Ohio University Press.

Gentile, E. 1996. *The Sacralization of Politics in Fascist Italy*. Trans. K. Botsford. Cambridge MA: Harvard University Press (Italian original published 1993).

Gentile, E. 2002. *Fascismo. Storia e interpretazione*. Bari: Editori Laterza.

Gerards-Nelissen, I. 1971. "Otto van Veen's *Emblemata Horatiana*." *Simiolus: Netherlands Quarterly for the History of Art* 5: 20–63.

Giardina, A., and A. Vauchez. 2000. *Il mito di Roma. Da Carlo Magno a Mussolini*. Rome and Bari: Laterza.

Giatti, C. 2007. "Il sepolcro cd. 'Arieti' sull'Esquilino: nuove proposte di lettura del monument." *Archeologia Classica* 58: 75–107.

Gibbs, L. 2002. *Aesop's Fables*. Oxford: Oxford University Press.

Gladigow, B. 1972. "Die sakralen Funktionen der Liktoren." *Aufstieg und Niedergang der römischen Welt I* 2: 295–314.

Goodrich, P., and V. Hayaert. 2015. "Introduction: The Emblematic Cube." In *Genealogies of Legal Vision*, ed. P. Goodrich and V. Hayaert, 1–16. London and New York: Routledge.

Gravelot, H. F., and C. N. Cochin. 1791. *Iconologie par figures ou Traité complet des allégories emblèmes*. 4 vols. Paris: Le Pan.

Green, H. 1872. *Andrea Alciati and His Books of Emblems: A Biographical and Bibliographical study*. London: Trübner.

Haldon, J. F. 1984. *Byzantine Praetorians: An Administrative, Institutional and Social Survey of the Opsikion and Tagmata, c. 580–900*. Bonn: Rudolph Habelt.

Hallam, J. S. 1978. "Houdon's Washington in Richmond: Some New Observations." *The American Art Journal* 10: 72–80.

Haselberger, L., ed. 2002. *Mapping Augustan Rome*. Portsmouth, RI: Journal of Roman Archaeology.

Hennin, M. 1826. *Histoire numismatique de la revolution Française*. Paris: Merlin.

Holliday, P. T. 1993. "Processional Imagery in Late Etruscan Funerary Art." *American Journal of Archaeology* 94: 73–93.

Hughes-Hallett, L. 2013. *The Pike: Gabriele d'Annunzio: Poet, Seducer and Preacher of War*. London: Fourth Estate.

Hunt, L. 1983. "Hercules and the Radical Image in the French Revolution." *Representations* 2: 95–117.

Jenkins, R. J. H., ed. 1962. *Constantine Porphyrogenitus, De Adminstrando Imperio. A Commentary*. London: Athlone Press.

Jones, A. H. M. 1964. *The Later Roman Empire 284–602: A Social, Economic, and Administrative Survey*. Oxford: Oxford University Press.

Judd, J. H. 2008. *United States Pattern Coins*. 10th ed. Atlanta: Whitman.

Karkov, C. E. 2001. *Text and Picture in Anglo-Saxon England. Narrative Strategies in the Junius II Manuscript*. Cambridge: Cambridge University Press.

Keller-Dorian, G. 1920. *Antoine Coysevox (1640–1720): catalogue raisonné de son oeuvre*. 2 vols. Paris: Keller-Dorian.

Knels, E. 2019. *Der Salon und die Pariser Kunstszene unter Napoleon I*. Hildesheim, Zurich, and New York: Georg Olms Verlag.

Komnick, H. 2001. *Die Restitutionsmünzen der frühen Kaiserzeit: Aspekte der Kaiserlegitimation*. Berlin: De Gruyter.

Konrad, C. 2003. Review of T. C. Brennan, *Praetorship in the Roman Republic*. *Classical Journal* 98: 341–347.

Kontorovich, E. 2014. "When Fasces Aren't Fascist: The Strange History of America's Federal Buildings." *City Journal* (Spring 2014): 114–119.

Koortbojian, M. 2013. *The Divinization of Caesar and Augustus: Precedents, Consequences, Implications*. New York: Cambridge University Press.

Kraay, C. 1956. *The Aes Coinage of Galba*. New York: American Numismatic Society.

Kraus, C., and H. Obermair, ed. 2019. *Mythen der Diktaturen. Kunst in Faschismus und Nationalsozialismus*. Schloss Tirol: Landesmuseum für Kultur- und Landesgeschichte.

Krause, C. L., and C. Mishler. 2019. *Standard Catalog of World Coins 1801–1900*. 9th ed., ed. T. Michael and T. L. Schmidt. Iola, WI: Krause Publications.

Kübler, B. 1926. "Lictor." In *Real-Encyclopädie der klassischen Altertumswissenschaft*, ed. A. Pauly, G. Wissowa, and W. Kroll. XIII 1: coll. 507–518.

Kuttner, A. 1995. *Dynasty and Empire in the Age of Augustus: The Case of the of the Boscoreale Cups*. Berkeley and Los Angeles: University of California Press.

La Franchi, L. 1929. "Il fascio littorio sulle monete antiche. (A proposito di monete moderne)." *Rivista Italiana di Numismatica e Scienze Affini* 26: 5–20.

Lacchè, L. 2019. "'Also and Above All a Regime of Justice': Criminal Law and the Aesthetics of Justice under the Italian Fascist Regime." In *The Role of Architecture and the Visual Arts in Ideology and Criminal Law: Fascist, National Socialist and Authoritarian Regimes*, ed. S. Skinner, 9–32. London: Bloomsbury.

Lafaurie, J. 1981. *Les Assignats: et les papiers-monnaies émis par l'État au XVIII siècle*. Paris: Le Léopard d'or.

Landes, J. B. 1988. *Women and the Public Sphere in the Age of the French Revolution*. Ithaca, NY, and London: Cornell University Press.

Lange, D. W. 2005. *The Complete Guide to Mercury Dimes*. 2nd ed. Virginia Beach: DLRC Press.

Laureys, M. 1995. "At the Threshold of Humanist Jurisprudence: Andrea Fiocchi's *De potestatibus Romanis*." *Bulletin de l'Institut Historique Belge de Rome* 65: 25–42.

Lavin, I. 2005. "Bernini at St. Peter's: *Singularis in Singulis, in Omnibus Unicus*." In *St. Peter's in the Vatican*, ed. W. Tronzo, 111–243. Cambridge: Cambridge University Press.

Lawrence, R. H. 1883. *Medals by Giovanni Cavino the 'Paduan.'* New York: R. H. Lawrence.

Lazzaro, C., and J. R. Crum, ed. 2005. *Donatello among the Blackshirts: History and Modernity in the Visual Culture of Fascist Italy*. Ithaca, NY: Cornell University Press.

Leith, J. A. 1965. *The Idea of Art as Propaganda in France*. Toronto: University of Toronto Press.

Leith, J. A. 1968. *Media and Revolution: Moulding a New Citizen in France during the Terror*. Toronto: CBC Publications.

Linderski, J. 1986. "The Augural Law." In *Aufstieg und Niedergang der römischen Welt* II 16.3, ed. W. Haase, 2146–2312. Berlin and New York: Walter de Gruyter.

Loskoutoff, Y. 2001–2002. "*Fascis cum sideribus* V: L'héraldique du cardinal Mazarin dans les ornements gravés pour le livre." *Revue française d'héraldique et de sigillographie* 71–72: 5–38.

Loskoutoff, Y. 2002a. "*Fascis cum sideribus* I: L'héraldique du cardinal Mazarin et son symbolisme dans les beaux-arts." *Gazette des Beaux-Arts* 144: 39–64.

Loskoutoff, Y. 2002b. "*Fascis cum sideribus* III: Le symbolisme armorial dans les éloges du cardinal Mazarin, ses prolongements dans les mazarinades, chez Corneille, Racine et La Fontaine." *Dix-septième siècle* 214: 55–98.

Loskoutoff, Y. 2003a. "*Fascis cum sideribus* II: Les devises du cardinal Mazarin." *Journal des savants*: 169–132.

Loskoutoff, Y. 2003b. "*Fascis cum sideribus* IV: The Longueils, Mazarin and Maisons." *Revue de l'Art* 114: 19–28.

Loskoutoff, Y. 2007. *Rome des Césars, Rome des papes: la propagande du cardinal Mazarin*. Paris and Geneva: H. Champion and Diff. Slatkine.

Lushkov, A. H. 2015. *Magistracy and the Historiography of the Roman Republic: Politics in Prose*. Cambridge: Cambridge University Press.

Maffei, S., ed. 2012. *Caesare Ripa* Iconologia. Torino: Giulio Einaudi editore.

Majanlahti, A., and A. Osti Guerrazzi. 2014. *Roma divisa, 1919–1925. Itinerari, storie, immagini*. Milan: Il Saggiatore.

Majeska, G. P. 1984. *Russian Travelers to Constantinople in the Fourteenth and Fifteenth Centuries*. Washington, DC: Dumbarton Oaks.

Manning, C. E. 1985. "'Liberalitas'—The Decline and Rehabilitation of a Virtue." *Greece & Rome* 32: 73–83.

Manson, A. J. 2015. *Rationalism and Ruins in Roma Mussoliniana: The 1934 Palazzo del Littorio Competition*, diss. Columbia University.

Margolis, R. 1988. "Matthew Boulton's French ventures of 1791 and 1792: Tokens for the Monneron Brothers of Paris." *British Numismatic Journal* 58: 102–109 and plates 28–30.

Marshall, A. J. 1984. "Symbols and Showmanship in Roman Public Life: The Fasces." *Phoenix* 38: 120–141.

Martin, T. G. 1980. *A Most Fortunate Ship: A Narrative History of Old Ironsides*. Chester, CT: Globe Pequot Press.

Mathisen, R. 1979. "Resistance and Reconciliation: Majorian and the Gallic Aristocracy after the Fall of Avitus." *Francia* 7: 598–603.

Matthews, M. 2008. *Caesar and the Storm: A Commentary on Lucan,* De Bello Civili. *Book 5 lines 476–721*. Bern: Peter Lang.

Maury, A. 1904. *Les emblèmes et les drapeaux de la France: le coq gaulois*. Paris: A. Maury.

Mazard, J. 1965. *Histoire monétaire et numismatique contemporaine, 1790–1963*, Vol. I: *1790–1848*. Paris: E. Bourgey.

Mazzoni, C. 2010. *She-Wolf: The Story of a Roman Icon*. Cambridge: Cambridge University Press.

Mears, D. S. 2018. *The Medal of Honor: The Evolution of America's Highest Military Decoration*. Lawrence: University Press of Kansas.

Middeldorf-Kosegarten, A. 1975. "Fasces." In *Reallexikon Zur Deutschen Kunstgeschichte* VII, ed. O. Schmitt, 461–496. Munich: Metzler.

Miller, J. J., II. 1964. "The Designs for the Washington Monument in Baltimore." *Journal of the Society of Architectural Historians* 23: 19–28.

Minor, V. H. 2006. *The Death of the Baroque and the Rhetoric of Good Taste.* Cambridge: Cambridge University Press.

Mommsen, T. 1848. "De apparitoribus magistratuum Romanorum." *Rheinisches Museum für Philologie* 6: 1–57.

Mommsen, T. 1887. *Römisches Staatsrecht* I³. Leipzig: S. Hirzel.

Montaner, E. 2007. "Politics and Diplomacy: Emblems during the War of Devolution in the Minority of Charles II of Spain." *Journal of the Warburg and Courtauld Institutes* 70: 287–306.

Mosher, S. 1945. "Let Well Enough Alone." *The Numismatist* (July 1945): 732.

Musante, N. 2016. *Medallic Washington: A Catalog of Struck, Cast and Manufactured Coins, Tokens and Medals Issued in Commemoration of George Washington, 1777–1890.* 2 vols. Boston and London: Spink.

Nice, A. 2017. "Dummy Rods? Observations on the Consular *Fasces.*" *Latomus* 76: 3–34.

Nippel, W. 1995. *Public Order in Ancient Rome.* Cambridge: Cambridge University Press.

Nuttall, P., G. Nuttall, and M. W. Kwakkelstein. 2020. *Filippino Lippi: Beauty, Invention and Intelligence.* Leiden and Boston: Brill.

O'Brien, P. 2004. *Mussolini in the First World War: The Journalist, the Soldier, the Fascist.* Oxford and New York: Berg.

Östenberg, S. 2021. "The Arch of Titus: Triumph, Funeral, and Apotheosis in Ancient Rome." In *The Arch of Titus: From Jerusalem to Rome—and Back*, ed. S. Fine, 33–42. Leiden and Boston: Brill.

Painter, B. 2005. *Mussolini's Rome: Rebuilding the Eternal City.* New York: Palgrave Macmillan.

Pannuti, M., and V. Riccio. 1984. *Le Monete di Napoli.* Naples: Edizioni Nummorum Auctiones.

Panofsky, E. 1939. *Studies in Iconology: Humanistic Themes in the Art of the Renaissance.* Oxford and New York: Oxford University Press.

Paribeni, R. 1942. "Lictor." In *Dizionario epigrafico di Antichità Romane* IV 33, ed. E. De Ruggiero and G. Cardinali, 1041–1044. Rome: A. Signorelli.

Patterson, R. S., and R. Dougall. 1976. *The Eagle and the Shield: A History of the Great Seal of the United States.* Washington, DC: Department of State.

Pedullà, G. 2018. *Machiavelli in Tumult: The Discourses on Livy and the Origins of Political Conflictualism.* Cambridge: Cambridge University Press.

Petersohn, J. 1998. "Über monarchische Insignien und ihre Funktion im mittelalterlichen Reich." *Historische Zeitschrift* 266: 47–96.

Pierguidi, S. 2007. "Sulla fortuna della *Giustizia* e della *Pazienza* di Vasari." *Mitteilungen des Kunsthistorischen Institutes in Florenz* 51: 575–592.

Pierik, E. 2019. *Lictors in the Roman World*, MA thesis, University of Western Ontario.

Pinckney, P. A. 1940. *American figureheads and their carvers.* New York: W. W. Norton.

Pokorny, J. 1959. *Indogermanisches Etymologisches Worterbuch*. Bern: Francke Verlag.

Porter, J. R. 2019. *Plautus'* Asinaria: *A Grammatical Commentary for Students*. Online publication. Saskatoon: University of Saskatchewan. Accessed July 30, 2021, at academia.edu/39572020.

Praz, M. 1964–1974. *Studies in Seventeenth-Century Imagery*. 2 vols. Rome: Edizioni di storia e letteratura.

Premerstein, O. von. 1935. "Laureati fasces." In *Real-Encyclopädie der klassischen Altertumswissenschaft*, ed. A. Pauly, G. Wissowa, and W. Kroll. XII 1: col. 1014.

Purcell, N. 1983. "The *Apparitores*: A Study in Social Mobility." *Papers of the British School at Rome* 51: 125–173.

Ramsey, J. T. 2016. "How and Why Was Pompey Made Sole Consul in 52 BC." *Historia* 65: 298–324.

Ratcliffe, J. 2014a. "Some Comments on the Longevity of the Fable of Bundled Arrows in Inner Asian Cultures and Its Reception in the West." *Eurasian Studies Journal* 3.2: 1–24.

Ratcliffe, J. 2014b. "Untangling the Myth of the Fasces, Fascism and Aesop's Quarrelling Sons." Unpublished manuscript, via anu-au.academia.edu/JonathanRatcliffe.

Raw, B. 1976. "The Probable Derivation of Most of the Illustrations in Junius II from an Illustrated Old Saxon *Genesis*." *Anglo-Saxon England* 5: 133–148.

Rawson, E. 1985. "Theatrical Life in Rome and Italy." *Papers of the British School at Rome* 53: 97–113.

Rebecchini, G. 2013. "Rituals of Justice and the Construction of Space in Sixteenth-Century Rome." *I Tatti Studies* 16: 153–179.

Reghini, A. 1934. *Il Fascio Littorio*. Rome: Stabilimento tipografico Ambrosini.

Reilly, B. 1991. *American Political Prints, 1766–1876: A Catalog of the Collections in the Library of Congress*. Boston: G. K. Hall.

Rentsmann, W. 1876. *Numismatisches wappen-lexikon*. 9 vols. Halle: Riechmann.

Resnik, J., and D. E. Curtis. 2011. *Representing Justice: The Creation and Fragility of Courts in Democracies*. New Haven, CT, and London: Yale University Press.

Riddell, F. 2018. *Death in Ten Minutes: The Forgotten Life of Radical Suffragette Kitty Marion*. London: Hodder & Stoughton.

Rifkind, D. 2006. "Furnishing the Fascist interior: Giuseppe Terragni, Mario Radice, and the Casa del Fascio." *Arq* 10: 157–170.

Rinaldi, O. 1954. *Le monete coniate in Italia dalla Rivoluzione Francese ai nostri giorni*. 4 vols. Mantova: Casteldario.

Ripa, C. 1603. *Iconologia overo Descrittione di Diverse Imagini cavate dall' antichita, et di propria inventione*. Rome: Lapido Fazij.

Ripley, J. 1987. "Coriolanus's Stage Imagery on Stage, 1754–1901." *Shakespeare Quarterly* 38: 338–350.

Ronnick, M. V. 2021. "In Search of Helen Maria Chesnutt (1880–1969), Black Latinist." *New England Classical Journal* 48: 110–121.

Rosenberger, H. T. 1948/1950. "Thomas Ustick Walter and the Completion of the United States Capitol." *Records of the Columbia Historical Society, Washington, D.C.* 50: 273–322.

Rosivach, V. J. 1980. "The Genealogy of Latinus and the Palace of Picus (*Aeneid* 7.45–49 and 170 ff.)." *Classical Quarterly* 30: 140–152.

Ryan, W. G., ed. 2012. *The Golden Legend: Readings on the Saints. Jacobus de Voragine.* Princeton, NJ: Princeton University Press.

Salvatori, P. S. 2008. "L'adozione del fascio littorio nella monetazione dell'Italia." *Rivista Italiana di Numismatica* 109: 333–352.

Salvatori, P. S. 2012. "Liturgie immaginate: Giacomo Boni e la Romanità fascista." *Studi Storici* 53: 421–438.

Samter, E. 1909. "Fasces." In *Real-Encyclopädie der klassischen Altertumswissenschaft*, ed. A. Pauly, G. Wissowa, and W. Kroll. VI: coll. 2002–2006.

Savage, K. 2018. *Standing Soldiers, Kneeling Slaves: Race, War, and Monument in Nineteenth-Century America.* 2nd ed. Princeton: Princeton University Press.

Schäfer, T. 1989. Imperii insignia. Sella curulis *und* Fasces. *Zur Repräsentation römischer Magistrate.* Mainz am Rhein: Von Zabern.

Schäfer, T. 2003. "Zur Rezeption römischer Herrschaftsinsignien in Italien und im Imperium Romanum im 1.–2. Jh. n. Chr." In *Propaganda, Selbstdarstellung, Repräsentation im römischen Kaiserreich des 1. Jhs. N. Chr.*, ed. G. Weber and M. Zimmermann, 243–273. Wiesbaden: Steiner.

Schrijver, F. M. 2012. *The Early Palaiologan Court (1261–1354)*, diss. University of Birmingham.

Scott, A. G. 2018. *Emperors and Usurpers: An Historical Commentary on Cassius Dio's Roman History, Books 79(78)–80(80) (A.D. 217–229).* New York: Oxford University Press.

Scott, P. 1992. "Stephen Hallet's Designs for the United States Capitol." *Winterthur Portfolio* 27: 145–170.

Scott, P. 1995. *Temple of Liberty: Building the Capitol for a New Nation.* New York: Oxford University Press.

Scuccimarra, L. 1999. "Il fascio rivoluzionario. Genesi e significato di un simbolo." *Storia amministrazione costituzione. Annale ISAP* 7: 227–258.

Scuccimarra, L. 2010. "Il fascio littorio." In *Simboli della politica*, ed. F. Benigno and L. Scuccimarra, 23–44. Rome: Viella.

Shea, J. G. 1865. *The Lincoln Memorial: A Record of the Life, Assassination, and Obsequies of the Martyred President.* New York: Bunce and Huntington.

Sheriff, M. D. 1983. "Au génie de Franklin: An Allegory by J. H. Fragonard." *Proceedings of the American Philosophical Society* 127: 180–193.

Shoemaker, I. H. 1978. "Drawings after the Antique by Filippino Lippi." *Master Drawings* 16: 35–43 and 97–104.

Smith, P. H. ed., 1976. *Letters of Delegates to Congress 1774–1789*, Vol. I: *August 1774–August 1775.* Washington, DC: Library of Congress.

Stauffer, D. M. 1907. *American Engravers upon Copper and Steel*. 2 vols. New York: Grolier Club.

Staveley, E. S. 1963. "The '*Fasces*' and '*Imperium Maius*.'" *Historia* 12: 458–484.

Stewart, J. H. 1951. *A Documentary Survey of the French Revolution*. New York: Macmillan.

Stumpf, G. R. 1991. *Numismatische Studien zur Chronologie der römischen Statthalter in Kleinasien (122 v. Chr.–163 n. Chr.)*. Saarbrücken: Saarbrücker Druckerei und Verlag.

Sumi, G. S. 1997. "Power and Ritual: The Crowd at Clodius' Funeral." *Historia* 46: 80–102.

Summers, R. G. 1970. "Roman Justice and Apuleius' *Metamorphoses*." *Transactions of the American Philological Association* 101: 511–531.

Syme, R. 2016. "How Many '*Fasces*'? Approaching the Roman Revolution." In *Papers on Republican History*, ed. F. Santangelo, 255–271. Oxford: Oxford University Press.

Tassi Scandone, E. 2001. *Verghe, scuri e fasci littori in Etruria: contributi allo studio degli insignia imperii*. Pisa and Rome: Istituto Editoriali e Poligrafici.

Taylor, L. R., and T. R. S. Broughton. 1949. "The Order of the Two Consuls' Names in the Yearly Lists." *Memoirs of the American Academy in Rome* 19: 1–13.

Taylor, L. R., and T. R. S. Broughton. 1968. "The Order of the Consuls' Names in Official Republican Lists." *Historia* 17: 166–172.

Tea, E. 1932. *Giacomo Boni: nella vita del suo tempo*. 2 vols. Milano: Ceschina.

Thoen, P. 1970. "Aesopus Dorpii, essai sur l'Esope Latin des temps modernes." *Humanistica Lovaniensia* 19: 241–289.

Thomas, C. A. 2002. *The Lincoln Memorial and American Life*. Princeton, NJ, and Oxford: Princeton University Press.

Thomasson, B. E. 2009. *Laterculi praesidum*, Vol. I: *ex parte retractatum*. Göteborg: Bokförlaget Radius.

Torelli, M. 1982. *Typology and Structure of Roman Historical Reliefs*. Ann Arbor: University of Michigan Press.

Treggiari, S. 1969. *Roman Freedmen during the Late Republic*. Oxford: Oxford University Press.

Tymkiw, M. 2019. "Floor Mosaics, *Romanità*, and Spectatorship: The Foro Mussolini's Piazzale dell'Impero." *Art Bulletin* 101: 109–132.

Vadalà, D. 2016. "A Bundle of Rods: Transmigration of Symbols and Spatial Rhetoric in the Architecture of Modernity." *California Italian Studies* 6: 1–28.

Van Horn, J. 2017. *The Power of Objects in Eighteenth-Century British America*. Chapel Hill: University of North Carolina Press.

Vauxcelles, L., A. Fontainas, G. Gromont, and G. Mourey. 1922. *Histoire générale de l'art français de la Révolution à nos jours*. 3 vols. Paris: Librairie de France.

Verheyen, E. 1996. "'Unenlightened by a single ray from Antiquity': John Quincy Adams and the Design of the Pediment for the United States Capitol." *International Journal of the Classical Tradition* 3: 208–231.

Vittori, M. 2006. "Storia e simbologia del Fascio Littorio." In *Esoterismo e fascismo: storia, interpretazioni, documenti*, ed. G. De Turris, 15–22. Rome: Edizioni Mediterranee.

Volbach, W. F. 1976. *Elfenbeinarbeiten der Spätantike und des frühen Mittelalters*. Mainz: Wilckens.

Volk, K., and J. E. G. Zetzel. 2015. "Laurel, Tongue, and Glory (Cicero, *De consulatu suo* Fr. 6 Soubiran)." *Classical Quarterly* 65: 204–223.

Vovelle, M. 2015. *La révolution française: 1789–1799*. 3rd ed. Paris: A. Colin.

Wallace, R. W. 1967. "Salvator Rosa's Justice Appearing to the Peasants." *Journal of the Warburg and Courtauld Institutes* 30: 431–434.

Weaver, P. R. C. 1972. Familia Caesaris: *A Social Study of the Emperor's Freedmen and Slaves*. Cambridge: Cambridge University Press.

Weigel, R. D. 1995. "Roman History in the Age of Enlightenment: the Dassier Medals." *Revue numismatique* 150: 231–239.

Weil-Garris (Brandt), K., and J. F. D'Amico. 1980. "The Renaissance Cardinal's Ideal Palace: A Chapter from Cortesi's 'De Cardinalatu.'" *Memoirs of the American Academy in Rome* 35: 45–123.

Welch, K. E. 1990. "The Praefectura Urbis of 45 BC and the Ambitions of L. Cornelius Balbus." *Antichthon* 24: 53–69.

Wills, G. 1984. "Washington's Citizen Virtue: Greenough and Houdon." *Critical Inquiry* 10: 420–441.

Wilson, M. B. 2021. *Dictator: The Evolution of the Roman Dictatorship*. Ann Arbor: University of Michigan Press.

Winkler, M, M. 2009. *The Roman Salute: Cinema, History, Ideology*. Columbus: Ohio State University Press.

Wiseman, T. P. 2021. "Walls, Gates and Stories: Detecting Rome's Riverside Defences." *Papers of the British School at Rome* 88: 9–40.

Wunder, R. P. 1974. *Hiram Powers: Vermont Sculptor*. Taftsville, VT: Countryman Press.

Index

For the benefit of digital users, indexed terms that span two pages (e.g., 52–53) may, on occasion, appear on only one of those pages.

Note: classical authors and Roman emperors are here listed by their conventional English names; the supporting material in the notes has not received indexing.